NINE LIVES

Ruth Brooks

Pen Press

© Ruth Brooks 2013

All rights reserved

No part of this publication may be reproduced, stored in a retrieval system, or transmitted in any form or by any means, without the prior permission in writing of the publisher, nor be otherwise circulated in any form of binding or cover other than that in which it is published and without a similar condition including this condition being imposed on the subsequent purchaser.

First published in Great Britain by Pen Press

All paper used in the printing of this book has been made from wood grown in managed, sustainable forests.

ISBN13: 978-1-78003-067-8

Printed and bound in the UK
Pen Press is an imprint of
Indepenpress Publishing Limited
25 Eastern Place
Brighton
BN2 1GJ

A catalogue record of this book is available from
the British Library

Cover design by Jacqueline Abromeit

Excerpts from "We Remember Your Childhood Well" © Carol Ann Duffy 1990 and "Valentine" © Carol Ann Duffy 1993. Reproduced by kind permission of the author c/o Rogers, Coleridge & White Ltd., 20 Powis Mews, London W11 1JN

To 'Thomas'

Acknowledgements

I am grateful to Katy Clarke for mentoring the first draft of this book, and for encouraging me to write about what I know.

Thanks are due to Lynn Ashman, Director of Pen Press, and to all who have contributed to the production of this book. I am particularly indebted to my editor, Claire Spinks, for her ongoing support and meticulous care with the editing process, and her patience with my many revisions.

I would like to give my heartfelt thanks and appreciation to all the youngsters who came under my wing during my thirty-five years as a Home Tutor, especially those who feature in *Nine Lives*; and to acknowledge the work of all my colleagues, who were as committed as I was - they too achieved tiny miracles. Briefly sharing my children's individual journeys has been both humbling and inspiring. It has been a privilege to write their stories.

Author Profile

Ruth Brooks is a passionate advocate of child-centred, special provision for children who are struggling either in, or out of school. She has four children of her own, including a daughter with learning difficulties. Her interests include coastal walking, gardening and the environment. In 2010, she participated in an event called 'So You Want To Be A Scientist', organised by the Radio 4 programme, *Material World*, and was awarded the title 'BBC Amateur Scientist of the Year' for her research on the homing distance of snails. Best of all, she loves playing with her grandchildren and being very un-grown-up.

Also by Ruth Brooks:

A Slow Passion: Snails, My Garden and Me – Bloomsbury Publishing, 2013.

Imagine! An Educational Reading Game for 5 to 8 year olds – Claire Publications.

Author's Notes

Nine Lives is set in a fictitious sea-port somewhere in the West Country of England. All the names of places, children and their family members are false, and I have changed their appearance, nationality and ethnicity. The family structure – for example, whether the child is the youngest or eldest in the family, and the number and gender of siblings – has also been altered. However, these are the stories of real children. For authenticity, the child's gender and age remain the same, and each story is a true depiction of his or her particular problem. In addition, as emotional and behavioural difficulties are often intrinsically linked to the family dynamic, I have not altered this, while at the same time making the family unidentifiable. I have also juxtaposed pupils I taught many years ago, in different parts of the country, into the present time-frame of the narrative. Other characters in the book have been similarly disguised.

Nine Lives

Cassie
Harriet
Jack
Thomas
Wayne
Aisha
'Ivan the Terrible'
Bethany

CASSIE

First Visit – Monday, 6th October 2003. I hear the screams the minute I open the car door, though I've parked fifty yards away from the house. It sounds as if someone's being throttled. A sobbing. Another scream:

"Let me out! Let me out!"

No. 15 is in a row of narrow terraced houses. The gate opens into a neglected patch of front garden, littered with crisp packets, drink cans and a discarded mattress with a dark stain in the middle.

I knock. The screaming intensifies. There are two voices now, both raised in raucous fury.

"You're not going anywhere, my girl!"

"Yes I am, let me go! I HATE you – let me *out!*"

The door's suddenly yanked open. A tall skinny woman in her late thirties, with thin lips and a smoker's complexion, glares at me.

"You'd better come in. But she won't see you. She says she isn't having it."

Her voice is flat and rasping. There's a chilling impassivity in her expression. Behind her, Cassie is sitting on the bottom step of the staircase.

"Let me out! Tell her to go away, I didn't want her to come. I want to GET OUT! I want Dean, I'm going to Dean, *now*. I won't see her, you can't make me. I HATE you...!" The words are hurled out, punctuated by long shuddering sobs.

I can't believe such a small person can make so much noise. In spite of the tear-stained face, it's clear that Cassie's a very attractive girl. She has long, blond hair, which hangs forward like a safety curtain. Her eyes, hostile and wary, stare through it, daring me to come any nearer. Her six-month pregnancy is evident, but she does not hold herself protectively or proudly, like many teenage mothers. I'm struck by the curious disconnection with her own body – as if, with the convulsive jerking of her head, she's disowned the burgeoning new life in her belly.

"Cassie." I try to keep my voice low and calm, but I have to shout over the cacophony. Cassie's mother has joined in, and looks as if she's about to hit her daughter. I manage to yell, "Cassie, you don't have to have tuition. You don't have to do anything you don't want to do. If you—"

"Yes she does!"

Her mother turns on me, angrily. She takes a couple of steps towards Cassie, bringing her face close to hers, threatening. "I'm not having you go back to him, that no-good druggie… RIGHT!" She moves to the hall telephone, as Cassie tries to escape again. "I'm calling the police!"

"Shut up, shut up, *shut up*!" Cassie shrieks. She runs out of the hall into the front room. I follow her. I'm hoping for a breathing space in which I can talk to her.

By now, I would have expected Cassie to have exhausted herself. She should have dissolved into heaving sobs, like the abating storm of a toddler tantrum. But there's still a force nine hurricane – more hysterics, lasting at least ten more minutes. She looks demented. Unexpectedly, I find myself admiring her strength and her energy. Yet there's also a real worry – how will this affect the baby? The two feelings churn uncomfortably in the pit of my stomach.

"Cassie—"

"Go away!" For the first time, she looks straight at me. "I don't want you, I don't need *you*." There's a brief silence while she takes a choking breath.

"I can see that," I get in quickly. "And I want you to know that I'd rather not be here if you're not happy about it…" Cassie glances at me briefly. "…and you can see how upset I am. I'm sad for you, because *you're* so upset."

I pause, waiting for some reaction. Perhaps I'm getting somewhere. But no, Cassie jumps up without warning and rushes from the room, fending off the restraining arms of her mother.

There's a loud banging on the door. "Police!" calls an authoritative voice. Cassie and her mother scuffle by the front door, Cassie trying to keep it closed. Her mother yanks on the handle, elbowing Cassie roughly aside.

A police sergeant wedges his foot into the narrow crack and forces the door open. Cassie's mother allows him to slither round, and slams the door shut. She screams:

"I'm keeping her here. She's got to do her education."

"Let go of my arm, you bitch!" yells Cassie.

The sergeant has seen it all before.

"Wait a moment," he says. "You can't stop her if she wants to go. She's free to walk out of her own front door."

Cassie's mother turns on him viciously. "I'm reporting you!" she shouts. "You fucking… I'm her mother! I've got rights! She's underage. Her so-called boyfriend's a druggie and he's made her pregnant. He should be in prison. He's a paedo!" She makes a sudden lunge towards the phone he's holding and tries to grab it.

"Right! I'm arresting you for foul language and for obstructing a police officer."

He steps nimbly out of her reach and makes a hurried S.O.S. call to his station. Then, with exaggerated emphasis, he opens the front door. Cassie squeezes through, and flounces out. I catch a glimpse of her rushing down the road.

By some miracle of diplomacy, Sergeant Woods eventually restores calm. Cassie's mother introduces herself as Ms Sanders. At least I know how to address her – the education office warned me that she's changed her name three times in two years. The sergeant suggests that we sit down for a few moments. He asks Ms Sanders to make us all a cup of tea. And off she goes, smiling, as if the last forty minutes were nothing but a small hiccup in her daily life.

"Listen," says Sergeant Woods, as soon as we were alone, "Just watch your step with that woman. I can't say much, obviously. But this isn't the first time she's called me in. Twice she wanted me to bring Cassie home from Dean's – her boyfriend's. Twice she's screamed down the phone that we've got to prosecute Dean for underage sex. The truth is, she won't leave the girl alone. She's always in her face. She won't accept that she really loves this boy and wants to be with him."

I'm wondering what I'd do if Cassie were my daughter. Wouldn't I be tempted to lock her up for her own safety? As if reading my thoughts, he continues, "The trouble is, that woman doesn't work, hasn't worked for years, just sits around reading magazines and watching TV. She ought to get a life for herself, give Cassie some rope."

There's a knock at the front door. Cassie's mother opens it looking as if butter wouldn't melt in her mouth. Reinforcements have arrived in the shape of WPC Carol Johns. She's come expecting trouble and is surprised to be offered a cup of tea.

"You can have mine," I say quickly. I make my apologies. I need to have a talk with Cassie's mother, but at another time. Just now I can't wait to get away. I hurl myself out of the front door and down the path.

The Copper Kettle is half way across town, on the way to my next pupil. I sit in the window seat with the mellow October sunshine streaming through and warming my shoulders. I'm making a To Do list in my diary:

- Ring line manager and report.
- Ring Ms Sanders and try to speak to Cassie if poss. Keep the contact going with both mother and daughter.
- Write report of incident for police, as requested by Sgt Woods.

- Write report for education office in case further incidents follow or more action needed by the Ed. Dept., social services etc.

I sip my tea, watching the busy movement of shoppers in the high street, and I reflect on the curious nature of this work I do, that I've done now for thirty-four years. Work that I enjoy so much, I couldn't imagine doing anything else. Yet of all the jobs in the teaching world, home tuition must be the least valued – and the loneliest.

Home tutors support children who, for a variety of reasons, mainly exclusions, don't attend school. These children need one-to-one tuition for as long as it takes to turn them round and set them on their feet again, hopefully in the direction of full-time schooling.

Last June, our line manager called an extraordinary meeting for our team of twenty tutors working in the area. To our dismay, we were all told that there would be little or no work for us next year. A new school for children with educational and behavioural difficulties (EBD) was being built, and expected to be ready next year. It would take most of the children who would now qualify for home tuition.

The new Pupil Referral Units (PRUs), set up for children who were disruptive and unable to settle at school, were already up and running. They took some of the children who normally would have come to us. Even with the PRUs, we still had a heavy workload. However, changes were creeping in.

Back in June, we were already working under a new initiative from the government – all children out of school must have twenty hours education per week. This had to include the basic subjects: English, maths and science. For these, tutors were assigned to a child for between five and ten hours per week. Any spare hours would be in the form of a 'package'. This included IT skills, outings with a Link Worker, visits to a Youth Centre. Naturally, local authorities were trying to avoid paying tutors to deliver twenty hours of individual tuition. The truth was that we were becoming far too expensive.

So wherever possible, a pupil was sent to a PRU. These were mainly for pupils with behavioural difficulties, but alongside these were a few specialist units, taking in very small numbers of school-phobic children. Though I supported the idea in principle – children need to be with their peer group wherever possible – there were problems. Some of these kids needed extra tender loving care, and that care had to be *individual.* The sad fact was that most children were not ready to be packed straight off to a PRU after being kicked out of mainstream school.

It was very different when I first started teaching children out of school, thirty-four years ago. After headteachers at the end of their tether had excluded a child for disruptive or bullying behaviour, he or she would be assigned to one of the home tuition team. During that time, which I always think of as 'tender loving care time', I saw a miraculous improvement. Children would have the chance to gather their forces, to reinvent themselves, to make good any educational deficits, and, with luck, to get to grips with the underlying emotional issues that were usually at the root of the problem.

Sooner or later, wonderful changes could happen. The child's new positive attitude, increased confidence and self-esteem indicated that it was now time for a return to school. In nine out of ten cases, he or she would settle back happily and succeed.

With the more recent cost-cutting initiatives, the danger was that a child would be placed too soon in the PRU, or into a school for educational and behavioural difficulties. This was a recipe for disaster, for the child simply continued the same patterns of disruptive behaviour, disturbing more settled children. Or, because of a too-fragile sense of self, he or she would be vulnerable to peer pressure, leading to new dysfunctional behaviours – drugs or theft. Then the child would find it all too much, and drop out. Or worse, get excluded from the PRU or school. A double failure. At this point the home tutor would be called in, to mop up the failures of the system, trying to deliver education to small egos so fractured and disillusioned that many were already headed for a life of crime or self-destruction.

At that June meeting, it seemed as if things were moving even further away from us. Children would, in future, be placed as soon as possible into the new LBD school. And the PRU's would still take as many as possible, though they already were bulging at the seams. All kinds of questions bubbled up in our minds as we listened aghast to these new proposals. But they all boiled down to two major issues: was this really the best way forward for the kids? And where did that leave us, the tutors?

Since 1990, as a single parent, I had been bringing up the youngest of my four children on my own. A few weeks ago, he left home to live his own life; the other three are also away, two of them abroad. The house feels empty and unnaturally tidy. Even the cat is spooked out by the eerie silence. Yes, I admit it: I'm feeling lonely.

Throughout the last thirteen years, the responsibility of my role as provider gave my days meaning and focus. But recently, there has been no work at all. None of the tuition team has the luxury of a proper contract. We get paid an hourly rate, but only for the actual contact time with children, and this can vary widely. So I'm facing a dilemma. Do I sit tight and wait for another pupil to come my way? Or should I start looking for a completely different job, thereby jeopardising my chances of more tutoring? Maybe I should throw myself into different projects, to fill the aching void of empty nest syndrome? Tempting. But courses and volunteering, however absorbing, don't pay the bills.

So yesterday, when I had a call from the Education office, saying that Cassie would need some support, I was delighted. And though so far she's been as elusive as a leaf in the wind, I have a new pupil. I'm back in the swing of things, doing the job I love. Cassie has appeared in my life and somehow, we'll find a way of working together.

Tuesday, 7th October. I'm back at the scene of yesterday's drama, trying not to cough, as Ms Sanders, seated opposite me in an armchair by the window, smokes cigarette after cigarette, and tells me about her daughter.

"She's always been wild, never settled at school. And then when her stepfather – *you* know. Well!"

She leans back with an air of triumph as if she's solved the problem to her satisfaction.

"When was this…this *incident* with her stepfather?"

"About two years ago. But he done it before that, it started when she was in primary. I don't know exactly when. I wasn't there, you see."

Carefully, I place my mug of tea down on the carpet. This revelation makes me feel hot and faint. And the settee where I'm sitting is sagging and uncomfortable and covered in dog and cat hairs. I'm beginning to itch.

"I was out working," Ms Sanders says. "Every evening I had my little job. Six till ten, it was, in Sainsbury's down the road. It was always down to me to pay the bills. He didn't work, not regularly. Just sat around in the day, watching telly."

She leans forward and lowers her voice. "It was the same with my first husband. Couldn't hold down a job. I'm telling you, I kept the family together. Never spent nothing on myself. It all went on Cassie. She never lacked for nothing, toys, books..."

Her tale continues, in a low monotone. Now and then she stubs out a cigarette on an ashtray perched on the arm of her chair. She's looking, not quite *at* me, but at some point near my left ear, as she leans back in her seat, puffs out a cloud of smoke and gazes around the room. I sense a performance repeated many times, over several years, for the benefit of social workers and whoever will listen.

I lean forward with difficulty. "Cassie should be here by now. She said she'd give it a try when I spoke to her on the phone last night. She promised. Would she be coming straight from her foster home?"

Ms Sanders coughs and cackles. "How do I know?" she shrugs. "Your guess is as good as mine. She's a law unto herself, that one."

"Is her foster home far away?"

"No. She just has to get one bus."

I'm feeling very disappointed. I'd had an encouraging conversation with Cassie at her foster home last night. I managed to persuade her to try one session only, suggesting that we meet just to discuss her educational needs, so that she could feel control in that area, at least. She seemed adrift in a life rapidly spinning out of control. I was thrilled when in the last minute of the phone call she'd agreed to be here at 9.30 a.m.

"I'll wait five more minutes."

In view of what her mother's just told me about her stepfather, I wish now I'd had time to read her file, which is kept at the office. In most cases I prefer to see the child in person before doing this. When I meet her for the first time, it's helpful to me to have no preconceptions. She unfolds, fresh, in front of me. I feel her energy – or lack of it. I note her body language and facial expressions, her attitude towards school, her family, and towards me. Occasionally, in that first visit, the child will tell me about some traumatic past event. And somehow, the way she tells it is the first brush stroke, a clue to the whole picture, in a way that no dry file can ever match.

Yet often the file in the office can be a very vital first port of call, especially with pupils who have a history of violent behaviour. I need to know if I will be in any personal danger. I'll also learn if the child has any pet hates, such as female tutors! Or maybe he or she just hates tutors in general and has gone through half a dozen already.

The phone rings in another room. Ms Sanders heaves herself up, coughing. In spite of the smoke, it's good to have this chance to talk to her. She's been very forthcoming about Cassie's problems. However, she does seem to have a very difficult relationship with her daughter; she doesn't speak of her with any affection, which is disturbing. But it's towards Dean, whom Cassie met a year ago, that she vents most of her anger and blame. Until she'd met him, 'Cassie'd been no trouble'. But once she started seeing Dean, her behaviour and attitude deteriorated. She dropped out of school just before last Christmas, and started staying round at Dean's, who was living in a squalid room in a shared house. She stole money from her mother's purse to pay for his drugs and started 'using' herself. Then she got pregnant. Dean was twenty-two. It was 'totally disgusting,' said Mum, unemotionally. She's always wanted Dean prosecuted, but the police just don't seem to care.

The phone call seems to be taking a long time. I look round the room, wondering where, in this complete mess of old magazines, dirty cups and plates, and clutter of every description, Cassie and I could spread out some books. There's a coffee table, laden with a scruffy hairbrush, newspapers, an open can of Coca-Cola and a huge pile of other detritus. We could clear that, I suppose. But this is not a good workplace. The air of total neglect, the cloying smell of smoke and sweat and dog make me feel like giving up before we've even started.

"Sorry about that," Ms Sanders returns, clutching her mobile. "That was the social. They were asking about her education, if it had been fixed up again, after yesterday. So I said yes, you were here now. And then I was asking them about a protection order. To stop her seeing Dean. That's what she needs. Why they didn't do it months before – would've saved all this hassle! They're going to see about it."

She plumps herself down heavily, looking pleased with herself, and lights another cigarette. Her mobile rings again. She listens, expressionless.

"Right. I'll tell her. But I'm not happy about this, not happy at all. If she misses her education, I'll hold you responsible." She switches off the phone.

"That was her foster mother. Cassie left an hour ago. I reckon she's at Dean's. I bet she never meant to come. I knew she wouldn't turn up. That woman's too soft with Cassie, lets her do exactly what she wants. Lets her see Dean at all hours. If I could only get my hands on that boy—"

"How long has Cassie been at the foster home?"

"She walked out of here a month ago. She'd just told me she was pregnant and we had an almighty row when she told me who the father was. She went straight round to Dean's and told him I'd thrown her out. Lying little bitch. So I rang social services to get her home, but she wouldn't come back. They fixed her up with this foster home. But they'll be throwing her out soon, they only take young children and they've got three of them. They just took her in as an emergency, like."

Any tuition with Cassie is going to be difficult, even if she does decide to turn up. Her foster home doesn't sound any more suitable a venue than her own home.

"Well, I'd better go now." I stand up. "I'm so sorry it hasn't worked out today. Maybe she'll have a change of heart? I'll try and talk to her again tonight."

"And so will I," says her mother grimly, as she opens the front door. "*And I'll be having words with that Dean if I can find him. He's rotten. I could tell you a thing or two…*" She launches into a blistering attack, saying she's got proof that he's been involved in a ritual abuse gang. Did I know that he…?

"Goodbye!" I run back to the car, shocked and sickened.

4.p.m. I've just spoken to Cassie's social worker, Mrs Hicks. She must know Cassie well, and I'm hoping she might persuade her to have her tuition session tomorrow. I'm also worried about Dean. Is he really the monster that Ms Sanders believes he is? If so, then Cassie could be in serious danger. I take a very deep breath and repeat her last vitriolic words. They've been haunting me all day. A silence, then Mrs Hicks explodes:

"All I can say is that I've known Dean for a long time. He's just a very inadequate young man, who lacks confidence and self-esteem. He's somehow managed to miss out on the most basic education. But he really loves Cassie as far as he's capable of loving anyone. He wants to live with her. But he can't seem to get himself together enough to keep down a regular job. He's not a bad lad, underneath."

"So he's not the devil Cassie's mother says he is?"

I hear Mrs Hicks struggling to be diplomatic.

"She hates Dean because he's come between herself and her daughter. She makes up stories about him and in her mind she's come to believe them. But you should know that she herself has problems that go back a long way. Just don't believe everything she says."

We agree to stay in touch.

I ring Sally, my line manager, to report on this morning's 'no-show', and book a time to study Cassie's file. I really need to know what I *should* believe.

I ring the foster-mother, who sounds friendly but harassed, and ask to speak to Cassie. I can hear a toddler crying.

"I don't want to talk to her." In the background, Cassie sounds as if her mind is firmly made up.

"Tell her I just want a quick word," I say urgently. "I won't keep her long."

There's a pause. I hold my breath. Then Cassie comes to the phone:

"What do you want?"

I tell her I was disappointed not to see her today.

"I changed my mind, okay? I don't want no tuition."

"But why, Cassie?"

"Because there's no point."

"I'm really sorry to hear that. There's a lot we could do that would really help you catch up on things you've missed at school. You could tell me what's most important for you to work on. You don't have to do anything you really don't enjoy."

There's a silence. I expect her to cut me off.

"It's no use." An impatient sigh. "I can't do it. There's no point."

Another silence. What else can I say to persuade her?

"I've got to go now," she says, finally.

"Keep in touch, Cassie."

She puts the phone down. I feel sad and empty, as if I've just lost something important to me.

Wednesday, 14th January 2004. "I want hair like *that*," pouts Cassie, "not this disgusting greasy stuff."

Against all the odds, I've got Cassie back again!

She's pulling distractedly at strands of her hair, while waving a magazine at her new foster mother, Andrea Cullen. She jabs at some photos of teen models with startlingly white teeth and unnaturally shining hair. Mrs Cullen, sitting next to her on the settee, peers at them critically.

"Give it time," she says, soothingly. "You've just had a baby, remember?"

"Bloody hell," growls Cassie. "How could I forget!"

"Well, your hormones have to settle down first."

"And how long will that take?" demands Cassie. "I had him two weeks ago and I still look like shit."

"Two weeks is hardly any time. It can take a few weeks." Mrs Cullen smiles at Cassie, and pats her reassuringly on the arm. "But you're doing so well. You've really bounced back!"

"I can't wait *weeks*." Cassie's near to tears. "I want to look nice *now*! I want my hair to look shiny!" She throws the magazine across the room, folds her arms, and hunches down into the settee.

"Give it time," Mrs Cullen says, patiently. "You have to get your strength back first."

"Yeah, right," snaps Cassie, "Like getting about two hours sleep last night."

Mrs Cullen continues to pacify and reassure, nodding sympathetically. Cassie's certainly getting along well with her newest foster mum, with whom social services have placed her since the birth of her baby. But so far, she hasn't said a single word to me. A few minutes ago, she opened the front door to let me in, clutching a can of hairspray, a packet of cigarettes, and the magazine that caused her so much grief. She gave me a fleeting,, unwelcoming glance, then led the way into the sitting room, where she plonked herself down on to the settee, next to Mrs Cullen.

In her mid-forties, Andrea Cullen has an open expressive face that invites confidences. Shrewd eyes twinkle at me, with laughter lines and a firm mouth set ready to smile at any moment. She looks like everyone's ideal mum. She has a husband, Bill, and two grown-up daughters living nearby. At the moment there's only one other short-term foster-child – Lee, aged three. It sounds as if it's just the kind of family Cassie needs just now.

"Welcome!" There's a barely disguised wink as Mrs Cullen waves me into the armchair opposite.

"So how do you feel about having tuition now, Cassie?" I'm hoping to make the question sound conversational, to keep the charge out of it.

She shrugs, sinking further down into the back of the settee. "I'm knackered."

"I expect you are."

I wonder if my ambivalence shows in my voice. All my natural instincts baulk against tutoring this young mother so soon after giving birth. Surely she needs at least four to six weeks recovery time? Two years ago, I'd tutored a schoolgirl mum whose baby was four weeks old – but that was exceptional: her English GCSEs were in three weeks' time. For any mother, however mature, and in the very best of circumstances, a new baby is a shock to the system.

Yesterday, Sally, my line manager, rang and said that Cassie was now available for tuition again. It was urgent and should start right away. When she told me that Cassie had specifically asked for me, rather than a new tutor, I felt gratified, and childishly elated. Yet today, I'm seeing the reality. There she sits, exhausted, so vulnerable and unready. What she needs most is rest, guidance, counselling, lots of help and tender loving care. But surely not tuition? Not yet.

"Well, we'd better make a start. Where can we work, Mrs Cullen?"

"You can work in here today. Though normally I like to keep it free for myself, and for meetings. And please call me Andrea."

It's a lovely room, exuding comfort, good taste and elegance. The settee and two armchairs are covered with deep crimson velvet, the light beige carpet is new, still shedding its pile, and smells deliciously of clean wool. Family members smile out from photo frames, early daffodils in a tall blue vase grace the windowsill.

"Have you any work from school, Cassie? I could look through that first."

"No. It's all left at school."

And it will take forever to get it back again. Once a pupil is excluded, it's a case of out of sight, out of mind. There'll be a relieved washing of hands – one less nuisance in the class to cope with.

"Well," I say brightly, "I've got some work with me. But first I'd like us to sit down together and do a work plan."

"Whatever."

Andrea vacates her seat, and I take her place. Cassie moves a foot away from me. Her sideways glance is hostile and suspicious.

"How long do I have? Darren's due for a feed soon."

As if on cue, there's a sudden wail from the room next door. Cassie jumps up immediately, and returns a minute later with a tiny bundle.

"Oh do let me see him!"

Cassie gently pulls the blanket away from the tiny face. Baby Darren peers out at the world with that knowing, wise expression peculiar to the newborn. His skin is peachy smooth and there's a silky crown of fair hair. He looks healthy and well cared-for.

Up to this moment, lulled by his mother's arms and the change of scene, he's been quietly gurgling – 'a – a – a,' in his engaging baby language. But now he decides he's hungry, and the gurgles change to short staccato cries. His little mouth puckers and roots from side to side.

"I've got to get his bottle," says Cassie. And then, to her foster mother, "What shall I do with him?"

"Can I hold him?" I ask, eagerly.

Cassie lowers Darren rather too rapidly into my arms.

"He needs changing," she says over her shoulder to Andrea, as she disappears into the kitchen. "I'll do it after, okay?"

Andrea sits down next to me. "I hope you don't mind working in here. There's only the coffee table. But I couldn't even think of offering you Cassie's room. It's in one hell of a mess. I've never seen anything quite like it. And I've been doing this for a long time."

"Here is fine. Thank you."

I'm lost in another world. Did I read somewhere that babies have that delectable newborn smell – like the purest honeycomb from the finest bees – to ensnare their mothers into instant bonding? Somehow, I don't think we'll get much work done today.

"How's Cassie doing, generally?"

"Well…" Andrea sounds cautious. "She seems to be coping. She can change a nappy, thank goodness. And she's learnt to make up the feeds correctly."

"She didn't want to breast-feed, then?"

"She did it for a week, then gave up, with no explanation at all. But he's taken to the bottle like a duck to water. You'll see in a minute. He drains it in one gulp."

"And are they bonding?" Darren's stopped in mid-grizzle and shut his eyes. He looks adorable.

"They seem to be. She spends a lot of time holding him and talking to him. She can tell the difference between a hungry cry and a settling-down cry."

"I'm glad. I was worried."

I tell Andrea about the first time I'd visited Cassie, the hysterics that seemed to go on forever. Darren opens his eyes and starts rooting around my jumper for food. I lift him up and place him over my shoulder.

"And has he regained his birth-weight?"

"Well, the health visitor was very pleased with his weight yesterday. He does seem to be thriving."

Is it my imagination, or has Andrea sounded cautious in all her responses?

"Are you all right with him for a minute?" she asks suddenly. "I just want to peep round the door to see if she's managing. I don't want her to think I'm checking up on her, but she does sometimes get sidetracked. Unfortunately, there's a mirror in the kitchen!" Andrea tiptoes into the hall.

There's an enraged yell from Darren – the service round here is just not good enough. I get up and joggle him around the room, patting his back. He nestles between my neck and shoulder, soft and warm. I make goo-goo noises, grinning fatuously. I'm suspended in that dreamy, timeless state of wonder, of reverence for a new life. Tuition seems a lifetime away.

As I move around the room, I take a peek at the book titles. There's astronomy, history, nature, gardening, archaeology, rug making, health care, prizewinning novels. An entire shelf filled with nursing manuals and medical textbooks. All stacked neatly in two floor-to-ceiling old pine bookcases.

Cassie's back with the feed. Darren downs his bottle in one long guzzle. Then she changes his nappy with sure, deft movements. Is this really the same girl? It all looks too good to be true! She places him carefully in his carry-cot next to the settee.

"We'd better begin, Cassie," I say, trying to keep the reluctance out of my voice.

"Okay," she shrugs indifferently, then looks at Andrea. "What shall I do with him?" She indicates the sleeping Darren.

"He can stay here, by you," I say firmly, "then if he cries you can see to him right away."

I look at Andrea for confirmation. She nods. We're both thinking the same thought: Cassie must be the first one to care for him, whenever possible.

"The first thing we must do is prepare a work plan, Cassie. Together."

I write 'Cassie – Individual Education Plan' at the top of a blank sheet of paper. What can I teach her, how much learning can she cope with, in the cotton-wool fog of new motherhood?

I tell her that many children find maths difficult, and don't like to ask for help. Or they may have missed so much school that they've fallen way behind.

"What do you think you need to concentrate on most?" I ask her. "Is there anything really important that you missed at school? Or that perhaps you didn't understand?"

Cassie twirls a tendril of hair round and round her fingers.

"I've missed loads of maths and stuff."

"Any particular topic that you find really difficult in maths?"

"Fractions. I could never get my head round them."

"And what about adding, subtracting, multiplying…"

"Oh, I dunno, do I?" She's fidgety and uncomfortable.

I make a few notes. "And English? Did you like it?"

"It's okay. Better than maths. I used to like writing stories and illustrating them when I was at primary.."

At *primary* school! Poor kid, what's she been doing since then?

"Writing stories is a lovely thing to do. What other types of writing did you do at secondary school?"

"Nothing. We just did worksheets. And we read boring books and stuff."

"What other subjects did you like? Science, craft, art, P.E?"

"Science is crap."

"Is it?"

"Yes. And history. Who wants to know about dead people?"

"What about art?"

"Can't draw."

"Art isn't just about drawing, there's design, painting, experimenting with colour – all sorts of things that aren't just drawing."

Silence.

"Craft? Do you like making things? Sewing, woodwork, pottery...."

"I started making a bag before I left. Wait there...."

Cassie springs to her feet with sudden energy, and nips into her downstairs room next door. She returns waving two brightly hued rectangles of felt. Geometric shapes in shiny material with sequins dotted about are glued, or sewn on. I admire it.

"Would you like to finish it, maybe sew a strap or a handle on to it?"

"Maybe."

"Anything else you'd like to do, in our time together?"

"Dunno."

So far there's been just a glimmer of hope. I tell her we've run out of time and she heaves a sigh of relief.

"Are you going to have a sleep before the baby wakes up?" I ask.

"No. I'm going to have a fag. Then I'm going to wash my hair. *Again*. I washed it yesterday and it's crap."

"Well, you've done well to stay awake, Cassie. And I'm looking forward to seeing you tomorrow."

Thursday, 15th January. "I'm afraid you're in here today." Apologetically, Andrea leads me into Cassie's room. "I've got a meeting at ten with Lee's social worker. We need the lounge. And I've got Lee home from playgroup today, so I hope he doesn't disturb you."

Cassie's bending over Darren's carrycot, placed in the middle of her bed.

"He's just gone to sleep," she informs Andrea.

"That's good. You can expect some peace and quiet for a while."

"Yeah, right, like doing tuition!" glowers Cassie, resentfully. "I want to have a bath. And I need to shave my legs. They're minging."

"Now, Cassie," warns Andrea. "Remember what we were talking about last night?"

Cassie flounces down sulkily on the bed. This is not a promising start. And when I look round the room, my spirits sink even further.

"Believe it or not," says Andrea, "she had a reasonably successful tidy-up last night. What on earth's happened to it today, Cassie?"

"It just got in a mess somehow..." Cassie shrugs, indifferently.

I glance round. There's an area clearly designated for the baby, with a chest of drawers and a nifty-looking trolley with a changing mattress, and shelves beneath for nappies, wipes and other small baby necessities. Yet, on the trolley, Cassie's dirty underwear is mixed up with her clean clothes, and scattered everywhere amongst little baby vests and bibs. Her creams and potions and sprays are jumbled up with Darren's talcum powder and cotton wool balls. A dirty nappy, a half-finished feeding bottle, the dregs of two mugs of coffee, tissues and magazines layer the floor.

"Where shall we work, Cassie?"

Cassie moves reluctantly towards the settee under the window. She picks up some magazines, a sleepsuit, a hairbrush and a plate with a half-eaten slice of toast, and flings them down on the floor.

"And you'll need some file paper. Remember? You said you had some."

"God!" Cassie looks round helplessly. "I dunno where it is, do I?"

"You had it ready this morning," says Andrea patiently.

Cassie swears. She flounces off to the kitchen and appears with a pad of file paper and a pencil case. With a martyred air she sits down heavily on the settee.

"Sorry there isn't room for a table, even a coffee table." Andrea's looking stressed this morning.

I'm used to working on my lap and I'm sure Cassie will manage it too, I reassure her.

Andrea retreats with a sigh, leaving the door open. I glance at Cassie. She's staring down into her lap, stony-faced. She still hasn't made eye contact. What on earth can I do with her? *Stories*! Cassie used to like them. I'm glad that at the last minute, I grabbed a couple of teenage fiction books from my store cupboard.

"Choose a book to read, Cassie."

I spread them out in front of her, on the edge of the bed, which is touching our knees. She looks at me suspiciously.

"I'm not reading. I hate reading out loud."

"No, you don't have to read. I'm going to read to you. So choose a book."

Cassie picks them up one by one and flips through the pages.

"This one."

She's chosen a teen romance, written in 1960, called *The Forbidden Path*. I keep some old-fashioned children's fiction, partly for their excellent themes, which never age, but mostly so that children might glean some insight into their grandparents' way of life. It's disturbing how many kids think that mobile phones and microwaves and computers have been around forever. In this boy-meets-girl story, her parents don't approve, because they're snobbish prigs and don't like his clothes and the way he speaks. They forbid her to see him. She has to dream up all kinds of schemes to meet him in secret. Her parents lock her in her room – oh, happy days! There's no swearing and no sex except a chaste kiss along a moonlit path in the wood. Not even a hint of naughtiness – '*and then he...*'. Will Cassie find it deadly dull? Well, she chose it. And with synchronicity working in its usual mysterious way, the story line echoes the Romeo-and-Juliet plot in Cassie's own life.

I begin the story. I'm so engrossed in it myself that I forget to look at her. After two pages, her unnatural silence unnerves me. Her head is bent down, the curtain of hair shielding her face. Is she asleep? I stop reading. Immediately she peers round at me.

"Go on then!"

I continue, now and again glancing at her to include her in the shared experience. Now something curious is happening. Not only is she listening with rapt attention, but almost imperceptibly, she's moved closer towards me, sucking her thumb. When I stop to turn a page, or pause for breath, she looks at me with an unfathomable expression.

"My throat's getting dry, Cassie. Would you read just this tiny bit, to give my voice a rest?" I indicate about ten lines of text.

She hesitates. For a moment I think I've lost her. Then, tutting, she grabs the book and starts to read. She stumbles over a place-name, and the words 'sympathetically' and 'character.' Yet she can scan the page well, and she puts expression into the short dialogue between the boy and girl.

I thank her for her help, and carry on reading. She doesn't want me to stop.

"We'll carry on tomorrow," I promise.

I give her a point for helping me read. My point system, which I started thirty years ago and could no more relinquish than give up chocolate, is really for my own use. It consists of an encircled '1' which is placed in one of three columns which run down the side of the page, alongside the day's work plan. The columns are headed: 'Ready', 'Session Work Completed,' and 'Homework Completed.' The word 'Ready' doesn't just include being able to get out of bed in the morning in time, but also keeping to our agreed break times, and for completing the session. As the columns fill up with points (or don't, as the case may be), I can see at a glance how a pupil is doing. A full column indicates steady progress under that heading. Primary kids are intrigued by this, and like to see their points mount up. I give them a small prize when they've achieved thirty points. Teenagers generally are indifferent. It's babyish. Yet those who have never gained a good mark or a 'smiley face' sticker at school are often quite chuffed to watch their points grow, although of course they pretend they don't give a toss.

And now Cassie's suddenly looking sideways at my file.

"What's that you're writing down?"

"I've given you a point, for helping me read. You get one point for every piece of work you do."

"Oh." Do I detect a flicker of interest in her voice?

I've decided to kill maths and English with one stone today. I tell Cassie we're going to make two shopping lists. I take a piece of paper and rule a line down the middle to make two columns. The first column is headed 'Cassie's items' and the other one is headed 'Cost of items'. I get another piece of paper and do the same for Darren.

I hand her the paper with her name on it first. I'm hoping to give her the subliminal message that *her* needs are important, at a time when her world has been turned upside down. When it might seem to her that all the professionals seem to care about is how the baby is doing.

She greets this idea with little enthusiasm.

"What's the point? I can't go shopping. Andrea won't let me out by myself."

"You will, soon. Just think, if you could buy anything you wanted with your allowance, what would you spend it on?"

At the top of her list, Cassie writes 'Dean'. She looks up at me to see my reaction. I nod. Underneath, she writes 'trainers, hair gel, glitter jeans'. She stops, chewing her pencil. She adds 'present for Andrea', "because she's helped me with Darren" but says she doesn't know what to buy her. She yawns and sighs. Just the act of thinking seems to wear Cassie out. After much frowning she says, "A photo frame?"

"Great idea!"

She runs out of ideas for herself, so we move on to the next column to estimate the cost of the items.

"Dean." Her fingers rest lovingly on the word. "He's priceless."

She flings down her pen. "It's not fair. They won't let me see him, not even supervised? Just because he's on probation? And he's hardly even seen Darren yet. Like he's going to snatch him or something?"

It all sounds very harsh to me, but then I don't know the full story. Perhaps there's more to this than Cassie's telling me. I murmur soothing platitudes and get her on to the subject of trainers.

"They cost £120."

"That's a lot!"

"You don't believe me, do you? Look, they're in here!"

She dashes across the room and with remarkable homing instinct finds a catalogue hidden under a pile of baby clothes on the floor. In an instant, she's found the page.

"There!" she says triumphantly. "I really want those, and – wait there – there's a top I want." She's about to get sidetracked. Flicking through the catalogue, she finds pictures of skinny teen models and comments on the different hairstyles. With difficulty, I get her back to the thorny subject of budgeting. Could she write down what else she'd like from the catalogue, and next to it, what it costs?

This is a laborious process, punctuated with much page flicking, exclamations of approval or disapproval of the latest fashions displayed. Twice she jumps up to look in the mirror and clutch at her hair. She drops her pen and scrambles around at the bottom of the settee. But after twenty minutes she's completed her half of the exercise.

"Can I have a break now?"

It's five minutes' short of the forty minutes we'd agreed, but Darren could wake any moment, so I let her go. She bolts into the kitchen to phone a friend and make herself some hot chocolate. I look at her work. Her writing is that of a much younger child, large and rounded, but clear. There's a good grasp of basic spelling rules. Maths is weaker. She can add, but her subtraction is shaky. She uses her fingers, as she has no idea how to set out a simple subtraction sum. Place value and borrowing are complete mysteries. Not for the first time, I'm wondering how any child – even one like Cassie who has missed a lot of school – can reach the age of fifteen without having the least grasp of how to take £26.78p from £50.36p.

I'm determined to carry on with this. I can see she's bored with this exercise and feel I'm in danger of flogging a dead horse. On the other hand I sense a strong need for continuity. Completing an exercise, however boring (as long as she doesn't find it distasteful or too difficult), is one of the ways Cassie can be 'held together'. If I'm not careful, I'm going to be so discouraged by her lack of enthusiasm that I'll end up trying to please and placate her, offering to change the exercise at the first sign of boredom. We'll then end up with a jumble of disjointed and unfinished pieces of work. All these, as messy and incomplete as Cassie's room, could just compound the chaos in her mind.

When she comes back, I ask her: "So what about Darren? What does he need now?"

Cassie looks as if she's about to throw her pen across the room, then changes her mind.

"*For godssake!*" She pulls the paper towards her, and writes rapidly and carelessly: 'Nappies, cotton-wool, cream, more bibs, nappy liners, dummies."

"Anything else?"

"No. Andrea gets it all. Social services pay for it. All the nappies and his clothes and everything."

"Well, what about extras, things that social services wouldn't buy?"

Cassie thinks hard, then writes, 'teddy,' 'fluffy cat.' She looks at her watch. "How much longer have we got?'

"We'll just write down how much these items cost, and then see what the total comes to."

With much huffing and tutting from Cassie, the exercise is finally completed. It's almost time to stop. Just time for a quick maths game. I give her two points for her work and praise her for persevering. Not too much praise, she can't take it yet. Unexpectedly, I feel pleased with today's session.

"See you tomorrow, Cassie."

She follows me into the hall to see me out. I seem to be winning her over at last! Pride comes before a fall. Cassie suddenly glares at me.

"I'm only doing education so I can see Dean. My social worker says I have to. She's minging. I hate her. I'm going to get another one."

She opens the front door dramatically. "Bye."

"Goodbye Cassie."

The door's slammed shut. I scuttle humbly down the path. Cassie's words ring in my ears. Can she really sack her social worker, just like that? And am I next for the chop?

Friday, 16th January. Cassie went on strike this morning. At one point she left the room and refused to come back.

After this gruelling and exhausting session with Cassie, I know the answer is, as ever, to grab some personal space. On the way to my next pupil I instinctively know my survival depends on a breather by the pier.

As I drive along, I'm wondering where I'm going wrong. Should I try a different approach? Would it be better to—

Brakes screech, a horn blasts in my ear.

"Wake up! What d'yer think yer doing? IDIOT!"

I'd just seen a parking place opposite the newsagent and aimed for it. Without warning or signals. Then I'd made a hash of reversing into the space. My bonnet sticks out at a jaunty angle, nudging the van driver's nearside front wing.

His van has pulled up alongside. He leaps out bristling with black stubble and righteous indignation, and peers through my window. The van has stopped in the middle of the high street, leaving a trail of tooting, irate drivers stretching as far back as Boots the Chemist on the corner.

I'll not mess with him. Bulky, with close-cropped hair, he's mean-eyed and menacing. Gracefully, I admit that there might have been some slight error of judgement on my part – but what awesomely speedy reactions he's shown, managing to stop so promptly! He storms back into his van with a parting shot: "Woman driver!"

And now, back to my original mission. I make a beeline for the newsagent's. Chocolate. My need for chocolate increases, on a scale of one to ten, in direct ratio to the amount of stress hormone released. This is definitely a two-large-bars day. With a few chocolate brazils and exotic chocolates thrown in.

Back in the car with chocolate and newspaper, I munch my way through half a bar and congratulate myself on my willpower. The paper is full of gloom and disaster, but I need peace and serenity. So I head for the Pier Café. In a seat by an open window inside the café, I watch the waves lash and eddy around the pier supports far beneath. The syncopated rhythm is soothing and hypnotic. Half an hour later, I'm restored. With time for a quick stroll along the seafront, I take long, deep breaths. I 'breathe out' the last pupil, and 'breathe in' the next. I want to be fully present for Thomas, without any lingering residue of this morning's angst.

It's hard, this process of switching between each child, shaking off the effects of stressful or challenging behaviour, in order to fully receive what is being offered *now*. It's hard but essential.

Charity shops are my particular solution. They give me time to think. And there's nothing to equal the triumph of finding the unexpected bargain that might act as a teaching aid. It could be a counting game, map, jigsaw... anything. How all this works is still a bit of a mystery to me. Perhaps it enables me to view seemingly intractable pupils in a more positive way. In buying something for tomorrow, I'm looking to their future. Suddenly there's an opening, like a doorway in a secret garden, through which I might glimpse new pathways, new choices.

Monday, 2nd February. We've almost finished reading *The Forbidden Path* – a tale of thwarted love. The heroine's mother has found out about secret meetings in an abandoned genuine Romany caravan in the woods. The two lovebirds are innocently painting the rotten timbers, and restoring it to its former glory. But mother suspects the worst and issues a dire warning.

"What's 'illeg...' 'illy' something?"

"Illegitimate."

"Whatever. What's it mean?"

I stare at Cassie. Is she having me on? In the fifties – and even the sixties – the word 'illegitimate' lurked darkly, deep in the consciousness of every adolescent. It was spoken in a hushed whisper among friends huddled together in school changing rooms. Just knowing the word was a badge of honour, a sign that you'd put away childish playground games and crossed over the bridge into a secret, adult landscape, where, like oak trees looming out of the fog in a pitch-black forest, new words would suddenly pop up – disturbing and exciting. Just knowing the word 'illegitimate' along with 'intercourse' and 'bastard,' earned you kudos amongst your friends. And the word held a fearful warning: it was what happened if you went 'too far'.

Yet this one word would probably have summed up many thirteen or fourteen-year-olds' worldly knowledge. Sex education in those days was gleaned over a period of several years, in a triad of learning curves: a) plants and rabbits did it, b) humans did it, and c) humans did it for fun! And most 1950's teenagers would have looked as blank as Cassie does now, if they had heard any of the Anglo-Saxon words that colour the everyday conversation of Cassie's contemporaries.

"So what does it mean?" persists Cassie.

"It comes from the word 'legal'."

I tell her how things were in those far-off days, hoping she won't take it personally. But no, she's looking at me uncomprehendingly, as if none of all this touches in any way on her own life story. I may as well be talking about mummifying the dead.

I'm glad for her that she'll never know the pain of having her baby, only two days old, whisked away for adoption. But I'm also sad that Cassie's childhood has ended so soon.

Friday, 13th February. Cassie's had to miss four tuition sessions in the last ten days. She's had meetings with her social worker, the child protection officer, a Link worker, the health visitor. All this has interrupted the flow of our work together – she's distracted and fidgety.

So far, almost imperceptibly, we've been making some headway. I've divided the week's work into roughly four subjects: maths, English, science, and arts and crafts. Cassie is still struggling with maths. I'm determined that she should have at least some idea of the four basic operations. But her idea of a good session is to rush through as many worksheets in her workbook as possible. It's a primary-level workbook, but she makes many careless errors. And there remain glaring gaps in her knowledge – she still refuses to write down a subtraction sum, saying she'll 'do it in her head'. Multiplying and division are quite beyond her, as she doesn't know her multiplication tables.

We have to go right back to the very beginning, so today I've started with a multiplication card game. By some miracle there's a tiny patch of uncluttered floor, and we're kneeling down, taking turns to find matching pairs. Cassie's actually enjoying this new game. The habitual scowl on her face has been replaced by a barely disguised smile.

"What's six eights?"

"Go back to one you know, Cassie. Like five eights?"

"I dunno, do I? Tell me."

"Try eight fives instead then. You know the five times table, don't you?"

"Yes, but…"

"Then all you have to do is to swap the numbers round, and say eight fives instead of five eights."

Cassie looks doubtful. "Can I do that? It won't be the same, will it?"

"Try it!"

After heavy breathing and laborious counting on fingers, Cassie finds out that, magically, the two answers are the same. Archimedes himself could not have looked so amazed at this discovery.

"I never knew that," Cassie says.

"So *six* eights are…? Just add another eight to forty!"

Still uncertain, she does so, then snatches up two cards.

"They match, look!"

She puts another winning pair on her pile, touchingly triumphant.

There's a sudden jangle of ring-tones. Cassie's mobile, hidden under a pile of clothes on the bed, interrupts us.

"Cassie, you promised you'd leave your mobile with Andrea." This means several precious minutes wasted.

"Sorry, I forgot. But I won't speak to her. I'm bloody fed up with it!"

I stare at her, mystified, as she answers the call. She holds the phone well away from her ear. A woman's voice, persistent and hysterical. I pick out the words 'lover boy', 'baby', 'danger'. Cassie's turned pale.

"Shut up, shut up, *shut up!* I'm not talking to you. Leave me alone!"

She switches off the mobile, and remains stock still for a moment.

"It's my mum. She keeps threatening me. She's going to get a care order for Darren, so she can have him instead of me. But I won't let her."

The phone rings again and at the same time Darren, who's been peacefully asleep in his carrycot on the bed, wakes up with a hungry shriek. Cassie snatches him up as if he's about to be abducted by aliens. She rushes next door, with baby and phone, to tell Andrea. I follow her into the lounge.

"Can you keep this phone for me? She won't stop ringing. She's doing my head in."

I offer to hold Darren while Cassie prepares his feed. She marches into the kitchen, full of righteous indignation. Darren's calmed down and is gurgling at me disarmingly. He can now focus on my face, and if I wriggle my fingers, his gaze follows the movement. He looks healthy and well fed and contented. I cradle him in my lap, marvelling at how his cheeks have filled out. He seems to have doubled in size.

"So what's been going on?" I ask Andrea.

"Well, the social worker has set up a supervised meeting at the family centre for the three of them to meet – Cassie, Dean and the baby."

"Has Dean seen the baby yet?"

"Just once, soon after he was born. But Cassie wasn't allowed to be there."

"That seems very hard!"

Andrea's look suggests I'm being naïve.

"We have to be absolutely sure of what we're doing, in our dealings with Dean. He's not violent, not a criminal. But he's on probation for theft, and he's still into drugs. If he starts passing them on to Cassie, that will go against her as regards keeping Darren. This is a trial period for her too, to see if she's fit to look after the baby."

"Does he seem pleased about Darren? Is he taking an interest?"

Andrea looks doubtful. "It's difficult to know. The trouble with Dean is that he's unpredictable. He'll suddenly decide to do something, without rhyme or reason. Like after he'd known Cassie for a couple of months, he just disappeared up north to stay with some relative, to look for a job. Cassie was heartbroken. And then, just as suddenly, he came back again after three weeks. And though I say he's not naturally violent, he gets into fights. Lets people wind him up. He's very immature."

"Cassie told me her mother is trying to get a care order so that she has sole custody of Darren."

"Yes, but she won't have a chance. She's too unstable, and everyone knows it. But such is her hold over Cassie, that the poor girl's terrified."

"What a horrible mess. Yet at least Darren seems to be thriving."

Andrea gives me a quizzical look. Her mouth has set in a firm line.

"There are concerns."

"Oh?" My heart thuds uncomfortably.

"The health visitor was here yesterday. She was appalled by the state of Cassie's room. And the baby has quite a bad nappy rash. Cassie isn't changing him as often as she should."

"Oh dear, that's awful!"

"Anyway, we shall see." Andrea ends on a warning note – Cassie's just returned with the feeding bottle. She flops down on the settee. Gently, I place Darren in her lap. He drinks in long, gasping draughts. She's stroking his head, smiling down at him.

This image of mother and baby, as close to a medieval painting of a Madonna and Child as I've ever seen, will haunt me in the months to come.

Monday, 23rd February. "Andrea, keep this phone for me!" Cassie holds out her mobile, pleadingly, as I enter the hall. I've never known a girl *volunteering* to be parted from her phone, and I'm amused. And mystified – she's certainly not trying to please me. In fact, she looks frazzled.

"It's my mum! She rang ten times yesterday? And like, she was crying down the phone? She wants me to come home to live with her. One moment she's being all nice, like, 'I love you Cassie!' and the next she says she's going to get her solicitor onto me!"

Andrea takes the phone. Her voice is calm and controlled, but I can see that she's as fraught as Cassie.

"Just try and concentrate on your education, dear. I'll answer any phone calls."

As I follow Cassie into her room, Andrea nudges my elbow, and whispers, "I'll have a quick word, later."

The room's looking, if possible, even more like a bomb-site than usual. The carrycot is missing from its usual place on the bed. I've a sudden fear that something's happened to Darren.

"Where's the baby, Cassie?"

"Andrea's got him."

Cassie slumps down on the settee. She looks exhausted, with dark rings under her eyes. How can writing practice and division have any meaning, set against the backdrop of Cassie's everyday reality – the drama of threatening phone calls and constant visits from the professional care workers?

"What would you like to start with today, Cassie?"

"Dunno. What's the point, anyway?"

If I get drawn in to this, I'll end up feeling as hopeless as Cassie. To make matters worse, last week was half term, so we're both suffering from broken continuity.

"Have a look at this, Cassie. I'd love to know what you think."

By a happy chance, whilst medicating myself with chocolate and charity shops the week before last, I found a magazine that's just right for Cassie. The photo on the front cover caught my eye – three teenage graces, all munching apples, their glossy tresses swirling around their shoulders. The caption read:

'Eat Your Way to Healthy, Shiny Hair! - see p.15'. Cassie snatches the magazine from me. Alas, I forgot to cut out the article first.

Cassie thumbs through till she finds the problem page. I let her read for a few moments, then, promising to leave her the magazine, I find the article. Three stunning super-models smugly reveal the secrets of their shiny locks. Natasha starts her day with a glass of water with a smidgeon of fresh lemon, followed one hour later (after her morning jog), by a small bowl of organic muesli, with yogurt and honey. For lunch she has a large salad and toasted Feta cheese. Tammy prefers her main meal at lunchtime, and favours steamed fish, or an organic chicken leg. Mimi loves raw food...and so on. All three models are scrupulous about their five daily portions of fruit and vegetables. Not a whiff of a McDonalds in the whole article. I'm impressed. Will Cassie find them inspiring role models? How about planning a healthy eating plan for herself, for just three days?

To my relief, Cassie takes up the challenge. She 'hates' science, so I've abandoned the textbooks for the moment. But they do contain some interesting sections on health. Perhaps this might be a way in? One thing's certain – Cassie has a healthy appetite.

For ten minutes there's a blissful silence as Cassie writes down suggestions for the magic formula which will un-grease her hair. I've also bought along a colourfully tempting 'Five Veg.' brochure from my local surgery. Cassie, who'd heard of vitamins but wasn't sure what they were, is fascinated by the magical effects of vitamins C and D. I tell her in graphic detail what happens to the long-suffering intestines through lack of fibre, and how runners eat a mound of pasta before the London Marathon. All good stuff. It's got Cassie interested enough to write down a sample menu for herself. But she's struggling. Not with ideas, but with the act of writing.

"My wrist hurts!" She flings down the pen. She's been holding the pen by wedging it between her middle finger and forefinger, so that she's either gripping it too tight and using her wrist to move the pen along; or she lets the fingers flop, and loses control.

"Try holding the pen like this, Cassie."

I show her the tripod grip, with thumb, forefinger and middle finger together, encircling the writing end of the pen, fairly close to its point. Cassie says it doesn't feel right, she's tried it before, her primary school teachers kept on about it.

"Try again. It might work this time."

She perseveres and makes some headway. She admits her wrist hurts less, yet it's still painfully slow. I watch her carefully. She'll think of what she wants to write, but then there's a long pause before she transfers the thought to the page. Her brain signals don't seem to reach the tiny muscles at the end of her fingers, which should move the pen up and down and round. Clearly, there's a problem with her grapho-motor ability, a fairly common problem with younger children, rarer in Cassie's age group. What she needs is loads of practice. Sadly, Cassie lacks both the time and the motivation to devote herself to half an hour a day of writing *something,* no matter what, maybe a diary, a letter, or just copying out something that interests her from a magazine. Her mind and concentration are all over the place. Already she's bored and wants to stop.

Andrea comes in and asks if I'd like a cup of tea. She tells Cassie that Darren's grizzling and working himself up for a feed. Cassie disappears into the lounge, and Andrea motions for me to stay.

"I hope you don't mind, but we might need to cut short Cassie's tuition today. The health visitor's coming this afternoon. I want Cassie to have an almighty clear-up in here."

Maybe we need to get over the hurdle of the half term break before we gather up some new momentum. Cassie's definitely had enough education for today.

"I'll help her, if you like?"

"*Would* you?" Andrea flops down suddenly on the bed. "That would help me too. I've also got a meeting with social services at twelve about a new child they'd like me to take in, next week."

"Heavens! You've got a lot on your plate – you've still got Lee, haven't you?"

"Yes, but he's no trouble. It's Cassie who's the main problem just now."

"She seems very exhausted. I managed to get a little work out of her – but only just."

"She met Dean secretly yesterday afternoon."

"But she's not allowed out of the house by herself, is she?"

"We've just relaxed the rules, at the beginning of last week. We thought it was a bit hard on her being in all day, as it was half term and there isn't much for her to do here. She's allowed out, unsupervised, for two hours at a time, on Monday, Wednesday and Friday."

"With the baby?" There's a hollow, sinking feeling in my stomach.

"No, she's only allowed to take Darren out if I'm with her, or together with some other responsible adult."

"Will that change, soon?"

"She has to prove that she can be responsible for herself, first."

"Thank God for that!"

Andrea gives me a long look. Am I over-reacting? Am *I* bonding too much with Darren?

"Anyway, she was good as gold on Monday and Wednesday. On Friday, she was due back at five, but by half-past she wasn't home. I was getting worried, so I asked Bill if he'd go and look for her. I had a rough idea where she might be. There's a café where all the kids hang out. And there they both were, huddled together at a table, so deep in conversation that they didn't even notice Bill coming towards them. He says they looked as if they were hatching some plan."

"Oh no! No wonder she can't concentrate with all that happening – and her mother ringing all the time… And poor you, having to cope with it all."

"That's not all." Andrea says grimly. "She's become very lax about making up Darren's feeds for the night. Twice I've had to wake her at about two in the morning to prepare a bottle. Last night she refused to get out of bed. I had to make up the feed myself. Then she asked me, not very politely, to feed him for her. She was too 'knackered'."

"But that's not like Cassie, is it? They seemed to be bonding so well."

Andrea shrugs and sighs. "I just don't know what's happening with Cassie. Several times lately she's left me to pick him up when he cries. And then there's the nappy changing – she has to be reminded about it constantly."

"Do you think it's some sort of natural reaction from the birth, like post-natal depression?"

"I thought of that, but she's too lively in other ways. She'll prance around the house listening to her music, which is so loud the neighbours have complained. Then, if I take her out shopping she's wheedling about some new outfit she wants me to buy. Yet when it comes to making out a shopping list for Darren, she can't be bothered. She's always running out of nappies and liners and cotton wool. I've told her, all she's got to do is give me a list, and I'll get anything she needs…" Andrea's shoulders slump. She shakes her head.

"What a shame. All that work Cassie and I did on shopping lists for Darren."

"She *could* do it," says Andrea sadly. "She *could* do a simple shopping list if she were more concerned about Darren..."

Cassie clearly isn't coping as well as she should be. I try to put this thought out of my mind. After all, Cassie's apathy could well be due to tiredness and anxiety. Surely this is just a blip in the bonding process?

For the moment, let's just tackle that horrendous mess in her room.

Wednesday, 25th February. "Oh Cassie, what on earth's happened to your room?"

The exclamation bursts out of me before I can stop myself. All Monday's careful tidying and sorting, dusting and cleaning has descended into chaos. Cassie gazes round the room blankly. "I dunno."

"But it's terrible! How can it get like this in two days?"

I'd felt pleased with Monday's efforts. Tidiness, I've discovered, falls into a spectrum of abilities that can broadly be defined as organisational. This includes managing our time so we're not always late for appointments, and knowing how long a task will take. Tidying up comes under spatial organisation – being able to make order out of our personal space, including our possessions. Teenagers are notoriously bad at this. There's so much going on in their lives that having to tidy their rooms is very low in the list of priorities. As they mature, their natural pre-disposition for order or disorder 'will out' and they'll settle into one camp or another. The good news is that tidiness can, to some extent, be learnt.

Every time I sat in the middle of Cassie's horrendous mess, I'd wondered if her mum had ever shown her how to tidy up. Anyone who's ever asked a three-year old to put away toys will know the frustration of seeing him or her wander around aimlessly. It can often end in tears or defiance. The child just doesn't understand what's meant by 'putting away', or 'tidying up'. It's too abstract. But try saying 'Let's put all the teddies in the big basket', or 'Can you put all your cars on the shelf – let's pretend it's a long car-park!' Hopefully, the child will associate tidying up with fun.

On Monday, I had tried putting this theory into practice with Cassie. The challenge was to break down into bite-size, manageable chunks, the mammoth job of making order out of chaos and yet to respect her boundaries and possessions, and her age. I asked her what she'd like to sort out first.

"Darren's trolley," she said. "My health visitor always watches me change him."

Even this was easier said than done. The trolley had to be tidied shelf by shelf. As each layer was cleared, I wrote out a step by step reminder of what we did. We worked side by side.

"Step by step is best for learning anything, Cassie. When I was your age I wanted to make my own clothes. Design things the way *I* wanted them, and I didn't know how until I discovered an 'easy steps' sewing pattern. I learned how to cut it out and then put it together. It was wonderful. I felt so pleased with myself."

Cassie gives me a withering look. "Sad."

"It worked, Cassie, I felt great!"

As she made headway in ranging Darren's toiletries into neat rows, I saw a slight flush of triumph on Cassie's face. I had left on a high that day.

So, my plan for today was to combine I.T. with English, and get Cassie to type up the tidying-up plan we'd written down as we went along.

I'd arranged with Andrea for Cassie to have an hour on the computer this morning. Now, having seen the room in this state, I was having to reconsider what was best tackled first. What would make most impact on Cassie? Typing up a theoretical plan (which obviously hasn't even scratched the surface of her consciousness) or another practical session of room sorting?

"My health-visitor's coming again this afternoon," says Cassie, conversationally, "so I suppose I'd better clear up a bit in here."

The decision's made for me. After all, Rome wasn't built in a day. We begin an action replay of Monday's session. I get Cassie to read out what she has to do, step by step. I want this to be *her* achievement, not mine. She potters along with it in a desultory fashion, stopping every few minutes to tell me the latest on Dean.

"We're going to get a flat together, when I'm sixteen."

"When's your birthday, remind me?"

"November 15th. And no one can stop us, not my mum and not that minging social worker neither."

There is a rare moment of silence as Cassie folds up some little vests and jackets. She's deep in thought, in another world – of Dean, and freedom, and happy-ever-after.

"We're going down the council, to get put on a waiting list."

"Oh?"

"Yes. You have to get points, but we'll have enough by then. They have to give you somewhere if you're homeless."

"Well, that's some time ahead," I say guardedly.

There's a tightness in my throat. I look at her. Is she trying to tell me something that Andrea should know about? But she's still in dreamland, gazing into space.

Darren's crying in the lounge. Cassie ignores him. The crying stops suddenly.

So far Cassie's sorted half the trolley. Already she's fidgety. She jumps up to look in the mirror, and tweaks her eyelashes. She dashes to her wardrobe and pulls out a skirt, which she holds up for my inspection.

"Look what Andrea got me yesterday! It's well lush. I love it."

"Very nice." I'm weary and worried I might sound snappy. "Let's see how much more you can do in the next ten minutes, then we'll have a break."

"Where shall I put these clothes?" Cassie holds out the folded baby things.

"Where do you think they should go?" I suck in a deep steadying breath.

"In here?" Cassie points vaguely at the chest of drawers.

She goes towards the drawers, then stops. "I'm knackered. I need a fag. Can I have my break now?"

"Now Cassie, you know the rules. You've been good about keeping to the break times so far. Only five more minutes!"

"God, it's like a bloody boot-camp in here!" She dumps the baby clothes in a pile on top of the chest of drawers and looks round helplessly.

"What shall I do next?"

"Look around and see what needs doing. Or look at the plan." I hold it out to her. Cassie snatches it and reads from the list.

"'Pick up my dirty clothes and put them in the laundry basket.'"

She wanders round the room, finding clothes on the settee, the bed, and the floor, but progress is painful. She picks up her hairbrush and brushes her hair vigorously.

"I'm going to grow it really long. Dean likes me with long hair. And I might dye it black."

"Cassie…"

"I need a shower. Is it break time yet?"

"Just about," I sigh.

"Great! I'll be back in five minutes…"

"CASSIE!" She's just about to dump the clothes back on the floor. "Put the clothes in the dirty linen basket!"

"Oh, yes. I forgot."

The pile finds its rightful place and I heave a sigh of relief. I concentrate on holding my voice as level as possible.

"When you've had your shower, what will you have to do next?"

She looks round the room, yawning. She shows little interest in her surroundings. She is outside of it, uninvolved, although it is her room. Hers and her baby's.

"Um. I could make my bed. And tidy my shoes…"

"Good!"

Cassie has her hand on the door handle, "But I won't have time. I've got to see my solicitor at eleven o'clock."

"WHAT?"

"I thought Andrea told you. She was going to. She's found me a solicitor so that my mum can't get custody of Darren. And so that I can get my allowance. Mum is taking all of it, the bitch. She got it for looking after me while I was pregnant. But I'm living here now. She's well out of order. See you in five minutes."

I stand still, clenching my fists, as I hear her light footsteps on the stairs. I survey the room, defeated. Making the bed and tidying her shoes will make scarcely a dent in this almighty mess. I've a sudden urge to open the window and fling out every shoe, every item of clothing on the floor, all the soggy make-up tissues and unwashed coffee mugs. I want to scream and holler: 'It's all too much, it's too hard!'

There is fear, too, in this room. It's so palpable that were I to unclench my fists and clutch the air around me, I can imagine grabbing handfuls of it.

I recoil, thinking of Cassie's early experiences. And suddenly, being in the room, Cassie's room, is like swimming in a murky, midnight sea, and feeling something slimy brushing against your palms.

I feel stuck, and powerless. Forget all my fancy theories. Whether or not Cassie lacks innate sorting skills, whether or not she learnt to tidy up at her mother's knee – all of this is just a minuscule part of a huge problem. Cassie's like a teddy bear, coming apart at the seams. There's no one there to put her together again. To stitch up the torn fur.

Where was her mother when Cassie needed her most? To love her. To care for her, to hold Cassie in her thoughts. *And to keep her from harm.* How lucky the child who has such a parent! That child will carry throughout her life a somatic sense of invisible arms wrapped around her. She'll feel safe in a protective embrace. But Cassie's had to cope alone with the devastating effects of sexual abuse. No wonder she's all 'over the place', unable to hold anything in her own thoughts for more than a few moments. For Cassie, to actually slow down and *think* is dangerous. It's the last thing she wants to do. The chaos in this room reflects the chaos in her life – and this in itself is a protective arm she's had to conjure up for herself. It shields her against the jumble of painful memories and feelings which threaten to engulf her at any time.

How can Cassie 'bond' with English and maths, when there's such an arid landscape in her inner world? How can she bond with anything?

Andrea's sitting on the settee in the lounge, when I knock and go in, cuddling Darren. His eyes are watching her lips move, as she coos and talks to him. He half smiles, but of course it could be wind.

I offer Andrea her computer back, there won't be time this morning if Cassie has to see her solicitor before the end of the session. Andrea says the appointment isn't till twelve, she always works around my tuition sessions. Cassie's just trying it on. I should have guessed, but by now I've lost faith in the tidy-up plan– it no longer seems relevant.

Cassie stomps downstairs in a flurry of talcum powder, dripping-wet hair and soggy towels. Andrea passes Darren over to her.

"He's done a nice big packet for you to deal with."

"Shit! Not now, I've got to dry my hair!"

"NOW, Cassie!"

Andrea fixes Cassie with a gimlet eye, and even Cassie recognises that there's no wriggling out of this one. Sulkily, she takes Darren into her room.

I tell Andrea about Cassie's plans to get a flat with Dean. She smiles wryly and says she's heard all about it. Dean will be on probation for another year, however, and Cassie will still have to prove she's a good mother. It's highly improbable that they'll get on a housing list.

"Cassie's got a supervised meeting with Dean tomorrow afternoon," Andrea calls after me as I leave the room to see if Cassie's finished Darren's nappy change. "It won't affect you directly, but she might be a bit restless in the morning. I thought I'd better warn you!"

Cassie's trying to do up the poppers on Darren's babygrow. His little legs are kicking like pistons and she keeps trying to grab them and stuff them in the legs of the little garment, but it's like trying to line up two moving targets. Cassie turns suddenly and sees me trying to keep a straight face.

"Very funny," she scowls.

I want to suggest that she just holds out the leg of the babygrow and waits – sooner or later Darren's leg will land inside it. But no, she has to find things out for herself. Suddenly, watching Cassie, I don't feel like laughing. She doesn't talk to her baby or make eye contact. There's no play or loving touch. She might as well be tying up a parcel with string. And Darren's clearly not happy. He screws up his little face and cries, tossing his head from side to side. What's happened to that loving mum of just two weeks ago?

As soon as he's dressed, Cassie whisks him up and takes him back to Andrea, then returns fairly quickly. I guess there's been some stern prompting from that direction.

"I'll do a bit more clearing up then, shall I?" says Cassie.

"What you're going to do is to clear as much of this room as you can in the next ten minutes. I'll time you. And anything that doesn't get done will just have to stay that way. You can choose whether you live in a mess or not, but don't expect your health visitor to be impressed."

"Oooh! What's rattled your cage?" Cassie rolls her eyes at me. "How long do we have after that? I've got my solicitor…"

"Your solicitor's meeting is at twelve. After you've tidied up we have half an hour and I'll tell you then what we're doing."

Cassie opens her mouth, then gives me a sidelong look and shuts it again. She moves round the room in silence, picking things up from the floor and stuffing them into drawers. I sit on the settee making some notes, letting her know I'm there if she needs me but that I'm not going to do it for her.

I, too, am going through a process. I've been trying to climb mountains with Cassie. I've wanted to lift her up by the very force of my will and my enthusiasm, but the terrain is too steep, criss-crossed with too many crevasses and sheer cliff-faces. What can I – and Andrea – do for Cassie, with so many odds stacked against her?

Suddenly my role has shrunk. All I can do is to be here, showing that I'm hanging in, whatever happens. That I *care*. Maybe if I'm lucky, I can give a little nudge here or there, in the right direction along the path. Maybe the climb will be too difficult, we might never reach the top. Even so, I can still point to everything that is beautiful and fascinating along the way. Hardest of all, I have to be there, still holding her in my thoughts, even when she turns her face away.

"What are we doing now?" asks Cassie. "I can't do any more."

The room looks little better than when we started, but she's so right – she *can't* do any more. Not just now. And maybe not for a long time to come. A lot of good things have to happen to Cassie before she can successfully tidy her room.

"I thought you might like to finish your bag? I can show you how to do back-stitch."

To my surprise, Cassie jumps up and unearths the bag from under her bed.

"I showed it to Ella. She thought it was lush."

Ella manages a boutique in town. She's also Andrea's daughter and a frequent visitor. She's one of the few people to whom Cassie relates.

I get out my sewing kit and a cushion cover I've been working on for about fourteen years. It comes in handy for sewing sessions such as this.

"Let's see what you've done so far."

Cassie's done no more since she last showed me her handiwork. The bag's still in two halves, ready to be stitched together.

"Now, what stitch you do next depends on how professional a job you want to do. If you want it to be really neat inside as well as out, you'll have to learn a hemming stitch as well as back-stitch. But if you just want to sew it up quickly, and you don't mind seeing ragged edges on the inside of the bag, I can just show you a back-stitch." I demonstrate on the cushion cover.

"Mmmm." Cassie frowns, stares at the cushion cover, then considers her bag. "I think I'll do it neatly."

"Right." I try to hide my amazement. "Well, first of all you have to turn the material inside out, and then this is what you do..."

Cassie catches on quickly. Her stitches are careful and even, though she's never hemmed anything in her life. I'm struck by the contrast between the deft movements of her fingers when she sews, and the awkward, clumsy grip when she writes. I know that fine-motor and grapho-motor coordination are different skills, but I've never seen it demonstrated so clearly.

"Those stitches are nice and neat, Cassie."

For ten blissful minutes, we sit hemming, side by side on the settee. Cassie doesn't speak. She's concentrating hard. Now and again she'll peer at my stitching, to compare it with hers. Once she looks at me, watchful, with that strange unfathomable expression I've seen when we're reading together.

It's a magic ten minutes. The sun's streaming through the window, warming my back, and making the sequined patches on Cassie's material sparkle like crystals. The scent of spring wafts through the open window. A blackbird flutes loudly in a nearby tree, and there's a fainter, answering call in the distance. Will Cassie remember this moment, when times are hard for her?

"My fingers hurt." Cassie puts her sewing down.

"Then stop. We can do some tomorrow."

"Can I design another bag, *now?* I want to make one for Ella."

"Sure. Go and find some paper."

Cassie comes back with some A4 computer paper and some coloured pencils. She sits down next to me and begins to draw. She knows exactly what it should look like, she says, but she's 'no good at drawing.' I tell her it can be as sketchy as she likes – it's just a guide to enable her ideas to take shape.

Suddenly, it's there on the page – she's visualised the finished article. She colours it in carefully, her tongue sticking out. There's a fine sense of design and colour, and she thinks three-dimensionally; she's done a separate sketch of what it will look like when it's open.

"I like the way the strap follows the shape of the sides, Cassie. I think it will look really good when it's made up."

I'm excited. I've caught a glimpse of something very special. There it is, that tiny spark inside the candle flame. That essence deep in the core of Cassie's being that by some miracle remains vital and undamaged. How to keep it alive?

"How about having a wander round the charity shops next week," I suggest, casually. "We could look for remnants of material that you could make into a lovely bag."

"Yeah, whatever."

"I'll speak to Andrea and find out what day would be best."

"I need a new pair of jeans. Can you ask Andrea to give me some money? She's well stingy, she won't let me have any. I know the pair I want – we could go into *proper* shops. Charity shops are minging, they're for drop-outs and bag-ladies."

"Bye Cassie."

"See ya."

Friday, 27th February. Andrea opens the door, looking dreadful, holding a screaming Darren over one shoulder. Her eyes are like slits in a puffball, with dark shadows. Usually so smart and well groomed, today she's abandoned the neat little jacket and elegant skirt, in favour of an old jumper which she's put on the wrong way round, and jeans with a hole in the knee. For a moment I have an irrational sense that the real Andrea has been kidnapped.

"Come in," she yawns, "Cassie's still in the bathroom. I've called her – she knows you're here."

She leads me into the lounge, and sits down heavily on the settee. She reaches down to the floor for Darren's bottle. He opens his mouth and she pops the teat in, but for some reason this makes him even angrier, and he works himself into an almighty rage. He's now purple in the face.

"I just don't know what to do with him. He's had me up all night – I've fed him and changed him but each time I've put him down he just won't settle."

"Won't Cassie—"

"Cassie! She refuses to get up. Short of dragging her out of bed I can't make her. Last night, the first time he woke up, I took Darren plus the bottle in to her. I yelled at her to wake up. I shook her. But she just refused point-blank to sit up. Meanwhile, Darren was getting so frantic, I couldn't risk upsetting him any more so I took him into our bed and fed him myself. Bill was not impressed – he didn't get much sleep either...ssshhh, shhh, Darren, it's all right, there now, ssshhh..."

Darren's heartbroken cries subside into hiccupping shudders, and he rests his head on Andrea's shoulder. I rub his back.

"He seems very unsettled compared to how he was in the first few weeks."

"Yes, he's not happy," sighs Andrea. "The health visitor said just the same thing on Wednesday. She noticed how he became much calmer when I was handling him. All Cassie does now is feed and change him. Then she passes him over to me right away to burp him and cuddle him."

"I saw that on Wednesday. She was handling him like a parcel – I couldn't bear to watch."

"He's started to cry even when Cassie picks him up." Andrea shifts Darren off her shoulder and puts him on her lap, feet towards her stomach, cradling his head with one hand while she strokes his cheek with the other. "And then he'll often stop when she passes him over to me. But the most worrying thing of all is that when the health visitor weighed him on Wednesday, he'd lost half a pound. That's a lot from a baby who weighed nine pounds a week ago."

"That's *really* worrying." There's an iciness in my stomach.

"But it's all wrong, I can feel it's all wrong. It's Cassie I'm supposed to be fostering, not Darren!"

"And what about this other child you said you were going to have?"

"I've had to say I can't have her. I felt terrible, letting them down at the last moment. They're desperate for short-term carers, but I can hardly cope with Cassie and Darren at present. Thank goodness Lee seems fairly happy here."

"So did the health visitor talk to Cassie, try to get her more involved and concerned about Darren?"

"She's going to send someone round to give Cassie individual parenting classes, starting next week. But I think it's almost too late." Andrea tickles Darren's chin and cheeks. His eyes, the colour of the sea where it meets the sky on a misty day, gaze up into her own eyes. He's quiet now, but his cheeks are flushed and he moves restlessly. We both fall silent. I'm trying to shut out my dismal, negative thoughts.

"I'll call Cassie for her lesson."

I shout up the stairs: "Cassie, you're fifteen minutes late!"

"Fuck! One minute, okay? Keep your hair on!"

"Hurry up! I'll be in your room."

I settle down on the settee in Cassie's room and get out some maths worksheets. They're straightforward simple division and multiplication questions, and will give Cassie more practice on her tables. For later, when she's had enough maths, I've bought a fashion catalogue along, with five pages of bags in it. I want to build on Cassie's interest, maybe encourage her to do some more designs.

There's a distinctive smell coming from the corner of the room. It's strong and very unpleasant. Underneath the baby trolley lurks a dirty nappy. Next to it, a lime-green stain is slowly seeping into the carpet.

Cassie bounces into the room, unexpectedly bright-eyed and bushy-tailed.

"Look what Dean gave me!"

She holds out her left hand, coming closer as I squint at it.

It glitters on her finger, a silver ring with a diamond in the middle, surrounded by tiny rubies.

"It's my engagement ring. He gave it to me yesterday, at the family centre. We were just sitting there, talking in this room, and he suddenly gets out this box and puts this ring on my finger! It was like, weird, like being in EastEnders or Coronation Street or something? Don't you think it's lush?"

"I think it's lovely. Can I have a look?"

Cassie shoves her hand closer to my face. The ring is far too large, it wobbles about on her slender finger. The sunlight streaming through the window catches the diamond, and tiny rainbow prisms dapple the walls next to us. To my un-expert eye, it looks like the genuine article.

"He's been saving up for it for ages. Weeks and weeks," says Cassie proudly. "All his benefit money, he told me."

"Well! You have had a lot of excitement, Cassie – so many things happening all at once. How are we going to bring you down to earth this morning?"

"Dunno." She twirls the ring around her finger, then shoves out her arm and moves her wrist from side to side, watching the diamond sparkle. She lies down suddenly on the settee, shoving me away with her feet. Still admiring her ring, she sucks the thumb of her other hand.

"Can't wait to show my friends at my old school."

"Do you still see them, sometimes?"

A shadow passes over Cassie's face. "Not now. I can't, can I? Shut in here like a prisoner. But Andrea's going to get their telephone numbers from the school and I'm going to invite Carly and Emma round."

"Let's do some maths," I say brightly. "Then, after your break, we'll do some art and design."

"Can't I do that now?" Cassie yawns, "I'm not in the mood for maths."

"Maths first. Look, Cassie, you've only four points to go, then you've got your thirty points – you'll get a prize!"

I'm still clinging to my points system like a drowning woman to a piece of driftwood. Even to me, the words sound ridiculous. Nonetheless, Cassie slowly swings her legs down to the floor, and without a word, grabs the nearest maths sheet and begins work.

I take a deep breath. If nothing else, Cassie will have learnt most of her tables; she can divide and subtract, so long as there isn't a row of noughts at the top – these still freak her out. Yet, in the final reckoning, I seem to have taught her very little.

The smell coming from the nappy on the floor is becoming more pungent by the second. I'm hanging on as long as possible before I say anything, and I can feel the pressure building up inside. Any moment now I'll explode. It's like vowing never again to ask your teenager, before he swans out of the house for the fourth evening that week, if he's actually done *any* homework? You hold your tongue for three nights then out it comes in a rush: "How do you think you'll pass your exams/ hold down a job/ learn consideration for others?"

"What do I do now, this sum's got more bloody noughts in it!"

Cassie holds out the worksheet as if it's a bomb.

"Well, you can't borrow from the tens, because there aren't any, so you have to go along the row, all the way along to the 'thousand' column. Borrow from that, cross out the 9 and put 8 above it. Take the 1 all the way along to the first 0 and make it 10. Now you can take away, see?" I demonstrate – slowly – on a scrap of paper.

Cassie doesn't see. Her eyes widen. She peers suspiciously at the tiny 1 as if it might be a weapon of mass destruction. "Where's that come from?"

I try to explain. She looks at me warily – am I mixed up in some conspiracy to confuse her, to test her to her limits?

"Look, Cassie, let me show you the 'short cut' way. Just cross out the noughts in the tens column and the hundreds column, and put nines instead. Then you can borrow, all along the row." I show her. "Just do it – and don't worry about understanding *why* just yet. When you've done loads of these, and can do them in your sleep, you'll suddenly understand – in a flash! Trust me."

Trust. A leap of faith for Cassie – trying to bond with the unknown. For her, it must feel like leaping off a cliff. For me, it's like scattering seed on parched ground and trusting that the rains will fall and that one day, the desert will be a carpet of blooms, shimmering under the sun in all the colours of the rainbow. Just now, teaching Cassie maths seems as crazy and irrelevant to me, as the rogue number 1 in her sum must seem to her. Yet we both need to plod on, making 'as if' our guiding mantra. For unless we act *as if* it will all come out well in the end, we might as well give up now.

Cassie says she'll do the easy sums, without the noughts. There's another silence for five minutes.

I urgently need a break for the simple reason that I'm about to be sick. *Don't mention the nappy.*

"We'll stop for five minutes. You can have your break now."

"I'm going for a fag," says Cassie. "My brain hurts."

"Before you go, Cassie, what is the procedure for dirty nappies? Perhaps we should amass them in a huge stockpile, there'd be no need for new nuclear power stations in this country. Then, we could pipe the gas to the Iranians, stop their nuclear energy programme getting out of hand."

"You what?" Cassie's mouth falls open.

"What are you meant to do with Darren's dirty nappies – look, there, on the floor!"

"So? I forgot, didn't I? Shit, it's only one nappy. There's no need to look like that!"

"It stinks!" A whine has crept into my voice.

She scowls, picks it up, and marches off to the kitchen with a martyred air. I hear a rubbish bin lid banged down. There's a brief pause, then music blares out from a local radio station.

The lounge door is ajar. I peer round. The television's on, and Andrea's in front of it with her eyes closed, Darren asleep on her lap. She opens one eye.

"Sorry to disturb you. Cassie's on her break."

"That's all right." Andrea eases herself up and places Darren carefully in his carrycot. "I've got to remind her to make up some feeds in advance. She could do that now – if you don't mind her break being a bit longer?"

"No, that's fine. I'll make up the time at the end. I'm not in such a rush today."

"I'll make you a cup of tea. I could do with one myself."

"Thank you." I sink gratefully into a corner of the settee, next to the carrycot, watching the gentle rise and fall of Darren's breathing.

There's a pile of old newspapers on the floor. Tuesday's local rag is on top, I glance idly at the headlines. The usual mix of the dramatic and the pathetic, the sublime and the ridiculous: 'Midnight raid on jewellers'; 'Benefit man exposes himself to speed camera'; 'Are we creating Godless society?' asks new vicar;

'Milk float runs amok down Windacre Hill.' Suddenly another heading catches my eye:

Education authority to cut back on out-of-school provision for excluded pupils.

Due to a massive overspend last year, the authority is now looking to cut back on what many consider non-essential provision for children who should by rights be in school. Many children receive ten hours or more home tuition. But there is concern that, for the rest of the time, they are on the streets, stealing cars and getting into drugs. 'They have too much time on their hands,' said a spokesman for the authority. 'Moreover they are being rewarded for bad behaviour, by being singled out for extra attention. It's a soft option. They should either be forced to remain in school, in accordance with the government's inclusion policy, or be put on a stricter regime of discipline and law-enforcement than is currently in place...' Plans are being put forward to rationalise the budget of all sectors of out-of-school provision, including tutors, Link workers, Outward Bound courses... The authority is working in conjunction with the borough council and social services to see where alternative provision can be made.

The Tribune interviewed several members of the Borough Council to hear their views. Mrs June Bagshott said:

"It's a disgrace. In my day, they would all be in Borstals. Now we're paying for them to fly off to Australia to go surfing!"

Councillor Colonel John Hawes agrees: "Bring back the birch, I say. There were fifty children in my class and we were flogged regularly if we spoke out of turn. And it never did me any harm!"

Councillor Evans was of the following opinion: "We need more Anti-Social Behaviour Orders. And every hooligan on an ASBO should be made to do community service wearing a distinctive uniform. I suggest an eye-catching bright orange. Then justice to the poor victims of muggings and theft would not only be done, but BE SEEN to be done!"

"Do you fancy a slice of my home-made fruit-cake?" calls Andrea, from the kitchen.

"Yes, please."

I throw the paper down on the floor. The article makes me fume. That sinister word – 'rationalise'. And that last comment. Community service might be a good idea, with the right support in place. But standing out, shamefully, in an orange uniform! How can kids be turned round, and reinvent themselves during what might be a life-changing experience, if they're being stared and jeered at?

Not for the first time, I feel that my very existence is threatened. Does anyone out there actually understand what we tutors achieve? Every week, we spend ten hours or more individual time with our children – far more than any schoolteacher or social worker can ever hope to achieve. More quality time, sadly, than some kids spend with their own parents. Moreover, we see them in their home environment – in the very soil which nurtures them. Why then aren't we valued for our unique contribution? Why are we always bottom of the heap when it comes to funding?

I can hear Andrea in the kitchen, patiently reminding Cassie for the umpteenth time to sterilise Darren's bottles more thoroughly, and Cassie's reply: "Bloody hell, I've done it, haven't I?" Andrea, too, is at the sharp end of the care system.

I sit, brooding. There's a huge problem in society, and it's getting worse. Yet draconian measures are not the answer. There are so many different issues underlying the current explosion of anti-social behaviour. We need to re-examine every strand of the fabric we call our society. We need to start at the very beginning, with Darren…

"Cup of tea?' Andrea passes me one, and sits down next to me with her own cup. "And before I forget," she says, "Cassie's got another appointment with her solicitor on Monday morning, but it's at 11.15. It's the only time she could fit Cassie in. Will that be a problem for you? Could you come just before 9a.m?

"Yes, that's fine. It must be urgent, if she's got another meeting with Cassie so soon after the last one!"

"We've got to get this sorted out quickly," says Andrea. "Cassie's mother's still hassling her, ringing between eight and ten times a day."

"What does she want, exactly?"

"Well, she's putting up a fight to get custody of Darren on the grounds that Dean had a sexual relationship with Cassie when she was only fourteen, and also that Dean is not a fit person to associate with her, because he has no means of supporting himself."

"But that could apply to any two young people with no money who want to be together."

"True," agrees Andrea, "but that doesn't stop her. She's already been to court to try and get a Resident's Order to prevent Dean and Cassie living together. Surprisingly, according to the solicitor, the under-age sex isn't an issue – unless Cassie herself makes a complaint."

"She's not likely to do that! You've seen the engagement ring?"

Andrea chuckles. "Amazing, isn't it? It shows that Dean must feel a lot for Cassie. And this is what's most important at the moment – their relationship, how it can develop in the best possible way, given the circumstances."

"So is Dean having some kind of counselling or help?" I wriggle deeper into the settee, luxuriating in this rare moment of comfort.

"Well, in order to be a 'fit' father, Dean will be required to sign up for anger-management courses. He'll also have to have counselling and drug-rehabilitation. Only then will he prove his commitment to Cassie and his child." Andrea sips her tea, thoughtfully. "Meanwhile Cassie is desperate for more supervised contact with him. Of course she'd prefer it to be completely unsupervised, to be able to see him when she wants to. This is why she's so unsettled. And she's not in contact with her mother, because she can't trust Mum's motives. It's very sad, and a complete mess."

"Poor Cassie – what a lot for her to cope with, just trying to get her head around it all! No wonder she can't concentrate on maths. I get very discouraged sometimes." It's a relief to unburden myself to Andrea. "I'm making so little headway with basic subjects."

"What you're doing is crucial!" exclaims Andrea. "Continuing her education is one of the conditions of her keeping Darren, *and* being entitled to the supervised contact with Dean. It's hard going, I know. To me, caring for Cassie feels like going one step forward and two steps back just now, but we have to have faith."

"I know." Yet I'm uneasy. Faith can move mountains, but can it move Cassie?

"You've done well today, Cassie." I tell her, at the end of the session. "Look – I've given you two points for your maths, and another one for the bag design you've just finished. That means you've only got one more point to go, you'll have got thirty in all!"

"Wow. Big deal." Cassie sticks out her tongue and squints at me mockingly. Yet I can tell from the way she helps me pack up my books, and the spring in her step as we walk to the front door, that she's secretly pleased.

"Be ready for your session on Monday, and you'll get a point right away – even before you've done any work! Or, how about making my day, and doing a maths worksheet for homework? You could give me the shock of my life."

"In your dreams!" Cassie half-smiles. For two seconds her habitual scowl has gone, like the sun escaping from a dark cloud.

"Oh, and we're going shopping next week, remember? We'll look round the charity shops for some material?"

"Yeah, cool."

"Enjoy your weekend, Cassie."

"Bye."

As the front door closes behind me, I hear Darren crying once more.

Monday, 1st March – 4.a.m. I wake with a jolt, sick and dizzy, my heart thumping. I'm surfacing from a crazy dream about a green nappy.

Now I realise what the green in the nappy was trying to tell me. I break out into a cold sweat. It's far too early to ring Andrea. I toss and turn until 7 a.m., knowing that she's usually up by then. Then, I dial her number. There's no reply. I leave a message: "Andrea! I noticed a nasty green stain on the carpet in Cassie's room. It was seeping out of Darren's nappy. I'm not sure how long the nappy had been there, under the trolley. Cassie put it in the bin. But I was wondering if it meant Darren had a tummy upset. Look, I'm sure if there was anything wrong, you'd have discovered it long before now. Sorry if I'm interfering…"

Interfering! I'm getting too involved, that's what. My job is about Cassie and her education, isn't it? Of course it is. So why am I constantly worrying about Darren, as well as Cassie? The rational answer is, of course, that they're inextricably linked, but deep down, there's much more to it. The truth is that Darren has stolen my heart. And I cannot get the dream out of my head.

Am I stepping over some line here? Professional boundaries – a framework of ethical, moral and social guidelines. They give parameters within which to work, safely and with confidence. They're like stone walls. I have always respected them. Yet sometimes these boundaries can be unhelpful, even injurious.

Once, I attended a review meeting set up to consider a new educational placement for an eight year old girl who had been excluded for persistently stealing money from her schoolmates and from her teacher. Present at that meeting were the head of her current school, the educational psychologist and the girl's mother, who watched me like a hawk.

Clearly, the headteacher didn't know what I knew. The little girl, Julie, and I worked at the kitchen table at Julie's home. One day, while her mother answered the phone, the child rushed to the kitchen cupboards, looking for food. The cupboards were almost completely bare. I discovered that her mother, a wraith-like woman on a permanent, stringent diet, rarely bought any food except for coffee, teabags, milk, crispbreads, and occasionally a bag of apples. At the meeting, we all sat round, solemnly talking about the next step in my pupil's education. I was asked how Julie was getting along with her maths and English. I told them, and added, almost in passing, that I wondered whether there might be any difficulties at home which could be contributing to her behaviour at school?

Shock! Horror!

"You are not here to talk about anything but Julie's education," the psychologist said, icily.

Which are genuine stone walls, and which are constructed from someone else's imagination, or fashioned out of their own hidden agenda?

9.45 a.m. I'm sitting outside Andrea's house, wondering where everyone is. There's no answer when I knock. I've hammered hard, imagining Andrea maybe in her bed after a wakeful night with Darren. And no doubt Cassie too, sleeping because no one's woken her. There's no reply when I ring their number on my mobile.

At lunchtime, there's still no answer when I ring the house. With gnawing anxiety, I go home. Whatever I eat seems to stick in my throat. Sitting down with claim forms and report sheets, I jump when the phone rings. It's Andrea.

"I'm so sorry I haven't rung you before – I haven't had a chance. Cassie and I have been in the hospital all morning with Darren…"

I sit down on the floor, weak at the knees.

Yesterday afternoon, Darren's temperature soared. Andrea called the doctor, who found Darren was severely dehydrated. A bemused Cassie and Darren – with Andrea in attendance – were whisked off to casualty in an ambulance. Darren was dangerously ill.

I start telling Andrea about the green nappy. "I should have mentioned it on Friday," I wail. "This could have been prevented."

"Rubbish!" says Andrea. "And I got your message, by the way. I knew about the green nappies – who changes them half the time? I do! Babies *do* have green nappies sometimes. Even so, Darren did seem much more fretful than normal, so I'm the one who should have realised there was a problem. The poor little mite was in a terrible state, everything coming out both ends non-stop!"

"So what caused the tummy upset?"

"I'm afraid Cassie's really to blame – she hasn't been bothering to sterilise the feeding bottles."

"Oh no, that's awful!"

"Yes, the health visitor's been informed. She's coming first thing tomorrow to give Cassie an emergency parenting session, which means tuition will have to be cancelled. Sorry about that, but Cassie'll see you Wednesday morning as usual."

"I could fit her in tomorrow afternoon?"

"No, she's got a supervised visit at the family centre with Dean. It would be unfair on her to make her miss that."

"Wednesday, then. And while I remember, can I take her shopping on Friday morning? We've got a long-standing date with the charity shops!"

"Yes, so long as nothing else comes up in the meantime. Cassie seems to attract more visits and appointments than any other child I've ever fostered."

"I'm so shocked by what's happened. Will Darren be okay?"

"He seems much more settled," says Andrea cautiously.

"Can I speak to Cassie?" I want to keep contact, let her know that it's 'business as usual' as far as tuition goes, whatever's been happening in the meantime.

"She's asleep, last night was too much for her. To do her justice, she was worried sick about Darren."

"Just give her my best wishes, tell her I'm looking forward to seeing her on Wednesday."

Wednesday, 3rd March. I'm humming along to Classic FM, tapping my fingers on the steering wheel. As I wait at the traffic lights, I jig around in my seat. A car in the next lane pulls up alongside. The driver nudges his passenger, who stares at me, rolling his eyes. He taps his temples, slowly and meaningfully. I stick out my tongue at both of them.

I don't care what they think. It's a glorious day. The cherry trees lining the main road are unfurling their delicate pink and white blossom. The early morning sunshine casts a misty glow through the slender branches. A muted buzz of energy fills the air, a gentle stirring. Yet spring still holds back, as if curbing her own excitement – waiting for the perfect moment to leap on to the stage.

I'm looking forward to this morning's session. Seize the day! Why wait till Friday for our trawl round the charity shops? My mind races ahead, planning other activities which might, by a leap of the imagination, be termed educational. A consumer survey on the relative value for money provided by Oxfam compared to Save the Children? Or a tally, listing the pathetically few individually owned shops in the High Street? (As far as I remember, there isn't a single greengrocer, baker, or butcher to be seen – they've all been gobbled up by the supermarkets and chain stores). We might call in at Ella's boutique, one of the few remaining clothes shops under private ownership, and show her Cassie's bag designs. If all goes well, and Cassie hasn't died of boredom by now, I could treat her to a hot chocolate in the Portside Café. We could watch the big ships come in from far-off shores, and imagine foreign lives.

But there's to be no shopping trip with Cassie today, or Friday – or ever.

A frantic Andrea greets me at the door with the news that Cassie's done a runner. At some time between midnight and dawn, Cassie fled silently from the house, leaving behind her sleeping baby. Police enquiries into Dean's whereabouts revealed that his rented room was empty. They would also like to interview him in connection with a raid, late last Sunday night, on a jeweller's shop in town.

Meanwhile, the two lovebirds have disappeared without trace.

Tuesday, 16th March – 9 a.m. Andrea phones and invites me round for a cup of tea. Cassie's still not back, but she has some more news. She'll tell me when she sees me.

Intrigued and anxious, I hop in the car and race off to Andrea's house. It's been over two weeks since I last saw Cassie. Full of gruesome fears for her safety, I've been ringing Andrea almost daily.

Darren's fast asleep in his carrycot on the settee, blissfully unaware of his uncertain future. Andrea sits me down next to him. Today, on the coffee table in front of us, there are cake and biscuits, as well as a pot of tea. It feels like a wake.

"So have they been found?"

"Yes," replies Andrea. "They're in Wales."

"Wales?"

"Cardiff. Dean's got an old school-friend living there. This friend shares a rented flat with his girlfriend, and they've got a spare room. They wanted to sub-let to make some extra money. Dean somehow heard about it, and fixed it all up, long before the last supervised meeting with Cassie. That's when he told her he was going to go away, and asked her to come with him."

"Why did he want to leave the area anyway?"

"Goodness knows. That's Dean for you. Never stays long in one place. But as it turned out, from his point of view he got away just in time; the police thought he might be mixed up in the jewel theft in the High Street.

"Good grief! And is he?"

"Probably not, apart from Cassie's ring. That was definitely knocked off. But the police have caught the three men who broke into the shop. They're all mates of Dean, they've been seen together with him in town, so of course he was a suspect. They most likely sold him the ring, telling him it had fallen off the back of a lorry. Dean's always on the edge of any trouble. He's weak, easily sucked in. Fair game for anyone who wants to get rid of something quickly. They might have palmed more stuff off on him. No one knows, yet. Nothing's been found. If he's charged with anything, for the moment it will only be for receiving the ring."

"So what made the police think of searching for him in Wales?"

Andrea laughs. "It was probably Cassie's fault. If Dean had been on his own, he might have had the sense to keep a low profile for a while. Get a casual job somewhere, no questions asked, but about a week after they arrived, Cassie decides she's fed up with sharing a house. She persuades Dean to march off to the Housing Department, and demand that they're put on the waiting list for a flat. So of course, people start asking questions."

"No! Well, it was only a question of time, I suppose."

We drink our tea in silence for a while, each with our own thoughts. So, Dean will have broken his probation order – on several counts – and may have to face charges connected with the robbery. Cassie will come back into the hands of social services. This time, a new authority will be responsible for both Dean and Cassie. Does the fair city of Cardiff know what's it's in for? Is it prepared, I wonder?

"I expect they'll find her another tutor," says Andrea, glancing at me sympathetically.

"I suppose so."

"You did your best. We both did."

"Yes." I feel crushed by the sudden turn of events.

Andrea hands me Cassie's work folder. "You'd better keep this."

I flip through it quickly. There's precious little, really – just a few maths and English worksheets. some healthy eating plans and her bag designs. I'll have to take it into the office and hope it somehow reaches her next tutor.

I've been putting off the question I most want to ask. I take a deep breath. "So what will happen to Darren?"

"He'll be fostered, either by me, short-term, or by someone else."

"Couldn't you keep him, Andrea? I mean, keep him forever?"

"I only do short-term fostering."

"But he's bonded with you." My voice quavers.

Andrea looks at me compassionately. "He needs a long-term placement, which I can't give him. Hopefully, he'll be adopted."

"Couldn't you adopt him then?" I plead wildly. "He's so settled here."

"Oh dear, I can see you'd be a hopeless foster parent! You'd never give them up!"

But Andrea says this kindly, and pours me another cup of tea. "Bill would leave me if I even suggested adoption. He's still waiting for the day when he can whisk me off for an exotic holiday somewhere, at a moment's notice. By the way, Cassie left this note for me. She must have written it in a great hurry."

The handwriting is large and scrawling and almost indecipherable.

"Dear Andrea. I'm sorry, I can't do it it's too hard."

So, here it is. The final severing of the links between Cassie and her baby. The chain, at first as solid as iron, has slowly but inexorably turned into paper. Fragile and tenuous. And now it's snapped.

Darren wakes up with a sudden, high-pitched shriek of surprise. His little arms and legs start moving as if someone's just wound him up. His flailing fists land on the bright yellow and purple plastic baubles stretched out on a string in front of him. Bells jingle, rings collide and rattle. In a few weeks, he'll start associating these sounds with the random movement of his hands. How I'd love to be there when this happens! To witness Darren's first sense of his own power. Wild thoughts flash through my mind: *'What if? Could I...?'*

Andrea's watching me. "You'd love to adopt him yourself, wouldn't you?" She smiles at me, sadly.

"Me? No, I..."

"Admit it. You've loved this baby from the moment you first set eyes on him! That's really why I invited you here. To say goodbye to him."

Andrea lifts Darren out of his cot and passes him to me. I hug him close, his cheek close to mine.

'Goodbye, little one. I hope you find a loving home. I don't want you to end up like your mum, history repeating itself generation after generation. Will I, in a few years' time, get a call from the office, asking me to tutor a little boy who can't cope in school? Realise with a shock, when I turn up at your house, that it's you?

As I leave, Andrea places Cassie's bag, three-quarters finished, in my hands.

"I found it on her bed, in the jumble of things she must have been rummaging through, deciding what to take with her. Poor child, she must have been in emotional turmoil. There's a note. She'd pinned it to the bag. I put it inside, for you to read later."

I drive down the road a little way, out of sight of the house, then stop and read the note:

'Dear Teacher. Please finish this for me. From Cassie.'

Of course I will. I'll sew it up, carefully, with neat stitching. It'll be a fine bag when it's finished. A work of art. I'll keep it for you, Cassie.

HARRIET
༄

Wednesday, 22nd October 2003. I have been tutoring Harriet, a private pupil, since the beginning of September. She's an engaging ten-year-old, with long, dark, shiny hair. Her mother, originally from India, is a pharmacist, working with her two brothers who own a large pharmacy. Her English father is an orthopaedic surgeon. Harriet's parents are high-achieving professionals, and they want Harriet to be like them. Her mother keeps a steely eye on what goes on in our weekly sessions.

Mr and Mrs Bailey are keen for her to gain entry into *the* local private school, a school with an excellent academic reputation. There's a very difficult entrance exam. A scholarship would pay all her fees, a bursary half. Her parents intend for her to 'go for gold' – the scholarship. They've enlisted my help.

I'm not against private schools if they fit the need of a particular child – smaller classes, a more relaxed system, more practical and outdoor work. (Yet how desperately these conditions are needed in *all* state schools.) I'm convinced there's a strong case for special schools for those with severe learning difficulties, and other disabilities. But I have the feeling that many private schools are high-pressured learning factories. They're not child-friendly: they satisfy the needs of ambitious parents. This seemed the case with Harriet.

Today, Harriet and I are wading through some past maths papers. There are six whole months before the entrance exam, but Harriet's mum wants to be well ahead of the other parents, who will all spend a fortune on coaching. There's fierce competition for entry into St Bede's.

It's hard to guess what Harriet herself thinks, wants or feels. She always tries hard, and works willingly, if not enthusiastically. She ploughs through tests on automatic pilot, only stopping when she's not sure about the method. Then she sits back with a little sigh. Harriet's passivity can be disconcerting. At the end of a long day when I've had a constant battle to win pupils' hearts and minds, the smooth progress of my session with her feels like tobogganing on Dartmoor. After the hard slog up the hill, the easy ride down the slope is great – but I'm still half expecting to collide with rocks.

I suspect that Harriet herself doesn't have many strong feelings about going to St Bede's: she's been programmed to do as she's told.

We work through half a paper before it's time to stop. She's not sure about the next question – division of decimals. (Nor am I, so I'll have to mug up on them over the weekend. I find it amazing that she's doing work that, with luck, I might be doing with some of my more able kids at GCSE Foundation level.)

She's looking tired – no wonder, she's been at school all day – so I suggest a maths game for the next few minutes: a fun fraction and decimal game. Harriet is laughing, looking relaxed for the first time, when Mum comes in, and seeing a trail of dominoes stretching round the dining room table, looks faintly disapproving. She isn't paying me good money to play silly games.

We finish, and I'm quizzed about Harriet's progress today. Harriet escapes to get a drink, but her mum wants to keep me talking for an extra fifteen minutes before she hands over my fee. At last I can leave. I take deep breaths of gusty autumnal air, my feet rustle through deep piles of sycamore leaves, stroll along wide pavements, past secret driveways with tantalising glimpses of gabled roofs and mullioned windows. Then the houses and streets nudge together in a companionable way, and I'm outside my own front door. My cat miaows loudly and accusingly – it's half an hour past her tea time. A few minutes later, sitting down with my cup of tea, cat installed on my lap, I'm wondering why I'm teaching privately. Every September, I vow "Never again!" Of course I know why. The financial lot of a home tutor is not a happy one. September and October are lean and hungry months. And if I'm honest, private pupils are often a relaxing break from the emotionally draining work with excluded, disaffected pupils.

Yet deep down, I know this is not really my kind of teaching. I'm so used to dysfunctional families that functional ones can freak me out. Harriet is bright, motivated and self-disciplined. She lives an ordered life with parents who love her and want the best for her. Harriet will forge her own path in life, whether or not she has a tutor to get her through her exam. She's destined for success. She doesn't need me.

Or maybe, in some ways, she does? We shall see...

Wednesday, 19th November. Harriet is grappling with division of decimals again – or rather I am. They keep popping up like cockroaches as problems in her test papers. Harriet finds them easy but boring, so she makes careless errors. I find them almost incomprehensible but fascinating. They're ugly, alien creatures. In real life, do we divide decimals by decimals?

We now have a five minute break halfway through the session, a welcome diversion for both of us. Mum's brusque entry with the tray of drinks and her equally brisk exit demonstrate her deep disapproval. Dereliction of duty. Though I've assured her that the extra minutes will be tagged on at the end.

I sip my tea. An aroma of freshly chopped herbs and exotic spices wafts tantalisingly from the kitchen – curry tonight. Mrs Bailey is a superb cook, I've discovered. Pharmacy and cookery, ideal partners. I'm hoping she allows time in Harriet's busy schedule to share this wonderful skill with her daughter.

Last week, I asked Harriet if she belonged to any clubs or did any after-school activities.

"Oh, yes. On Monday I go to Chess Club, on Tuesday it's Guides, Wednesday, you come, on Thursday I have a piano lesson, and on Friday I just stay in. I have to do extra piano practice and get most of my weekend homework done. Oh, and Saturday morning I have a swimming lesson." She sounds quite matter-of-fact. Doesn't every ten-year-old have such a regime?

Harriet's opening up and trusting me a little more. Last week she also confided that she'd love to have a dog, but with both parents working there's no one to walk it. She also has the passion, typical of a girl of her age, for horses and ponies, and longs for one of her own. Immediately after this revelation, she nipped upstairs and came down with a sketchbook. Page after page of horses, all shapes, colours and sizes, most of them in full gallop across a vast grassy plain. Sometimes there were hills in the background, or ploughed fields with red earth. Lovely drawings, graceful and flowing.

Would she like to go riding? I asked. Harriet frowned. Her best friend at school goes, but it's on a Saturday morning when there's a swimming lesson. Over half term – her eyes sparkle – swimming was cancelled. Instead, she'd been to the stables with her friend and fed and groomed the horses.

"If I had a horse, he'd be a bay with a white blaze down his nose and very friendly and I'd ride it every day!"

"Perhaps Mum will let you go riding when the swimming lessons finish?"

"Hmm. Maybe." She shrugged. "Mum and Dad say that if I get a scholarship I can have riding lessons."

I changed the subject. I'm in danger of stirring things up in this highly regulated family. But I'm feeling angry. Why wait nine months before allowing Harriet to do something that really fires her? Indulging a passion shouldn't be a future reward for academic success. NOW is the moment. And they could afford to buy her a pony.

In our break today, Harriet suddenly remembers something else she wants to show me. First she checks Mum's whereabouts – we can see her at the end of the garden taking down the washing. Harriet dashes upstairs and returns with a cat litter tray, which she places carefully on the table. There's a cardboard lid with large round holes at regular intervals. With a magician's flourish, she removes the lid.

At first, all I can see are a flat stone, a piece of bark, some twigs and moss lining the bottom of the tray. She lifts the bark and dozens of sleeping woodlice leap into frenzied activity. "They live on top of my wardrobe," says Harriet proudly. "Mum and Dad don't know, Mum hates creepy crawly things." Harriet loves watching them run about and tries them with different leaves every day to find their favourite menu. At night, she covers them with a muslin cloth "so they don't get cold but can still breathe." I'm impressed. We watch the woodlice, until the back door rattles, and Harriet runs upstairs to hide her secret.

Half an hour later, after the usual de-briefing session with Mrs Bailey, I'm walking away down the sweeping gravel drive. My feet scrunch to the melodic rhythm of piano scales. Harriet has already begun her one hour's daily practice.

Wednesday, 4th February 2004. Incessant, dreary rain drips down my neck as I walk round to Harriet's house. I'd much rather be at home in front of my wood-burning stove, hugging the cat and my book.

Inside the front door, I take off my shoes, careful not to spatter muddy drops on the deep-pile cream carpet. As I look for somewhere to hang my dripping coat, the study door on my left opens. Dr Bailey steps out and advances towards me, hand outstretched.

He's at least six foot three, with the physique of a Rugby player, fair hair, slightly florid complexion. He reminds me of one of the characters in the *Carry on Doctor* films, which my friends and I, as oh-so-innocent teenagers aeons of years ago, loved so much. Yes! He looks exactly like the gung-ho doctor played by Leslie Phillips, only much larger and more intimidating. The very walls of the spacious hall seem to shrink back as if struggling to contain his expansiveness.

"Good afternoon," I shake his hand, and mutter something suitably inane about glad to help, etc. Harriet skips out of the living-room door opposite.

"Daddy's home today, he's got the *whole day off*, haven't you, Daddy! Daddy?" Proud, excited, her voice holds the words aloft, as if displaying a rare treasure.

"Considering I didn't get in till one o'clock this morning, and considering I have jet-lag, not to mention having to type out a very long report before tomorrow, I hardly count this as a day off." But he's hugging her affectionately and smiling.

Mrs Bailey joins us. "He's been away for four days, in New York for a conference. And he's very tired, Harriet. You mustn't bother him while he's in his study."

"But you'll still take us out, won't you, Daddy? Daddy? *Please!*"

Harriet jumps up and down in front of him. She's tall for her age, but at the height of her jump she hardly reaches his shoulder. Mrs Bailey looks on indulgently. Standing at either side of him, she and her daughter look like twin dolls, with the same dusky skin, the mother's darker, both slender and willowy.

Their large brown almond-shaped eyes contrast with his, small and twinkly blue.

"Of course we'll go out. We're going to a very special restaurant, and we're going to eat, and talk, and eat some more, and talk some more…"

He catches his wife's eye and grins. In turn, they glance surreptitiously at me. I blush. This last salvo of information has been aimed directly at me. I've been dropping rather heavy hints about the importance of family conversations.

For about three weeks now the family has made a point of sitting together for a meal one evening a week, depending on Dr Bailey's operating schedule. It's been difficult, Mrs Bailey told me. You never know when someone's going to smash their leg in a motorbike accident. But they've both kept to the spirit of it, and she's had the sense not to make Harriet feel that the arrangement isn't some sort of exercise undertaken solely for her benefit. It's a fun family occasion which they all enjoy.

Dr Bailey disappears into his study, Mrs Bailey returns to her beloved kitchen. Harriet and I start work.

I've spent most of the weekend trying to get my head around simultaneous equations. I can hardly believe that Harriet's supposed to understand these. Normally only my brightest kids, fourteen and upwards, would be tackling algebra at this level. And then, mathematically-challenged as I am, professional ethics would compel me to give over my sessions to a maths-whizz colleague who gets really turned on by this stuff. I might yet have to do this for Harriet, if her understanding outpaces mine. For now, however, she's struggling, and thankfully, I'm still two steps ahead.

We spend half an hour going through the test paper. One good thing about finding maths difficult is that when I teach, I can navigate slowly and thoroughly, aware of the usual black holes in comprehension, where panic is likely to grip. I've been down them so often. Breaking everything down into minuscule, manageable steps, with constant practice and repetition, is how I cope. I find it works wonders with pupils who fear maths.

But for Harriet, there are no gremlins. She's plodding away now, in her usual systematic way, and I watch her in wonder. Watching different sorts of minds at work is a never-ending source of joy and fascination to me and I suddenly realise that the test is an extension paper, for the scholarship kids. No wonder it's hard!

After the break, it's creative writing. For the last few sessions, I've concentrated on developing Harriet's imagination by getting *her* to think up a title for a different story or description. This was a challenge for her; to find the subject, map out the narrative, discuss story lines, choose vivid descriptive words. Last week she made up four titles – a big leap forward. I'd like to get her to develop her ideas for homework, but she already has homework from school every night.

Today's subject is: 'Imagine a date far into the future: describe a typical day at school, or at home, or with your friends'. Harriet draws a spider-gram, and on the threads writes: 'no school, everyone having computer lessons'; 'no cars.'; 'all children have their own helicopters and landing pads'. She's still hesitant, but not nearly so panicky when she sees a blank piece of paper. Her ideas are really good, and I tell her so. She writes down: 'no green spaces, skyscrapers everywhere'. I'm really excited, she's doing amazingly well. I encourage her to develop these ideas, putting in some descriptive detail, otherwise her eventual story will consist of a series of bald statements without embellishment.

Today, I've bought a tape-recorder, so whenever she thinks of a really good word, or idea, she can record it immediately. Sometimes with children like Harriet the *mot juste* is lost somewhere in the process between the thought and the written record. Speaking is instant, and seems to work for Harriet. She can voice the idea currently in her mind, and also grab that precious gem just behind it, waiting in the wings. Harriet, so competent in other ways, has a real problem with retrieval from her memory when it comes to accessing stored vocabulary.

For next time, I ask Harriet to think up some really funny, amazing, descriptive words that could go in her 'Future' story. She doesn't have to write them down, it's just for a game we might play next time. She says she'll have a go, and I leave her the tape to record them on.

Dr Bailey comes out of the study as I'm putting on my coat, and again thanks me profusely and embarrassingly for my services. Truthfully, I reply that tutoring Harriet is a pleasure, but I escape with a sense of relief. The rain has stopped. I take deep gulps of the cool damp air, as dusk closes around me and the street lamps shimmer in the mist. The Bailey household is a hothouse, and it's not just the central heating.

Wednesday, 10th March. I enjoy geometry. It's visual and elegant, and unlike many maths concepts, I can understand it. Luckily, it's come up on the test paper today. For Harriet, it's new learning, so for once I'm ahead of the game.

Harriet's working in her usual methodical way, measuring angles with her new protractor; but she seems a bit deflated. When I point to a mistake, she sighs and looks on the brink of tears.

In our break I ask her about school.

"It's okay. Except that Katy won't be my friend anymore." Tears fall. I sympathise. Ten is the prime age, especially amongst girls, for sudden shifts in alliances and friendships. The time when your best friend who's played with you constantly since you started school together, suddenly 'breaks friends' and goes off to play with someone else, not just today, but every day. Or worse, she joins a gang or secret club, and you're not invited. And it's heartbreaking, like the end of the world.

"Could you invite her to tea?" I suggest, lamely.

Harriet shakes her head, silent, miserable. Then in a rush, the words tumble out: "She doesn't like me anymore. She asked me to tea and I couldn't go because I had Chess Club, and then another time she asked me and I had a piano lesson and then she didn't ask me anymore and she asked Elli instead. And now the others are being horrid to me."

More tears. I find a tissue. "What a shame."

Poor Harriet. I'm wondering what's causing her isolation. She's not the only one hoping to get into St Bede's. There are four other young hopefuls in her class. And the academically biased state primary school she attends is favoured by more affluent parents, so it's not a matter of being perceived as too 'brainy' or too 'posh'. It seems that Harriet's unavailability is being misinterpreted as being anti-social or even stand-offish.

I want to ask what the other children do after school? Do they play together at each other's homes, invite each other to stay the night? But it seems too pointed a question just now.

Mrs Bailey seems preoccupied as she counts out my fee. I feel even more nervous than usual about approaching her, but Harriet's despondent mood has definitely affected our session together. I take the bull by the horns.

"Harriet seems a bit upset today. Maybe something has happened at school?"

I wait to see if she's mentioned anything about Katy to Mum. I've no wish to be Harriet's number one confidante.

"Oh yes. She's fallen out with Katy. Such nonsense. They argue and make up all the time. I tell her to just wait. It will blow over."

"I'm wondering if Harriet had more contact with her friends out of school…?" I'm treading on difficult ground here. "Perhaps she'd widen her circle of friends and not be so dependent on Katy. She'd be part of a group…"

"And what are you suggesting, exactly?"

I'm unprepared for this directness. Mrs Bailey has a defensive, steely glint in her eye. "I'm just wondering if she had more free evenings, she could go round to play with her classmates, or have them round here…"

"Ah, that will indeed be possible one day, when she starts at St Bede's. Then she will choose to drop Chess Club perhaps. But now she is very good at chess and next month there is a competition. She can tell them at the interview that she has entered for chess competitions and who knows, maybe she will win! And that would be impressive, I think."

Mrs Bailey seems to be pinning all her hopes and expectations on Harriet getting into St Bede's. She's blinkered to any present social and emotional cost.

"And," she adds, as she very politely edges me towards the front door, "Harriet meets lots of nice girls at Guides. I'll see you next week."

She holds open the front door.

What about just hanging around, playing with the friends she's chosen? Inventing crazy games, sharing secrets? The words explode in my head, but I say nothing. I retreat, feeling cowardly and frustrated.

Wednesday, 17th March. "Mum's lying down, she's got a headache," whispers Harriet, as she opens the door.

"Poor Mum," I whisper back.

We tiptoe into the living room where Harriet, conscientious as ever, has laid out her test papers, coloured pencils, pen and paper. She's been drawing ponies again and proudly shows me some new sketches. The bay with the while blaze takes centre stage. In the background are stallions and carthorses grazing in a paddock.

With Mum out of the way, Harriet also wants to show me her latest wildlife collection – a tray of snails and slugs, covered with a rigid plastic sheet with air holes. I'm impressed by Harriet's breadth and depth of knowledge about their body parts and functions, even waxing lyrical about their love-lives. She strokes the snails' shells, pointing out how the pattern on each is different. The snails all have names: 'Snouty, Slimy, Speedy, Crinkly.' I'm loath to break the spell, but duty calls. I'm not getting paid for this.

Descriptive writing today. We've been discovering adjectives, and making a collection. Each week we add to an ever-increasing list under the headings 'Sound words', 'Sight words', and so on. The game is to see who can collect the most unusual and vivid words under one heading. Harriet's winning, of course. She's working with more verve, less like a robot. And she seems much, much happier this week.

Harriet now chooses ten adjectives from her list, and we find a suitable noun to go with them. She hasn't a natural affinity with vocabulary, and I'm enjoying her willingness to have a go.

The subject on the English test paper is 'Describe someone you know well. This could be someone in your family, a relative, a neighbour or friend, or anyone else you choose'.

"Guess what?" Harriet's face lights up suddenly.

"What?"

"I'm going riding now!"

"Really? That's wonderful, Harriet." I can see she's dying to tell me all about it, but I have to keep her on track. "Now, who do you want to describe in your piece of writing?"

Harriet puts down her pen and wriggles back happily in her chair. She's still in the world of horses and ponies.

"What happened was, the swimming lessons, there were ten of them and they all came to an end and we had to go up to a higher group. But this group starts at eight o'clock in the morning and Mum said there was no way she was getting up at that god-forsaken hour on a Saturday morning. So I said could I do riding instead and she said yes!..."

"Wow, that's great. Now, your writing..."

"...and Katy goes, so Mum takes her too, or I go with Katy's mum. And we're in the same riding group and afterwards we groom the ponies. And then Katy comes back with me to play or I go and play at her house."

I can't remember seeing Harriet quite so animated.

"So," she finishes, with a deep, contented sigh, "I think I'll describe Katy."

Harriet picks up her pen and without prompting, draws a spider-gram. On the radials she writes: 'Katy's nice, she's kind and happy. She says funny things. She makes up jokes. She tells me secrets. She's my best friend'.

Wednesday, 24th March. It's all systems go on the creative writing front. This week's subject is: 'Imagine you are transported to a far, unknown planet. Describe it in as much detail as you can'. It's not on the test paper: I've just thought of it as I walked round to Harriet's. It probably reflects a deep-seated desire to escape to some far-off place, after this morning's difficult session with Bethany, my school-phobic pupil.

Harriet's chewing the end of her pen, gazing into the garden. Through the open window wafts the scent of daffodils. A robin chirrups on the branch of the apple tree, red breast-feathers bright against lime-green buds. Harriet tap-taps her foot. There's a buzz of energy, an excited tingling. Sunlight shimmers on the polished table and on the Dresden ornaments. Even the books on the shelves seem to quiver. Nature's stirred at last, leaping into action as if she has far too many jobs to do.

We watch Mrs Bailey weeding one of the borders, carefully easing dandelions and forget-me-nots away from the base of the daffodil stems. I feel my toes twitching to be outside.

I introduce the exciting topic of the mysterious planet.

"Let's think of some alien creatures that might live on the planet. What might they be like?"

Harriet hesitates. I wait. I've learnt that she likes to think before voicing her ideas. She looks puzzled.

"Not like anything on earth? They might have to adapt to a different atmosphere, like the air might be thinner, or thicker?"

"Yes! Excellent idea. And so…?"

"Umm..." She's struggling to make, for her, a giant leap of imagination.

I prompt her a bit more.

"Can you describe the atmosphere and how it might affect the aliens?"

Suddenly Harriet's love of all creatures great and small kicks in. "Can I draw them?"

"Of course."

"They're small and furry, a bit animal and a bit like humans," she says, doing a rapid sketch. "And they have *huge* noses because the air's so thin. And they've got kangaroo legs, lots of them, because they need to jump long distances to find the food."

Other species of aliens begin to appear: enormous creatures with double-faced heads that can look in two directions. Others with dozens of eyes on stalks. She's doing amazingly well, as if her imagination muscles have suddenly flexed. The drawing helps. I'm curious to know if she can translate the striking drawings into the written word.

Next, I ask Harriet to consult her ever-growing list of adjectives, and to match up her mental picture of the alien's nose or eyes with a suitable describing word.

"Let's find one that's really unusual or funny or vivid!"

Harriet discovers some highly original combinations.

"Spreading cabbage ears. Sly mysterious octagonal eyes. Purple plump passionate noses. Gawky great giraffes' necks."

She's just cottoned on to the joys of alliteration, and liberally seasons her aliens with them. The effect is so much more lively and colourful than her usual bland, factual prose that I let her gallop away in this new direction.

Harriet finishes her description with minimal prompting. The scientist in her is coming to the fore. She wants to draw diagrams of her creatures, with explanations of their attributes, and full colour-coded labelling. She laughs loudly over her word combinations, so loudly that, Mrs Bailey, back inside from the garden, pokes her head round the door to see what's going on.

"So what is happening?"

"We *are* working, Mum," says Harriet, blithely. "We're just doing adjectives."

"Hmm." She darts a suspicious look at Harriet, then at me. Her expression clearly shows that she thinks I'm an *agent provocateur*. However, she sees that Harriet is engaged in some kind of writing activity that matches the strict work criteria. Her head disappears back in to the kitchen. A rather malevolent Cheshire cat without the smile.

Lately, Mrs Bailey has seemed grumpy and preoccupied. I realise that she hasn't brought out our usual refreshments. I wonder if I'm in the doghouse. I know my ways must seem mysterious to her. I don't do what a tutor *should* do, which is to work through test papers, or the occasional textbook exercise.

I watch Harriet carefully labelling her aliens. Come to think of it, now that Harriet's simmered down a little, I notice that she looks a bit tired and strained around the eyes. As if by telepathic communication, she puts down her pen.

"I wish Katy could come to tea today instead of y…" She stops herself just in time.

"Couldn't Katy come tomorrow and do her homework while you have your piano lesson?"

"Mmm. Don't know. She might distract me."

"Oh, I see."

I let it be. But I'm wondering if Harriet, though mentally robust, might be physically overloaded by one after-school activity after another. Plus homework. Plus piano practice. It's great that she's doing riding now, but when does the poor kid just chill and daydream? Mrs Bailey brings in a tray of drinks, although by now it is almost the end of the session.

"I'm so sorry, I forgot your tea. I've been so busy, it just went out of my head!" She places the tray down with a sigh. Unusually, she has brought a cup of tea for herself.

"Oh, that's all right, it's very welcome at any time."

Mum hovers while Harriet gulps down her orange juice. I look at my watch. "It's time to stop now, Harriet."

Mum checks this with the mantelpiece clock. "Yes, indeed it is."

"Can I go outside now?" Harriet asks.

"Yes, but put on a coat. And your outdoor shoes."

Like a spring colt, Harriet darts out through the kitchen to the back garden. A moment later she's soaring high on her swing.

Mrs Bailey is sipping her tea thoughtfully. "And how is she getting on?"

I tell her that Harriet is doing very well, but seems tired. Then in spite of trying to button my lip, or at least to be tactful, I proceed with all the delicacy of a herd of stampeding elephants.

"She seems to be under pressure, maybe doing too much? Perhaps having a friend to tea might give her a break, then she'd have more energy to do her homework and her piano practice?"

Silence.

"Pressure!" The word explodes like a cannon shot. "Don't talk to me of pressure! Do you know I haven't a minute to myself? For three weeks now I have no cleaner. She used to come twice a week. So now I am hoovering and cleaning every day. And my gardener has a bad back. For four weeks now he hasn't been round, and the weeds are everywhere, and already the grass needs cutting."

I make sympathetic noises. I can see that she's not angry with me; she's just feeling overwhelmed. I finish my tea and stand up, but Mrs Bailey, glad of a willing ear, rushes on:

"Yes, you know, in Bombay – now it is Mumbai of course – in my parents' house we never had any problems. My father was a civil engineer. My mother didn't work. There were six of us children. We had a housekeeper who stayed with us for twenty years. She and her husband lived in the grounds. He did all the maintenance. And we had a full-time gardener. He stayed for twelve years."

I edge towards the door. "It must be very frustrating for you."

"Yes it is. Very frustrating." We both move into the hall and she opens the front door, handing me my fee in an envelope. "So, where am I to find another cleaner? And a gardener?"

I shrug and spread my arms wide. "You just can't get the staff these days."

"No, you can't." Mrs Bailey shakes her head vigorously.

Wednesday, 21st April. "How was your camping trip?" I ask Harriet, as I unpack the essential ingredients of today's tuition session. "Was it good?"

"Sort of." She shrugs, pulling a face. "Some bits of it were good." She's not prepared to elaborate. I ask what else she's been up to during the Easter holidays.

"Um…playing with Katy, doing my piano practice. Riding. Doing some test papers…"

"Test papers!" I exclaim before I can bite my tongue.

"Yes, Mum and Dad say the entrance exam's getting very near, so I have to keep at it." Harriet sounds resigned rather than resentful. She shows me the maths extension paper she's just been working through. "I'm stuck on these."

'These' are Speed, Distance and Time.

"I can do some of them in my head, but then they get difficult."

I show her the triangle formula. It fascinates her and the worried frown lifts, her face brightens. In turn, I'm fascinated by how speedily she grasps the idea – just like that! – and by the comfort she gets from the formula: Speed ÷ Distance x Time.

Full of confidence now, Harriet bounces through the questions, and it's time for our break. Mum sets the tray down on the table and peers over Harriet's shoulder at the now completed test paper.

"Ah yes! I wanted Harriet to finish the paper. She said she wasn't sure about one question, and I told her you would surely know the answer." (Such touching faith!) "And now, would you please mark these other papers Harriet has done?"

From a drawer in the bureau next to the table, she extracts a thick wad of at least ten test papers and hands them to me. It will take me hours to go over them, even with the answer sheets, as I'll also have to check her workings to see if she's used the right method. Trying to hide my dismay, I ask if her class teacher could mark them?

"It is not part of her duties," says Mrs Bailey. "She might do it eventually, but it would take her some time to get round to it."

"Right," I say, "I'll take it home, and mark it in time for next week."

"Maybe if you are passing this way, and if you manage to mark them sooner, you could drop them in, so Harriet can study them in time for the next lesson?"

I murmur something non-committal, then remark how hard Harriet's been working during the holidays. I try to keep the disapproval out of my voice.

"Ah yes, well you see," she places her arm round Harriet's shoulders and looks down at her fondly, "Harriet understands that all this is just for a short while. She can tell herself that *now* it is worth putting all her effort into the exam. Afterwards, she can relax. It is only for less than one month."

During this homily, Harriet has been watching her mother, with a special look that catches my heart. In it, I see duty and a strong desire to please. But there's also love, and faith. It's an expression I see so often in a child's face as they watch and listen as mum or dad make decisions for them, an open steady gaze, a touching trust that this parent really does know what's best. A look that's both haunting and humbling. What power we as parents yield over the children in our care!

Mrs Bailey goes off to cook, and we settle down to look at the next English test paper. I feel that Harriet deserves a break from imaginative writing, so I'm pleased to see a question on factual reporting. By a happy coincidence, one question asks: 'Describe a recent trip you have made with your school, parents, or with an organisation you belong to, such as Guides, Church group, or similar'. Although depressingly Establishment, it suits Harriet.

Would Harriet like to write about her recent Guide trip? She's not very enthusiastic, but can't think of anything else. Mechanically, with a sigh, she makes notes on the radials of her spider-gram and after much pencil chewing, begins to write:

We camped in a wood near Barnstaple. I was sharing a tent with Susie. We had to put the tent up all by ourselves because the parents who came on the trip with us were busy putting up the big tent with the food and tables in it. It was hard putting up our tent, because it was raining and the pole kept getting stuck in the nylon material. Susie kept grumbling. She said I should have a new tent that had poles that slotted together in an arch instead of this one with straight poles that Dad got out of the attic.

At last we had the tent up, and I just wanted to put a battery in my torch and hang up my new pockets so that I could put my wash bag and torch and notebook in them, but we had to go outside in the rain and make a stand out of branches to put plates and cups on and a tripod for hanging the cooking pots over the fire. All the children had a competition between tents to see who could make the best and the strongest tripod. It was quite fun tying the branches into place with twine but we got cold and wet looking for the branches in the wood. Me and Susie were the last to finish. Susie is quite bossy and kept telling me my branches were too short.

Then the rain stopped and our pack leader said we had to cook outside on a fire to save gas and the planet. We all had to gather firewood. This time the branches had to be VERY dry, but most of them were soggy wet. We really had to hunt for the dry ones in ditches and under fallen trees and they had to be old and snap easily. We made a barbecue with bricks to go under our fire.

Then we had to light the fire. Our pack leader wanted us to do it without matches. She had a flint but the spark wouldn't catch on to the wood. Then she tried the matches, but they kept going out. She went away to find more matches. In the end Sarah's mum said bugger this, we'll all die of starvation and she found some old newspaper. She poured a tiny bit of paraffin on to the newspaper and stuffed it into a long cardboard tube that tinfoil goes round. Then she lit it with her cigarette lighter. Suddenly it went WHOOSH and there were huge flames that leapt all around. Sarah's mum got her coat sleeve singed. She looked REALLY scared as we were standing a bit too close and said DON'T try this at home. Jane our pack leader came over and told Sarah's mum off because of Health and Safety and Sarah's mum went off home in a strop.

It took ages to cook sausages on the barbecue, but the baked beans in the pan on the tripod were quicker. We had to wait till nearly dark before the potatoes cooked in the ashes. They were burnt on the outside and raw inside.

We had to wash up outside by torchlight and then it was time for bed. I wanted to go to sleep but Susie kept flashing her new torch on and off doing signals to Emma in the next tent and talking.

It was the same the next day and the next day, just getting firewood and cooking and washing up in cold water.

The best bit was a Badger Hunt. We looked for setts in the wood. I found some badger droppings and some fox trails. We saw two deer in a field. We had two competitions to find things you can eat, and the other was who could spot the most wild birds and insects. I won easily as I had 42 creatures on my list.

It rained every day and in the end we stopped saving the planet and cooked inside on the camping gas stoves in the big tent. Susie got homesick on the third day and her dad had to come and collect her. Kerry had an asthma attack and had to go to hospital. It happened at midnight. She woke up choking for breath. It was because we'd been out at night on a bat watch and the cold damp air had hurt her lungs. Amelia fell into the stream but she was okay just very wet. Her mum had to bring some dry clothes as her other clothes were all soaking from all the rain.

We were in the wood for five days before Dad and Mum came to get me out. THE END.

Wednesday, 12th May. As I draw up a chair to begin our lesson Mrs Bailey bustles in, waving a brochure of St Bede's for my perusal, no doubt to impress upon me the gravity of this last session with Harriet and the full weight of my responsibilities. The entrance exam, which takes place over three days, begins next week.

The brochure shows full colour photographs of an old manor house with modern additions: a gymnasium, assembly hall, tennis courts, and scenes of neatly dressed, industrious, smiling children engaged in various activities. The superb facilities, and the brochure itself – lavish, glossy and worthy of a chain of luxury country hotels – indicate a healthy revenue in fees.

Last Friday, Harriet and her parents visited the school. She points to a small lake in the spacious grounds, where she saw a pair of nesting swans. She was shown the classroom she'll be in, and the dining room and kitchens. Her eyes light up as she describes the science labs. She's excited and interested. *Good.*

The hour flies by. We check her latest test papers. I remind her to pace herself, to read the questions through twice. Be thorough, show your workings. Don't rush. Allow equal time for each question, you can always go back and finish it if you find time at the end. In maths, do the easiest ones first. Just have a go! And, I'm thinking, *'Have fun, little girl, as much as you can, don't take it too seriously.'*

Cautiously, I ask Harriet how she's feeling about the exam.

"Okay." A typical shrug, a smile, and she quickly begins to tell me about her latest riding lesson. Her first proper gallop, along a wide grassy track. And she might start jumps soon.

It's time to finish, but I find myself trying to prolong the session. I enjoy working with Harriet. Her quick mind, willingness, capacity for sustained effort and her passion for nature are all a delight.

As I gather my things, I savour the aroma of fresh thyme and sage, cinnamon and coriander wafting from the kitchen. For the last time, I gaze through the long windows into the garden. There's Spice, the haughty family cat on the patio, sunbathing – crouched like a sphinx on a stone bird table mounted on a pillar. There's the apple tree, its base circled by a ballerina skirt of puffy rose-white blossom. The immaculate, bowling-green lawn.

Reluctantly, I turn to leave. Mrs Bailey rushes out of the kitchen and hands me a foil-covered dish, hot from the cooker. "It is a *vegetable* curry. I know that you are a vegetarian. Put it in the freezer if you do not wish to eat it tonight. And thank you for your help with Harriet."

"Thank you," I say, touched.

"And this is for you too." Harriet has crept up behind her mother, and hands me a large flat box wrapped in pink tissue paper.

"Shall I open it now?" I ask.

Unexpectedly, she shakes her head. "You can open it at home," she says shyly, "with your curry."

Mrs Bailey promises me she'll let me know how Harriet gets on in the exam. I want to press her on this, and add 'whether or not she gets the scholarship', but I don't want to end on a negative note. She should get the results during the week following the tests. I tell Mrs Bailey that I shall be thinking of Harriet all next week.

At home, I carefully open my present. It's a watercolour painting. The detail must have taken her hours. In the foreground, two swans are nesting on a reedy mound in the centre of a small lake. In the background rises the moor, a mass of bracken-covered hills and grey, craggy tors. A white stallion with flowing mane gallops towards me, just about to jump over a rocky stream fringed with flag irises and rushes. *Wild and free.*

Will Harriet ever be as happy and free as the stallion in the painting? And will Mrs Bailey remember to tell me her results?

Friday, 16th July. It's been over two months since Harriet's last tuition session and I haven't heard a peep from her family. I'm longing to know if she's at least gained a place at St Bede's. And I'm feeling miffed at the lack of contact. Although most probably she's been accepted – she's so bright, they could hardly have refused her – it looks as if she hasn't managed to get a scholarship.

After work, I have to go to the bank in town. As I walk up the High Street, I suddenly hear a high excited voice behind me.

"Look, Mummy! There's my tutor!"

I spin round. Mrs Bailey is walking a few paces behind me, looking at me as if she can't quite place who I am. Harriet's at her mother's side, smiling at me. She, at least, remembers me.

I'm holding my breath, hardly daring to ask the all-important question. Then I feel righteous indignation rising inside – damn it, Mrs Bailey *should* have informed me.

"I hope it all went well with St Bede's?" My words sound abrupt, even rude, to my ears. Harriet's eyes dart to her mother's face, as if wondering what the correct reply should be.

"Ah yes," says Mum, "I'm so sorry. I meant to contact you, but we have had a very busy time at work. And what with one thing and another…but yes, Harriet did very well. She got a bursary."

One of two, I remember. Half Harriet's fees will be paid.

"But that's fantastic!" I'm so excited I'm almost jumping up and down. "Well done, Harriet. You must be so proud of yourself."

She nods, looking shyly pleased, although there's also something muted in her pleasure. She's looking at her mother for reassurance that she is, in fact, entitled to be proud. Maybe I'm being hypersensitive, but I also detect a slight reserve in Mrs Bailey's response. They were going for gold: the full scholarship. Have Harriet and I been made to feel as if we've failed to make the grade, in spite of this remarkable achievement? She's reached joint second place, beating three hundred other applicants, the brightest and best in the county.

"Yes, indeed," concedes Mrs Bailey. "Harriet has done extremely well. And she is looking forward to starting in September. Of course, she is realising that she will be amongst the cleverest children, so she will have to work very hard to keep ahead."

"Well, I'm thrilled. It's the most exciting news I've had for a long time. You've made my day, Harriet!"

Her smile broadens, her large almond shaped eyes light up. Suddenly she bursts out, "And guess what? I'm going to get a pony!"

"Wow! Really, when?"

"Soon. When the holidays start, so I can ride it lots and lots in the summer!"

"Yes, that is the plan." Mum is smiling indulgently at Harriet. "It will be very expensive and very time-consuming, but it is what Harriet wants and we have promised it."

"That's really great." I watch Harriet's face. Her joy and excitement are unmistakeable. Yet there's a wary look, too. Perhaps she wonders if this pony will ever actually materialise.

"Well, we must get on," says Mrs Bailey. "We are on the way to order Harriet's school uniform. We have left it as late as possible because she is growing so fast. By September, she'll be squeezing herself into a doll's jumper and skirt." We all laugh at this image.

"Well, goodbye then Harriet. Enjoy your pony!"

"Yes, well…" Mrs Bailey pauses a moment to rummage for something in her handbag. "Harriet understands that the pony mustn't take over her schoolwork. She must remember that in no time at all she will be taking her GCSEs, so *now* is the time to put in all the effort and the groundwork…"

Suddenly I catch Harriet's eye. I wink.

Checking to see that Mum is still preoccupied with studying her shopping list, Harriet winks back.

JACK

∽

Thursday, 9th October 2003. As I drive along the seafront, there's an irritating drizzle; not full-on enough to warrant the windscreen wipers, and on my ancient Fiesta I don't have the luxury of intermittent mode. I'm on the way to see a new pupil. Karen, the administrator at the office, rang yesterday to ask if I would tutor Jack, who's had a serious accident and has been off school since the beginning of term. He's only just come out of hospital and is in bed. He, as well as his two younger brothers and older sister, have learning difficulties.

The O'Neills live on a less-favoured council estate on the east side of town, between the railway station and a huge complex of industrial works. Clay is the main industry here, and if I'm ever running even a smidgeon late, it's inevitable that I'll be stuck behind a massive truck transporting raw material from the nearby quarries. Today, fortunately, I'm on time.

No one's around when I knock at the front door. After waiting for a couple of minutes I go to the back of the house, under the side passage which divides the house from next door, and find Mrs O'Neill taking in the washing. The rain's now coming down in buckets, and we both dash into the kitchen via the back door, where I introduce myself. Mrs O'Neill is a stout woman of about forty. She's wearing a shapeless floral skirt and a frayed pink jumper, her grey hair straggles down to her shoulders. She looks harassed, as if her appearance is the last thing on her mind. Straight away, she leads me through the opposite door which opens directly into the living room.

Jack is lying on a bed, which is taking up a good deal of the small living space. He's propped up with three pillows, a soft foam sling around his left arm. His right leg is in plaster and raised on to two cushions. He looks pale and listless. I say "Hello, Jack" and tell him that I'm his new tutor and that I'll be helping him with his work until he goes back to school. My heart's going out to this youngster. I want to give him the message right away that I'm a positive phenomenon, in what must seem a sudden series of bewildering, scary and often painful changes in his young life. I mention school as an anchor in the hope that Jack, from the beginning of our working relationship, can keep alive the concept of normality – of classmates, playtimes, football at break. So often we forget, when children's lives turn topsy-turvy, that the child somehow thinks that *all* the familiar, good things in his life must be ending, buried under a pile of plaster casts, injections, discomfort, anxiety and uncertainty.

"Hi," says Jack. His voice is flat, and he hardly glances at me.

His mother asks if Jack needs anything. In a small, high voice he asks for some lemonade, but says he isn't hungry.

"Just a little toast?" urges Mrs O'Neill. "You haven't had any breakfast." Jack shakes his head.

While we're waiting for Mum to return with the lemonade, I start unpacking my bag, and spreading various items out on the coffee table by the side of the bed, a jigsaw, some games, coloured pencils, felt tips, toy animals and some Lego. I've no idea what developmental level Jack has reached, and for the moment I don't care. One thing is certain, he's not in a fit state to do 'formal' work. I suddenly feel an irrational sense of anger and intrusion; I shouldn't be here so soon after such a traumatic event. Almost simultaneously I transmute this rebellion into a determination – I'll justify my presence by aiding, in whatever way I possibly can, Jack's recovery process. So today I need to find out what he can *physically* do, as well as finding out what his interests are.

While I'm displaying all my materials, I'm also reassuring him.

"I expect you're feeling quite tired and fed up just now. So you don't have to do any hard work. The most important thing is for you to get strong again. Look! I've brought loads of things for you to play with. You can choose."

For the first time Jack looks at me directly. There's no mistaking the relief in his face. He smiles, a burst of sunlight that's totally disarming. The smile emphasises his delicate features, and almost translucent skin. He really does look dreadfully pale. From what I can see of him, he's also very tiny for an eleven year old.

Mum's back with his drink. She puts her arm around Jack's shoulders and gently levers him into a more upright position. The tumbler is a baby's feeding beaker, with a straw in it. Jack can hold the tumbler with his right hand, his left arm lies uselessly on the bed-covers. He drinks about half, then sinks back into his mother's supporting arm. He's still incredibly weak. Mum carefully sets him back on to the pillows.

"Right, I'll leave you to it," she says. "Are you all right using that table?"

I'm warming to this mother, with her open, homely features and soft Irish accent. She has a calm and soothing way with her. She looks exhausted and worried, yet she's there for Jack.

"We'll be fine, won't we, Jack?"-

He nods and points to my bag. "What else have you got in there?"

"I've got a book to read to you." I take it out and show him. "I've chosen it especially for you."

He's looking at me expectantly now. At least that heavy listlessness has lifted a little.

"Now, you've had an accident, and that wasn't fun, was it?" He shakes his head. "So while I'm here, you're not going to do anything that's too hard for you. If I do make a mistake and ask you to do something you can't do, or don't like doing, will you tell me?" He nods, fixing me with large, solemn eyes, deep blue like his mother's. "So I'm going to read to you for a little while. Is that okay?" He nods, half smiles, and wriggles a little further down the bed with a little sigh.

I'm not going to suggest that he reads out aloud. This book would probably be too difficult, and besides, I don't want to put him under the slightest strain. Even presenting him with an easy reader might seem a bit like a test. Not yet. All my instincts are telling me to lead very gently into these tuition sessions. In fact, I'm a bit wobbly in the knees myself. I'm struggling not to feel crushed by the enormity of what's happened to Jack. He needs toileting as he can't get out of bed, he has to be washed, changed and fed. There are also the physiotherapy sessions at the hospital, visits to the doctor and chemist for painkillers, liaison with his teacher. How, with three other children, does this family cope?

"What's the book called?" Jack is struggling up from his semi-reclining position, craning to see the picture on the front cover.

"It's called *Danny, the Champion of the World.*" I show him the picture. "And guess how old the boy in the book is?"

"Eleven, like me?"

"He's nine. But he's only five when the story begins." I show him the illustration of Danny as a baby and as a little boy with his dad.

I start reading. Jack is showing me in every way that he's not to be pitied. He settles down in the bed now, with a half-smile of anticipation, shimmying his shoulders sideways towards me so that his head almost touches the book. I glimpse the strength in him, the strong recovery instinct.

I've chosen the book just for this reason. Jack's accident happened as he was walking to school. For the first few days of the new term, his dad had walked him there. But Jack, seeing his friends making their own way without parental supervision, begged to be grown-up enough to join them. Reluctantly, for they were fairly protective, they agreed. It was only a short walk anyway, about half a mile along the road, with no roads at all to cross.

On the very first day of this new independence, there'd been a good-natured scuffle on the edge of the pavement. Jack stepped off the kerb, just as a wide truck hit the edge of it, trying to avoid a car coming from the opposite direction, which was swerving into the middle of the road. Jack broke a hip, thighbone and elbow. It had been a lucky escape – no head injury – yet what a tragic blow to

Jack's confidence. I imagine him that morning, striding out from the protection of the parental wing. That sense of adventure and power as he set out for school with his friends. All suddenly shattered. And for the next few months, there'll be no skate-boarding or football or cycling. No daring deeds that always herald the pre-teens – that stage of burgeoning maleness that likes to measure its own courage and physical strength against that of the peer group.

In the classic Roald Dahl story I've chosen, there are no gentle maternal figures fussing and administering. Jack will be blessed with much tender motherly care in the next few weeks; but through Danny's father and in Danny's adventures he might also absorb a little male energy and courage, as well as enjoying the excellently drawn character of Danny's father, who has single-handedly and lovingly brought him up. The power of it, this raw energy that's the very essence of Jack's age and gender! The accident has robbed him of it for now – yet perhaps he can feel just a little of it through a fictional character?

We read, and then play some games that Jack chooses. He can only use one hand, and too much movement is a strain. So we play word-rummy and Tummy Ache, a perennial favourite, with two sets of food cards – yummy and disgusting. His word recognition is that of a seven to eight year old, but considering his condition his concentration is admirable. We play I-Spy and then he wants to play with my miniature animals. He makes a Noah's ark.

He's looking weary. I say goodbye till tomorrow, and knock on the kitchen door to tell Mum I'm off. She is busy sorting out the mountain of washing that came off the line. I ask if there's anything urgent I need to know about Jack – for example, is there any position he's not supposed to get into? Is he on any medication that might suddenly need topping up? And what does he really feel about having a tutor so soon after coming out of hospital?

"I did think it was a bit soon," admitted Mrs O'Neill. "And I was surprised when they sent someone so quickly." (So am I. Often a pupil is out of school for months without a tutor, having somehow slipped through the system.) "But Jack wanted you to come. He just sort of accepts it, just as he's putting up with the pain, and the bedpans, and not being able to move properly. He just puts up with things. He's never been a complainer."

"He seems a bit…flat." I say hesitantly. "Not at all surprising."

"The spirit's gone out of him," sighs Mrs O'Neill. "Partly it's the pain, partly the shock. But it's a good job you're here. He needs something to take his mind of the pain. And, to be honest, it gives me a chance to have a break away from him, to get on with a few things. Not that he's a demanding child – in fact, of the four of them he's by far the easiest – but I need a chance to get myself together, like, if you see what I mean."

Friday, 10th October. Dad opens the door for me. He's medium-height and very heavily built – I guess at least seventeen stone – making his plump wife look positively petite. His shock of black hair contrasts with high colouring and piercing blue eyes that appraise me shrewdly as we shake hands. I sense that he's mentally judging whether I'm a fit person to tutor his son.

He takes my jacket and hangs it up on a stand already bulging with coats. There's hardly room to move in the tiny space at the bottom of the stairs, and we both do a polite dance as we try to avoid bumping into each other. Before he opens the door into the living room, I ask how Jack is today.

With a catch in his voice, Mr O'Neill tells me that Jack had a bad night with the pain, and might not be able to do much today. "Tis a terrible thing that's happened."

I nod. There's a lump in my throat just thinking about what Jack's going through.

He coughs and continues quickly, "I'm afraid Ryan and Sean are at home today. Both ill with a tummy upset in the night, so we've kept them in bed. They'll not bother you."

He wants to talk, perhaps to relieve his anxiety. The family are originally from the Irish Republic. They came over to England three years ago for the work, and to be near his brothers and sister who live in the West Country. He's not in work at the present, he tells me. He hurt his back six months ago while doing heavy lifting at the quarry, and though it's on the mend, he has to be very careful. He's on 'the sick' but this will run out any moment and he'll be looking for another, less strenuous job. "But 'tis a good thing, so it turned out." It enables him to take and collect the three other children from school and to carry Jack to the bathroom and do the shopping. Mrs O'Neill doesn't drive, so she'd be a bit stuck without him. His voice wobbles a bit and he coughs again. He opens the door to the living room.

Jack's lying down, looking, if possible, even more listless and fragile than he did yesterday. It's very clear to me now that my role here is to be a companion, a distraction from the pain – and even an entertainer. Jack is not yet ready to tackle the worksheets the teacher has conscientiously prepared and sent home for him. Yet there's education in everything, including entertainment.

Would Jack like me to read to him again? He nods and tries to make himself comfortable. I ask if I can help settle him into his pillows. He nods again, and I lift his shoulders and puff up the pillows behind him. I read for about fifteen minutes, showing him the illustrations and talking about the story: what might happen next to Danny?

I've bought some animal puppets today, and I make them do various actions, getting Jack to guess the appropriate action words. I can now note on my record sheet that Jack has covered verbs (parts of speech as required by National Curriculum KS2), but far more importantly, Jack might vicariously experience the fun and freedom of movement. The animals run, jump, spring, growl and slither. "Where might the animals be?" I ask. "In the jungle," he replies promptly. In no time at all we've got a mini-drama under way. I fix the lion puppet on to Jack's right hand so that he can be King of the Jungle.

After forty-five minutes Jack needs the toilet. "Ask Dad," he whispers. The kitchen door is open and I can see Mum and Dad sitting at the kitchen table surrounded by a mound of washing-up still to be done. Mum is slowly peeling potatoes. Dad's just sitting. Both look utterly wiped out. I explain Jack's need, and Dad stiffly heaves himself up and fetches a camping-style port-a-potty. I make myself scarce and sit on the bottom step of the staircase, writing ideas for Monday's lesson.

There's a sudden commotion upstairs. It sounds like a pillow fight, thumps and bangs and squeals of laughter. The door's flung open and two pyjama-clad figures spill out on to the landing, arms raised in combat. They see me and stop in mid-blow.

I introduce myself and ask their names. The older one is Ryan, aged eight, and the younger is Sean, seven. They're as alike as identical twins, with their mother's fair colouring. We chat amiably about bikes and fishing, and school. "But we're both too ill to be at school today," they chorus, a comical double-act.

"But you seem to be making a remarkable recovery," I say.

They nod happily, the irony quite lost on them. Mrs O'Neill comes out of the kitchen, and tells them off roundly. They both scuttle back into their bedroom.

"I do hope they weren't being a nuisance?"

"Not at all," I reassure her, "it's been a pleasure to meet them." I ask about the eldest child, Sinead. Does she enjoy school?

"Ah yes," Mum says proudly, "she's top of her class, she got a maths prize last week."

All the O'Neill children go to a special school for children with mild learning difficulties, some with behavioural problems. Sinead was in mainstream children until a year ago – she's now thirteen – but she was being bullied and teased because she was slow at 'catching on, like'. After a 'statementing' process that seemed to take forever, she was moved; and now she's making rapid progress. Jack has always had problems with reading and writing, so have the youngest two. All are now thriving. I'm thinking how good it is to hear about children happily placed in a special school when so many have been closed, or merged with schools for those with profound learning difficulties. This is part of the government's 'Inclusion Process'. Fine in theory, but intelligence covers a wide spectrum, and wherever a child belongs in that spectrum, he has a right to have his needs met. These include the need for friendship and acceptance, and to fit in.

Since the original Warnock report I've had strong doubts about this 'one size fits all' policy. It seems as if we're trying to tailor the child to the school, instead of ensuring that the school is the right one for the child. Even with personal teaching assistants and other concessions to their learning difficulties, there will always be children who feel out of their depth intellectually – and worse – a misfit socially. I've supported just such children in schools, and with them, gone through agonies at playtime when no one asks them to play.

Jack loves the animal puppets, so I let him play with them, fitting them in turn on to his hand. We try to imagine how each animal would move in the jungle. He makes the monkey climb and swing from the treetops. We think of words to describe what the tiger does, and come up with 'stalking, hunting, pouncing', while Jack mimes the action. I write all the words down for him to read in some future session when he's feeling stronger.

"Will you bring the puppets next time?" he says, as I leave. I promise I will.

Friday, 17th October. Jack looks stronger today. He's sitting upright in bed when I arrive, eating some toast. He's also totally absorbed in listening to the tape we made last week.

We'd developed last Friday's antics with the animal puppets first into a play, and afterwards into a story about an enormous lion, who isn't, in fact, as fierce as he looks. The lion is angry because he can't find his son anywhere in the jungle. He asks Tiger to help him, but Tiger wants the son for himself, because poor Tiger hasn't got a son of his own.

As Jack told me the story, I wrote it down. When it was finished, I read it back to him, then we both read it through together. Jack recognised most of the words – I wrote only the words he chose. He worked out the rest either from the context or from memory. (For reluctant readers, it's so much more fun to read out loud their very own story.) On Monday we made a tape of the story. I was the narrator, but Jack supplied all the sound effects – growls, monkey-chatter, the pitiful cries of the lost little lion, the wind howling through the trees. I wrote these down as directions in the story.

Today, as I settle myself down by his bed, he's listening and following both the story and the directions on the page with his finger. He growls, whistles and cries in turn, with appropriate actions and facial expression. He's not Jack any more, he's a creature of the jungle! His voice is stronger, too, and he has more colour in his cheeks.

This is the joy of one-to-one teaching. To have the freedom to follow the moment, letting one activity lead naturally into another, like the flow of a river into a lake. Watching, fascinated, as a child's interest in one topic, such as fishing, can spread ripples over the lake. The lake is full of fresh-water fish, but maybe the Loch Ness monster lurks within its depths...

This lake has outlets in more rivers, and some of them flow into seas, and now there are whales and dolphins, seals and sharks, trawlers to catch the fish, and big ocean-going ships too. The seas are surrounded by cold countries, hot deserts, fjords and mountains. Where will it all lead? In optimum learning conditions children, if left to explore, are so much more efficient and imaginative in leading themselves where they want to go, than we admit. Or allow. Instead, we often impose on them our adult, linear, ordered way of learning. Do we, as we grow older, lose this childlike delight in mental exploration, or is it knocked out of us at school? And today, how many teachers have the time – or the courage – to spend several weeks following where the class decides to go? Or even to share their own interests with the class? I still remember a history teacher who was passionate about architecture and British constitutional history – and brought them both alive, to bored and cynical fifteen year-olds, by a series of visits to London: to the Houses of Parliament to watch Question Time from the public gallery, to the Inns of Court and the old coffee shops in the City, to the magnificent grandeur of St Paul's Cathedral. Suddenly, all that dry old stuff was real. Through her enthusiasm, we could almost hear the crackle of the flames and smell the charred buildings of The Great Fire. Over those few weeks, how many delightful twists and turns were made in our explorations!

Today, I want to follow Jack's lead as much as possible. I also want to see how confident Jack is with numbers. We play some simple adding and subtracting games. He's fairly sound on number bonds to twenty, and counting to one hundred. However, multiplication tables are a mystery to him. He hasn't yet grasped the concept of multiplication as repeated addition. Even the idea of 'lots of' twos or threes or fours is impossible for him to fathom out. He's still very much at what Piaget – a pioneer educationalist – describes as the concrete, non-abstract stage of understanding.

I dash back to my car and find a set of small coloured cubes, a set of 'ten' sticks, (ten cubes stuck together), and a flat square, made up of one hundred cubes. I gather up ten of Jack's teddies and other soft toys, and play a sharing game. The small blocks are sweets. We start with the two times table, giving all the toys two sweets each until all ten have an equal share. Now it's easy for Jack to see that ten times two is twenty, if he looks and counts. But if I ask him what nine lots of two are, he will have to look and count all over again. He's still not ready to just subtract two. I can see we'll have to have lots of teddy bears' picnics until what is now just a glimmer of understanding becomes certain knowledge. And I mustn't assume that just because a child 'sees' it once, that he'll know it for next time. I must be patient, not rush him. Gently, softly, like the river flowing into the sea.

Today, when Jack needs the toilet, Dad comes in and carries him through to the loo opposite the kitchen. This is progress. It means that Jack can now stand for short periods with support. I'm moved by the way this giant of a man cradles Jack, so small and fragile, as gently in his arms as if he were a newborn baby. When they return, there's a broad smile on his dad's face.

"He stood up without holding on to me at all!' he says proudly.

Jack's getting his strength back far more quickly than any of us could have hoped – a testimony to the loving care of his family as well to his own powers of recovery. With a pang, I realise he'll be ready for school in a few weeks. So, now is the time to build up his educational strength, so that when he does go back, he'll be top of his class!

Wednesday, 22nd October. Instead of steps up to the front door of Jack's house, there's a brand new ramp. The concrete has hardly set and is damp in patches. Mr O'Neill opens the door.

"There's a surprise in the living room!"

Jack's sitting up in bed, grinning triumphantly. The small, cluttered living space has shrunk even smaller, due to the majestic presence of a wheelchair, wedged between the settee, behind me, and the bed.

"I can go out now!" says Jack.

"He's been out to the shops yesterday," Dad looks proud, and relieved. This is a new stage in Jack's recovery.

"Got some fresh air at last," adds Mum, bringing in some lemonade.

Jack does look much healthier. His face has lost that hollow, wan appearance and his cheeks have filled out a little. The waif-like translucence has gone.

Jack drinks his lemonade and I sit down and prepare for the session. There's barely room for my chair and the small coffee table. The arm of the wheelchair's poking into my elbow. The living room bulges with toys, an extra-large television, newspapers and magazines in piles next to it. The set of shelves in the alcove by the chimneybreast is crammed with mugs, a china money-box pig, toys, photos, notepads and pencil cases, schoolbooks, and a pair of sandals. Ryan has had a birthday on Sunday, and cards from family and school spill over from the mantelpiece to every available surface. Propped up against the television are a pile of new, bulging, carrier bags, and rolls of Christmas wrapping paper. It's all a glorious muddle, with warmth and heart.

"I went to the corner shop!" Jack wipes his mouth on his sleeve and launches into an account of his outing yesterday. "And I met Gary and Peter, and they pushed me along. Peter tried to have a ride on the back, but Dad said not to. And the lady in the shop gave me two Mars bars, free!"

"Mmmmm. Yummy."

"And after school we're all going to the park with my brothers and sister!"

It's difficult to settle him down and I hardly want to. Yet I also want to build on yesterday's progress. Then, because he's now so much stronger, we did some writing. First, we played charades, miming an action word. I wrote these down in his drawing pad, which doubles as a workbook. I ruled lines on the blank page with enough space in between for a beginner writer; notebooks with narrow lines can be quite cramping and even intimidating. Jack filled a whole page with action words.

While I'm thinking what to do today, Jack says he wants to draw his wheelchair. It's a tricky choice. He rubs out a lot, but perseveres and comes up with a large, bold sketch. I admire it. "The wheels really look as if they're going along! Would you like to label the wheels and the other parts of it?"

He puts his head on one side, and, like an artist, looks appraisingly at his work. "I think I'll keep this one like this and then I can colour it. I don't want to put writing on it. But I'll do another one next to it."

The second drawing is equally careful. Once again, I'm impressed with his concentration. I write out a list of wheelchair parts: wheels, brakes, headrest, seat etc. on a spare piece of paper and ask him if he can write the word next to the corresponding part on his drawing. He can, with elaborate arrowheads pointing to each item.

Time has flown this morning, it's well past our usual break-time. Dad comes in and carries Jack to the toilet. Jack says he can hop on one leg, but Dad won't let him.

Sinead, Jack's elder sister, is off school today. She's had a dentist appointment and it's too much of a palaver to get her back to school again.

"Show the tutor your stars," prompts Mum, coming in with a cup of tea and some biscuits.

Sinead leaps upstairs, and comes down with three English worksheets. The last four exercises include several simple word patterns, for example, boat, goat, moat, and a short description of a country scene, with blanks to fill in with the appropriate word. The teacher has commended Sinead's neat writing.

I admire the work. Mum peers over my shoulder. "She's such a hard worker, just look at all those ticks! And the stars at the bottom of the page!"

"*And* a smiley face," adds Sinead, pointing.

Jack wants to see. Sinead explains the exercises. "See! Bright, sight, fight, might...... see Jack, look – they've all got 'i g h t' at the end." She dances round the room with the worksheets, still exulting over her page of ticks and stars, then skips upstairs again.

Sinead has given me an idea. Jack and I play a 'word race' which I've found to be popular with most children. It's much more exciting than just writing out lists of word patterns. I divide the blank page of his workbook into two wide columns. I write *Jack* on top of the first one, and my name on top of the other. I rule lines for eight words in each column and number them. At No.1 in my column I write 'wheel,' and in Jack's first space, I write 'brake.' The one who can write the most words with the same pattern is the winner. Jack catches on quickly. Triumphantly, he shouts "Make!" "Peel," I say.

We write down our words. Jack's writing is large and non-cursive, but the letters are well-formed. He follows with 'cake' and 'take' and has soon filled in the eight blank spaces. I have only found six words, so Jack is the winner.

I'm wondering if Jack can now say the two times table without using the counting blocks. But he has a problem with sequencing, so I give him the blocks to set out on a tray, and he has fun arranging them in pairs, "like marching soldiers".

I really must do this every day, I tell myself. One of my weaknesses is following up on really vital learning reinforcement. Sometimes I assume that just because I'm bored out of my mind with some repetition exercise, then the child must also be fed up with it. Not so. The child often loves the routine and the predictability of it, just as a three-year-old will beg you to read the same bed-time story every night for weeks. 'Water on a stone'- my mantra. I mustn't forget it.

Jack is leaning back now, sinking into the pillows. I read half a chapter of *Danny*. His eyes are closing. I shut the book, quietly collect my things, and tiptoe out of the room.

Monday, 3rd November. There's no reply when I knock on Jack's door. I wonder if I've forgotten some important hospital appointment. Then I hear voices, faint thuds getting progressively louder, laughter.

A moment later, Jack opens the door, a triumphant smile stretching from ear to ear. He's on crutches, and eager to demonstrate his new skill.

"Watch!" He hops back into the living room and completes a ceremonious circuit of the tiny space, weaving his way between his bed, wheelchair, and settee. The crutches look too big for him, his 'good' leg is almost on tiptoe as he moves, but this is great progress.

"He'll be back at school in no time at all," says Dad. He and Mrs O'Neill are standing in the kitchen doorway, watching.

Suddenly, I feel the familiar heartache that I've been fighting for thirty-five years. It heralds a child's return to school. This is what I hope and aim for, the ultimate successful outcome. This is the reason I'm here. Yet there's always that sense of loss. I can anticipate it, cerebrally, but emotionally it always catches me out.

His mum tells me they're hoping that Jack can manage just a couple of hours a day at school, initially, building up to whole mornings. But first, he needs to consult the orthopaedic surgeon as to how the hip-bone, femur and arm are mending. They have an appointment at the hospital next Wednesday, then they'll know for certain if Jack will be fit for the rough-and-tumble of school life.

Jack begs me to read *Danny*. We're just getting to the exciting bit where Danny has to rescue his father from the deep pit, the man-trap in the wood that the evil and despicable landowner Bunce has prepared. Before half term, the chapter where, hardly able to reach the gears or see above the steering wheel, Danny slowly but skilfully drives a car seven miles to the dark wood, had Jack bouncing up and down in his bed, eyes shining, while he steered an imaginary car. Maybe there's a healing synchronicity, for this road-injured child, in Danny's dramatic car-rescue. It's amazing what suddenly pops out of the printed page, somehow finding you exactly as you are at that precise moment, and telling you what you need to know.

I pretend I have a cough, and ask Jack if he will read a very short paragraph for me, to help me out. He reads two or three lines easily but stumbles over some unfamiliar words. I help him say them, and he continues right to the end of the paragraph. He's pleased with himself.

Jack is now confident with the two and three times table. He's just grasped the idea of multiplication as 'lots of' *things* – that don't have to be blocks or teddies or sweets. We play a three-times-table pairs game. Jack has to pick up the question card, for example 6 x 3, and tell me the answer before he's allowed to look for the corresponding answer card. He has an excellent memory for the positioning of the cards in the random spread on the table. This helps him remember where the 'right' card is. This spatial memory is a strength. It will be useful to him in later life and needs to be encouraged.

Jack's now ready to tackle the English worksheets sent home by his class teacher, and we're working through them, gradually. They're boring and disjointed. Bite-size bits of information – everything in school today seems to be bite-size. Prepositions, word-endings, suffixes. I shudder when I see nine year-olds trying to get their head round subordinate clauses, when some of them are still beginner writers, struggling to spell simple words, and to formulate their thoughts into coherent sentences. Can subordinate clauses really foster a love of the language, even in the brightest child? Where is the *heart* in English these days? Back in the golden age when I was at school, we all learned to write by *writing*, however imperfectly, and didn't start to analyse what we'd written till the words we read and wrote were felt deep inside us, poetry in our bones and our soul. And then, it was almost a joy to discover 'parts of speech', like saving the icing on the cake till last.

Still, Jack will feel good if when he returns to school he sees that he's kept up with his peers, so I find the least odious worksheet. Adjectives. Now adjectives *are* really quite useful and colourful things, even for a beginner writer, so I don't mind having a go at these. First, they need to come alive. We play a game: I have to choose an object in the room, and without saying what it is, I describe it, using as many different words as I can, bringing in all the five senses. So the clock over the mantelpiece would be round, flat with a shiny clear cover. It would feel smooth to the touch. It would also have a faint regular sound (the trick is not to give too much away). It has a pale blue surround and is about fifteen centimetres in diameter – I indicate the appropriate size with my hands. And so on, while I try hard not to peep at the object.

Jack guesses in the end, then chooses his object, staring hard at his lemonade mug. I remind him – does it make a sound, does it smell? We take turns, and by end of the session he knows that adjectives are not just sight words like 'red' or 'big'. His perception of everyday objects has expanded to include all five senses. And now the worksheet will come alive.

As I leave him, he's busy sniffing any objects that he can reach.

"Ugh – that's disgusting!" he says, pointing to something on the floor, "Smell that!"

"No, thank you. I'll take your word for it! Bye, Jack. See you tomorrow."

Thursday, 20th November. Jack's been seen by the specialist. His bones are mending well and he should go back to school 'when he feels ready'.

However, the class teacher has cautioned that Jack's class is a lively and often unpredictable bunch, and there's no guarantee that he won't be knocked over if he happens to be in the firing line when two kids decide to fight over a nicked rubber. So his return to school has been put on hold, and meanwhile I can continue to build up Jack's confidence in spelling, writing, reading and maths.

He can now count, with help, to one hundred. Yet he has little grasp of the range of numbers, how they grow, or what they represent. The number three thousand is meaningless to Jack. I borrow an idea from that classic *How Children Learn* by John Holt. I buy a till roll, and we begin to write the numbers in, starting at No. 1. Each day, we add between fifty and a hundred more, depending on Jack's mood and interest level. As we say the numbers, I relate them to something meaningful to him. How many miles to Bristol, where his aunt and uncle live? He guesses, and I show him on my roadmap. How much would a battery-operated racing car cost, how much might a family spend on the weekly food bill? His mother, coming in at this moment with a drink for Jack and a cup of tea for me, obligingly tells us what how much they spend on a family of six. Jack's eyes widen in amazement. The neighbour up the road is selling his car for £450, which is exactly how far we've reached in our numbers for today.

We count to one hundred, then in hundreds to a thousand. I show him the thousand cube block . He can't believe that a thousand small blocks could fit inside. He peers into it and taps it and looks at me suspiciously. I place a flat, hundred-square block of cubes in front of him and get him to count the cubes. One hundred, agreed? He nods. Now I get him to place nine more of these squares on top of the first. Hey presto, we have another block of a thousand! Jack looks at me as if I've produced a rabbit out of a hat. He's still not quite convinced that this isn't some clever adult con trick, so tomorrow we'll play the game again until he 'feels' the concept.

Jack has been reading small bits of *Danny* with confidence, so I've bought along some easy readers with good story lines. I'm probably a dinosaur in that I'm a fan of reading schemes, where children progress from one carefully graded book to another, and where each book introduces new words very gradually, with constant repetition. There was good old *Janet and John* in the sixties, and the Rainbow series in the seventies, both irritatingly male chauvinist and White-Anglo-Saxon-Protestant, but they did the job.

Suddenly, these were supplanted with 'real' books. The theory was that children should regulate their own reading readiness, so there were many books with pictures only, for the reception classes. Children could see that stories could be told without words, and hopefully develop an interest in books without feeling threatened by the words and having to read them to a teacher. (On the continent, school doesn't start until children are seven, so they're not expected to start reading until then.) The 'real books' were great for children with a natural affinity with language, but confusing for the less able, as they were having to grapple with new vocabulary every day, while the teachers found it difficult to keep tabs on the words they had learnt. On the other hand, some teachers felt that reading schemes were too competitive – a child would get discouraged if her friend was leaping ahead with Yellow Book 1, while she was still stuck on Red Book 2.

I can see arguments for and against reading schemes, but I was sorry to see the end of the Rainbow books, which had they been updated to make them more multiracial and less 'daddy-is-reading-the-newspaper-while-mummy-is-doing-the-washing-up', would be colourful, fun and engaging. A few schemes, like the excellent and funny *Fuzz Buzz* series, were still available, though often hidden away in school stock-rooms. I'm still trying to find a set of them for myself.

For Jack, I'm using the *Puddle Lane* series, which is just right for him. These are strong and exciting stories, all centred on the happenings in the picturesque lane of the title. There are monsters breathing fire, a friendly wizard, a cat that turns green, and other wonderful characters. Best of all, on one side of the page, there is an easy version to the text for beginner readers. Since he discovered old Mr Go-to-bed of *Puddle Lane*, Jack's confidence in reading out loud has soared. Jack's not just making up lost ground – he's forging ahead. Sinead, watch out – your younger brother is about to catch you up!

Tuesday, 25th November. Christmas begins early in the O'Neill household. It started at the end of October. Over the last few weeks the pile of carrier bags propped up against the shelves in the corner alcove has been growing impressively, spilling sideways against the end of Jack's bed. Christmas cards in boxes are stacked up in wobbly towers against the fireplace surround. The whole family are already in a fever-pitch of excitement. A plethora of aunts, uncles and cousins from Ireland will be coming to stay, as Jack can't travel.

Since the shops started piping Silent Night at the beginning of September, I've found it difficult to bond with Christmas. I have a sneaking sympathy with Scrooge, but at least he didn't have to put up with non-stop TV commercials for grotesque-looking monsters and Bomb-Your-Neighbour computer games. So I'm forcing myself to enthuse over Jack's desire to do a wish-list for Father Christmas. However, it's a good, if rather unimaginative, teaching opportunity. Meanly, I tell Jack that maybe that Santa might deal with his list more quickly if he can read the words.

Jack chews his pencil and disappears into happy dreamland for a moment. After ten minutes, the list consists of:

battry modl rasing car play stashen game

Lego car traners

Futbol play tent

Ball wot bonses high Lego crane

"And there's some more," says Jack, "but I can't remember them. I thought of them yesterday, but I've forgot."

His spelling actually shows progress. The silent 'e' in *crane* and *game* are a new development from our 'word race' games. The double *t* in *battry* is hopeful, as is the *y* ending. *Futbol* is interesting, as below, he has spelt *ball* correctly. I ask him about this. It turns out that Jack believed the word 'football' to be a totally separate entity – a thing-in-itself. It reminds me yet again never to take it for granted that children make automatic connections in their learning of spelling, or in any other learning.

We finish *Danny* today, and talk about the characters and the plot. He's really enjoyed it. There's also satisfaction for him in completing a book that's more grown-up than the ones he's read at school. He's impressed with the number of pages it has – an interest developing from our number roll, now up to 857.

Jack can now walk without help to the toilet. He hauls himself around quite capably with the aid of his crutches. He's being encouraged to place the injured leg lightly on the ground and to very gradually increase its load-bearing. He's doing all this naturally and sensibly and it's great to see him so mobile.

While Jack is out of the room in our break, I show Mum his Christmas list. She laughs and says she's bought most of them already. I marvel at her efficiency, and she adds that she's also got most of the other children's wish-list presents, plus those for all the relations. "I start as soon as Christmas is over, ready for the next Christmas."

"Amazing," I say.

We do some more numbers on the roll. For the remainder of the session, there's another English worksheet to do for school. It's on capital letters for proper nouns – essential knowledge, but lacklustre. However, that's how I'm feeling today, and can't think of a way of enlivening the exercises. Tomorrow his sister will take the completed worksheet in to the teacher.

I've slipped a note in with it, asking her to send back some comments, and a Smiley Face sticker. Keeping up the links with his teacher and his class is becoming increasingly important as the time draws near for his return.

Monday, 1st December. After being in bed with flu-like symptoms all Thursday and Friday last week, I'm still feeling a bit groggy. I need to be gentle with myself, and plan an easy session.

Jack opens the door for me and swings himself on his crutches back into the living room. He's able to use his injured leg much more now, and seems to have gained an inch in height over the last five days. He tells me he's been out shopping in his wheelchair and brought presents for all the aunts, uncles, cousins, and two sets of grandparents.

"That must have cost you a lot of money," I comment.

"Oh, we help him out," says Mum, as she moves Jack's breakfast tray away, and burrows amongst the piles of papers on the shelves for his workbooks. "He only buys little things anyway – bars of soap, notepaper, that kind of small gift. We help all the children out."

"How many people are there on your Christmas present list, Jack?" I ask idly, as I unpack my bag – then regret it, as Mum beams, sits down on the bed next to Jack, and begins counting on her fingers:

"Well now, not including all the children's presents to each other, let me see…"

Jack looks at her fingers and begins counting all the relations. After twenty, Mum gives up, saying she knows there are more. "And Auntie Joyce and Uncle Tom who live in Bristol!" Jack bounces up and down in the bed, loving this game.

I'm feeling a bit dizzy, trying to work out the permutations of a family of six who all give to each other and then also to about five hundred other relatives. I give up, and start rummaging in my bag for this morning's work. Mum takes the hint and disappears into the kitchen where I hear her and Mr O'Neill arguing about who she's forgotten to mention.

I've brought with me a county jigsaw of the British Isles. Jack hasn't heard of a county. Neither does he know where Scotland, Wales and Ireland are, though he does know Ireland is separate from England, somewhere across a big sea, because he goes over there for his summer holidays. He's not alone in this lack of geographical awareness. Many otherwise intelligent children haven't a clue about the location of London or Edinburgh, let alone the countries of Europe. Yet we assume they know this, as if they should have absorbed the knowledge somehow by osmosis. There used to be a subject called geography until fairly recently, or at least in most primary schools such learning might be deemed important enough to be covered under the subject General Knowledge. But today, though lots of facts are being shoved – sorry, *delivered* – into children's brains, such as how draw a pretty picture with a computer mouse and how to draw up a mini business plan, much common and useful knowledge, particularly about where we live in our own country and also in relation to elsewhere on this globe, is being neglected.

I'm also keen to see how Jack tackles jigsaws, which involve spatial awareness, manual dexterity, patience, planning and organisation. This one has over a hundred pieces, with no distinctive figures or animals to provide clues as to how it fits together. Just a plain wooden jigsaw, with each county in a different colour, and the name of the county marked out in bold letters. The name of the county town, designated by a large black dot, is marked in contrasting colour with smaller letters. Will he find it too boring, too difficult?

Jack begins by finding all the outside edges – "I know how to do this." He notices that the whole map is surrounded by blue sea, so finds all the blue pieces and puts them in a separate pile. He finds the edges of the blue pieces and makes the frame of the jigsaw. He works inwards, fitting all the blue pieces together, so he now has the shape of the British Isles in outline.

He hesitates. It's a mammoth task. However, by referring constantly to the picture on the lid, and by studying each gap intently, then scanning the pile of pieces still to be fitted for the one that fits in the gap, he completes over half in twenty minutes. Then he tires and gets a bit bored.

Now I've tried this jigsaw with much older children of so-called normal intelligence who attend mainstream school. Many find it incredibly difficult. They don't know where to start, or they seem unable to use the cover picture as a guide. It's as if, for them, the picture and the pieces bear no relation to each other. Some children pick up a piece from the pile and then try to find the appropriate gap – a very laborious process. Some start in the middle, and don't see the significance of the edge pieces. Many just give up, saying they're bored. Jack, on the other hand, is methodical, shows the ability to use a model (the lid), a good eye and feeling for shape – he literally runs his finger round the edges of the gap to reinforce what his eyes are telling him. He also perseveres. Best of all he's really having fun with it, before he runs out of steam! I'm bowled over by his spatial abilities.

Mel Levine, in his book *A Mind at a Time* has some fascinating comments about spatial perception:

Spatial perception has always intrigued scholars ranging from philosophers to cognitive scientists. The various features and relationships within a display of simultaneous information together represent its perceptual content. Highly specific features come together to form a complete image or a pattern. They include such vivid variables as the relative sizes and locations of component parts, an awareness of what's in the foreground and what's in the background, three-dimensionality, symmetry versus asymmetry, and left versus right. Another feature of spatial perception is known as wholepart relationship. What goes with what? How does the whole relate to its constituent pieces? So, in gazing meaningfully at a portrait or scanning a bus map, one surveys its parts and their relative positions, almost at the same time discerning which of the parts connect through various linkages with other points in space. When perusing a map of Alabama, we observe that certain towns are part of a particular county and that a group of counties comprise the whole state map. We have discovered an essential whole-part relationship. Interestingly, there are some young children who become confused by these whole-part determinations; they seem to have a weak sense of such crucial relationships. As a result, when they write there may be as much space between letters as there is between words.

Jack has an unusual strength here. It calls into question the whole subject of what actually constitutes intelligence. And how can we recognise, value and appreciate gifts other than literacy or numeracy, how can we foster them when we discover them and give them the recognition they deserve, within our present education system?

We have a break, and when he is rested, Jack wants to finish the jigsaw. He does so with renewed vigour. We then find Scotland, and Wales. He finds Ireland, surprised that you have to get to it by crossing Wales. He thought it was across the sea from Devon. I ask him to find London (the main cities are also marked), Bristol – where his aunt and uncle live – and Manchester, because of the football team, of course. We talk about the North of England, how long it would take to drive up there or go by train, by coach, by plane? Imagine if you walked, how long would it take? How far in miles? Can he point to the different counties, if I say them? Can he find his own county? So much rich material here, so much more time we could spend on it.

We play more multiplication table games. Jack now has a fairly good grasp of the two, three, four and five times table, by using the blocks. I'm curious to know if he can make the transfer to more abstract thinking. There's always a danger that we assume that just because children can say a multiplication table by rote, they actually understand what it means. Often they don't 'see' groups of three, four, or whatever, in their minds' eye; it's just parrot learning.

I get out the blocks and ask Jack to lay out the four times table in rows of four and to tell me when he's got to forty. He does this easily. I then test him on various multiples, seeing if he knows them without looking at the blocks.

Then I ask him to check his answers by counting the rows. I realise that he's only just beginning to see the connection between the rote learning and the concrete evidence given by the blocks. I'm convinced that we rush children too much when we're trying to teach them the four basic operations – addition, subtraction, multiplication, and division. They need so much more time to play – literally – with new concepts and to try them out in different situations, with attractive material that can be made into shapes and towers or used in their own games.

Jack is on the cusp of abstract thought. He's one of the lucky ones – he's at a special school which recognises that he needs extra time. What about the not-so-lucky children in mainstream schools, having targets at key stages imposed from outside – by schools which are all fighting for the best place in the league tables?

Monday, 8th December. Jack's edgy this morning – abstracted and unable to concentrate. It's not the jittery buzz of pre-Christmas anticipation; he looks worried and unhappy.

Unusually, ten minutes into the session, he gets up to go to the toilet. Perhaps he's unwell? He seems to be spending a very long time in there. He's left the living room door, which connects to the small rear hallway, wide open. The kitchen door, opposite the loo, must be open too – I can hear muffled, angry voices.

I've not known the O'Neills to row while I've been here. It's generally a very harmonious household, but today there definitely seems to be some discord in the air. I busy myself catching up on Jack's lesson plan notes. Mr O'Neill's booming voice reaches my ears, however, and I'm unable to switch it off.

"Will you listen at all?" The thump of a fist on the kitchen table. "I tried, didn't I, and it had gone already."

Mrs O'Neill's voice, higher and sharper than normal: "You could have gone for that other one at Harris's!"

Expletives pepper the air. "Will you not hear me? Will I be having a job that pays half what I earned at the quarry for longer hours altogether?"

I get up and silently pull the door to. A few moments later Jack enters the room, white-faced. I'm sure now that he went into the toilet to listen. Children are drawn like magnets towards their parents' rows. Jack has definitely heard and understood most of it, and feels upset; his world threatened.

I abandon the English worksheets just for now. We'll wait till the atmosphere lightens, or till Jack perks up a bit. Somewhere deep in the recesses of my bag, there's card, glue, glitter, gold spray and scissors. We'll cut out some shapes and make Christmas decorations.

I hope this will work as a distraction for Jack. Christmas is fast approaching – it's time for us both to get into the festive mood!

Tuesday, 16th December. I'm waiting on Jack's doorstep, stamping my feet to keep warm, watching a robin foraging in a frost-laden flowerbed and wondering if I've forgotten one of Jack's hospital appointments.

I ring the bell again. This time I hear voices at the top of the stairs, and Jack's high, insistent, "No! Let me do it! I can do it!" A couple of thuds follow, the second fainter than the first with a silence in between, a slow drum-roll. I peer through the frosted glass. Jack comes into view on the lower stairs. He's placing his good leg carefully on each step, and bringing the injured leg down next to it. Out of focus, Jack looks like a tiny elderly gnome, bent nearly double as he descends.

He flings open the door with a triumphant flourish. He's flushed with the effort, and his eyes sparkle.

"WOW!" I exclaim. "That was fantastic. Is that the first time you've done that?"

"Yes, but I've climbed up before. That was easy. But Dad carried me down last time."

The living room looks unnaturally, eerily spacious. The bed has gone.

"Dad and Uncle Paul took it back up last night. I can sleep in my room now."

"And isn't it just great to be back with your brothers." Dad appears at the kitchen door, beaming.

"Yes, except that Ryan's got his things all mixed up with mine on my shelves and Sean's got his clothes all mixed up in my drawers so there's no room for mine…" He doesn't look the least bothered, just happy that things are back to normality. This new, lively Jack is such a contrast to the listless shadow of a child I'd first seen in September.

Mr O'Neill's in good mood, too. He reminds Jack that he's off to his new job in a minute, so will Jack be needing anything from upstairs before he goes?

Jack doesn't need anything but I'm wondering where Mum is; there's no reassuring hum of activity in the kitchen.

"Will Mrs O'Neill be in before you go out?" I ask.

"Oh, she'll not be long, she's just popped out to the shops, she should be back by eleven at the latest."

This is tricky. Dad's either forgotten, or is not aware of The Golden Rule: there *must* be an adult – parent or carer – present in the house during all tuition sessions.

"I'm sorry," I say, "but there must be someone here with Jack while I'm tutoring him."

Dad looks stricken. He's just got an agency job at the pottery – a subsidiary of the quarry which has pottery retail outlets – packing Christmas orders for sending round the country.

"Am I to get the sack for being late on my second day! Or maybe they'll not keep me on after Christmas, they'll think I'm too unreliable altogether. Holy Mary, will half an hour matter at all?"

This is a terrible dilemma. Dad's job versus professional ethics.

"Would there be a neighbour who'd pop in for a while?"

Dad scratches his head and looks doubtful. "They're all at work or taking the kids to school and going on to the shops…"

"Mrs Jenkins!" Jack suddenly pipes up. "She never goes out!"

"Glory be, she's eighty if she's a day, she'll hardly make it across the road," snaps Dad. His usual good humour has deserted him utterly, and I can hardly blame him.

"Please try her," I urge.

Mr O'Neill heaves an almighty sigh, grabs his coat. I watch him cross the road and knock on the door of the house opposite.

"Why does she have to come?" asks Jack.

"Because there has to be another grown-up in the house while I'm here teaching you."

"Why?"

"In case I go off with the family silver," I reply, my stock answer to younger kids when this uncomfortable situation crops up, as it inevitably does from time to time.

Jack's brow furrows. He looks round the room hopefully. "Do we have any silver?"

Both Dad and Mrs Jenkins are both smiling when they return. Yes, she does walk with a stick, and she's nearing eighty, but she's perfectly *compos mentis*, sociable and glad to help.

Dad has to leave. I ask if I can make a cup of tea for Mrs Jenkins, and leave her chatting happily to Jack. When I return any ice has been broken and Jack's showing her his work.

At last we settle down to work, with Mrs Jenkins comfortably installed on the settee. All this extra space in the living- room! I just have to make use of it while it lasts. Is there some law, a skewed domestic version of Parkinson's Law, which decrees that objects naturally gravitate to fill up the amount of space available?

Jack seems to be in a bubbly mood today, and so am I, so I suggest we do some acting games. I wait for the inevitable groan I usually get from children of this age, or "I can't do acting, Miss!", but Jack's face lights up and he looks at me expectantly. What a joy this child is!

Yesterday we started a worksheet on adverbs, but Jack looked confused and bored, as well he might – the examples were deadly dull: 'Tom ran quickly down the road', 'The old lady walked slowly to the shops'.

First, Jack has to know what a verb is. "I'm going to act a doing word, a verb," I say. "Can you guess what it is?"

I run round and round in the new space, looking and feeling like a demented chicken. I suddenly remember Mrs Jenkins – there she is, transfixed, a captive audience. Warning: do not try this at home with disaffected teenagers, they're apt to think you've suddenly lost it. Worse, you're met with a stony silence telling you you've died. Worse still, you get a yawn, and "whatever," as they hunch back into their hoods and produce their mobile phones from their pockets.

"Running!" shouts Jack. He turns and grins at Mrs Jenkins, who nods appreciatively.

"Right!" Now I'm crawling on hands and knees and Jack shrieks with delight.

"Crawling, like a baby!"

"Now it's your turn."

Jack chooses 'hopping', nearly overbalancing in the process, and I guess the word correctly.

I tell Jack that the doing word doesn't have to be very active, it can be a very small movement. I wiggle my finger. Between us, we sleep, snore, clap, jump, slide, scratch, read, hiccup, sneeze, fidget, swim, eat and drink.

Adverbs turn out to be even more entertaining for Mrs Jenkins. Jack and I try to remember all our previous actions, and then do them slowly, quickly, lazily, loudly, crossly, sleepily, happily, sadly, noisily, bumpily, hungrily. We finish with a flourish, two chimpanzees scratching their armpits hungrily and noisily.

"Well, well," Mrs Jenkins shakes her head in wonder. "I never did anything like that when I was at school!"

Now Jack can tackle the worksheets, which he does easily. Mum returns loaded down with carrier bags just before I'm due to leave, and I have to explain Mrs Jenkins's presence.

"Oh dear," says Mum, hugely embarrassed. "I didn't think…and I'm so sorry we had to drag you out of your house, Mrs Jenkins."

"Don't worry about me, dear. I haven't had such an entertaining morning for years!"

Jack sees me to the door.

"Would you really do it, you know, that thing what you said in there?" He's narrowed his eyes, looking at me speculatively, and jerks his head towards the living room.

"What was that, Jack?" I reach up for my coat.

"*You* know. Thieving. Nicking our silver jewels and stuff. Would you?"

I drop my coat, shocked. "Of course not, Jack. Never! Never in a million trillion years!"

"Then why did Mrs Jenkins have to come over?"

"To prove it, so she can tell everyone I'm not a thief."

Jack's face clears, like cloud shadows scudding away over a sunlit cornfield.

"Oh." A pause while he thinks this over. Then, "Bye, see you tomorrow."

Friday, 19th December – Jack's last session. "What's different in here, then?" demands Jack, as I enter the living room. He's sitting on the settee, eyes mischievous, his lower body wrapped in a duvet.

I'd have to be blind to miss it – a whacking great Christmas tree against the far wall where Jack's bed used to be. A real one, not plastic. There's a golden angel, its gauzy wings brushing the ceiling. Silver and gold baubles, tinsel strings, lights, little robins, shiny reindeer…

"It's magnificent! Who made it so beautiful?"

"We all did. But I did all the snow on the branches – look! – and all those chocolate round things up there." He makes as if to get up and show me, but seems to change his mind. He sinks down deeper into the settee again. Instead, he points to where they are on the upper branches.

Mum pokes her head round the kitchen door. "Okay?" She winks at Jack then disappears again.

"Are you cold?" I ask, as I unpack my bag.

"Yes, *very* cold. I think I'm getting flu!" He shivers and shudders exaggeratedly. He pretends to study the tree, glancing slyly at me out of the corner of his eye.

Now Dad comes in from the kitchen, fusses around picking up some old newspapers, collects a few dirty cups, and winks at Jack. Then he too goes back into the kitchen.

"Oh dear!" I play along. "Perhaps you should see a doctor, be in bed?"

An explosive snort as Jack collapses into hysterical laughter. "Yes, yes, get the doctor, please doctor come quickly, I'm dying!"

Now I am a little worried. I don't remember Jack behaving quite like this before. Is he suffering from post-traumatic shock syndrome?

With a flourish, Jack suddenly lifts the duvet away from his legs, and stands up, stretching his arms out wide. He marches, goose-step at first, then speeds up till he's almost trotting. No crutches, no sticks. The plaster's off!

My dropped jaw and astonished expression provide the reaction Jack was hoping for. Luckily he can't see the tears prickling behind my eyes.

"Watch!" Jack stands on his good leg, lifting the injured one behind, then swaps over, ballet-style. "Look, I can balance!"

"Jack, do be care…" Should Jack be doing this at all?

The injured leg is thinner than the other one, but strong and straight. Jack canters round and round the room, a colt in springtime, revelling in the sheer joy of movement.

Mr O'Neill comes in. "Will you just see how he walks now, would you ever believe he's been in plaster for so long?"

"I'm going to play football today, aren't I Dad?"

"Oh no, you're not," says Mum, overhearing from the kitchen.

"But isn't he just grand altogether!" Dad can't stop gazing at his son as if he's just scored a winning goal in the cup final.

"He sure is," I agree.

"And won't you be raring to get back to school now?" Dad lifts is son up triumphantly, and Jack wraps his legs round Dad's ample waist and hugs him tight. "Tis high time to get back in there, into the swing of things, see your friends…"

Every word reminds me that this is the last day of term and my final session with Jack. It's going to be very hard to say goodbye to this engaging, courageous child, with his quiet sense of fun, his thoughtful and equable nature. A kid who uses every last ounce of his brainpower. And how I shall miss the warmth of this expansive, loving home.

It's a finishing off day. We gather all Jack's work into a folder to show his teacher, celebrating all the stars and smiley faces I've dolloped onto every worksheet. There's just enough time to make a long paper chain and a concertina decoration out of silver foil, until finally it's the end of the session.

I give Jack my Christmas gift to him – a small Lego kit – and he thanks me shyly and places it under the Christmas tree, where it nestles humbly at the bottom of a three-foot mound of huge wrapped boxes of every shape.

Mum bustles into the room, wiping her hands on a towel. "Have you given your teacher her present?"

"Oh no, I forgot." Jack dives behind the settee, surfacing with a flat rectangular box. He wants me to open it right now, and I'm perfectly willing, because if it's what I think it is…

"*Chocolate*! Mmm! Thank you very much, Jack. Just what I wanted," I say truthfully.

I ask Mum and Dad to let me know how Jack gets on at school. I don't expect Jack to contact me – I have to let him go now. By the beginning of next term I'll be just a distant memory. But I'm happy. With a family like the O'Neills, and with his own gifts, he'll be fine. He's one of the lucky ones.

I say goodbye, and as the front door shuts behind me, I hear Jack's voice, loud and strong:

"Dad, *please* can I go round to Sam's and play football in his garden?"

THOMAS

Tuesday, 13th January 2004. *"Qu'est-ce que c'est?"*

"C'est la fenêtre!" answers Thomas promptly.

"Et ça?" I point.

"C'est mon cahier!" Thomas grins at me triumphantly. He's nonchalantly slipped in the possessive article – clever boy. I don't remember teaching him that. He's certainly done the homework I set him yesterday. He knows all ten words on the list, including whether it's *'le'* or *'la'* before the noun.

Unusually, languages are a high priority on the curriculum of Thomas's primary school, and he's taken to French like a gourmet to truffles. He's a natural. I ask him to recite the days of the week for the pure pleasure of hearing him pronounce *'mercredi'* and *'vendredi'*. He rolls his r's at the back of his throat like any nine-year old French kid.

Thomas would love to visit France this summer, but that might be a problem. Thomas is dying.

A week ago, the office rang me, giving me details of his circumstances, warning me that it wouldn't be easy. I called round to see him, and began working with him that very afternoon.

Thomas has leukaemia. He first contracted it when he was three. For five merciful years he was in remission. A year ago, it recurred. He's been fighting it ever since. Two months ago, he started spiralling downhill, and now school is too much for him. My brief is to keep him occupied and interested as much as possible.

"To keep his brain active, until the end," says his mother. Mrs Cartwright doesn't mince words; she believes in calling a spade a spade.

The 'end' is expected soon – in four to six weeks, to be more precise.

Thomas loves maps as much as he loves languages. We pore over a map of France. I've written down a list of the major towns and rivers for him to find. He does this with quiet enthusiasm, competently finding his way around the index at the back of the atlas.

Considering how ill he is, his concentration is remarkable. I watch him, frowning slightly, as his finger moves over the pages. Slender fingers on fragile, stick-like wrists. His face is sallow and sickly. As he bends his head over the book, I notice the blond hair, thin and wispy where it's grown back after the last bout of chemotherapy. There will be no more chemo, or radiotherapy for Thomas. It will no longer halt the cancer.

Mrs Cartwright bustles into the kitchen, asking if I'm ready for a cup of tea. I say I'm always ready. Thomas isn't hungry or thirsty, but she offers him a high-energy drink which will help to keep his strength up. One of the symptoms of the disease at this stage is that Thomas has lost interest in food.

Thomas takes a few sips of his drink, then shakes his head, pushing it away. Mrs Cartwright doesn't insist. She simply removes it and rubs his shoulder in a semi-hug. She turns away to the kitchen sink to wash the lunch dishes. She's a tall, well-built woman, with well-defined black eyebrows and a firm mouth. All her movements are brisk and definite, as if there's no room in her life for dithering.

As I gratefully sip my tea, I show her Thomas's work.

"Look, Mum! I've found ten rivers and towns. That's all of them!"

Mum looks over his shoulder. "Clever boy, well done!"

She smiles encouragingly at both of us. Particularly at me. Then she goes upstairs to hoover the bedrooms.

Thomas is beginning to wilt. I wish he'd had more of his high-energy drink. I'm worried sick that all this might be too much for him. Maybe he just needs a bit of fun?

I put my box of games on the table and ask Thomas to choose. We play Connect 4 – Thomas wins every game. Then, Tummy Ache, and Tops and Tails. In this last game, the cardboard characters are cut out into sections: head, torso and legs. The winner is the one who's assembled the most completed characters. It's visual, easy and funny. I'm hoping to make him laugh – and he does. It's more like a burbling chuckle. His small frame shudders a little. Even laughter is too tiring for Thomas.

Tuesday, 20th January. I've arrived at Thomas's house at the peak of a sibling squabble. Seven year old Paul is home from school. Yesterday, in the playground, he sprained his ankle. However, that doesn't stop him chasing Thomas round the snooker table in the living room, jabbing at him with his cue.

"Thomas said I cheated, Mum! He said I potted the ball with my finger!"

"You did, you DID! I saw you!" Thomas is leaning against the table, flushed and indignant.

"No I didn't, I just went like *that*…and my hand sort of slipped." Paul pulls a face at his brother.

The argument rages on. Mrs Cartwright is keeping out of the way, peeling vegetables in the adjoining kitchen. I watch and marvel at the normality of this domestic scene. Paul's not pussyfooting around Thomas. No allowance is made for his illness, no ground expected or conceded on either side. Nor does Paul seem to be attention-seeking, as might be understandable in a family with a sick child. It's just a brotherly scrap with no hidden agenda.

Mr Cartwright comes downstairs and smiling, says, "Ready, Paul? Time to go off to the doctor, get your ankle sorted out."

No recriminations on the squabble, no comment about the noise level. The boys' father is a tall, gaunt-faced man, in his late thirties. His hair looks prematurely grey. Soft brown eyes, tired and strained with dark rings, gaze affectionately at both his sons, lingering anxiously, for a split second, on Thomas. Yet he still manages to smile at all of us, and make me feel welcome in his home.

With Paul safely out of the way, Thomas calms down, and we go into the kitchen to start work.

"Thomas's teacher called round yesterday with some fraction worksheets." Mrs Cartwright hands them to me.

I glance at the worksheets. They're not difficult; but I'd planned to play games with Thomas today. Surely that would be best for him?

"This is what his class will be doing today," says Mrs Cartwright, meaningfully, as if reading my thoughts.

I can see that I'm on a rapid learning curve here. Thomas needs to feel part of school life. This fraction worksheet will connect him to his teacher, his classroom and his friends.

Thomas sails through the worksheet on equivalent fractions. He's logical. He sees right away why he has to multiply the numerator and the denominator by the same number, "Well, it makes sense, doesn't it?" he says. I'm impressed. Most children just do it as a leap of faith, and don't understand *why* until much later. And even some of the fourteen and fifteen-year-olds I've worked with have struggled to get their heads round this topic.

Half an hour later, and Thomas is flagging at last. We play Fraction Dominoes until break-time.

"What's next?" asks Thomas, wiping the juice from his mouth with his sleeve. He looks at me expectantly. His eagerness is touching, and very poignant. I'm so used to dealing with resistance, this takes the wind right out of my sails.

There's another batch of French worksheets. Thomas wants to do one on colours. This requires nothing more than colouring in some shapes and objects, but soon Thomas is white with exhaustion. Yet he won't give up until he's quite finished. This youngster won't admit defeat.

Would he like me to read him a story?

"Yes, please," Thomas smiles with relief.

I've chosen a classic storybook: *Old Peter's Russian Tales*. It's my own precious copy, given to me as a childhood present. It's full of myths and legends and universal truths. Thomas chooses a story called 'The Old Man and the Sea'. It's about a very poor fisherman, who lives in a hovel that's falling to pieces. He hears about an amazing fish who can grant wishes. His wife, naturally enough, would like some repairs done to the leaking hut. She sends her husband down to the sea to make her request. This is granted, but the wife is never satisfied; she wants ever bigger and better homes. It's like a latter-day Property Ladder TV programme with a different ending.

The story is ideal for guessing 'what happens next?' and 'how will it end?' Children always enjoy the repeated refrains and the moral message. Thomas listens, entranced, to the wisdom in the story. In his wide brown eyes, I see reflections of his own inner wisdom, a deep understanding far beyond his years.

Thursday, 29th January. The town is full of mad drivers, all hell-bent on getting somewhere fast, even if it means jumping red lights and cutting me up. I arrive at Thomas's house fifteen minutes late, flustered and apologetic.

There's a car race going on here, too, in the living room. Wooden Brio tracks and bridges form an intricate road system across the floor. Thomas is playing with his youngest brother, Andrew.

I perch on the arm of the settee, not wanting to interrupt. The two boys are totally absorbed in their game. Andrew's a chubby-faced four-year-old, with the family's blond hair and brown eyes. There's a special rapport between these two: Thomas, the patient teacher, Andrew the hero-worshipper.

Andrew's too young to go to school, but goes to a nursery three days a week. Today is one of his home days. I feel tempted to include Andrew in our tuition session. I could find – or invent – a game for them both to play together. As usual, I'm vacillating between my natural inclination to keep within boundaries – I'm not here to teach Andrew – and an overwhelming urge to seize the moment, to let Thomas lose himself in a world of make-believe. Surely I'm justified in bending the rules?

However, Mrs Cartwright appears from the kitchen. Gently but firmly she prises the two boys apart, with promises that they can play together later. She steers Thomas towards our workstation, the kitchen table.

Today, there are six new English worksheets. Thomas chooses a worksheet on synonyms, and launches into the exercises with his usual eagerness. His handwriting is small and neat, his tongue poking out as he forms the words. After only twenty minutes, he's tiring fast, but he reaches for his third worksheet. This one's on antonyms.

"You don't have to do *all* the worksheets today, Thomas!"

"I'll just do this one, then."

There's a determined gleam in his eyes. For a few more minutes, there's no stopping him. Then he slumps. His head rests on his crooked elbow, as if on a pillow. His eyes are closing.

"Shall I just check what you've done so far?"

I ease the worksheet away from under his arm. Thomas yawns, and sits up again. I give him a Smiley Face sticker and three points. Plus an extra one, for stamina. He's quietly pleased with himself.

"How about a guessing game now, Thomas? I'm going to act out doing something, and I wonder if you can guess what it is, and then act out the opposite action – the antonym. Would you like to play?"

I put my head down on my crossed arms, and snore. Thomas grins, repeats my action, then springs upright. He spreads his arms wide, and looks round the room, as if amazed to find himself awake.

"Sleeping and waking!" he says, triumphantly.

We carry on merrily with this game for a while. I cry, Thomas laughs; he stretches, I hunch myself into a ball. I shout, he whispers. I shiver with cold, Thomas mops his brow. Then we take it in turns to think of an abstract word like 'good,' or 'dangerous,' and see how quickly we can say the opposite.

"I've got an idea," says Thomas. "Guess what the opposite of this is."

He points to the kitchen door. Opposite of 'door?' I'm stumped. I make a few outrageous guesses. Little snorts and snuffles of mirth shake Thomas's body.

"It's *black!* It's a white door, see?"

But now Thomas is beginning to wilt again. Mum bustles to the rescue with his high-energy drink. After only five minutes, he seems to revive, and is raring to have a go at the science sheets his teacher's left for him.

I sift through them to find one that is easy, not for Thomas, but for me. One of the problems of doing science at home, is the lack of proper apparatus. In any well-equipped classroom there would be scales, balance springs, test tubes, pressure gauges. So often, teachers trying to be helpful send home worksheets like these, all of which require some form of exact measurement.

A worksheet on forces looks promising. But hold on – we need a Newton-meter, (a spring scale which stretches according to how much force is applied.) Foiled again! Oh, well, for the moment let's just introduce the concept of 'pushes and pulls'. For a few minutes we push and pull books and other objects along the table top, but this is well boring. I shall be asleep in a minute, even if Thomas is still hanging in there.

Wait! There's a ready-made laboratory already set up in the living room! We tiptoe in.

"Can we play too?" I ask Andrew.

He's still crouched on the floor, like some giant traffic controller, coordinating an ever-proliferating network of roads. Lorries and cars are lined up, obligingly waiting for their big moment in our experiment. Andrew is happy to welcome us into his world.

"Just watch for a moment, while I explain what to do."

We begin with parallel tracks, about two metres long. I'm careful not to upset Andrew's arrangement. I place two cars, of equal size, at the beginning of each, and ask the two boys to push the cars along by tapping once with their little fingers. The cars stay put.

"How can you get them moving? What if you use your next finger, your thumb, the whole hand? What if you don't just tap, but push?"

Both boys weigh about the same, I realise with a pang. I have to ensure that this doesn't turn into a test of power and strength. Andrew naturally wants his car to go the fastest and the furthest, but Thomas won't be drawn into a competition. His approach is remarkably scientific, and he gradually increases the pressure until a really strong shove has his car hurtling along the track. It's all obvious stuff, really. Yet it's fun – and satisfying. What we're finding is that there's a law of physics behind the smallest everyday action.

"Can you speed your cars up now? Can you slow them down? Can you find different ways of doing this?"

Andrew wants a race, but he exerts so much force that his car spins right across the room, scudding into the skirting board.

"Now, how about changing direction?" I suggest.

A moment's silence. Both boys stare at me.

Then, with a jubilant whoop, Thomas grabs a curved length of track and sends his car along it. We watch how the curve slows it down.

"What would make the cars go *really* fast?" I ask in breathless tones, milking this for all it's worth.

Andrew draws his arm back ready to thwack-start his car.

"But with only the GENTLEST of pushes!" I add quickly, restraining him.

There's another, much longer silence. Thomas's brow furrows, deep in thought. He gazes round the room, searching for inspiration. Andrew watches his brother, exaggeratedly copying his movements. He frowns fiercely. His head rolls as he looks around the room. He peeks at me sidelong, as if asking: 'Am I doing it right, this *thinking* business?'

"I know!" Thomas moves his car to the top of a slope. "Look, I'm hardly touching it!"

We all clap as the car whooshes down the track, getting faster and faster.

"So what's happening, here? What do you think makes the car go faster?"

"The wheels!" shouts Andrew.

"The slope, of course," says Thomas.

"But what if you push the cars *up* the slope, will it go?"

I give Andrew another car and point to another slope with the same gradient as Thomas's. With their initial shove, both the boys' cars go up a little way, then roll down again.

"So what's pulling them down, *apart* from the wheels and the slope?"

They're stumped. I pick up a soft teddy from the armchair. "What will happen if I throw teddy up into the air?"

"He'll fall down!" They chorus.

"And what if Thomas throws this ball into the air?" I hand Thomas the ball. He throws it up and catches it deftly before it lands. I give Andrew a turn. He misses his catch, and insists on repeating the throw till he gets it right.

"Now what if I throw this car up really high? But I won't, because it's a bit heavy."

"That will come down too, on my head!" shouts Andrew, delightedly.

"So what is it that's making everything that goes up, come down again?" I'm really enjoying this.

Andrew goes off to find more teddies to throw. But Thomas says suddenly, "I know! It's something beginning with 'g'…"

"Yes! G…gr…gra…?" I prompt.

"Gravity!" says Thomas exultantly.

"Well done!"

We spend the rest of the session experimenting with slopes of different gradients, and sending the cars racing down. I leave the boys to carry on with their own discoveries while I talk to their mother.

For the last half an hour, I've been vaguely aware of her presence in the kitchen. Once or twice she was chuckling to herself – over something on the radio, maybe? As soon as she sees me, she puts the kettle on.

"I enjoyed the physics lesson." She beams at me.

"Yes, it worked quite well." I say, complacently. "Of course, I had to improvise. Normally if I were in school, I'd have had the proper equipment, like…"

"A Newton-meter, a force meter, a spring balance, and possibly a large magnet." There's a mischievous twinkle in Mrs Cartwright's eyes.

My jaw drops. "Are you a teacher?"

"God, no. I couldn't bear it. I just did physics at university. Don't look so horrified. I thought you covered four of the five effects of forces on objects very well!"

My mind's racing. "Where does the large magnet come in?" I ask feebly.

"Well it's a force, just as gravity is a force. Worth a mention. I've got a large magnet, if you'd like to play with it tomorrow."

"Yes, please."

I'm wondering how I'd be feeling if I'd made a complete hash of that physics lesson. Teaching all subjects to all children, aged six to sixteen, I'm sure that one day I'll make some heinous blunder and be found sadly wanting by some smart parent, expert in his or her field.

The session's now at an end. I'm keen to be off – I've got some photocopying to do. But Thomas's mum seems anxious for me to stay and to give me a bit of family history while we have a cup of tea.

She and her husband met as students at university, both studying physics. He chose meteorology as a subsequent career, and now researches weather patterns at the Met. Office in Exeter. She, being more gregarious, and having good organisational skills, chose to go into office management, also at the Met. That was where she was working until Thomas became ill. It was hard to give it all up. She misses the company, the adult conversation.

She tells me about her difficult move down from Bracknell, when the Met Office relocated to Exeter recently. The house prices suddenly rocketed as hundreds of employees descended on the city. She talks about Andrew and his playgroup, and Paul's ankle, now mending well. About almost everything except Thomas.

Reluctantly, I have to leave. I say goodbye to Thomas. Tomorrow, I tell him, we'll do magnets! Plus, pins, needles, compass points and anything else we can possibly magnetise. We'll have fun!

Thursday, 5th February. By the front door of Thomas's house, a few early daffodils have burst into bloom. Their lovely yellow heads turn towards the afternoon sun. They bask languidly against the warmth of the brick porch, like a row of sun-worshipping grockles propped up against the sea wall.

"Isn't it much too soon for daffs to be out?" I say, as Thomas's mother opens the door. "I'm sure they don't usually appear until early March."

"Don't ask me. I'm a newcomer. In Bracknell, spring was always a bit later generally. I just assumed everything was always earlier down in this part of the country."

She takes my coat and ushers me into the kitchen. Thomas is writing, slowly and carefully, at the kitchen table, his head bent over a maths worksheet I gave him for homework yesterday. Any homework is entirely optional, but Thomas is always keen to do it. In fact he asks for it – and if I forget, he reminds me again.

He looks even paler than usual, with a jaundiced hue to his skin. He smiles at me, but his eyes are dull.

"I've only done half a worksheet. I was too tired to do it yesterday, and then I thought I'd do it in the morning, and I thought I'd do it much quicker."

"That's all right. Things often take longer than we think. Especially if it's something new, like algebra."

"I *can* do it," says Thomas stubbornly. "It's not hard, it just took me longer."

"Can I see what you've done so far?"

Reluctantly, he hands me the worksheet.

"This looks really good. I can see that you've sorted out all the x's and the y's. And you've remembered to multiply first. Well done!"

I stick a gold star halfway down the page. Next to it, I write 'Excellent Work.' I'm amazed at the level of maths. This seems very advanced for Year 5. But Thomas's school streams children in maths, and Thomas is in the top group. Many parents are hoping to send their children on to prep schools.

Let's do something less intense. Ah! Word Bingo in French sounds just the job. I ask Thomas to pronounce each word as he picks up a card from the pile. He does this gleefully, once again showing off his superb pronunciation. As well as the rolling of the r's, he has a nifty way of pronouncing the e-acute as in *clé* – a vowel sound much tighter and sharper than any English equivalent.

Thomas's mother comes in with a bag of washing. She loads the machine, and then puts the kettle on. I ask her where Thomas acquired his superb French accent.

"It was on a family holiday in Provence a couple of years ago," she tells me. Thomas was the only one in the family who dared to go into the local *boulangerie* and ask for the morning baguette. She and her husband Barry are typical Brits. Won't even open their mouths unless they're sure the words will come out just right.

"He's got a very good ear."

Mum nods, proudly. "He can do Scots, Irish and Welsh. You should hear him in Wales when we visit my sister in Haverfordwest! You'd think he was Welsh-born."

"Would you do Welsh for me, *please*, Thomas?" I plead.

Thomas obliges promptly. He launches into an *Under Milk Wood* performance. Then, hardly pausing for breath, he takes us on a world tour of accents. He crosses the Irish sea to Dublin, circumnavigates the globe to Australia, doubles back to Spain, where he executes a perfect 'Manuel' as in *Fawlty Towers*. He comes to rest in France, rolling his r's with a flourish. It's an awesome performance. We both clap hard. Thomas smiles sheepishly.

"That's so good, Thomas. What's your secret?"

"It's because he's musical, too," Mum cuts in. "That probably explains it. Before he became ill, he was having recorder lessons at school. And private flute lessons." She hesitates. I sense there's more on the subject of Thomas's musical ability, but abruptly, she changes the subject.

"The school's sent some geography worksheets. Maybe you could help Thomas with them?"

"I'd love to."

Mum makes me a cup of tea and hands Thomas his favourite Pudsey Bear Mug. Poor Pudsey, sitting up looking so sad, with a red and white bandage across one eye. A few years ago, this mug would have been found in every service station along the motorway. It sold in thousands, to raise money for Children in Need. Mine got broken and I've been looking in charity shops ever since for a replacement. While Thomas sips his drink, his mother seems totally absorbed in watering some herbs on the windowsill. Yet I can feel the sudden tension in the room.

Thomas has lost his appetite. He eats very little at family mealtimes. Chewing is difficult for him, even when the food is cut up very small. This high-energy drink, supplying vital nutrients and vitamins, literally keeps Thomas going. And now his mum, so calm and capable at other times, seems to fall to pieces as Thomas lifts the mug to his lips. All her anxiety, normally diffused amongst a dozen small household concerns, suddenly sharpens to a point. Like a laser beam, it hones in on Pudsey. It gauges the angle that Thomas has tipped the bear towards his mouth. If it's at the correct angle, that's good news – most of the drink will go down. But if poor Pudsey has only leaned forward a little way towards Thomas's lips…

Each sip is painfully slow, but today, Thomas has managed at least two-thirds of the drink. Mum relaxes. Thomas wipes his mouth on the bottom of his sweater. He rolls a few more r's, which makes us both laugh.

I'm curious about his musical talent, which has been mentioned so casually.

"Did you take any music exams, Thomas?" I ask.

"Um, yes. I got up to Grade 4 in flute."

I'm following my own train of thought. Thomas has so much talent! It *must* be developed in the future.

"And will you be able to continue your music lessons at your next school?"

There's a sudden chill in the room. I have the sensation of falling …falling… into a deep dark cave.

Thomas is gazing at me, wide-eyed. A host of emotions sweep across his face, like cloud-shadows across a cornfield. He looks puzzled, confused. Then, for a split-second, there's a flicker of hope.

He turns to his mother, now hovering nearby with the medicine bottle. He looks at her, questioningly, but doesn't speak. In the silence, my words hang in the air. My heart thuds.

Mum places the bottle down very carefully on the table.

"Well now," she says conversationally, "if Thomas *were* to go to a secondary school, it would most probably be to Dame Alice Leggatt Comprehensive. It's got an excellent reputation for all subjects." She continues to talk calmly, while measuring out two large spoonfuls of a sickly pink liquid. I hardly hear her. I'm drowning in waves of guilt. What a gaffe! For God's sake, the boy's got terminal cancer. What could be more plain to see? Am I in complete denial, or what?

I'm furious with myself for my lack of tact. Then suddenly, with a force that frightens me, my anger turns towards Thomas's mother. I asked a fair enough question – a reasonable query about his next school. Yet it seems that Thomas has been so programmed to expect his own death that he dare not even *think* for himself. He has to defer to his mother for an answer. Why? What's the harm in letting him at least *imagine* a future?

Thomas is sitting quietly, waiting for the session to continue. The incident seems to have passed over him with no lingering effect. His mother glances at me briefly before she leaves the room. I can't read her expression.

I scan the geography worksheets. They're blank maps of all the continents and waterways of the world. Here's a nice one – a blank map of Europe, with all the countries ready to be marked and coloured in.

There's a junior atlas in my car. I'm glad of the chance to escape for a moment, to compose myself outside the front door. I take a deep breath.

Thomas finds the right page in the atlas, and very carefully fills in all the names of the countries, and writes the capital cities next to the big black dots. He's enjoying this – his eyes have lost that leaden look and his cheeks have a faint, rose bloom. He wants to do another worksheet for homework. Where will he choose to go, out of all the continents of the world, all the seas and oceans? He decides he's like to visit the United States.

"That's a lot of states to label and colour in, Thomas!"

"I can do it," he says. "I *want* to do it."

"Well, just do what you can, we can finish it tomorrow. And I'll leave you my atlas overnight."

Sunshine streams through the glass panel in the front door. I stand in a diamond patch of light in the hall, putting on my coat. Mrs Cartwright runs downstairs to see me out. She'll look forward to seeing me tomorrow, she says. Half-past one as usual? Her tone is friendly, but faintly guarded. I don't feel comfortable with her. My *faux-pas* still sits uneasily in my stomach.

Outside, the daffodils are still following the sun. They stand proudly – uncaring and aloof. A mutual admiration society. Suddenly, I hate them. How dare they strut and preen, so smugly wrapped in their own self-importance? I want to kick them, trample them down into the earth.

Wednesday, 11th February. On Monday, Mrs Cartwright drove Thomas over a hundred miles to visit a healer in Gloucestershire. The result was dramatic. His healthy cell count, which was almost non-existent, has increased significantly. It's unbelievable progress. Thomas has lost the pasty, sallow look. His complexion looks almost normal. He's more alert, his movements quicker.

Dare we hope? Mrs Cartwright, as she moves efficiently around the kitchen, unpacking the morning's shopping, looks cautiously optimistic, almost happy.

Thomas shows me the geography homework he's done. Not only has he completed North America – all the states beautifully coloured in – but he's halfway through South America. At this moment, in tiny, circular movements, he's outlining the coast of Chile in blue.

"What colour shall I do the Andes mountains? Should they be the same as the rest of Chile?"

"It's up to you. What would look best?"

"I think I'll do them dark brown. As a contrast. With white tops, where the volcanoes are."

I let him carry on while I unpack my bag.

"I'm going to do Africa next." Thomas's eyes are shining today.

"Great! Now, do you want to finish what you're doing, or shall we do some maths?"

"Let's start with maths. Let's get the boring stuff out of the way. It's decimals and I don't like decimals."

"Well, I promise it won't be boring – we're going to play a decimal game first."

It's a board game, clearly de-mystifying the multiplication or division of decimals. Thomas catches on immediately. He's now ready to tackle the worksheet. He sails through all the exercises so quickly that I'm wondering how we're going to fill the rest of the time today. When it's time for his energy drink, he downs it in two gulps.

I steal a glance at his mother. She's pottering about, her expression impassive. But today there's a lightness in her step.

"*Now* I can finish my map!"

Thomas pulls South America towards him with the self-righteous air of one who has postponed gratification for the sake of future reward. For a while there's silence except for the light chafe of pencil on paper. The sun streams through the window, creating a golden patch on the pine table. The box of coloured pencils shimmers like a casket of jewels.

Thomas says his wrist aches – "Just a little bit."

I haven't got a book on South America – he's so far ahead, I can't keep up with him. Instead, I show him some books about North America that I found in the library yesterday. He's entranced with the beautiful scenery, and fascinated by photos of children who live in different parts of the country. He wants to read every profile – about lifestyles as unlike each other as Thomas's is from theirs. Children smile out of the pages, inviting us to try rodeo riding, to skate on frozen lakes.

"I'd like to do that!" says Thomas, we turn each page. "I'd love to see the Rocky mountains, the Niagara Falls!"

Today, it's almost possible to believe that one day he just might do it.

Monday, 23rd February. I'm eager to see how Thomas is progressing, after the dramatic improvement in his energy before half term. It seems a long time since I saw him last.

"He's a bit tired today," says Mrs Cartwright, as I step into the hall. "In fact, he's gone back to sleep on the settee."

Her face is drawn and strained. My heart sinks.

"Should I leave it for today?"

"Well, let's just see how he is first."

Quietly, she opens the living-room door. Thomas is curled up under a duvet, his breathing shallow.

"Thomas, your tutor's here," says his mother, softly.

His eyes flicker awake. For a moment he looks puzzled. He sees me and tries to get up. Swiftly, I kneel down by the settee.

"Hi, Thomas. You can sleep some more if you like. I can come back another time. Or I can wait in the kitchen for when you feel ready."

But Thomas is already swinging his legs down to the floor.

"I'm awake now! I just fell asleep. How long have I been sleeping, Mum?"

"About an hour, dear. You didn't have enough sleep last night."

Thomas holds out his hands towards his mother. She helps him to his feet. Beneath the sleepy flush, that pasty look has returned to his cheeks. There's been a setback.

Thomas leans heavily against his mother as we walk into the kitchen. He collapses into the chair. This doesn't look promising.

"Mum, can you get my maps down from upstairs – the ones I did yesterday?"

"He's been working very hard over half term," says Mum, returning with some worksheets.

"Look!" says Thomas proudly. "I finished South America and then I did all the oceans of the world, just for a change. And now I'm doing Africa. But it's taking me ages. It's got about fifty different countries in it. I bet *you* didn't know that, Mum?"

"I certainly didn't!" replies Mum. There are dark smudges under her eyes.

"Nor did I. But I do now. And some of them are really tiny and hard to find. But some of them are enormous, like South Africa. That one was easy. But I can't find Chad anywhere." His large eyes fix on me, expectantly.

I settle down next to him. His mother glides silently away, giving me a 'thumbs up' signal as she leaves us. Soon all the missing countries have been slotted into place.

"Now I'm going to colour them all in. I like doing that last, because when I say all the names, I can see a different colour for each one." Thomas frowns at me. "And I don't mean just thinking 'well, I'll do it yellow, or brown.' It's not like *choosing* a colour on the spot. That's what my dad thinks I do. It's different for me. Every country has its own colour in my head, and it never changes."

He gives me a doubtful look. "I bet you don't believe me."

"Oh, but I know exactly what you mean!" I exclaim. "For me, all the days of the week have their own colour, and *they* never change either."

Thomas nods eagerly. "And numbers, do you see coloured numbers?"

"Yes, numbers – and names. For example, I see your name, Thomas, as white with a blue edging."

"I see it red," says Thomas. "And 'Chad' is bright purple."

"Well, my colours aren't very bright," I admit. "Monday is pale mauve, Tuesday an ochre yellow, the exact colour of a newborn baby's poo. Wednesday is khaki – a soldier's uniform in World War Two. Thursday is like Monday, but deeper and stronger. Friday is light creamy-beige, Saturday is white, and Sunday is a deep magenta with a hint of purple in it."

I watch with amusement as Thomas's mouth drops open and his eyes widen like saucers.

"Baby's poo!" he says, awestruck.

"Yes," I sigh. "I wish I could change it, but it's been like that for about forty-five years now, so I reckon I'm stuck with it."

"I've never met anyone else like me who does that," says Thomas, gazing at me wonderingly.

Synaesthesia is the name given to this strange ability we both have. The dictionary defines it as 'a sensation in one part of the body brought about by a stimulus in a different part'. For Thomas and me, it seems to happen in our brains rather than anywhere else. Apparently, it's rare, inherent in only about one per cent of the population. There are even a few 'odd bods' who experience words as *tastes* instead of colours. For years I assumed that everyone saw words in this way. For me, apart from being an interesting conversation piece, it's an utterly useless gift. I'd swap it for whizz-kid computer skills any time.

But for Thomas, it's an extra dimension in his life. He's now contentedly crayoning, pausing now and again to whisper under his breath. Then he shuts his eyes, while a kaleidoscope of different countries, each bathed in its own distinctive hue, appears like magic on the screen of his mind. Fixed and unchanging, for all time.

Friday, 5th March. Maps have been neglected this week. There have been two extra hospital appointments. And early yesterday morning, Mrs Cartwright rang to cancel my visit that day. She and Thomas were just setting off to Gloucestershire, to see the healer once more.

"It would be good if we could keep him alive for his birthday," she adds, minimalist as ever.

Thomas is putting the finishing touches to Africa when I arrive.

"Done!" Thomas throws down his pencil with a triumphant flourish.

I admire the neat labelling, and say how clever he was to find all the different countries.

"Did you find it difficult, matching the colours in your head with the right colouring pencils?"

"Yes, I did. Mum had to go and buy me some more. Look!" He shows me a posh new box of proper artist's crayons, an expensive German make. "There's sixty-eight different shades in there!"

"They're lovely. Just look all these different greens!"

"And the blues, and the reds. And they've all got names, see? 'Ultramarine, viridian." His tongue lingers on each syllable as if on a choc ice.

"Can I try some of them out?" I find some blank paper and we both doodle along contentedly for a while.

"I want to do Australia next," says Thomas. "I'm saving Asia till last."

"Why?"

"Because it's got Mount Everest, and all the highest places in the world. And the coldest. *And* the wettest!"

Thomas has been fascinated by a TV programme about extreme conditions.

"So what would you like to do next?" I ask, as Thomas places his pencils carefully back into the box. "Some more maps, or some maths – or French?"

"I think I'll do *le frrrrrrançais, aujourrrrrrd'hui.*" He rolls his eyes and his r's at me dramatically. He knows it's always good for a laugh.

There are some oral exercises in his French textbook. There's a conversation between two children, strangers to each other, who meet on the swings in a park. New vocabulary is introduced – the kids ask each other their names, where they live, and which apparatus they like best.

"I'll be Pierre and you be Anabelle," says Thomas.

We spend a few minutes in amiable conversation. Anabelle doesn't like the roundabout, it's too fast. Pierre loves the swings best, he likes to go really high. Suddenly, I can't cope with this nonsense. For heaven's sake! Playing on the swings? Boating on the lake, whizzing down the slide…and what is Thomas doing? Thomas is stuck here with me, that's what! Does he too, feel the injustice of it?

But Thomas is dreamily formulating sentences in his head, or looking for words with r's in them, rolling them under his breath.

He completes the worksheet entitled *'Le Parc'* and then chooses one on *'Les Saisons'*. But suddenly, there's a change in him: one moment, he's writing *'L'hiver'* in his small copperplate handwriting; the next, he's gazing into space. He must be thinking, working something out. I carry on making some notes, but when I look up again, two or three minutes later, Thomas hasn't moved. He's as still as a statue. His eyes are open, but trance-like and far away.

"Thomas," I whisper softly. "Thomas? Are you stuck on something?"

He jumps, startled. He looks at me as if I've just appeared from nowhere.

"Oh, sorry. I…I just went off in my head somewhere. Where was I up to?"

"You were just about to write down the French word for this season – see?" I point to the picture.

"Oh, yes. *Le printemps*." He picks up the pen, drops it. "I think I'm a bit tired."

"Have a rest then, Thomas. How about lying down on the settee?"

"Yes, please."

I help him out of the chair into the living room, and on to the settee. I lift his legs so that he can lie down. I go to the bottom of the stairs and call up to Mrs Cartwright. She sprints down.

"Don't worry," she says, seeing my stricken face. "He does this from time to time. He just needs his special drink."

Rapidly, she makes up the magic cocktail. Pudsey Bear once more reports for duty. To my relief, Thomas downs most of the drink.

Now he's more alert, and wants to go back and finish his worksheet. Yet when he tries to get up, he sinks back again against the cushions.

I turn to his mother. "Should I go? Hasn't he had enough for today?"

She shakes her head. "No, stay. It takes a while for the drink to work."

"I'll tell you what, Thomas," I say. "You can finish the worksheet later. Because now, I've got a new game I'd like to try out on you."

There's a coffee table nearby, and his mum quickly moves it into place. She finds a chair for me.

"Now, look at this, Thomas!"

A few years ago, I invented a story-telling game. I produced it in rough form, on home-made cards, and tried it out on primary-age pupils. To my delight, the kids pronounced it 'wicked' and 'ace'. And with the reluctant readers, it achieved its objective – to get them interested in stories and vocabulary. For the past few months I've been producing it in a more polished form, and now I might have a publisher who's interested. But first, he wants it informally trialled, with various age groups and levels of literacy.

"Will you be my guinea-pig, Thomas? Would you like to be my Game Tester?"

He nods, making a heroic effort to sit up.

"Just sit back," I say. "Look, I'll pick up the card from the pack and hand it to you. Then you point to where you think it goes on the board. Easy!"

"*Peasy.*" Thomas sinks back with a little sigh. I've engaged his attention. He's looking at me eagerly. "What's the game called?"

"I haven't given it a name yet. Maybe when you've played it, you can help me think of a name?"

It's a simple game, yet subtle enough to stretch more able children. As new energy gradually seeps into him, Thomas proves a worthy game-tester. He makes helpful suggestions, and is kind about my rough drawings.

"So what's the verdict, Thomas? Do you like it?"

"*Wicked.*"

Thursday, 18th March. It's an evil day, with gusty wind and spiteful lashing rain that's found every gap in my so-called waterproof raincoat. I'm shaking the drops from my umbrella as Mrs Cartwright opens the door.

Thomas's condition has been fairly stable, with no marked decline in his strength and energy. In fact, there's been an improvement this week. Which is just as well, for this Saturday, Thomas will be ten years old. A big party's planned, with relatives and friends coming from far and wide.

"How's Thomas?" I ask, routinely, lulled into optimism.

"He's had a bit of setback. His leg was hurting quite a lot last night. He's a bit off-colour."

She's mistress of the understatement. Translated, this means that Thomas is very poorly. I feel my heart freeze, and close up.

"Barry's just helping him get dressed. He'll bring him down in a moment. Would you like a cup of tea while you wait?"

"No, thank you."

I wait in the hall. My legs are shaking. There are steps on the stairs. Mr Cartwright carries Thomas down, cradling him like a baby. Thomas looks frailer than ever, but he just manages a smile. His dad looks completely wrecked. His hair seems much greyer since I last saw him, and his face is ashen, with dark stubble on hollow cheeks. He barely nods in my direction and takes Thomas into the kitchen, where he lifts him into a chair. He comes out again, brushing abruptly past me in the hallway.

Mrs Cartwright beckons me into the kitchen. She says conversationally, "Barry's home to help today. There's a lot to do before Saturday. Thomas has invited the whole of his class, so we're preparing food for an army! You can begin – don't mind me, I've just got a couple of things to do in here."

I sit down with Thomas, who's eager to show me his work – a completed map of Australia.

"It was easy-peasy! There's hardly any states – just Queensland, and New South Wales and some others. Not like North America. That was well hard. But now I need to do more to Asia. It's got so many countries, and I've only done half of them. Can I do Asia first?"

Thomas gets out his pen and the box of splendid crayons. He settles down to work with a little sigh of satisfaction. I offer to help him look up the countries in the Atlas, but he wants to do it on his own. I sit by him, watching him choose the exactly the right shade. I have a sudden sense of being suspended in time and place. Thomas's bent head, the colours, the two of us sitting here at this table – all suddenly move into sharp focus. I'm dimly aware of rain buffeting the window pane in sharp angry bursts. Of Mrs Cartwright, opening cupboards and checking items against a shopping list. The cupboards and the worktops, the fridge, the cat-basket on the floor suddenly seem hazy, unreal. But Thomas and I are in a separate bubble – a reality bubble. Here, inside it, everything is crystal clear.

Mr Cartwright pokes his head round the door, and asks for the shopping list.

The bubble gently evaporates. Its edges merge into the surrounding haze and all is as it was.

Mrs Cartwright goes to the door and gives her husband the list. He mutters something, and she answers sharply. They both glance in my direction and move into the hall. There's an argument. He's protesting.

"He should be in bed, for Chrissake."

Her reply is inaudible, the tone soothing and matter-of-fact. Then the words become distinct again, as she reminds him to collect the vacuum cleaner, and to bring back a crate of soft drinks.

She's the organiser, the one who copes. Dad's the emotional one, who can't cope and is caving in under the strain. So it seems. Yet, he's the carrier of crates – and of Mum's unexpressed angst. Both of them parcelling up the burden and carrying it between them in their own fashion.

Mrs Cartwright bustles back into the kitchen. She rests her hands lightly on Thomas's shoulders.

"Drink in about thirty minutes, then, dear?"

"Mmmm."

She bends down and nuzzles her head against his.

"Oh *Mum,*" says Thomas, embarrassed.

His eyes are scanning the Himalayas, his fingers tracing the contours of their dizzy heights.

"Look," he says delightedly. "See how high they are. See this purple? This is the highest colour you can get."

His mum smiles at me and goes upstairs.

"And guess how high Mt Everest is?" I point out the highest mountain on earth.

"Nearly seven miles," he says promptly. "I know. Dad told me last night. That's as far as to my Nan's house!"

I'm well prepared today. I have a general book on Asia, and beautiful picture books about India, Russia and China. But Thomas wants to label all the countries in the continent before he allows himself the indulgence of reading about them.

"I'll stop if I feel tired."

It's the first time I've heard him mention the T word. Even now, he says 'if' not 'when'.

"But I *won't* get tired," he turns to me, his expression teasing and mischievous, "because I want to finish this today."

Thomas works steadily. He finds nearly all the countries. As he writes their names, he puts his other hand on the covers of the books I've brought, as if to say: 'I know you're there. I'll be with you in a minute'.

But by the time his mother's back to make up his drink, he's running out of steam again. His face is very pale. There are dark circles under his eyes which I haven't noticed until now. He manages a third of his drink.

"I'll have it in a minute, leave it over there."

"Just one more sip," pleads his mother.

"I'll be sick," says Thomas, as if he really means it.

His mum sighs and removes the cup. She spoons out his medicine, which he takes, pulling a face.

"I'll leave you to it, then."

A reassuring smile for me, another quick hug for Thomas. I hear her footsteps on the stairs, and a minute later, sounds of housework in the bedroom above.

I move Thomas's work to one side, before he can pick up his pen again. I point to the books.

"I really want to show you some of these pictures today, Thomas. You see, I'll have to take these books back to the library soon."

"Okay," he says cheerfully. "Can we find Siberia?"

"Why Siberia?"

"Because it's so cold. I want to find the coldest place on earth."

We flip through the book, until to my delight, there it is. The picture I was hoping we'd find. A group of incredibly robust Siberian males, clad only in swimming trunks, are standing around a square hole cut into several feet of ice. One man has already jumped into the freezing depths, and two comrades are standing by, ready to haul him out.

"Look, Thomas! They're all queuing up for their turn to jump in. Guess what the air temperature is?"

"*Extremely* cold." Thomas shivers dramatically.

"It's about minus 40°. That would be like stripping off inside a giant freezer!"

The next book, on India, is full of factual information: the biggest city, the longest river, the main industries. Thomas devours these facts with the appetite of any soon-to-be ten-year-old.

He asks, "Why are all those people in that river? Look, some of them are just putting their heads in, they're not swimming properly? And there's loads of others on the bank…"

"That's the River Ganges. For some people, the waters are holy. They make a long journey to bathe there. And they dunk the whole of their bodies in the river. It's a bit like baptising a baby in a font. But of course, in church, the vicar or whoever, only just wets the baby's head. Have you ever seen a font, Thomas?"

Silence.

I look up sharply, teleporting myself back from the humid shores of the Ganges. Thomas hasn't heard a word I've said. He's gazing into space, his eyes vague and far away.

"Thomas?"

Slowly, he comes back. "Sorry…did you say something?"

"I was just telling you about these people, and why they're bathing in the river."

"Oh." He frowns. He seems to be concentrating very hard on the picture. Then he blinks his eyes and turns away. He stares at the wall next to the kitchen door, where his mother has hung an efficient-looking notice board. There are hooks for keys, a shallow tray where beakers containing pens, felt-tips and pencils are neatly arranged. For a moment, Thomas looks intently at these, then that faraway look returns. The eyes half-close, then open again, unfocussed.

I'm frightened. Thomas is slipping away in front of me. He seems to have less substance, little bits of him breaking free. Like the tendrils of a cloud separating, floating off into the blue.

"Thomas!"

Suddenly, he's back, filling his own space again. He looks puzzled.

"Sorry, I forgot what you were saying. I was dreaming, I think."

"I think you were."

I look at my watch. It's time to finish, anyway.

"I'll leave you the books, shall I, to look at later?" I try to disguise the relief in my voice, but the forced brightness grates in my own ears.

"Yes, please. And when you come tomorrow, I'll have finished Asia, and then I'll have gone all the way round the world." He yawns and rests his head on his arms.

"Goodbye, Thomas."

He looks up briefly and smiles. "Goodbye."

"I'll see you tomorrow."

"Yes, see you tomorrow. Thanks for the books." He spreads his arms wider on the table, and lowers his head again. He shuts his eyes.

I call up the stairs to Mrs Cartwright to say I'm leaving now.

She runs down. "How time's flown this morning! I've been writing out Thomas's party invitations to his class."

"How on earth will you cope with thirty of them?"

"I've press-ganged six mums, each in charge of five kids. And of course Barry will be there, plus a couple of neighbours, and my mother and father are coming over too. We'll manage somehow." She smiles and adds suddenly, "And how are you?"

"Me? I'm fine, but Thomas is asleep, I think. He lost concentration towards the end."

"Ah!" She takes a sharp breath, and nods thoughtfully. She looks at me as if she's about to say something more, then stops. Instead, she opens the front door for me.

"See you tomorrow then," she says.

Friday, 19th March. The sun streaming through my window wakes me, and I'm up unusually early. The weather looks promising today – a clear blue sky with just a few light puffy clouds. I stand by my kitchen window sipping my morning tea, and enjoying the new splashes of colour in the flowerbeds. The pieris by my front gate has just burst into full blossom. Bunches of tiny, lantern-like white flowers perch atop the foliage, graceful as ballerinas. The leaves, at first a delicate pink, are just beginning to unfold. The shrub is at the peak of its perfection. I'm just wondering whether to take a photo of it when the phone rings.

"Best to leave the tuition today," says Mrs Cartwright. "Thomas is resting up, so he's ready for his party tomorrow. But he's fine." she adds quickly. "He finished his map of Asia last night. He told me to tell you. He'll show it to you on Monday."

By a stroke of luck, my local bookshop has a copy of the very book Thomas liked best – the one about Asia. I take it home and wrap it up. Later, glad to be outside in the balmy sunshine, I walk round to his house.

I pause at Thomas's front gate, not wanting to intrude. The place is a hive of activity. People I don't recognise are bustling in and out of the house with plastic boxes and trays of little cakes. Inside, loud voices call to each other. I hear laughter and someone singing in the kitchen as crockery clatters in the sink. A large, cosy lady gets out of her car carrying an enormous birthday cake. She introduces herself as Thomas's aunt. I hand her the present and send my best wishes for tomorrow.

Monday, 22nd March. There was no lesson today. Thomas died at five o'clock yesterday afternoon.

Saturday, 17th April. "He loved the book," said Thomas's mother. "The one about Asia. He took it to bed with him on Saturday night, after his party. He got his dad to read it to him."

We're sitting on my patio on a mild, sunny afternoon. At my feet is a huge box of Thomas's books, which I haven't had the heart to look at yet. Yesterday, Mrs Cartwright rang up to ask if she could bring them round. She wouldn't keep them. All Thomas's things – his clothes, his toys, everything – have already been stored away in the attic, ready for a sale she's planning. A fresh start. But she knows Thomas would have wanted me to have his books.

Mrs Cartwright might welcome a change of scene, I reckoned. A cup of tea in my garden. And a chance to talk about Thomas. Maybe I could find the right words, this time.

The last time I'd seen her was at Thomas's funeral. There hadn't been room in the church for everyone, so over a hundred people stood outside in the pouring rain. Yet she'd found a place for me, in a back pew. After the service, with rock-like equanimity, she greeted the weeping congregation as it filed out, shaking hands with white-faced little boys from Thomas's class and their distraught parents; with teachers, relatives and neighbours. When it was my turn, I couldn't speak.

Today, once again, I've failed miserably in my role of comforter.

"I didn't believe he would die, I kept pretending to myself that he'd be all right." Mrs Cartwright hands me yet another tissue. "And I just carried on as if…"

"I know that. You were in denial. You weren't the only one." She smiles at me encouragingly, the smile that used to reassure Thomas and me that we were both doing just fine. "But that wasn't a bad thing. You helped to give him what we – his family – were trying to give him. Normality. And you kept his mind active and alive."

Caring and perceptive, this remarkable woman has ended up telling me everything I so wanted to hear.

"He had the most amazing birthday!" she says. "*All* the children in his class turned up. Even one who'd just broken his leg was wheeled round in plaster! Of course, Thomas didn't do much rushing around. His right leg suddenly packed up altogether the day before. But that didn't stop him hopping round the snooker table on his left leg, determined to win the competition Barry'd organised."

"I can picture that so clearly. I'm just so glad he had his birthday."

"Yes, at least he had that. And we were sure he'd carry on fighting, but on Sunday morning, he seemed exhausted. He couldn't get out of bed, even with help. He went back to sleep. By lunchtime he was in a coma. It was all very quick, and very peaceful."

There's a long, long silence while I take all this in.

"There's a mixture of books in that box. Some of them are quite new. Sort them out at your leisure, and give any you don't want back to me. I'll have a good use for them."

"Won't you want them for the other boys?" The other *two,* I'm thinking, with a sick wrench in my stomach. *Three* no longer.

"No. It would be too painful for me to watch them reading Thomas's books. And it would be hard for them, too. They need to start afresh, with their own books and toys. There'll be other ways of keeping his memory alive…"

We sit, deep in our own thoughts, but it's a comfortable silence. Mrs Cartwright is making this so easy for me. She's helping herself to a piece of cake, and looking at me as if she really wants to be here, sitting in this patch of sunshine, hearing the shrill, laughing cackle of the gulls nesting on the chimney breast.

"What will you do now?" I ask. "Will you go back to work?"

"Not yet. First, there's something I have to do. What are you doing on Saturday, June 6th?"

"Goodness! I haven't thought that far ahead. What's happening?"

"A fête in aid of Cancer Research. I shall be organising it."

"I'll be there," I promise fervently.

"And tell all your friends. It's going to be an annual event. Just for this year, it'll be in June, but next year, and every year after that, it will be on the anniversary of Thomas's birthday."

"I'll keep that date clear every year."

Mrs Cartwright stands up. "I must go," she says. "I've called a meeting this evening, trying to get the Fête Committee together."

We walk round the side of the house to her car. She opens her door, and reaches into the back seat.

"Thomas would have liked you to have these." She hands me a large envelope. "His maps of the world…" For the very first time, I hear a catch in her voice.

"Thank you, I shall treasure them."

WAYNE

Monday, 19th January 2004. "It's these two – they're the same! Look, *look!*"

Bonnie jumps up from the floor, excitedly. In one hand she holds a picture of a cat. In the other she waves the corresponding word card. She gives me a beatific smile – her princess smile. Then she looks at me, waiting for my reaction.

I nod. Bonnie is as bright as fairy dust and loves to be wherever the action is – just now, spread out all around us on the carpet in a game of Matching Pairs. Bonnie can already read simple words aimed at Reception Class level and above. She's relishing every little bit of my reluctant attention. She wants it non-stop and undivided. The problem is, four-year-old Bonnie is *not* my pupil.

"Wayne!" I call sharply. "Look – it's your turn! Come and sit down here, next to me."

Wayne, aged six and three-quarters, is rushing round and round the room. Now and then, he picks up a toy in a purposeless fashion and flings it down again. Something hard with a glint of metal whizzes past – a Corgi collectable car. It misses my ear by two centimetres. I pick it up and put it beyond his reach.

"Wayne's being naughty again, isn't he?" lisps Bonnie.

Her face is flushed with triumph, not just at her card-matching success. She positively glows with the pleasure of being – yet again – one up on her elder brother. The problem is, Bonnie's a stirrer. And she shouldn't be here at all. Not here, in the living room, bang in the middle of Wayne's tuition session.

"Wayne!" I hold up a word card. "Let's see if you can find the right picture. Look! It's a *very* fierce animal…very BIG…and it has a long mane and it's the King of the Jungle!" I prowl on hands and knees around the settee, making unearthly lion-noises. (Saints alive, what *does* a lion sound like?) "Can you guess what it is, Wayne? And find the right picture card on the floor?"

"*That* sounds like an elephant. Not a *lion*," says Bonnie, scornfully. She pounces on the lion card, in a double-whammy of giving-the-game-away.

I'm pulling out all the stops here, and all I'm achieving is a dislocated kneecap.

Bonnie waves the card at her brother. She darts him a look that says: 'I'm-so-clever-and-you're-not'.

"Wayne! Come here!"

Wayne's now sitting down at the computer, which his mother has left on. With expert ease and superb mouse-skills, he's zapping some creatures on the screen. He's a stocky, slightly overweight child, with rosy cheeks and his sister's whitish-blond hair and pale blue eyes. Since I arrived this morning, he's had a permanently truculent expression on his face. And as another monster bites the dust, he looks positively vicious.

I'd like to leap over to the computer and turn it off at the socket, but I can't even see the socket beneath a tangled mass of trailing wires. I don't fancy an undignified scramble on the floor. That damn computer! It shouldn't be on.

I'd made a point, at the very start of our session, of asking Mrs Lewis to turn it off, together with the television, now flickering away at the opposite end of the living room. She'd tutted. She'd turn it off in a moment. She just wanted to watch the end of something-or-other. Then the phone rang. She leapt off to the kitchen, leaving me maddened by the subdued but incessant murmur of a chat-show. It must be a long phone call – she's been gone twenty minutes now.

"He's naughty, isn't he!" shrills Bonnie, goading Wayne with wide, innocent eyes. "He *never* comes when he's called. *I* do. I'm *never* naughty."

She tilts her head sideways, looking up at me guilefully, smoothing her frilly skirt over neatly-crossed legs.

This is the tuition placement from hell.

Recently, there's been a surfeit of exceptionally difficult excluded teenagers doing the rounds of the home tuition team. They tend to get passed around, as each despairing tutor collapses with exhaustion, worn down under a constant barrage of foul language and non-co-operation. I was sure one of these youngsters would be coming my way soon. I hoped not. My need for challenge and excitement was being fully met by Cassie. So when the phone rang yesterday asking me to start as soon as possible with Wayne, a Year 2 boy with Attention Deficit Hyperactivity Disorder, I'd been relieved, and delighted. I enjoy working with very young children.

A brief look through his file at the office revealed scant information. Wayne had been temporarily suspended for rushing round the classroom in an uncontrolled way, hurling or smashing everything in his path, including his classmates. His mother, Mrs Lewis, was a single parent who'd recently been moved by the council to a very pleasant village about four miles out of town. Wayne has a sister, Bonnie, and a father who left four years ago. He'd found someone else, started a new family, but he lived nearby and was still in sporadic contact with Wayne and Bonnie.

I've worked with many children with ADHD. They're very challenging, but rewarding. (And what is ADHD anyway, other than a label for a collection of behaviours and symptoms that can vary from child to child?) I'd soon have Wayne sorted out and back with his classmates.

"WAYNE! Come away from that computer this minute!"

Wayne is crouching low, his face two inches from the screen. Blood-curdling yells accompany each movement of the mouse. *I'm* a mouse. Unseen, unheard.

Suddenly my blood boils.

"Bonnie! Would you go and find your mother in the kitchen? Ask her to come here? I want to speak to her."

"What do you want to say to her?" Bonnie's eyes widen and gleam. She sniffs the air for mischief like a beagle at the hunt.

"Never mind," I snap. "Just get her please, Bonnie."

Bonnie fiddles with the cards on the floor.

"Bonnie!"

Slowly, Bonnie stands up and dawdles to the door, with a lingering, poisoned-arrow glance at her brother.

I'm alone with Wayne at last.

"Wayne! Come and sit down. Look, I've got something to show you!"

"I'm doing *this*," says Wayne, indignantly. "I'm winning!"

And I'm losing. I wait.

Mrs Lewis comes in, annoyed.

"Bonnie says you wanted to see me because Wayne's being difficult again."

"I never said....!" I take a deep breath. "Mrs Lewis, the television is on. I asked you to turn it off while I was tutoring Wayne."

"It's not doing any harm. It's turned down low – I can't hardly hear it. Can you hear it, Wayne?"

Wayne shakes his head, still zapping monsters, crowing lustily as they fall to their deaths.

"*I* can't hear it." Bonnie nudges up to her mother.

"It's distracting!" I say sharply. "The computer shouldn't be on either. I'd be grateful if you'd turn them both off, please."

"I was just going to use it myself. That's why I left it on, but the phone rang, didn't it? It was urgent. From Wayne's headteacher. What am I supposed to do? Refuse to speak to her? I've been bloody waiting for her to ring since last Tuesday."

Mrs Lewis glares at me. She stubs out her cigarette on an overflowing ashtray nearby with a vicious, jabbing movement. She crosses her arms. Pale blue eyes, fringed heavily with mascara, snap and blink.

"Mrs Lewis. Wayne has been suspended from school. His ADHD has made him unmanageable in the classroom. His attention span, for any task, is never more than a minute, according to his teacher's report. If he's ever going to improve his concentration, he needs a quiet environment, with no distractions. Certainly not a TV and a computer!"

The gauntlet has been thrown. Wayne, hearing his name, and the words 'teacher' and 'school', swivels round in his chair, watchfully.

Bonnie opens her mouth to say something. I put my finger to my lips and flare my nostrils at her. She looks up at her mother, and then back at me, uncertainly.

"I've got to use the computer. *Now*." rasps Mrs Lewis. "For Chrissake, it's only for five minutes. I've got to write to the Education. About them that suspended him. I need to get him settled. He shouldn't be out of school at his age. It's a disgrace! Are you telling me that I can't use my own computer in my own house? Seems to me that this is a priority. It's about Wayne, isn't it?"

I'm being sucked in, feet first. *When in a quagmire, lie flat along the surface. Move as little as possible.*

"Of course I appreciate your need to get Wayne's education sorted out. But it's not acceptable for *parents*..." – I take a deep breath, hoping the more neutral word will stop her seeing this as a personal attack – "...for parents to be present while the child is being tutored. It's distracting for him. And so is a computer that's on. And a television flickering in the background. His eyes are drawn to these, instead of the work I'm trying to do with him."

A pivotal moment. The ball could fall either side of the net. In the brief silence, Mrs Lewis purses her lips and sucks in a sharp breath. Her eyes narrow, as she glances down at the floor, at the scattered cards. She plays for time. I wait.

This is the first time, in a chaotic session, that I've had a chance to look at her closely. She's a thin, nervy-looking woman, in her early thirties. Her face, once pretty in a doll-like way, is prematurely lined and set in discontented creases around the mouth. She's wearing a skimpy skirt and top from a chain store currently beloved by teenagers. Bracelets jangle as she lights another cigarette. She takes a deep draught, and exhales, sending a cloud of smoke in my direction.

"It'll only take five minutes, for Godssake."

"I'm sorry. It's not possible. But as it's Wayne's first session, I'd like to end with a treat. Perhaps we could have a treasure hunt in the back garden – with your permission? You can use the computer then. If Wayne behaves himself, of course!" I raise my voice, making sure Wayne can hear me.

Mrs Lewis takes a long drag on her cigarette.

"Right. Well then, Wayne. You'd better get your arse off that chair pronto if you want this treasure hunt. Do your education with your tutor. Go on then! What are you waiting for?"

Abruptly, she crosses the room to the television and turns it off. I smile encouragingly at Wayne as his mother descends on the computer and clicks out of the programme. Suddenly there's a blissful silence.

"I'll leave you to it, then." She marches out of the room, trailing ash along the carpet.

"Good boy, Wayne," I say quickly. "I'm so pleased that you're ready to play some games with me!"

"I don't want to play *that* game." Wayne kicks at the cards laid out on the floor.

"That's naughty, Wayne. You're being bad again. Isn't he, teacher?"

I'd forgotten Bonnie. An added complication. A thorn in Wayne's flesh. I'm tempted to send her off, pronto, to her mum. But caution tells me to wait. One hurdle at a time. Mrs Lewis is probably still steamed up about the computer. There's no point in pushing her over the edge. Leave it for today.

"Now look, Bonnie." I kneel down so that I'm at her level. "You're not supposed to be here. Did you know that?"

Bonnie shakes her head, wide-eyed and watchful, sucking her thumb. I feel mean – she's just a baby, really - but I have to set out the ground rules, for Wayne's sake.

"I'm here just for Wayne, you see!" I catch Wayne's eye, including him in this piece of information. Willing him to stay still just long enough for me to set up some compromise working environment that includes Bonnie. Only for today, I hope.

Wayne's standing by the cards, scuffing them with his feet. The scuffs get more violent. Cards begin to fly everywhere.

"So, Bonnie. I want you to pretend to be a little mouse. If a mouse comes out of a hole in the wall, what might happen to it?"

"A big cat will eat you up!" Wayne yowls, with a remarkably accurate imitation of a cat in the full moon. He gives his sister a venomous look.

"Exactly. So can you hide somewhere while Wayne and I do our work? And be VERY, VERY quiet, so that the big cat can't find you? And if you're especially good, we might let you join in our treasure hunt. Now, where are you going to hide? Where will you be safe from the big bad cat?"

Bonnie runs behind the settee and peeps out.

"Quickly, Wayne!" I say. "Let's pick up these cards and give them to the mouse behind the settee, so she doesn't get too bored. If she peeps her head round again, the cat will get her!"

Together, we place the cards behind the settee.

"Now, little mouse, see if you can find all the *little* animals and put them on one pile. Then make another pile with all the *big* ones." I help her start sorting.

Now Wayne wants to join in Bonnie's game.

"I've got a secret, Wayne!" I whisper in his ear. I take his hand and lead him a safe distance from the settee.

Some lucky survival instinct prompted me to put some play dough in my bag this morning. I spread out some scrap paper on the floor and ask Wayne to make a big cat who will eat a little mouse if he catches it. This he does, with little skill but much gusto.

"Can you make the tiny mouse, too?"

This is quickly done. Then, he spends a few moments shaping a dog and a snake. Now he's fidgety. He wants to move, to run around.

"Come on then. Let's have a chase. Will you be the cat or the mouse?"

There's a furious chase along the floor. The ferocity with which the mouse is finally caught and pulverised leaves no doubt as to his feelings towards Bonnie. (Or me?)

I'm running out of ideas.

"Shall we make another animal?" I suggest, lamely. "We could do a gentle, quiet animal this time. Now, what shall I choose…"

Wayne makes his choice with surprising speed. "I'll make a lamb."

"Okay. I'll do…um….a slowworm." An easy get-out. My sculptural skills won't run to anything more complicated. I begin to roll the dough into a long sausage. There's a blessed moment of tranquillity. No sound, except for Bonnie chanting "Big one, little one," behind the settee, in a charming, non-attention-seeking little voice. Outside, a dog barks loudly.

Wayne's intent on fashioning his lamb. He gives it far more care and attention to detail than he lavished on the cat. I watch him. There's a strange, intense expression on his face. He's breathing heavily, almost panting with some internal process. The lamb looks odd. Wayne's elongated the neck, so that it's taken on the comical appearance of a baby giraffe.

"That's a nice lamb, Wayne," I say, rolling my slowworm into a coil. "Has it got a name?"

Wayne shakes his head. That strange expression is still there. He looks agitated. His eyes flicker to my face, and then away.

"So your lamb has no name. Well, I'm going to call my slowworm 'Slither'. Because that's what he does. In springtime, he comes out of his little hole in the grass…and he slithers along…like *this*." I uncoil Slither and make him creep along the floor.

Wayne watches. He's unnaturally still.

"Would you like a go? He can slither along – or you can coil him up again."

Wayne shakes his head.

"Then can you make your lamb gambol? Jump about and play? That's what your lambs does in the springtime, with all the other little…"

"No, he doesn't!" Wayne's next action is so rapid that I've hardly time to register what's happening. He picks up the plastic knife that comes with the play dough set. He seizes the lamb and cuts off its head.

"There!" he grunts, breathing heavily. "You're gone. Deaded!" He's turned pale, and doesn't look at me.

"Wayne!" I can't disguise my shock. "Why did you cut off the poor little lamb's head?"

"Because." Wayne squeezes the lamb into a ball. His expression is deadly serious – this is no light-hearted modelling game.

"Because? Because what, Wayne?"

Wayne shrugs and fiddles with the now pulverised lamb. Suddenly, he glances up and me and opens his mouth to speak…

"Teacher, I've finished, look!" Forgetting she's a mouse, Bonnie springs from her hiding place, clutching a pile of cards in each hand. Wayne gives her a sulky look and gets up. He wanders over to the door.

"I want a drink."

"Wayne, we haven't finished yet. And we have proper break-times for drinks. Just like school. You must wait until I tell you before you leave the room."

Wayne opens the door, looking at me challengingly.

"If you want a treasure hunt, you must wait for your drink."

He hesitates, swinging the door backwards and forwards.

"*I'm* being good. *I'm* waiting for my drink, aren't I?" Bonnie's back to her needling, goody-goody, lets-wind-Wayne-up mode. At any moment, this tuition session will disintegrate into chaos.

"Tell you what, Wayne. Let's have an action game. I'll start counting, and let's see if you can pack up the play dough neatly before I get to a hundred. And Bonnie, you've done so well sorting those cards into two piles. Well done! Now, how about picking up all the toys from the floor and putting them in that toy box. We can give Mum a big surprise when she comes in and sees it's all tidy in here!"

"What will she say?" asks Bonnie, sucking her thumb and smiling up at me. For a moment I catch a glimpse of the normal little four-year old hiding inside her.

"She'll say: 'Well done children! I don't have to pick up all the toys myself. I can hoover the floor now'."

"The hoover's broken," says Wayne, sullenly.

"Oh well," I say brightly. "Pick up the toys anyway, Bonnie. And Wayne, you start putting the play dough away in the plastic box. Then we'll all have a lovely drink, won't we? One, two, three, four…"

Thankfully, both children spring to their posts. I'm still counting when Mrs Lewis comes in.

"Eighty-nine, ninety…Just look how well the children have done… ninety-one, ninety-two…and they've both behaved very well….ninety-three, ninety-four…."

Mrs Lewis gives me a surly look. "I was going to tidy up in here anyway. Just hadn't got round to it."

Bonnie's face has fallen with disappointment at her mother's unappreciative response. I can see she'd expected that her mother would, magically, utter the very words I'd rashly predicted: "Well done, children…"

"Well done, both of you," I say with more emphasis than necessary. "Now you both deserve a break. Is that all right, Mrs Lewis? I try to divide up sessions with at least one or two breaks for children as young as Wayne."

"Whatever," shrugs the children's mother, Cassie-style. "Wayne, there's squash in the kitchen. You know where it is. Go and get yourself a drink, and one for Bonnie."

Wayne runs into the kitchen and comes back a minute later with two beakers and a large plastic drinks bottle full of some psychedelically red liquid.

"It's too heavy. I can't pour it."

"Here, let me." Sighing, his mother opens the bottle and pours out the drinks for her children. Her body language shows that even this simple caring act goes far beyond the call of duty.

She marches back into the kitchen. There's the sound of a kettle being filled. China clatters on the work-surface. I sniff the air hopefully, but after several minutes there's not even a whiff of a teabag, and my mirage of a mug of steaming hot tea slowly fades back into the desert.

Meanwhile, Wayne and Bonnie are working themselves up for a fight. It's 'You did!', 'I didn't!' over and over again. They're both bored. Wayne, in particular, is getting very restless. Curiously, I pick up the bottle of squash that's been left half-empty on the coffee table. I scan the list of ingredients: 'flavouring, acidity regulator (E331), sweeteners (E951, E954), preservative (E221, E202), Contains a source of phenylalanine' (whatever that is).

Phew! What a potent cocktail. All E-numbers can trigger allergic reactions in some children, but by far the worst offender is E202, which has been linked with eczema and hyperactivity. If I were Wayne's mother I'd avoid *any* colourings and preservatives like the plague. Should I say anything to her? Again, I'm treading this fine line between tutoring and becoming involved in health issues. Better to keep quiet for the moment. I'm not exactly flavour of the week just now. Wait for some more congenial time. Or maybe a word with Wayne's class teacher might be more effective?

Wayne's building up to a crescendo of hyperactivity. Time for the treasure hunt, but my heart sinks. It's started to rain, a weary, incessant downpour that's crept up silently and unnoticed, filling dips and hollows between the broken paving outside the patio doors. I stare gloomily at the small neglected patch of garden, hemmed in darkly on all sides by high straggly hedges that fight for space with overgrown conifers. The long skeletal strings of last year's bindweed tangle together, almost strangling a *viburnum tinus,* its pink-white flower heads the only visible patch of colour in that dismal scene. The door hangs loose from a battered, ivy-encrusted shed. There's a small area which has been fenced off with the sort of wire frame one sees on building sites. This is not an exciting venue for a treasure hunt on a wet, mid-January morning.

Wayne's now jumping on and off the settee, flinging cushions into the far corners of the room.

Desperately, I say the first thing that comes into my head.

"Let's play 'Simon Says'!"

To my relief, both children jump up and down expectantly.

"Right. Simon says: Pick up the cushions and put them back on the settee."

"Simon says: Put all the toys back in the toy box."

"Simon says: Sit down quietly on the floor with your legs crossed."

"Simon says: Lie down on the floor and go to sleep."

And at last, peace reigns.

Tuesday, 20th January. There's a loud barking on the other side of Wayne's front door. Thumps, and a menacing growl. My hand freezes in mid-knock. Oh Lord, no, please not another mad dog...

Dangerous dogs are one of the hazards of our job. In an age of health and safety, in which children's playgrounds are now considered danger zones, whether the home tutor lives or dies seems of no consequence at all. So often, we're at the mercy of a frisky Rottweiler, who's 'just playing', as it clamps its jaws round our hands. *Please, please don't let it be a Rottweiler – or an Alsatian. And definitely not a pit-bull terrier.* On the few occasions tutors meet, apocryphal stories abound. One colleague was unable to leave her pupil's house for two hours after the end of the session. A snarling Alsatian was barring the front door. The laughing pupil had nipped out of the back door, locking it. Luckily, a neighbour with a spare key heard her plaintive cries. Don't get me wrong. I like dogs – even large, over-affectionate ones – so long as they're biddable. I'm used to teaching with a black Labrador sitting on my feet and thumping its tail against the table leg.

"Hello?" My voice quavers. I daren't excite the monster by knocking again.

"Who is it?" snaps a voice from the other side of the door.

"It's me. Wayne's tutor."

The door opens a crack. A large brown head nudges the door open a little further. A grinning mouth pants, and gently slobbers.

"Come in," says Mrs Lewis. "He won't hurt you. He's only a puppy. He's a soppy thing. Wouldn't hurt a fly." (How many times have I heard that?)

I ease myself round the door. It's a St Bernard. Apart from his size, he doesn't look too menacing, although he's straining at the lead and she's struggling to restrain him. Any moment now I'll be hurled to the ground and squashed flat.

"Down, Brandy, DOWN, boy! Bad dog. *Heel.*" She whacks his rump. "He'll be all right in a moment. He's just saying 'hello'."

"Hello, Brandy!" Instinctively, I reach out my hand, then hurriedly withdraw it. The last tutor who made that mistake ended up in Casualty with three fingers out of action for six months. Instead, I arrange my features into a dog-friendly expression. I avoid his eyes.

"I didn't know you had a dog. He wasn't here yesterday, was he?"

"Yes he was. He was in the garden when you came. He stays out there when it's fine. Then I brought him in because it was raining."

"Will he be with us, in the living room?" *As well as Bonnie, the computer, the television…*

"No, he's not allowed in there. He crashes into everything. Wayne's in there," she finishes abruptly. "He's waiting for you."

In the living room, the TV is on. So is the computer, with Wayne installed in front of it. He ignores me completely as he zooms into a surreal landscape – a Hampton Court maze with high stone walls instead of hedges.

"Pow! Pow! Kill! Got you!" he yells, bouncing up and down on the chair.

Bonnie's sitting demurely on the floor, lining up her dolls for a tea-party. She looks up at me and calls out in a bossy little voice:

"Wayne, your teacher's here. You've got to have your lesson. You're not allowed to do the computer. Wayne, you're being *very* naughty. He's being a naughty boy, isn't he?"

Nothing has changed since yesterday. I might as well have saved my breath, trying to explain to Mrs Lewis why the TV and computer had to be off.

Fuming, I storm into the kitchen without knocking, forgetting Brandy, who hurls himself at me like a long-lost friend. Mrs Lewis is sitting at the kitchen table reading a magazine. Another television blares out in a corner of the worksurface. She looks up, startled. "Brandy!" She yells. "Heel! *Here*. Bad boy. *Basket!* Did you want something?"

"I …I just…" I'm pinned up against the kitchen door, with all the stuffing knocked out of me. "Wayne…"

"BRANDY! BASKET!"

Brandy unclamps his huge paws from either side of my neck. With a parting lick, he slithers down my front, and ambles across the kitchen into his basket – an understatement for the huge plastic thing which takes up half the kitchen floor. It rests on the blue vinyl like a container ship in dock.

"I need to have the TV and the computer off," I say, as evenly as I can, keeping a wary eye on Brandy. I want to keep in his good books.

Mrs Lewis curses under her breath, uncoils her legs from under the table, stands up, and walks very slowly towards the living room, showing who's in control round here. She turns off the television, and unceremoniously drags Wayne off his chair. Yelling, Wayne hurls himself flat on the floor, thumping with his fists and feet.

"Thank you. It would be so much easier if they were off *before* I arrive. Then we could avoid this performance every day."

Wayne's yells increase to ear-splitting level.

"Now he's being a very, *very* bad boy, isn't he?" Bonnie puts the boot in.

"And another thing," I take a deep breath, "I'm afraid Bonnie can't be in the room when I'm tutoring Wayne."

"She won't be no trouble. She's always good as gold. What's she been up to?" says her mother truculently, arms akimbo.

"It's against the rules to have another child in the same room as the one who's being tutored. It's too distracting."

"I want to be here! I want to be 'stracting!" Genuine tears are welling up in Bonnie's eyes.

I kneel down next to her. "Bonnie, I'd love to teach you too, but I can't. I'm not allowed. Tell you what, if you're a very good girl and stay with Mum, you can join our treasure hunt at the end of the session. Because – look! – it's a lovely day, so we can be outside. If Mum says that's okay?"

Mrs Lewis grunts. "Come on then, Bonnie." She grips Bonnie's arm a little too firmly, and pulls her out of the room.

"Did you hear that, Wayne?"

Wayne's stopped yelling, but is still face down on the floor, flailing angrily with fists and feet.

"Wayne, sit up please. If you behave yourself, we'll have the treasure hunt after the break. Remember how well you behaved yesterday? Look, you got a smiley face for playing 'Simon Says' so nicely. And after we played that game, we got out the blocks and you put them in rows of ten, all the way up to a hundred. You did really well – I gave you *another* smiley face! And here's the best thing, if you get ten smiley faces, you get a prize!"

At first, I'm talking to Wayne's prostrate body, but by the end of my speech, he's sitting up, mildly interested. Just enough to come over and inspect the smiley faces I've stuck on to a large chart with his name pencilled in.

"Well done! Look, I've only written your name in pencil. I'd love you to write it much bigger, in colour. What would you like to use, these felt tips, or these lovely wax crayons?"

Wayne's short stubby fingers are the same size and shape as the thick wax crayons. Breathing heavily, he begins to write his name. It's an effort. He struggles to hold the crayon steady, wielding it like a dagger, stabbing at the page. I show him the pincer grip – thumb, forefinger and middle finger clasping the crayon in a triangle – and he manages to finish the word.

"What about 'Lewis?' Can you write that too?"

"No."

"Show me the words that you know."

Wayne writes 'Cat, dog, mum, dad." His grip keeps faltering. I praise him for persevering. After much prompting, he manages 'See, me, I, TV, gam (for game). As he writes, he's never still, his whole body in a state of St Vitus Dance. Now, he flings the crayon across the room. He's down on his tummy again, banging the floor with fists and feet.

"You've done very well. Look at all these words you've written. And here's another smiley face!" He stops thumping for a second and peers round at me.

"Now, can you promise me something, Wayne?"

"What?" – belligerently.

"Sometimes people get a bit bored with doing one thing, don't they? Or they get tired, or find something too hard? Like you did just now with the writing. So, you went FLOP on the floor. Like this – look! I'm Wayne!"

I imitate his action, exaggerating wildly. Wayne stares, and laughs.

"Now, next time, can you say 'I'm a bit tired. Can I stop now?'"

Wayne looks at me suspiciously. Am I getting at him in some way, in that crafty sarcastic fashion adults talk to children sometimes?

I need to get through to him. It's crucial that Wayne stops behaving like a toddler having a temper tantrum whenever he's asked to do something he doesn't want to do.

Quickly, before he loses interest, I gather a few soft toys together from around the room.

"Look! All the teddies are at school, in their class. Here's Big Teddy..."

"Not Big Teddy. He's Honey."

"Right. Here's Honey. He's the teacher. And these others are the children in the class. What are their names?

"Ray Rabbit, Waggy, Fluff, Sima..."

"Okay. I'll be teacher, I'm being Honey. I'm going to ask Sima to write some numbers down on this piece of paper." I take Sima's paw and place a crayon in it. Sima writes all the numbers up to 10, but when I ask him to write 11, he flings the pencil across the room.

"Oh Sima," I say sadly. "That's not very clever. What should you say when you're getting a bit tired of doing something?"

"Don't know," says Sima.

"Can you help him say the right words, Wayne?"

Wayne shakes his head, sucking his thumb. For a moment he looks exactly like Bonnie. He watches my face, half-smiling. "Let's say it together. Ready, steady go! 'I'm tired, can I stop now, please teacher?' Oh dear, I can't hear you, Sima. Can you say it a bit louder? 'I'm – tired. Can – I – stop – now?'"

This time Wayne joins in. Now he wants to be the teacher. I pretend to be each of the class in turn. Wayne orders me to write, but I forget the magic words. Wayne prompts me. I vary the phrasing: 'It's a bit too hard – can you help me a bit?' I'm not sure whether he thinks it's just another game, or whether he might be getting some sense of what I'm after. At the very least, he'll understand that there's another way of reacting, when life gets tough. And it's fun, playing on the floor like this. For a moment, Wayne's stopped being a terrible toddler and has become a normal, rather endearing six-year-old.

After work, I call in to see Wayne's class teacher. I'm curious to know what she thinks is behind Wayne's bizarre behaviour. For example, might it be frustration at being behind the rest of his class with reading, writing and number work? Or is it the other way round: the hyperactivity is actually causing the learning delay?

The teacher, a bright-eyed young woman in her twenties, is busy putting up a display about dinosaurs on the classroom walls. She welcomes me in a rich, warm voice and says she won't be a minute, but she has to finish this before tomorrow morning. There's going to be a class trip to 'Dinosaur World'. She moves quickly and purposefully around the room. I admire her energy at the end of the day. I feel sad that Wayne will miss such an enjoyable outing, and I wonder how he could fail to respond to the charm and obvious dedication of this teacher. She sits me down in one of the little chairs, and I watch her pinning up the posters and the children's work with deft, practiced movements.

She introduces herself as Ann Harding, and immediately launches into an apology for suspending Wayne. She'd felt terrible about it, but she was at the end of her tether. It was after a four-week period during which Wayne spent the whole time throwing things around and hitting other children

She shows me samples of the little work he'd managed to do. In his English work-book, he'd written a few simple words in very large, wobbly printing, with many letters back to front, upside down, and with no gaps between the words. Yet wasn't this fairly common with 'beginner writers', I ask her? In reply, she shows me a story by her 'best' pupil. This little girl has written a whole page about a greedy monster – all in complete sentences, with neat, even writing and near-perfect spelling.

"That's totally amazing!" The child must be a genius!

"Yes," concedes Ann. "She *is* very good, but she's by no means exceptional."

"Do you think Wayne might have a specific problem? Dyslexia, for example?"

"It's too early to know for sure. True, his writing is more at a Reception class level than a Year 2 standard, but that could well be because he's so hyperactive. He's not getting the practice which is crucial at this stage. So he's falling further and further behind. It's a vicious circle."

"What's the rest of his work like?"

"He's quite quick at number work." Ann flips through one of his maths workbooks. "There's not much in here. He can do number bonds up to ten, even to twenty. But he hates to write the sums down. He starts fidgeting and playing up."

"What about other activities? Does he like making things, drawing, music..?"

"He loves building Lego models. And he's a star when we have our percussion band sessions, especially on the drum. He hates drawing or painting. He just messes about and disrupts the other children. He's got worse over the last month."

"That's interesting. Do you think it's because of their move? The family moved house three months ago."

Ann ponders over this. "It's possible, but I don't think so. Wayne was thrilled with the move. He seemed to love the new house – all the space, after being cooped up in a small flat. Plus he kept telling me about the friends he'd made in the village. At that stage, he was very lively, and sometimes difficult to control. But not manic – and *vicious*."

"So you think it all started about a month ago – the really bad behaviour?"

"Yes, and it was quite sudden. It almost happened overnight."

"Do you think it's something to do with his diet?" I tell Ann about the luridly coloured drink Wayne and Bonnie had in their break yesterday.

"That certainly wouldn't help. I've also noticed that he often doesn't have breakfast, so by ten o'clock he's starving, and reaching into his lunch-box for a chocolate bar."

"So his blood-sugar level would be going up and down?"

"Yes. But to be fair, he's not the only one. You should see what some of the children have in their lunch boxes! Pappy white bread with chocolate spread, crisps, sweets, biscuits, chocolate bars…"

"He'd be better off having a cooked school lunch, wouldn't he? He'd be entitled to free meals."

Ann snorts. "Have you been in schools lately? The school dinners are *appalling!* Fish fingers, and *turkey twizzlers*! I dread to think what part of the turkey goes into that rubbish." She rolls her eyes with horror and disgust, as if imagining the contents of the witches' cauldron in Macbeth. "And chips … chips with everything, every day."

"Not very nourishing, and very fattening."

"It's a scandal! Someone ought to start a campaign against it. The trouble is, we teachers see what's going on – we see what the children are eating – yet we're too exhausted to protest. What we need is someone with time and energy and vision to start a public outcry…"

"With enough *chutzpah* to take it to government level…"

"Exactly! But the parents need educating too. It's a massive problem…" Ann's warming to her theme, and I listen. This is evidently a subject she feels passionately about. She calms down enough to tell me about the projects the class are doing, and I make some notes. I'd like Wayne to do what his classmates are doing, as far as possible.

I thank her for all her help, and add, "I don't know how you keep sane, with thirty children to keep tabs on!"

"I don't! I'm heading for my first nervous breakdown. I've booked it for the end of June and beginning of July – Wimbledon fortnight!"

I drive home, deep in thought. Wayne still remains a mystery. I'm not too bothered about his immature writing. After all, he's not yet seven. On the continent, formal schooling doesn't start until that age. Before that, children play outside, ride their bikes, run about. Inside, they build towers, paint, make up their own games. They're free to explore their environment in an unstructured and pleasurable way. Yet, when they *are* taught reading and writing, two years later than their British counterparts, they learn surprisingly fast. By the time they're eight or nine, there's little difference between their performance and that of their peers this side of the Channel. As a bonus, they've had two years' extra play! Why, in this country, do we insist on such an early start? And then pile on yet more pressure by making them sit SATS at seven?[1]

Wayne seems bright enough. Just because he has immature writing doesn't mean he has a learning disability. It could be something as simple as delayed grapho-motor coordination. This often rights itself with practice and maturity. On the other hand, if there *is* a problem, it will be need to be addressed as soon as possible, and with specialist help.

It's a puzzle. Wayne's like a puppet whose strings have become all tangled up. If we can untangle them, we can find out which strings are moving which bits of him. Maybe some are missing, or need adjusting?

I'm also mystified by his mother's hostility toward me. Almost without exception, other parents – only too glad to share the problem of a recalcitrant, excluded youngster – do all they can to provide a suitable and calm learning environment. But Mrs Lewis seems to go out of her way to make things difficult for me. She seems to resent my presence as an intrusion. I can't understand the woman. She's making it far, far harder for Wayne. Somehow, I've got to get through to her, so that she understands we're both on the same side.

Wednesday, 21st January. Wayne lives in a small village about four miles out of town. His home is idyllically situated, being almost the last house along a very quiet road. Opposite, there are no buildings, just a willow-fringed stream, crossed by a wooden bridge. Over on the other bank, a stile leads into a meadow, lush with long, dew-dropped grass and clumps of celandine.

Just now, I'm prowling about by the bank, hoping I can't be spotted from the Lewis's house. I'm trying to find not-too-obvious places to hide clues for the treasure hunt. So far, I've Sellotaped pieces of card to low branches, stones, and to the side of the first step up to the bridge. On each card, I've written instructions which lead to the next clue – for example, the clue by the bridge will read: 'look under the top bar of the stile'.

Yesterday's hunt, in the Lewis's back garden, was a spectacular flop. I'd written some words – 'leaf, grass, shed, etc.' on cards, and let Wayne and Bonnie loose to hunt for these items. It was a fine, sunny day, and I'd reckoned I was on to a winner. I misjudged Wayne's capacity for mischief. It took precisely five minutes for him to find all the items on the cards. Then, bored, he swung on the rickety shed door and pulled it right off its hinges. He followed this by padlocking Bonnie into the large wire enclosure, which I discovered was Brandy's den. Brandy had been penned in there by Mrs Lewis, and wanted to get out. So did Bonnie, thus quadrupling the volume of noise: screams and frantic barking. Neighbours peering out of windows, Bonnie in floods of tears, Mrs Lewis storming out of the house asking me why I couldn't control her children.

---

1 *Except for Wales, where SATS have now been abolished for seven-year-olds.*

Today's effort has to be better. I need to redeem myself. I tape the last clue to a twig of pussy willow and hurry across the road to the house. Mrs Lewis opens the door po-faced without a word of greeting. She nods in the direction of the living room and goes upstairs. To my delight, the TV and the computer are both off! And Wayne's sitting quietly on the settee with his arms folded across his chest, in 'perfect angel' pose. There's no sign of Bonnie, though I'm half expecting her to leap out from behind the settee any moment. What a turnaround!

"Well done, Wayne. This is the first time that you've been ready and waiting for me. That definitely deserves a smiley face sticker."

Wayne stares at me. Am I imagining it, or is there a hint of disappointment in his expression?

"What are we going to do?" asks Wayne.

"Later, if you behave yourself, we're going to have a treasure hunt by the stream." Wayne jumps up and heads for the door. Seeing my warning glare, he sits down again. This is progress! "But first," I say, "just look at this. It's new. I want you to be the first to try it out for me, to see if it works."

It's a large slate with a magnetic pencil that, on contact with the magnetic surface of the slate, writes or draws with the lightest pressure from the user. It's ideal for the erratic letter formations of beginner writers. They can feel the movement as they write, without having to press hard to make a mark; they can experiment with letter shapes, mess about and doodle, and erase it all in a flash. For reluctant writers, some of whom have developed almost a phobia about committing pencil to paper, it's an instrument of freedom.

For a few minutes, Wayne makes marks and designs with the ring block and the solid round block that come with the slate. I get him to scribble with the pencil. How about a picture? Which letters of the alphabet does he know? Can he write any of the words he wrote yesterday?

As soon as he starts to fidget, I write a word in large letters. "Can you do what the word says?"

"J-u-m-p!" Wayne manages to sound the word out. Gleefully, he does so.

"Now another one. What does this word tell you to do?"

"S-k-i-p!"

He's released some of the pent-up fidgets. Let's see if he can manage some reading and writing, camouflaged in game form. I've prepared a sheet of card with ten instructions on it. Next to each one is a little sketch of the action required. Wayne now has to choose one of the word instructions, and copy it on to the slate.

"I have to do whatever you tell me, even if it's difficult!" I tell him.

He writes 'Jump', and adds, 'You've got to do it really high!'

I leap high in the air, forgetting that the last time I did this was over forty years ago, at school, in the sports day high-jump. There's a horrible crunch in my knees as I land.

"Ouch!" I wince. Wayne's eyes gleam with satisfaction.

We take turns to crawl, clap, sneeze, snooze, hide, run and slide. It's the first time I've seen Wayne animated. He seems to become 'himself' when he's allowed a lot of movement. Yet it's not the random rushing around typical of so-called ADHD children. Wayne's quite controlled, and he's showing that he can concentrate well enough when he wants to. I'm beginning to doubt whether he does have ADHD after all.

The treasure hunt proves to be more complicated than I'd expected. I suddenly realise that I can't just wander off with Wayne into the countryside, even though it's just across the road. Mrs Lewis has to come too. And that means bringing Bonnie. And Brandy, who would bark pitifully if left behind, annoying the neighbours – again.

Hastily, while Wayne's having his break, I prepare another set of clues. On the pretext of going out to the car to get something, I nip over the road and secrete this second set, in different hidey-holes, for Bonnie and her mother. Knowing that Bonnie would do everything she could to spoil things for Wayne by getting in his way, I've divided the family into two teams: Bonnie and her mother v. Wayne and me. There are two separate trails.

"Now, it's not a *race*," I emphasise, as we cross the road to the stream. "It doesn't matter which team finishes first, because both get a prize at the end."

The clues are so simple and precise that Wayne manages to read them with only a little prompting from me. He's raptly attentive, fascinated by the whole game – until, with a war cry, his mother suddenly moves the hunt on to another level. She whoops and shrieks at Bonnie to run faster. I call to her to slow down. I'm trying to point out to Wayne some tiny fish swimming amongst the reeds in the stream; and look! Here's one of the first signs of spring – a glorious fountain of snowdrops massed together on the banks. Left to ourselves, we'd be able to amble along, making discoveries, absorbing the beauty and peace of the scene.

However, Wayne wants to keep up with the opposing team.

"They're winning!" he says fretfully.

Mrs Lewis is racing towards the finish as if her life depended on it. And Brandy, all his rescue instincts suddenly coming to the fore, charges round and round in circles. He barks excitedly, certain that we want him to sniff out some hapless villager, lying injured and senseless, buried deep in the long grass.

"Come *on,* Bonnie!" shrieks Mrs Lewis. "Hurry *up*! Don't be so slow – we're on the last lap now!"

Bonnie runs over to us. "Look, I've found all these. How many have you found, Wayne?"

Crestfallen, Wayne counts the four cards clutched in his hand.

"It's not a *race*, Bonnie." I say, for the umpteenth time, through gritted teeth.

But Bonnie doesn't believe me. How can she, with her mother in full battle cry, her eyes glittering with manic determination as she drags Bonnie by the hand: from bridge, to overhanging branch, to ditch. She literally leaves no stone unturned.

"Slow down, Mrs Lewis!" I call. "It's not a competition. The children need time to notice things, to enjoy nature—"

"FINISHED!" she pants. "Look, we found the last clue. We found them all. Didn't we, Bonnie? Didn't we do well?" She's flushed and exultant. "That was good. I enjoyed that. I like being first!"

"No one is first in this game," I repeat, sternly, beginning to hate the sound of my own voice. "*Everyone's* a winner." Holy Moses, what drives the woman to behave like this, her triumph out of all proportion to our little game?

"Come on, Wayne," I sigh. "Let's find the next clue." I take his hand. Bonnie wants to come and 'help'. Luckily, her mother calls her over to throw some sticks for Brandy to chase in the meadow.

I just about manage to keep Wayne interested until the 'treasure' is found, in the hollow of an old oak tree. He grabs the chocolate lion, wrapped in gold foil. A happy smile lights his face.

"*I* won, didn't I?"

"We all won. But you were the best player, because you read all the clues by yourself."

"We're going back now," Mrs Lewis shouts from the bridge.

"Right, we'll be back in a moment," I call.

There's a pony in a field on the far side of the meadow. We race across to say hello. I pick a clump of the long grass and hold out my hand between the wires of the fencing. Wayne watches the pony's mouth curl, with delicate precision, around the tasty morsel.

"Do you want to feed him, Wayne? Look, you have to hold out your hand, and keep it flat, like this…"

Wayne shakes his head, suddenly very fearful.

"How about patting his neck, then? Like this… I can hold you up high…"

Wayne shakes his head again, watchful and uncertain. He's turned pale. I'm puzzled. Surely, living in the country, he's seen many ponies. There must be several children in the village who ride – there's a riding school nearby. Now he's grabbing my hand, and pulling me, urgently, away from the fence.

"I want to go home."

As we near the bridge, he looks again at the pony, and starts to run.

Back at the house, I let Wayne choose what he wants to do. He's done well today. He tells me he wants to play on the computer, but I stand firm on this one. The computer will have to wait till the session has finished. He wanders round the room, picking toys up and then flinging them down. He seems to have regressed again. Then he goes over to his toy garage under the window, and lines up the cars in a queue for petrol.

Suddenly, with a violent push, he scatters the cars. He dives into his toy box, and grabs some farm animals. He throws them all on to the floor. For a moment, he looks at them speculatively, his head on one side.

He picks up the horse. With a sharp, slicing movement of his finger, he slits its throat.

"There! You're deaded!" He kicks it viciously across the room.

I'm shocked, by both the action, and the murderous expression on his face.

"Wayne! What on earth was that about…?"

But Wayne has run off into the kitchen, calling to his mother that he wants a drink. And what bad luck – there's no time to pursue this. I've got to leave, *now*. Thomas's mother has asked me to come half an hour earlier as he has a doctor's appointment at three o'clock. Even without my lunch break it'll be a dash to get over there in time to give him a full tuition session.

Yet Wayne has unnerved me. A word pops into my mind and I censure it immediately – it's horribly inappropriate for such a young child, but it persists until I confront it head on: there's something chillingly *psychopathic* about his behaviour.

Monday, 26th January. "*'Now then,' said the magician, 'Listen to me. Some of the things in this room are part of my magic. If you come to see me, there are some things you can touch, and some things which you mustn't touch…'*"

I glance up from the story book. "Wayne, are you listening to me?"

Wayne's staring at the TV. It blinks, mockingly, beckoning his attention. I suppose I could just march over and turn it off. Yet some deep-seated sense of propriety always stops me turning off other people's appliances, without permission, in their own homes. It feels intrusive, like rearranging their furniture, or nosing into their cupboards. Besides, Mrs Lewis is here, too. She's at the computer, playing Patience.

I can't believe this is happening. I don't know whether to laugh or cry. There's something Kafkaesque about the scene – the woman's just sitting there, as if rooted. She's not even trying to prove a point, not casting surly, territorial looks in my direction. She's ignoring me completely. No, she's just *there,* as if she has every right, as if *this* is normality!

This has been going on for ten minutes, and Wayne is totally distracted. His eyes hover between the television, which unfortunately is showing a cartoon, and his mother's computer game. It's all quite surreal. For a moment I feel like an anthropologist landed in the midst of some previously unknown tribe, with a mission to learn their ways and customs. If I can only approach this scenario in the spirit of detached, scientific enquiry...

Wayne jumps up and dashes across the room to the computer. He leans over his mother's shoulder and points to the screen.

"Look, Mum! You can put the Jack on the Queen. There!"

As if on cue, a shrill voice pipes up: "Wayne, do your lesson. *Bad boy.* Wayne's being a *very* bad boy today, isn't he?"

I'd forgotten all about Little-Miss-Perfect, playing 'picnics' with her dolls behind an armchair. Bonnie's the last straw. I stop being an anthropologist. Shaking with fury, I leap to my feet.

"Mrs Lewis, this is impossible! I can't teach Wayne in these conditions!"

She swivels round. "What's the problem?"

"I've already told you – and you agreed – that the computer and television would be *off* when I arrived. How can I teach him when his eyes are distracted by what you're doing?"

"Bloody hell. I'm just sitting here quietly, aren't I?"

"You shouldn't be here at all!"

Her jaw drops. "You can't tell me what to do in my own house!"

"Mrs Lewis..." My voice wobbles with rage. "We've been through this many times. On Wednesday, it was bliss when I arrived. Both the TV and the computer were already off. So we were able to start tuition right away without wasting valuable time. And I noticed that Wayne behaved much, much better after such a good start. If you could turn them off on Wednesday, why can't you do it every day?"

Mrs Lewis stares at me blankly. "*I* never turned it off. Wayne must've."

Wayne's eyes ping-pong between his mother and me. I ask him, "Did *you* turn the computer and TV off on Wednesday?"

"Yes." Wayne gives me a sulky look. "And you didn't notice. You didn't give me a smiley face for it. So I didn't do it today."

"Oh, Wayne, I'm so sorry! I thought your mother had turned it off, so I didn't thank you. But I *did* notice, and I was very pleased. Really!"

Tight-lipped, Mrs Lewis turns off the computer with exaggerated sweeping movements.

"There! Satisfied?"

"Actually, no. I need to know that you will take responsibility for this. If Wayne turns them off, that's good, but I'd like you to check each time, please."

Mrs Lewis sucks in a long breath between clenched teeth. She averts her eyes as she moves towards the television and turns that off, too.

"Mrs Lewis, *please* can we have some agreement about…"

But she's gone. A second later, I hear the kitchen door slammed shut.

"Well, Wayne. You heard all that. If Mum forgets to turn off the computer and the TV I'll be very pleased if *you* remember. And each time you do, you'll get an extra smiley face for being so helpful. Okay?"

"Okay. Can I get one for Wednesday?"

"Of course." I make a big show of entering an extra smiley face in my folder. "And Bonnie, you go and play in the kitchen, like we agreed. If you're extra good, and don't disturb Wayne, I might play a quick game with you at the end. But Wayne will have to be good, too!"

Bonnie stands still for a moment, sucking her thumb, one hand on the back of the armchair. Then, with a look that plainly says: 'I'll be back, you can't get rid of me that easily!' she glides slowly out of the room.

This is all such a struggle, and now Wayne's restless. He wanders around the room aimlessly. He starts building a tower with his blocks, then gives it a savage kick, sending the blocks into the far corners of the room. I'd been hoping to do some writing with him today, but I'll have to abandon the idea. How can I *use* this restlessness, profitably? What I mustn't do is 'reward' his bad behaviour, immediately after it happens, by letting him off lightly – by avoiding learning situations which he finds challenging. That would be colluding with him.

Yet I'm stumped for ideas. I let him play for a while. Then I get out a game I've been saving for an emergency such as this. I open it and get out some picture cards. The pictures have words written underneath. Wayne edges a little closer. He glances at me truculently under long, fair lashes.

"What are you doing?"

"I'm sorting some cards. But it's a secret."

"Why?"

"Because," I reply.

"I can keep secrets."

"I don't know if I should tell you. Only well-behaved children keep secrets."

"I'm well 'haved. Look!" Wayne sits next to me on the settee, folding his arms across his chest.

"Well. It's for a game, but I'm not sure whether you're good enough. Let me see…" I look down at the cards and then at Wayne. "You see, to play the game, we have to look at these cards first."

"They're too hard. They've got words on." Wayne uncrosses his arms and stands up again.

"You don't have to read them all. They've got pictures on as well as words. I just want to know if you can see what's happening in the pictures. Each one shows something that's going to make a special sound. The words underneath are to help us if we don't recognise the object." I show him the first card. "I'll do the action. If you guess what I'm doing, can you make the sound this makes?"

I pull down on an invisible chain above my head. "Can you guess what I'm doing?"

Wayne looks at the card, then at me, puzzled. "You don't do it like that. You pull on the handle, like *this*. Like *this* handle, in the picture, see?"

"Oh dear, I forgot. I've got an old-fashioned toilet, you see. But well done, you understood what was happening in the picture. What would a flushing toilet sound like?"

Wayne makes a whooshing sound.

"That's right! Now this one?"

Wayne brushes his teeth with an invisible toothbrush. With the other hand he scratches lightly on the card I've given him.

"That's very good teeth-cleaning, and just the right sound. Your teeth must be sparkling. Can I see? Now, for this card, you'll have to be very quiet. Can you hear the clock ticking on the mantelpiece? Well, that is what the clock in the picture will sound like. Because I've got a tape here, that plays all the sound-effects of what's happening in these pictures."

At last I've caught his attention, but he's still jittery, his bottom bouncing up and down on the settee. Tremors pulsate through the cushions like the rumblings of an earthquake.

"Can you help me spread all the cards out on the floor?"

There's over a hundred of them: flushing toilets, teeth-cleaning children, babies crying, pianos playing, a wedding, a police car – several of each type.

"Have a good look at all the cards and see if you can work out what's happening in each. When you're ready, I'll start the tape. We'll both play together. As soon as you hear the sound on the tape, look at all the cards and pick up the one with the picture that matches that sound. The winner's the one who gets the most cards."

Wayne waits expectantly, his eyes shining. (This game has saved the day for me many times, when all else has failed.)

We're off. I'm still fumbling around, trying to distinguish between the wedding march and a disco band, but Wayne immediately forges ahead, arms whirling and flailing like windmills as his hands search and grab. He whoops triumphantly as he matches sounds and pictures with unerring accuracy. Soon his pile is three times as big as mine. Long before the end of the tape, he's found all the cards – there are none left on the floor – and he's sitting back on his heels, listening to the repeats.

"Wayne – you're amazing! I can't believe you've matched so many cards. Look at my pile and look at yours!"

Wayne accepts this accolade graciously, nodding and smiling like a maestro bowing to a devoted following at the Last Night at the Proms. It all comes so naturally to him that he doesn't see what the fuss is about. Yet his skill is quite awesome. I've played this game with children of all ages and abilities. Never before has a child shown such an exceptional ear for distinguishing different sounds with such accuracy and speed. My mind's already racing ahead with possibilities and plans for him. Music lessons are a priority.

"Can we play it again?" asks Wayne, eagerly.

"Yes, of course. I'll see if I can do better this time!"

Unfortunately, before I can shuffle the cards and spread them out again, Bonnie bounces into the room.

"Mum's got to go out," she announces importantly.

"So?"

"So, I have to be in here. You have to look after me."

Before I can digest this, Mrs Lewis pokes her head round the door.

"I'm just popping out, right? Down to the shop. I'll be back in a minute."

"Hang on! You can't do that. I mean, you have to be here."

"Christ, it's only for a minute. If I take her, we'll be twice as long. She'll be nagging me for sweets."

"But you can't take her either. I mean…" I'm starting to gabble. "You have to be here, if I'm with Wayne."

"For Godssake, you won't even notice I've gone, I'll be so quick. I just need to get Wayne some breakfast."

"I'm hungry!" whinges Wayne, rubbing his tummy.

"So'm I, very, very hungry," whimpers Bonnie, imitating Wayne.

"But it's eleven-thirty!" I snap. "Haven't they had anything at all to eat this morning?"

"Nothing. Wayne wouldn't get up. I had to drag him out of bed. Then he had to get washed and dressed. I kept telling him, 'you mustn't be late for your teacher'. And I'd run out of cereals, anyway."

"Surely there must be something in your kitchen that the children could eat without you having to go to the shop?"

Again, I'm being dragged away from the main issue, which is about not leaving pupil and tutor in the house, unaccompanied. I can feel myself hurtling, head first, down the helter-skelter of this woman's crazy reasoning.

Mrs Lewis shrugs. "Nope. We've run out of coco-pops."

"Milk? Bread?"

"No." She jabs her finger at Wayne. "He won't drink milk on its own. And I'm out of bread."

"But – but – there must be something in your cupboards…?"

"Nope. So I'll be off then, if it's okay by you…"

"NO!" I exclaim, "It's not okay at all. It's against the rules!"

"Rules?" Mrs Lewis curls her lip. "We're not at school, are we?"

"Those are the rules of the Education Department. They apply to all children out of school. They are in place to protect their vulnerability…" As usual, my pomposity grows in direct proportion to how much blathering nonsense I hear falling from this woman's lips. "I repeat, every child must have a parent, or someone *in loco parentis*, present in the house while tuition is taking place. I don't intend to break these rules, Mrs Lewis, which are there in the best interests of your children." I draw myself up to my full height, and finish my speech with a flourish of my hand.

"So, you expect my children to go hungry, do you?" snarls their mother. Bonnie starts to cry, crocodile tears. "I'm so hungry!" She peers up at her mother through her fingers. Then she gives me a look which says: 'that puts *you* in your place!'

"And I'm starving!" wails Wayne.

"There are only thirty minutes left of this session, Mrs Lewis. Perhaps you could find a stale crust of bread and a glass of water for Wayne. After all, if he's starving, he won't be too fussy…"

Mrs Lewis explodes air through her teeth. "Tssshhh! Come on Bonnie!" She leaves with her parting shot. "Just wait till I tell your office about this. It's cruelty, that's what it is. Cruelty to children!"

"Do. Please tell the office. I'd like them to understand the extreme conditions I have to contend with…"

Mrs Lewis doesn't listen. She drags Bonnie off towards the kitchen.

"Shall we have another round of the game now, Wayne?"

"No, I'm too hungry," he whines.

"Right. I'll read you a story instead."

I grab the first book from the pile in my bag. "Once upon a time, there was a VERY hungry giant. He was always so hungry that he ate little children for dinner and tea. Especially those who were fussy about their food…"

Wednesday, 28th January. As I drive along the road towards Wayne's house, I catch sight of Mrs Lewis and Bonnie coming out of the village shop. As they live only a few doors down, it's not worth stopping to give them a lift. I park the car, and we walk up the garden path together. Inside, Brandy's barking loudly.

A thought strikes me: "Where's Wayne? Is he still in the shop?"

"He's getting dressed – he'll be down in a minute. You can go in and wait." Mrs Lewis nods towards the living room.

She goes into the kitchen and I hear a riotous greeting from Brandy. As I unpack books and games, I'm feeling very uneasy. Wayne's just been left alone in the house. Would Brandy protect him from any danger? It's unlikely that there'd be an intruder, in this quiet location, but what about accidents? Children do such unpredictable things in the twinkling of an eye. What if Wayne fell downstairs, or tried to light the gas fire?

The computer and the television are both off, thank goodness. Wayne hasn't yet appeared, though I heard him come downstairs five minutes ago.

I knock on the kitchen door. The children are both sitting at the kitchen table. They're munching a Mars bar and washing it down with a large beaker of Coca-Cola.

"You said he'd got to have his breakfast first," says Mrs Lewis, "so he's having it. That's why I was in the shop, to buy his breakfast before you come." She flashes me a virtuous look, as if to say: 'There, I've done what you wanted. What more can I do?'

She could do a lot more than feed Wayne sugary empty calories, guaranteed to bring on a mega rush of hyperactivity. Just now, he appears fairly calm, but how long before the sugar begins to take effect? Today, I'm going to see. I look at my watch. I'll time it.

Wayne slides down from his chair. Bonnie follows suit.

"You stay here with Mum, Bonnie." I avoid her mother's eyes, but I can feel her indignation boring into my back as I usher Wayne out of the kitchen.

Today, I want to get Wayne reading, to increase his confidence before he returns to school. If he can find some area in which he can just hold his own, he might be more manageable in class. (I've also found an area in which he might actually excel – music. I've had some ideas about that too, but I need to talk to his mother first.)

Here's a book I just know he'll love. "Shall we read about the Griffle, Wayne? You like monsters, don't you? Well, this one's very friendly."

The *Puddle Lane* series has the story written on the left-hand page for the adults to read aloud to the child. On the opposite page, under the illustration, is a very simplified version of the story, one or two sentences in big print for the child to read.

At first, Wayne clamps his lips together when I point to the 'children's page'. I sound the words out very slowly for him, telling him he doesn't have to read if he doesn't want to, but soon the story sweeps him up. His eyes begin to shine. He joins in, hesitantly, just a random word here and there. Then as we reach the end, he reads the whole of the last page. It's only three sentences, but what a big step. I can feel goose pimples on my arms – that little *frisson* of delight when a child, in spite of himself, gets so caught up in a story that somehow the words spill out of him and suddenly, like magic, he's reading!

"Would you like to choose another book?" I ask him.

"This one. About the green cat."

"'Tim Turns Green'. That's the title. This is a good story too. It's about magic!"

"I know a *real* magician." Wayne begins telling me about a friend's recent birthday party. As he talks, his movements become more and more expansive. He waves an imaginary wand. He picks up a soft toy – a rabbit – from the floor and stuffs it down the front of his T-shirt. Then, with a yell and a wave of his wand, he makes it pop out of my left ear.

Suddenly, he throws the rabbit to the floor. He stamps on it, hard, with a ferocious expression on his face.

"There, you're dead!"

Now he's running round and round the room. For a moment I stare at him, quite mystified. Then I remember. I look at my watch. It's taken just fifteen minutes for Wayne's breakfast to make him completely 'hyper'. Yet I'm still not entirely convinced. Would it take that long for the sugar to work into his system? I need to do some more research on this before I jump to conclusions. Perhaps, in the cause of scientific discovery, I should eat a chocolate bar – no, two, because I'm bigger – for breakfast, with a cup of strong coffee, and see what happens? Tempting.

Meanwhile, what to do with Wayne? He's now jumping back and forth from the settee to the two armchairs, playing 'pirates'. Nothing I say or do calms him. He's a volcano in full flow, driven by his internal, fiery energy.

A lamp stand bites the dust, crashing down on to a Lego tower.

"What's going on?" Mrs Lewis stands in the doorway, arms akimbo. Behind her, Bonnie peeps round, wide-eyed.

"You can't control him, can you?" gloats Mrs Lewis.

I prepare to do battle. "How often does Wayne have a chocolate bar and cola for breakfast before he goes to school?"

"You what?" Her jaw drops.

"It's taken exactly fifteen minutes to transform the calm little boy I saw when I arrived, into a…into a…"

"A stupid gorilla?" suggests Bonnie, helpfully.

Yes. Nice one, Bonnie. "Is that Wayne's normal breakfast?" I ask.

"It might be. Most days. But that's not—"

"And for lunch?" I persist. "What does he eat?"

"He takes a packed lunch. But don't you try to—"

"And what's in that?"

There's a sudden silence. Mrs Lewis glowers at me.

"Sandwiches, sandwiches!" shouts Wayne, jumping up and down on the settee like a trampoline. "And choc bars," he adds, at the height of the next bounce. "Fizzy drink" – bounce – "crisps" – bounce – "jammy biscuits" – bounce – "jammy doughnut". He sinks down, suddenly exhausted.

"He never eats his sandwiches, does he, Mum? He always leaves them in his lunch-box," says Bonnie, putting the boot in and providing the final missing link in the evidence, neatly tying up the case beyond all reasonable doubt.

"So, Wayne has nothing but sugary, empty calories all day long?"

"Listen," says his mother, peevishly. "What's all this got to do with you? You're here for his education. I knew he'd be better off at school. I keep telling them, at your office, you can't manage him, either."

Thursday, 29th January. Wayne's not ready when I arrive. The television and computer are on. I turn off the computer at the plug, and switch off the TV. Sighing, I wait. A few minutes later, Wayne slides round the open door. He looks subdued.

"Have you had any breakfast, Wayne?"

"I'm not hungry." He gives me an uncertain look.

I leave it. We'll have a break halfway through the session. He can have something then, if necessary. I'm trying to structure his routine as closely as possible to how it would be at school.

For half-an-hour, things run smoothly. I persuade Wayne to write down some of the vocabulary from yesterday's sound-effects game, letting him choose the words. Soon, he has a respectably long list in his workbook: 'smash, glass, police car, bang, cuckoo, dog, bark, drum…' We play the game again. Today, Wayne's even quicker at matching sound and picture-card. He wins once more, easily.

"I'm hungry now," he says.

"Right. Go and ask Mum for something to eat and drink."

A few moments later, he wanders back in with a chocolate bar in one hand and a bottle of fizzy red liquid in the other. My heart sinks.

Maths next, using the counting blocks. I encourage him to do some simple subtraction. We sit on the floor with some of the teddies, having a picnic. The blocks, I tell him, are pretend Smarties. Each teddy starts with twenty blocks. They take it in turns to throw the dice, and to 'eat' the number of Smarties indicated on the dice. The first one to eat all twenty is the winner.

"We should have *real* Smarties," complains Wayne. "This isn't much fun."

I'm sitting with my back to the French windows that open out to the garden. The sun bathes me in a warm glow. It's the first time I've *felt* sunshine this year, and I'm enjoying the sensation. Wayne's been doing surprisingly well. His counting is getting better. He no longer misses out thirteen every time he counts to twenty. Tomorrow I'll see how he gets on with writing sums down. Maybe we...

"Wayne – what's the matter?"

Suddenly, Wayne's clenching his fist and fidgeting. He keeps looking up from the blocks, peering over my left shoulder and scowling at something.

Too lazy to turn round, I say, "Wayne, it's your turn to throw the dice."

It must be the chocolate rush starting, I decide. But now he stands up and stares out through the French windows into the garden. I follow his gaze.

His mother is sitting just outside, on the wide raised step below the windows. With her is Bonnie. Mrs Lewis is reading, very loudly, to Bonnie from a large picture book. She has her arm round her daughter, who's nestling in very close to her, and obviously revelling in this unusual amount of attention.

How tactless and mis-timed! Wayne must feel very left out of this cosy duo. Couldn't she have waited till after the tuition, and then read to both of them? Bonnie turns and catches her brother's eye. She sticks out her tongue at him. Instead of telling Bonnie off, her mother hugs her even closer. Then she, too, turns and stares through the window at both of us. She narrows her eyes. It's unmistakeable. The woman is deliberately needling her son. She *wants* to make him feel left out.

Wayne lets out a yell. It's a strange sound – rage mixed with anguish, like the indignant, surprised yelp of an animal in sudden pain. He springs to his feet, sending teddies and blocks flying. He picks up one of the bears, and flings it across the room. He dashes over to the windows, and bangs on the glass. He stamps his foot. He's now in a mega-fury that doesn't abate until his mother, with calculated slowness, dawdles through the story to the end. Even then, she continues to sit, hugging Bonnie, sharing little jokes with her, completely ignoring Wayne.

I stick it out till it's time to finish. I never abandon a session. It makes the child feel either too powerful, or rejected by the tutor. Yet whatever I do won't help Wayne today. He's feeling utterly abandoned by his own mother.

Friday, 30th January – 2 a.m. I'm sitting slumped at my kitchen table. I've been unable to sleep a wink, wondering what to do about Wayne – and his mother. Only pride is stopping me from resigning from his case.

Twice in my career I've given up on children, and each time I felt horrible afterwards. One child was thirteen-year-old Connor, whose language was so foul it would have shocked the most hardened recidivist. On the day Connor threatened me with a crowbar while calling me a bloody motherfucker, I decided enough was enough. My other failure was a GCSE girl, Erin. While I waxed lyrical about the wonderful imagery of Seamus Heaney, she sat at the table in a drug-induced coma, not taking in a word I was saying. I could have coped with Erin on her own – on the rare occasions she bothered to get out of bed. It was the bodies of her friends, lying stoned on the floor after last night's party, that got in the way. After each of these retreats, I suffered weeks of guilt, angst and despondency.

But I can't abandon Wayne. He's different – there's a lot of potential there. Underneath the truculent facade, he's a nice kid. Besides, how can I give up on someone so young? It's his mother who's the problem. If I could just win her over, we could all be working together. However, for some peculiar reason of her own, she seems determined not to work with me. We've reached a deadlock situation, and I can't see how it can be resolved. Except, perhaps, by bowing out gracefully and finding another tutor for Wayne, someone who Mrs Lewis feels more kindly disposed to. Yes. That's the only way. I'll ring Sally tomorrow and explain why I can't carry on and can she find someone else.

On the other hand, what about Wayne's feelings? After all, I'm making headway with him – of a sort. Slowly but surely, he's beginning to respond. It might be something as subtle as sitting down quietly for that extra minute. Or trying something he's been too scared to try before. Even the way he looks at me shows there's some rapport between us. If I leave him now, won't he see this as a terrible rejection?

At last, bleary-eyed, I come to a decision. At 4 a.m. I'm sitting at my computer, typing a letter:

Dear Mrs Lewis,

As Wayne's tutor, I have found his home environment almost impossible to teach in. It is preventing Wayne from making the most of the tuition sessions. If he is to make progress, both in his basic subjects, and in the management of his behaviour, I strongly recommend that the following conditions be met:

1. The computer and the television must be turned off *before* I arrive.

2. Wayne must be up and ready for the session.

3. He should have breakfast *before* I arrive.

I do not consider a chocolate bar and Coco-Cola a suitable breakfast for a child with ADHD. Similarly, sugary snacks throughout the day should be limited. Instead, the amount of nourishing food such as fruit and vegetables, wholegrain cereals and bread and pasta should be increased.

4. Bonnie should be kept out of the living room during the session. LEA funding does not include my entertaining her, or giving her childcare, concurrent with Wayne's tuition.

5. Any game you are playing with Bonnie, especially if it is of a distracting nature, should take place out of sight and earshot of Wayne, while he is being tutored. For example, playing with Bonnie just outside the French windows in full

view of Wayne, makes it impossible for him to concentrate and is very unfair on him.

 6. It is totally unacceptable to leave the house at any time while Wayne is being tutored.

Until these conditions are met, Wayne's ADHD is unlikely to improve. And while he remains hyperactive, he will not be able to learn. Therefore his return to school will be impossible until he settles into a pattern of more acceptable behaviour.

Given an improved working environment, I shall of course do everything I can to encourage Wayne's return to school, including the remedial help he needs with basic subjects.

Yours sincerely,

Tutor, Education Department.

Copies to: Sally Copland (Manager), Mrs Mary Holdsworth, Headteacher, Brooke End Primary School, Tom Green, Director of Education.

11.15 a.m. "Mrs Lewis, we need to have a talk. Is there somewhere quiet we could go – *without* the children?"

"I want to come!" says Bonnie, springing out of the living room into the hall, where I've cornered her mother.

"Just for a few minutes, please, Mrs Lewis? It won't take too long." I pop my head round the door, greet Wayne, and ask him to wait for me.

Something in my tone of voice persuades Mrs Lewis that she can't ignore me this time. She gives me a sharp look, and tells Bonnie to go back into the living room and be good, or else. Silently, she leads the way into the kitchen. We sit opposite each other at the table. I launch straight in.

"Mrs Lewis, I've drawn up a list of conditions that will help Wayne. I've already this morning sent a copy to Wayne's headteacher, to my line manager, and to the Director of Education. Would you read through it, please?"

I place one copy in front of her and keep one for myself. She reads through, in silence, stony-faced – until she reaches the list of names at the end. She flinches. There's another long, tense silence. Then she seems to crumple, like a balloon deflating. She puts her head in her hands and stares down at the table. I feel uncomfortable. By naming the other recipients of this letter, I feel as if I've hit below the belt, broken the Queensbury rules. Like threatening to 'tell tales' at school. It's a hollow victory.

For a long while there's no sound, except for Brandy snoring in his basket and the loud ticking of the clock.

"We're on the same side, Mrs Lewis,"

She swallows, avoiding my eyes.

"I want us to work together, for Wayne's sake."

She mumbles something, and I say I didn't quite hear her.

"He should be at school." She snaps, still hostile. For the first time she looks at me directly.

"Of course he should!" I exclaim. How can I get through to her? "He *should* be at school, with his friends. Not in disgrace. Not feeling different from them. And so you can have a break from him, too. All mothers need time for themselves."

Mrs Lewis opens her eyes wide and looks at me with a flash of recognition, as if for the first time I've said something that makes sense to her.

"It's a *job* I want! There's a job in town – at Russell's, you know, the Department Store? Cosmetics. My friend who works there told me about it. Health and Beauty. That's what I was trained in. That's what I did before I had them…" She jabs her thumb in the direction of the living room.

"That must have been very interesting. Was it at Russell's?"

"No, we hadn't moved down here then. It was in Oxford Street. In *London*," she adds, as if explaining the real world to a country bumpkin like me. "I used to advise customers about skin care and make-up and that." She gives me a sharp, appraising look. I'm suddenly conscious of my own unmade-up face and uncared for skin.

"It sounds as if you really enjoyed it."

"I loved it." There's a catch in her voice.

"What was the best thing about it?"

She sniffs, dabbing her nose with the corner of a tea-towel.

"The best thing was earning my own money. And meeting people – the customers. We had some well famous people come in all the time. You know *EastEnders*? And *Coronation Street*? Well, we had actors from them soaps coming in to buy stuff." She mentions a string of names I've never heard of. "You know them?"

I nod eagerly, though I haven't a clue who they are. I haven't even got a television.

"I knew them *personally*. They'd all talk to me, like I was a friend. Not posh at all, they weren't. Then me and the other girls, we'd all meet after work for a drink. We'd have a laugh."

"It must have been a great place to work in, with so many different departments and so many people working there."

"Yes. We were like one big family. There was always something going on. Clubs, Christmas party."

"It sounds fantastic." I mean it. Retail's suddenly become an attractive career move. "So when's this job coming up?"

"After Easter. The girl's going on maternity leave."

"Well, why don't you try for it?"

"What am I going to do with Bonnie?" Mrs Lewis gives me a withering look.

"Won't she be at playgroup by then? She's what, four? She could be there now."

"She started, but she hated it. She used to cry when I left her. Then, she'd just begun to settle down when they threw Wayne out of school. After that she wouldn't go at all. She screamed when I tried to make her. She hated the idea of Wayne being at home with me when she wasn't."

"Oh, what a shame – this job sounds just right for you!"

"I could pay a neighbour, I suppose," says Mrs Lewis pensively, "I just don't care if I don't make much money out of it. Anything to get out of the house! Washing, cooking, mopping up…I'm bloody stuck in this God-forsaken place!"

"Do you hate living here that much?"

"Oh, I dunno. They keep telling me how lucky I am to get this place. I was in a poky little flat, before. No garden. No pets allowed."

"So, no room for Brandy, then?" I chuckle at the image of Brandy crashing around in a tiny flat.

Mrs Lewis smiles for the first time. The atmosphere lightens.

"No, I got him the week after we moved. I'd always wanted a St Bernard."

"So there must be some good things about living here? It's a beautiful spot, with the meadow and the stream opposite."

"Oh, it's okay, I suppose. I like the house. Plenty of space. The kids each have their own room. And the village is all right – I've made a couple of friends here. It's just that it's so far away from everything. I can't get into town to the shops whenever I want to. Can't afford a car. Sometimes I feel so trapped. Do you know what I mean?"

"I do. Children are so demanding. Sometimes you're just longing for some adult conversation…"

"Yes, *yes!* I often go to the village shop not to buy anything but just to talk to Sheila. She runs it. I hear all the goings on in the village…" Mrs Lewis leans forward, lowering her voice, and giving me rather too much information about some neighbours down the road.

There's a sudden squeal from the living room, followed by the ominous sounds of a punch-up. We both prick up our ears for trouble, but it's gone quiet again. The children are being unnaturally good.

"So, are we going to work together from now on?" I ask lightly, trying to hide my anxiety. *If this should fail…*

We face other across the table, like two warring armies across the trenches. What's it to be, a Christmas Day truce with hostilities resuming on the morrow – or a permanent cease-fire?

"Are we on the same side over this, Mrs Lewis? Working together to get Wayne back into school again?"

More squeals come from the living room, followed by muffled giggles. There's a rhythmical banging sound. A percussive tinkle. There's a faint crash – and then a silence. What are they up to?

Mrs Lewis sits stock-still, staring at the wall behind me. Suddenly she waves her hand towards the typed sheet in front of her, with a gesture of surrender mixed with impatience.

"Okay, okay," she sighs. "I'll try to keep to…whatever you said."

"That's great! I just know it will help Wayne – you'll see!"

As we walk towards the living room, I brace myself for the sight of a disaster zone, but the worst that has happened is a smashed coffee cup, its pieces scattered over a wide area of the carpet. Wayne's holding a long piece of wooden Brio track, and Bonnie's got a metal spoon in her hand.

"We've been good," says Wayne, looking guilty.

"*Very* good," Bonnie echoes, wide-eyed.

"I was showing Bonnie the game we played. Making different sounds. Look! If I bang the door it sounds like a drum, and when Bonnie banged the cup it sounded like…"

"Like Tinkerbell! But I banged it too hard and it jumped off the shelf.."

We all look at Mrs Lewis, holding our breath.

"Doesn't matter. It was chipped, anyway." She says calmly. "Now, get on with your work, Wayne. Bonnie, you come with me."

Thursday, 12th February. As I open Wayne's front gate I can hear the banging of a drum – a real drum, this time. Accompanying this are the harmonious tones of a guitar, playing 'Nellie the Elephant.' Chrissie, the music teacher, is here. Wayne's singing along, in a pure choirboy voice, which moves me to sudden tears. The combination of rhythm and sound are so magical, that I sit down on the doorstep and listen.

Five minutes later, I knock on the door. Mrs Lewis opens it. "Come in," she says affably. "He's having his music lesson. He's really enjoying it. Chrissie said Bonnie could stay in and watch," she adds, looking at me warily.

"I'm so glad we managed to arrange it. Chrissie's really brilliant. She somehow manages to get all her children making music – and Wayne doesn't need much prompting!"

"Yes, he sounds quite good," says Mrs Lewis.

Talk about damning with faint praise – doesn't the woman recognise her son's talent?

The day after our show-down two weeks ago, I'd taken advantage of the uneasy truce which followed and broached the subject of music lessons for Wayne. Maybe there was a teacher in the village who could give him recorder lessons? Or if that was a bit too advanced for a six year old, how about the group percussion sessions (part of the Community Learning programme) held at one of the secondary schools in town every Saturday morning? Perfect for Wayne. And they didn't cost a lot.

Mrs Lewis's response was lukewarm. She couldn't afford one-to-one lessons. And how would she get into town, with no car? 'Bus?' I suggested. No, it would all take too long, she didn't have the time. (In other words, she couldn't be bothered.)

I'd been very disappointed. Then I'd remembered Chrissie, a peripatetic music teacher who works for the LEA. She's not part of our tuition team, as she usually works in schools, but in her spare slots she sometimes takes on individual pupils who are out of school. I rang her up and told her about Wayne. Then I rang Sally and persuaded her that Wayne was worth the money the Department would have to pay Chrissie. And Chrissie has turned up trumps. She's given Wayne three lessons so far – maybe started him off on a glittering musical career?

Chrissie opens the door. "You can come in now – we're just packing up."

Wayne is carefully putting all the different percussion instruments away. His eyes sparkle with interest. As he reluctantly consigns them into their boxes, he taps, strokes, rattles and bangs each one lovingly.

"Can you come tomorrow, Chrissie?" he asks, wistfully.

"No, this is your last one, Wayne. You're starting school after half term, remember?"

Wayne hasn't remembered. He looks desolate, eyes filling with tears.

"But you'll have music with your teacher at school – you can be in the class band!" Chrissie kneels down to his height and puts her arm round him.

Wayne and I help Chrissie carry the instruments out to her car.

"Can you have a word with his mother about music lessons?" I whisper urgently. "Maybe you can persuade her?"

"I'll do my best," she promises. "He certainly needs them. He's a natural."

Chrissie goes into the kitchen to say goodbye to Mrs Lewis, and Wayne follows me reluctantly into the living room, dragging his heels.

Mrs Lewis seems more affable now. I'm beginning to understand one of the reasons she's been behaving in such a hostile manner towards me. According to her skewed logic, Wayne should be at school. But instead, *I* was here, teaching him at home, a poor substitute for a full-time education. If she could somehow prove that I wasn't up to the job, if she could somehow make me go away, then – magically – Wayne will have to return to school!

But now, she *is* doing her best. An eerie silence greets me each morning – no blaring television, the computer off. Bonnie, still loudly protesting, is banished to her room or to the kitchen. There's even a suggestion of her starting a new playgroup after half term. An introductory visit last week proved satisfactory – little 'Madam' actually asked if she could join!

Cornflakes and Weetabix have replaced Wayne's chocolate fix for breakfast, with juice or milkshake instead of Coco-Cola. Chocolate bars and biscuits do creep in throughout the morning, I've noticed, but as a treat rather than the staple diet. Lunch now consists of sandwiches and fruit. This new pattern of healthy eating has calmed Wayne down considerably.

Wayne's teacher, Ann, and the headteacher, Mrs Holdsworth, have been very supportive to Mrs Lewis. As long as the conditions I set out are kept to, Wayne can return, on trial, after half term. I've noticed that he settles down more quickly now. He's more willing to have a go at new tasks. Last week I introduced some English and maths worksheets. He made his usual fuss at first; but then surprised me – and himself – by concentrating for a full twenty minutes! What an improvement on the twenty seconds of a month ago.

If I'd only tackled his mother head-on sooner, but, of course, it's easier to be wise with hindsight, and to forget how unapproachable Mrs Lewis was, from the very beginning – always holding me at arm's length. Even now, there's a kind of brittleness between us: our ceasefire could collapse at any moment.

All in all, I'm cautiously optimistic. Yet there's something that still remains a mystery – Wayne's strange and violent attitude towards animals. Today, I'm hoping to find out a little more.

Chrissie's a hard act to follow, so I need to grab his attention quickly.

"Would you like to play with my sand-tray, Wayne?"

"What's that?"

"Wait there and don't move. If you move so much as a finger before I come back from the car, we won't play!"

When I return with the heavy tray of sand, Wayne's sitting exactly as I left him.

"Well done! You've been as still as a statue!" This is progress, indeed.

"Can I move my fingers, now?"

"Of course you can. Give them a good wriggle. You'll need them in a minute."

Four inches of sand rest in a deep-sided blue tray. The sand can be hollowed out to reveal the blue base, thus forming a sea or lake or pond. It can be piled up into dunes or mountains. An imaginative child can be transported into another world, even without the addition of extra features. But the props I've brought with me will enhance any make-believe scene. There are some cardboard boxes of various sizes which can be turned upside down to make buildings, some Lego people, fences, gates and trees. There are some trucks, lorries, and cars. I keep my trump cards hidden until the last.

Wayne's eyes light up when he sees the sand. Immediately, he scoops out a lake and makes the smallest box into a boat. A man, a woman and a little boy and girl row across the lake. The boy throws the little girl out of the boat.

"'Oh dear'" says Wayne, as the Lego boy, "'You've gone. What a pity.' That's his little sister, he's pushed her over the side," he explains, looking up at me happily.

Wayne's having so much fun with the boxes and Lego people that I'm tempted to forget my original plan. Why spoil his fun – and mine – by getting too analytical? Yet, until I see how he plays with *all* my props – including the ones I've kept back till last – how will I know if my hunch is correct? Let's just see what happens:

"Look Wayne, some friends want to join in. They'll wait here outside the sand-tray until you want to play with them. See, they're lining up like at school, waiting their turn."

As well as a whale, seals, some fish and a crocodile, there are all the usual farm animals. Wayne barely glances at them.

"I want to play *this* game."

"That's fine, you carry on."

He reaches out for the whale. It upturns the boat. The whole family flounders in the water. An island magically appears in the middle of the lake and the family swim to it.

"They're safe now," says Wayne. "Not drownded." He looks relieved.

His eyes keep straying to the farm animals next to the sand box. His mood has suddenly changed. Now he's tense and agitated. Suddenly he seizes two sheep, and four of the lambs.

"You're coming with me!" He says, in a fierce, gruff, grown-up voice. He marches the animals into a truck. With a wide, sweeping movement, he covers the lake with sand. The boat family are scattered, the Lego father is commandeered as truck driver. He finds three more sheep and drops them into the truck. Now the truck is driven up to the biggest cardboard box.

"There's no door," says Wayne. He hesitates, uncertainly. He's visibly upset.

"Do you want one?" I ask.

"Yes."

"Shall I cut one out for you?"

Wayne nods, his face flushed, eyes as big as saucers.

"Big door or little door?"

"A very big one."

I quickly cut a large rectangle in the cardboard. Wayne's man gets out of the truck and tells the sheep to get out too. Now there's a running commentary. "You've got to get in there" – pointing to the box. "And you. And you. In *there*. Go on. You can't escape."

The sheep are lined up in the big box. There are some men waiting for them.

"You first," says one of the men. "I'm going to cut your throat." Wayne holds the lamb, and continues the running commentary, in a tight, expressionless little voice: "The man's got a big knife. He cuts its throat. The knife's very sharp. It hurts the lamb. It screams, 'Eeee! Eeee!' Look at all the blood coming out. It's on the walls, lots of it." Wayne pauses for a moment, his hand suspended in mid-air. His forefinger jabs at the walls of the box. He touches them lightly, and recoils with a look of disgust and terror. "Ugh, it's horrible, horrible red blood, all over the walls."

The little lamb lies in the palm of Wayne's hand. Wayne suddenly makes it writhe and twitch about, as if in agony. "Ha, you're not dead yet, all the blood hasn't come out." He pauses, staring wide-eyed at the lamb. "There, you're dead now. Where's the next one? It's your turn to be deaded. And you. And you. Ha! You're scared. But you have to be deaded, too. Cut your throat…"

White-faced and trembling, Wayne wipes clammy hands on his T-shirt.

I'm shaking, too. The scene has shocked me into silence. Wayne's in a nightmare world beyond my reach. Where has all this come from? What poison has crept into this child's mind?

I'm longing to bury my head in the sand. I wish to God I hadn't started this. I scramble around in my mind for reasons. Perhaps it's quite normal – all kids act out violent impulses, don't they, through play and games? No, not like this. Not with this cold, deathly fervour that reduces them to a trembling heap.

I'm out of my depth, but it's too late now. Wayne has just revealed for me a hidden part of his psyche. He's trusted me enough to show me something that's terrified him. I must, at least, acknowledge that.

"That's a very terrible thing that happens to the lambs, Wayne. Thank you for showing me. The poor lambs…"

Wayne nods, still clutching one of them. He twists and pulls at its neck. Stony faced, he stares down at the floor.

"I feel so sad for them. It makes me want to cry when I see the man kill them."

"He *had* to kill them," says Wayne.

"He *had* to kill them? Do you know why?"

Wayne laughs suddenly, an eerie, high-pitched hysterical laugh. It lasts a long time.

"For minced meat, of course."

"Minced meat?"

"And sausages. They all have to be *minced up* and cut up into *sausages*." As he emphasises each word, he bangs the hapless lamb hard against the side of the sand-tray.

"Poor lambs!" I exclaim. "Made into minced meat and sausages!"

"Where do you think your sausages come from?" asks Wayne, sternly. I stare at him. Whatever will he say next?

"I bet you thought they come from the supermarket. I bet you did. Did you? Do you like minced meat? Do you like sausages?"

"Not a lot," I say faintly.

"Sausages are my best dinner. And next best, is spaghetti hoops."

Suddenly he perks up. He's back at the sand tray, swishing the sand around with huge, sweeping movements. I'm not ready to let this go just yet. So near and yet so far – where did it all come from? If I keep on about it, will I risk upsetting Wayne even more? I take a deep breath.

"Well, I'm so glad you showed me what happened to the little lambs, Wayne. I'm still feeling very sad about them. I'm feeling that I'd like to draw a picture of them. Or sing a song…would you like to do a drawing of the lamb?"

Wayne gives me a sidelong, suspicious glance. He shakes his head. He's telling me, clearly, that the subject is closed. But he's calmer now, no longer trembling. The colour's returned to his cheeks.

I get out a box of crayons. They're special ones that turn into paints when you wet them. I fill an empty mug with water from the downstairs cloakroom and show Wayne how they work. I leave the crayons and a sketchpad by the sand tray and watch him. He plays with the crocodile and the whale, making them eat the fish. Then the family appear again and go fishing. Wayne keeps the farm animals strictly off-stage; their performance is over.

Wayne tries out the crayons, dipping them into the water and seeing how the colours change. He doodles experimentally, making shapes and circles, seeing how the colours run into each other and become different colours. He doesn't want to do a painting of any particular subject. He seems to be winding down, like a horse walking the last mile home, after a long, hectic gallop across country. Then, without looking up, he says conversationally:

"We watched this programme. About the place where all the animals go to be deaded." He makes a brief, token slash against the lamb's throat, but the sting seems to have gone out of the action.

"When was that? When did you watch this programme?"

"Don't know. We just watched it." Wayne puts the end of a blue crayon into the cup. "Look, it's getting darker. It's getting more blue." He stirs the crayon round and round the cup.

"Who did you watch the programme with, Wayne?"

"With Mum. And Bonnie." He places some more crayons next to the blue one in the mug, and jiggles them all about. The water slowly turns a muddy brown. He stands up suddenly.

"I want a drink."

"I want a drink, *please*." I say, automatically, my mind racing. "All right, go and ask Mum if you can have one."

Wayne runs off to the kitchen. He's had quite enough of crayons, lambs – and especially of me. I'd like to talk to Mrs Lewis. But for the life of me I just don't know where to begin.

Friday, 13th February. Once more, I'm facing Wayne's mother across the kitchen table. I've come early to thrash out this business of the slaughtered animals. Brandy, in his huge basket, sits grinning at us, his tail thumping like a metronome against the plastic sides.

"So, how did Wayne come to be watching this programme in the first place?" My words come out all wrong – accusatory and judgemental. I'd spent ages planning what to say. In rehearsal, the words were softer, more conversational.

"I thought he should see it. We watched it together," says Mrs Lewis, matter-of-factly, as if it were the most natural thing in the world to sit a six-year-old down in front of a documentary about slaughterhouse methods.

"But, for heaven's sake, *why?*"

Wayne's mother looks at me defiantly. "Well, he eats meat, doesn't he? We buy it at the supermarket. It's all wrapped up in neat packets. Wayne thinks – he *used* to think, before he watched it – that that's where it comes from, the supermarket. That's what I said to him. I said, when we were standing by the meat counter, and I was trying to get him to decide what he wanted for tea: 'Where do you think these sausages and this minced meat come from?'"

"But – but – surely lots of six-year-olds think their meat comes from the supermarket!"

"Exactly! It's wrong. He should know the truth. It's part of his education."

"But not for a child of Wayne's age! What time of the evening was this programme?"

"I dunno." Mrs Lewis shrugs dismissively. "Late, I think. It was one of those investigation programmes, might have been *Horizon*. So, about nine or ten o'clock? We stayed up to watch it specially."

My jaw drops. As long as I live, I'll never understand this woman's logic.

"I was with him all the time," adds Wayne's mother, as if this exonerates her from blame. "And Bonnie watched it too, but she fell asleep after the first bit."

Thank goodness for that!

"But can't you see how disturbing Wayne must have found it, those images of animals being killed?"

"They don't feel anything. It's all done professionally. They pride themselves. The knife is very sharp. They showed him sharpening it, and checking to see if it was sharp enough. They're dead the instant their throat's cut."

"But the *blood!* Wayne said there was blood all down the walls…And their poor bodies were still writhing and twitching, as if they were still alive…"

"'Course they're not alive! It's instant, I tell you. They explained that on the programme. Wayne was watching, listening to every word. It's, like, a reflex action, the muscles and that just carry on working for a while…"

"But – but – surely they don't just cut their throats? Don't they stun them with an electric current, or shoot them first?" With the cowardly, ignorant mind of a vegetarian, I'm grappling to understand slaughterhouse methods.

"Not on *this* programme," says Mrs Lewis, as if it were a point of personal pride that Wayne should see the whole gory process in its most extreme form. "It was from up *North* somewhere, not from these parts." Her scathing tone shows that the North/South divide is still very much alive and well. "Near *Birmingham,* I think it was. Perhaps they do things different up there." She says 'Birmingham' as if it were in some far-distant land. "Anyway, children should know what's what. That's real life, isn't it? How's it different from what he sees on the news? That's always full of wars and violence – like Iraq? He sees it every day."

"But why? I mean, why let him watch the news at all? When he's only six! Couldn't that wait until he's older?"

"Actually," says Mrs Lewis, dismissively, "he doesn't take much notice of it. He just looks at it for a moment or two, then he gets bored and goes away to play a game on his computer."

"Where he acts out all the violence he's just seen!"

"You what?" Mrs Lewis stares.

"Don't you *understand?* Children take in everything that they see and hear on television, or anywhere else for that matter. It goes into their minds and gets filed and stored there – just like a computer. And if it's especially violent or frightening to the child, the violence gets split off."

I'm beginning to shout. I lower my voice and grab two coffee cups, move one far away from the other, to a corner of the table. "It gets somehow parcelled up, and then it gets buried, deep inside the child's mind." I put the coffee cup under the table on the floor. "Because it's far, far too scary for the child to even think about…"

I've lost her completely, I can feel it, yet I lumber on, regardless, "But it never goes away. It lodges there, like a bomb, or a canker, in the child's mind. Because it's so painful for the child to have it lurking there, he tries to get rid of it…"

Mrs Lewis makes an impatient gesture, shaking her head. She half stands up, gathering up the dirty mugs.

"…*Please* let me finish. This is so important! The child tries in every way he can, to get rid of the horrible, scary thoughts and images. And do you know how?"

"For God's sake!" Mrs Lewis lets out a long-suffering breath.

"…He *acts it out*. He becomes aggressive and violent. Maybe he starts attacking other children. Or, he lets others act out the violence for him. As in violent video games…"

"There's nothing wrong in them games," sniffs Mrs Lewis indignantly. "It's only pretending!"

"But don't you see? It's like having a poisoned wound. If you don't treat it, the wound just festers underneath the skin until it gets worse and worse and gets into the bloodstream and poisons the whole body. You have to get the poison out of the body. What Wayne has seen, is festering in his brain like a wound."

Mrs Lewis stands up and goes over to the sink with the mugs and some dirty breakfast bowls. She looks over her shoulder.

"Do you want another cup of coffee before you start with Wayne?"

I put my head in my hands. "Mrs Lewis, hasn't anything I've just said made sense to you?"

"Well, I didn't know, did I? I just do my best. It's not easy, bringing up two children on your own, you know. Anyway, there's nothing I can do about it now, is there? He's seen the programme, and that's that!"

"Actually, you can do a lot. You can talk about it, let him grieve for the slaughtered animals. Maybe write a poem together celebrating their life. Don't you realise that Wayne's very upset about the lambs?" I tell his mother about the sand-play yesterday, and the previous unhappy encounters with the pony in the field, and the farm animals in his toy box. "Can't you see how badly he's been affected by that programme?"

Mrs Lewis glances at me briefly and looks away. She taps her fingers on the side of the draining board.

"And do you know what else you can do? You can make sure – absolutely sure – that Wayne watches only children's programmes from now on. Nothing violent, horrific or shocking. You'll find his behaviour improves. He won't be so aggressive towards other children – well, no more than any other six-year-old. And he'll be a much happier little boy. You'll see!"

There's a long pause. Mrs Lewis reaches for her cigarettes. With fingers that shake a little, she extracts one from the packet. She lights it and takes in a long deep drag, accidentally-on-purpose blowing a cloud of smoke into my face. She turns back to the sink and starts taking plates out of the draining rack. "He's in there," she says, nodding back towards the living room. "He's waiting for you." I'm dismissed.

I want to do everything possible to make Wayne's last session a happy, memorable one. First, I read to him. It's a beautifully illustrated book, with pop-up pictures about a farmyard full of happy animals. Ducks swim on the pond, geese cackle in the yard. Cows are being milked. But the stars of the show are the sheep. For the book is about wool production. So the sheep are very much alive, and will stay alive to the very end of the book - and to the end of their days. Their fleece will be sheered, carded, spun and woven into beautiful rugs and jumpers.

We sit together on the floor. Wayne watches me warily, as I begin reading and show him the lambs gambolling playfully next to their mothers. He feels he's being got at somehow. Even so, the story soon draws him in. The pop-up illustrations fascinate him. Before I've read the last sentence, he's begging me to read it again. And again.

After the story, I dive into Wayne's toy box and extricate soft-toy sheep. Who's going to be the sheep-shearer? Wayne throws himself into the action, showing a remarkable memory for the wool-production process. Towards the end, after all the sheep have been sheered, there's a hint of that haunted, sly look in Wayne's eyes. Oh no! Are the sheep for the chop, after all? But thankfully, Wayne sends them all back to their little lambs, waiting patiently to cuddle up to their mothers again.

"You haven't got enough wool on your skin yet," he consoles the lambs. "That's why you couldn't go with your mothers. But they're back now. Next year you'll be big enough and you'll be very, very woolly. And the farmer will make you into a jumper. Not saus..."

Wayne stops, glancing up at me briefly, then away. It's all still very painful. The words 'sausages' and 'minced meat' hang in the air like slaughterhouse knives. As they will for some time to come. Until happier pastoral scenes eventually obliterate – or at least coexist – with the shocking images in Wayne's mind.

We gather together all Wayne's worksheets, pictures and stories into a folder to show his teacher when he goes back to school after half term.

"Did I really do all that?" he exclaims, surprised.

We play Simon Says and other games till the end of the session. When it's time for me to leave, Wayne's mother is nowhere to be seen. I'd prefer to just slip away without seeing her again, but there's my timesheet to be signed, and Wayne's report to be looked at. Reluctantly, I go in search of her.

She's in the garden by the fence, chatting to a neighbour, a harassed young woman with a grizzling toddler perched on her hip. I apologise for interrupting, and wave the report sheet at her. She tuts, and says, "See you later," to the neighbour. The two of them exchange meaningful glances, with me in the firing line. I reckon I've become *persona non grata* in the road. Depicted by Mrs Lewis as the Tutor from Hell, my reputation is spreading like bush-fire through the village. One day, I'll be part of local folklore.

Mrs Lewis leads the way back into the kitchen. She scrutinises my time-sheet like an auditor checking ICI's yearly accounts. There's a nasty pause while she gets the calendar out and compares the dates. Even now, she'd love to catch me out, but she does soften a little after reading Wayne's report. It's positive and glowing: 'Wayne has made progress. He's quietened down. He can concentrate for longer periods. His grasp of number concepts has improved…'

"Hmmph!" She makes no comment as she hands me back the report. She's clearly pleased but won't admit it.

"Well, I wish Wayne luck the week after next, when he goes back to school." I move towards the door. I can see the neighbour still hanging about next to the fence, and Mrs Lewis fidgeting, wanting to join her again.

"Goodbye," I say, holding out my hand. She hesitates, then takes it briefly, in a limp handshake. She drops my hand quickly, as if it were a wet toad.

"I'll see myself out."

She nods. "Okay. See you in a minute."

I blink at her uncertainly. I'm always momentarily thrown by this local way of parting company. The words 'in a minute' can mean anything from seeing someone again literally in a minute, or more often, tomorrow, next week, next month or any time in the future.

"I hope not," I murmur. "I mean, I hope there's no need for any further tuition. I'm expecting him to settle back now."

"It's about time," says Mrs Lewis grimly. In part of her brain, she still thinks it's all my fault he's not at school *now*. She starts moving towards the back door, but suddenly stops still.

"I'll think about what you said. About the TV programmes."

I stand stock-still, holding on to the door frame for support. Is this a Road to Damascus deliverance?

"But I can't promise anything. I can't be checking all the time what he's watching in his room, after he's gone to bed, can I?"

"You don't mean…?"

"He always has the TV on. It helps him get to sleep. Of course, when I go up to bed, I turn it off. He's asleep, by then, usually, but how do I know what he's been watching in the meantime? Anyway, I've got to go…"

She dashes out into the garden, hailing the neighbour, leaving me gazing after her, open-mouthed.

Wayne follows me to the front door.

"I won't see you again, will I?" he says, pouting. He peers up at me accusingly through long lashes.

"Oh, yes you will. Because I'm going to visit you in school, after half term. To see how you're getting on. You can tell me about all the nice things you've been doing in your class."

Solemnly, Wayne slips his hand into mine for a moment. "Can I show you the big tunnel in the playground? It's new!"

"Yes, please. And I'll see all your friends, won't I?"

"Yes." His face brightens. "And you'll meet Sammy."

"Is Sammy your special friend?"

"No," – scornfully – "Sammy's the hamster, silly."

"Ah."

I walk to the gate. Wayne stands on the doorstep, still as a statue, a stocky little boy with wide blue eyes which follow my every step down the path. I open the gate, and wave goodbye before I disappear behind the high privet hedge. Slowly, Wayne raises his hand in salute.

I drive away, slowly. Generally, when a child returns to school, I feel a glow of elation and pleasure at the positive changes I've seen in them. But just now, I'm filled with foreboding. Will there be a successful outcome for Wayne? I doubt it – not for long anyway.

Unless his mother gets some urgently-needed parenting lessons and/or some therapy – best of all, a complete brain transplant – I reckon Wayne will be back home again in under a month.

Yet – who knows? He's a tough little boy. Deep down, he has strength of character, as well as talent. In the days to come, when I think back over our time together, I shall remember the highlights: his pleasure as he found the choc bar at the end of the treasure hunt, the sheep he reunited so tenderly with their lambs in our story session today. The card game, with all the different sounds.

And now, mingling with the cry of the gulls as I drive along the seafront, I can still hear Wayne's pure, choirboy voice, and feel the rhythm of 'Nellie the Elephant.' I hum along to the tune in my head, tapping my fingers on the steering wheel.

AISHA

༄

Wednesday, 24th March 2004. Thomas's death on Sunday has left me bereft. Dear, funny little Thomas, with his incredibly agile mind, his love of languages and colours and maps and his courage, right up to the end.

As well as this, there's been Cassie's sudden disappearance. I'm missing her, and baby Darren more than I could have possibly imagined. I've found it hard to fill the void between 9.a.m. and 11 a.m., unable to settle down to any useful activity. I wander around like a lost soul until it's time to leave for Bethany's house. And the afternoons, which I still think of as 'Thomas time', have become hollow. Empty spaces, filled with grieving…

So when Sally, my line-manager, rang me early this morning to offer me a new pupil, my initial reaction was one of relief. However, she'd seemed reluctant to give me much information over the phone.

"You'd better come in and read her file," she'd said, ominously. I'd hot-wheeled it round to the office there and then.

My heart was sinking by the time I'd finished reading Aisha's record . I was ready to refuse point-blank taking her on. After Cassie, it seemed to be a case of 'out of the frying pan into the fire'.

Aisha Mansur is fifteen. One of the youngest in her class, she's preparing for her GCSEs. In the opinion of the Educational Psychologist and her teachers, Aisha is very capable academically.

Aisha's past history was known and well-documented. And made horrific reading.

When Aisha was just twelve, the pimps who work the harbour and docks had got hold of her. In return for bribes, such as trainers and sweets, Aisha was 'groomed' and then passed round amongst paedophiles. She was prey to the dregs of humanity who hung around that area. To the casual workers who came to load and unload the huge vessels in the dock-yard. And sometimes, to so-called respectable 'pillars of the community'.

I'm finding this report gruelling to read. Sally is at her desk, and I'm tucked away in a corner of her office. I want to run away, to escape into the fresh air, but there are even more horrors to come.

It was also known that Aisha, when she was ten or eleven, had been sexually abused by one of her family. But what was still unclear was how long this had been happening, and who exactly was the perpetrator. The most likely abuser was an uncle, her father's brother. There was a lot of mystery surrounding the abuse. In short, a typical familial cover-up and total denial, into which Aisha had been dragged.

Shocked, I skim through the pages. There's some important information here about Aisha's family. If I'm to help her, I need to know as much detail as possible. Her cultural and religious background is bound to have significant influence on how she responds in the one-to-one tutoring situation.

Aisha's family are Muslim. Her parents had an arranged marriage. Nasser Udeen Mansur, Aisha's Iranian father, was doing Business Studies at a college in Marseille. Her French mother, Zainab, was one of a large family of dutiful daughters who stayed at home to look after the house and the menfolk. Both families were very devout. After their marriage the Mansurs moved to London. Soon after, they came down to this area to join a family printing firm run by Mr Mansur's three brothers and an uncle. The Mansurs are comfortably off, living in a new estate of smart executive homes on the hill above the harbour. Mrs Mansur wears a *hijab*, the traditional shawl and veil worn by Muslim women.

Aisha had been badly affected by her childhood trauma. Fortunately, at the age of almost fourteen, she had been rescued by the police from a young life rapidly spiralling into prostitution, but serious damage had already been done. Academically, she was extremely able, but she rarely attended school. Aisha began to drink and to self-harm, and was frequently hospitalised. Cruellest of all was her banishment from home.

Her parents hadn't known what was happening to their daughter. She'd told them she was going out in the evening with friends to school clubs, or round to their houses. Once the horror of Aisha's reality was exposed, there was only shame, not support. According to her father's beliefs, Aisha had disgraced herself and her religion. She was a pariah, not fit to live at home. The whole family were devout worshippers at the mosque. Her two older brothers, in their early twenties, also disowned her. Her mother, though distraught, was afraid of going against her husband's wishes. There was no one in the family to champion Aisha, or fight her cause. It was left to social services to pick up the pieces of Aisha's shattered life and to find her a foster-home. Most heartbreaking of all, Aisha now considered herself to be 'damaged goods'. Her self-esteem was so low that she sabotaged every effort made by teachers and social workers on her behalf.

The report is heavy reading. I'm desperate to have a break, to make myself a comforting hot chocolate in the little kitchen next to the office, but I'm due at Aisha's new placement in half-an hour, for our initial meeting. I must find out all I can, now.

A year ago, after a series of local foster placements had broken down, a foster family had been found who could cope with Aisha, and help her recover, but they lived thirty miles away. This meant a new school, which was very near her new foster home. For a while, all had gone well. Aisha liked her new school and her new family. She'd managed to get through two whole terms of year 10 and the first term of year 11. She'd begun her GCSE courses.

However, two months ago she'd started missing her old friends. Meanwhile, social workers had been working hard to keep the contact going between Aisha and her mother, by arranging occasional meetings between them. It must have taken a lot of courage on Mrs Mansur's part to defy her husband in this way, and agonising for Aisha to have these hurried, formalised meetings in the impersonal surroundings of children's centres and social services offices. What could mother and daughter find to say to each other? Yet they persevered. And social workers persevered. The result was that Aisha was allowed to see her mother on set occasions such as birthdays, as long as they met outside the family home. On that point, Mr Mansur would not be moved. Nor would he relent and meet Aisha himself.

So Aisha was moved back again, and yet another foster family was found for her. The drinking and self-harming, which had stopped for almost a year, now resumed with a vengeance. She started cutting herself. Her new foster family couldn't cope. So, as a last resort, a place was found for Aisha in a New Hope Home. New Hope is a company which specialises in finding placements for the most challenging children, for whom normal foster care is no longer an option. The company buys up houses which are large enough to provide full-time care and accommodation for up to six very disturbed teenagers. In this residential setting, they live under the close supervision of a team of carers working on a shift basis. There is a manager, with a deputy, appointed by New Hope. Both managers have experience of working with the most vulnerable children.

At last I close the file. For a few minutes I sit still. I can hardly bear to think about all Aisha has been through in her short life. Or what effect these traumas have had on her.

Sally glances up from her computer. "Grim stuff, isn't it? Can you cope?"

"One of us will have to. It might as well be me."

As I drive along to the New Hope Home where Aisha has recently been placed, my head spins with anxious thoughts. How can I best support Aisha in the next three months? Is she going to be in a fit state to take her GCSEs?

I'm almost there. I negotiate a steep right-hand turn into a narrow drive, which leads to a small gravelled parking area. I get out and look around. Belview is a detached 1900's house, situated in the older, more affluent part of the town. It's one of many old properties, hiding behind thick laurel hedges, which are spread out along beech-lined roads, high above the promenade. I walk up three curving brick steps on to a red flag-stoned porch. There's a big oak door, with small panels of stained glass set in the upper part. I knock.

The door is opened by an auburn-haired young woman in her early twenties. I assume she's one of the carers. I introduce myself and she nods silently. She shuts the door behind us, and bolts it. She leads the way through a spacious high-ceilinged hall, along a wide passage into a sitting room. Though I can see it's one of the smaller reception rooms of the house, it's large enough to comfortably contain two armchairs, two sofas and a large dining-room table, with a vase of fresh daffodils in the middle. In the corner, the wavy pattern of a computer screen-saver winks at me.

While I wait for the carer to go and find Aisha, I walk over to the window, which is draped with expensive curtains, and gaze out into the garden. There is a beautifully kept lawn, and flowerbeds, and shrubs interspersed with daffodils. I'd like to explore this garden . Perhaps when we have a break...

I'm suddenly aware that I'm not alone. The young carer hasn't left the room. She's sitting at the table, her chin propped up on her elbow. With her left hand, she's taking folders out of a canvas bag lying on its side on the table. Her movements are unhurried, languid. Her face is composed as she looks coolly at her work.

With a shock, I realise that this is Aisha.

"Hello!" I burst out, awkwardly, "I didn't realise that you were...I mean, I thought you were..."

"Hi," says Aisha, without looking at me. She continues to turn the pages in one of her folders.

I introduce myself again, and ask her where she'd like me to sit. I don't want to crowd her. She shrugs, so I ease myself into a chair at her end of the table, but at right angles to her. To break the ice, I chat inconsequentially while I unpack my work bag, making sure I leave a few gaps in my nattering, for her to reply if she feels like it. I remark how lovely a house this is, how I'd like to explore the garden, about all the early holiday makers I'd passed as I drove along the seafront. Finally I tell her a little about my experience of teaching GCSEs to Year 11 pupils. From the start, I want her to know that she's in good hands where her education is concerned.

I get out my lesson-plan folder. Aisha so far hasn't so much as glanced in my direction. I wait, though exactly what I'm waiting for I'm not sure. I'm beginning to feel a tightening in my stomach. This quiet composure, which should be restful, and even reassuring, as it's such a change from my usual stroppy teenagers, is somehow quite chilling. I decide to give her a few more moments before I leap in with more conversation. Perhaps she needs more time to tune-in to this session, and to remind herself what she was doing at school. After all, it's been a few weeks since she last did any work. Or maybe she's nervous, or shy.

I watch her turning the pages in her folder in that languorous fashion. Now I can see plainly that she's younger than I'd first thought. I'd assumed that she was about twenty-two. Her eyes are heavily made up with eyeliner and mascara and eye-shadow. The dark red lip gloss adds to the effect, making her look at least eighteen. She's a strikingly beautiful girl. Her hair is a mass of tight auburn curls which spread outwards and downwards from the crown of her head to her shoulders in an Alice-in-Wonderland style. Her skin is the colour of pale almond-shells.

She's of average height, with an extraordinarily mature figure resembling that of Marilyn Monroe. She's wearing a *kurta* – a kind of tunic top that is worn by Muslim women who are less strict about a total cover-up, and which is becoming very popular in Western cultures with women of all ages. Most *kurtas* are designed to enhance a woman's modesty – loose-fitting with long sleeves and a rounded or V-neck. Aisha's *kurta* is something quite different. It has long sleeves, but there the resemblance ends. Made of purple chiffon and satin material, it's tight-waisted and very low-cut in the bodice. It seems designed to show every single line and curve of her body. It's almost a parody – as if she's mocking Muslim fashion by using it to flaunt her attractiveness, rather than to cover it up.

Aisha has at last stopped turning the pages in her folder. Her chin is still cupped in her right hand and she's still gazing down at the table, making little smoothing movements along the varnished top with her other hand. I clear my throat.

"I thought that today, we'd start by making a timetable, Aisha. For the ten hours we have together each week. I've been told that you're doing seven subjects. Is that right?"

Aisha glances up at me briefly. She nods.

"That's quite a lot to fit into ten hours!" I say. "We're going to have to be incredibly organised and disciplined if we're to manage all of them equally. We may have to prioritise, to spend more time on some than on others. In that case, I need to know which subjects you find the most difficult…"

A short silence. Then, "I can do some subjects on my own," says Aisha, yawning.

"Oh? Like…?"

"French. I can speak it and write it quite well. My mother's French."

"Yes, of course. Are you bilingual?"

"No. I used to be when I was much younger. I haven't spoken it for ages. But I still remember lots of it."

"That's good. What about your coursework?"

"I did that last term. It was easy."

"Well, that helps a lot." This is beginning to sound hopeful. "What about your other subjects?"

Aisha tells me she's doing maths at Higher Level, English language, English literature, double science, and information technology (I.T.).

"Maths at Higher Level?"

I try hard to keep a panicky squeak out of my voice. I can teach maths at Foundation Level but I'm certainly not the best person to explain the intricacies of trigonometry. This means getting another tutor in for maths, which would leave me less time with Aisha.

"I can do it on my own," says Aisha. "I quite like maths."

"Do you?"

"Yes. It's quite relaxing."

I stare at her. "Really? And have you done your coursework yet?"

Aisha yawns again. "No, but I will when I get round to it."

"Right. And what about the other subjects? I.T., for example?"

"That's easy. I use the computer a lot. I can do that on my own, too."

"Well, that's very good to hear."

This is extraordinary. I've rarely come across a Home Tuition GCSE pupil who calmly tells me that they can manage three subjects on their own. I look at her sharply. Is she bluffing, I wonder? Or maybe she has no real idea of her own abilities? Perhaps her assertions are more wishes than facts. I try to read her expression, but she's looking down again, rolling a pen backwards and forwards along the table top.

"Well, that just leaves science and English. What about science? How are you getting on with that?"

"I don't like it. I can do it, but it's boring."

"What level are you doing?"

"Foundation."

I perk up. I enjoy science.

"But I might drop it," says Aisha.

"Oh," I say, disappointed. "Why don't you just have a go at it?"

"I'll see." Aisha shrugs and looks bored.

"Well, that only leaves English literature and language. Do you like English?"

"Ye – es."

"You don't sound very sure."

"I like some of it, like the reading and the oral work, but I don't like writing."

"How do you mean? Like you don't like the *act* of writing?"

"No." Aisha gives me a withering look. "I can write. Like, I'm not thick, or anything. It's just that…" she fixes me with large hazel eyes, "It's just, putting things down. Putting things into words on to the paper. I'd much rather *say* the words."

"I understand. Lots of people find it hard to get their thoughts down on paper."

"I *could* do it," says Aisha, slowly. "But half the time, I just can't be arsed." She sits back in her chair and looks at me appraisingly.

"I see. Well, let's look at what you've been doing at school. Can you show me some of the work you've done recently, towards the exams?"

Aisha passes me her folders, and sits back in her chair with her arms crossed, gazing out of the window. I'm feeling baffled. Her account of her progress in the different subjects started off with a bang and ended with a whimper. At first, she sounded supremely capable and in charge of herself. Now, I've no clearer idea of her abilities than I did at the beginning of our conversation.

Aisha's work is neatly presented and she seems to have no specific spelling difficulty, which was my main concern when she's said she didn't like writing. Her notes on I.T. and science are fairly comprehensive. Many of them are typed notes handed out by various teachers. I guess if she could just learn these and regurgitate them for the exams she'll be in with a sporting chance of passing.

The English folder has very little written in it. No hand-written notes on the set books, no creative or informative or 'argumentative' writing, all of which is on the English syllabus.

"Have you done any of your English coursework yet, Aisha?"

Aisha shakes her head.

Panic grips me. "You know that there are five pieces of coursework to hand in by Easter, don't you?"

"Yeah. I'll get round to it."

"Good. I'm glad. But you'll have to start soon."

I want to say more, but I mustn't start our working relationship by seeming to nag. I can still feel that rising panic in my solar plexus, and I know that this is as much about me, as it is about Aisha. Just because I was a little swot at GCSE level and always worried about getting homework done on time, doesn't mean that others can't work equally effectively by brinkmanship and a last-minute rush.

"Let's make out a work timetable, shall we? You can decide which subjects you'd like to do on which day, and how much time you need for each subject. Get some file paper, and we'll both write it down, so we know exactly what we're doing."

We spend the next half an hour on this activity. Halfway through, just when my head's aching with wondering how on earth Aisha will be able to pack so much learning and revision into ten hours a week, the manager, Sandy Harper, pokes her head round the door and asks if I'd like a cup of tea.

"Yes, please."

"I'm starving. I need some breakfast," says Aisha. She doesn't excuse herself as she leaps up and goes into the kitchen. This annoys me, but then I remember I hadn't mentioned any ground rules about break-times when we were discussing our work programme.

Sandy is a blond, sharp-featured woman in her forties, streamlined. She reminds me of a sinuous racehorse perpetually geared-up for action. Which I reckon could well be the case, in a house full of troubled – and troublesome – teenagers.

When she brings me my tea, she tells me that there are seven bedrooms in the house, which means that it can accommodate up to five youngsters, with two bedrooms for the two staff who are always on night duty. Just now, there are only three children here, including Aisha. She says she's glad because it gives the staff more time with Aisha, who's presenting quite a few problems.

"Is she?" I say, mystified. "I was impressed with her this morning. She seems very mature and keen on doing well with her GCSEs. And she's been sitting down and concentrating, which is more than I expected."

Sandy gives me a long, speculative look. "Is she telling you anything about herself?"

"No. But then I haven't exactly given her an opening. I thought it best to concentrate on her schoolwork."

Sandy nods in a guarded way. I ask about the set books for English literature and the anthology, which has sections in it for both language and literature. We really need to get started on all these, but Aisha said she'd left them all at school. Was that really the case, I ask Sandy, or is this one of those 'The-dog-ate-my-homework' excuses?

"It's probably true that they're still at school," sighs Sandy. "She's not very organised with her work. Plus, she tends to put things off till the last minute."

"I'll ring the school and ask to talk to her Year Head," I say, making a note in my diary. "She needs other books, too – textbooks for science and maths, and her workbooks. Perhaps the Year Head will be able to talk to all the subject teachers and get them to find all the missing work. And I need to know exactly what coursework she's done so far. She seems very vague about everything."

"She's very hard going," says Sandy. "In a different way from the other two here. They're both loud and in-your-face. We have to watch them the whole time to make sure they're not wrecking their rooms or trying to sneak out at night. But Aisha's very quiet – too quiet. It's difficult to know what she's thinking."

After the session has finished, Sandy asks Aisha to open the front door for me, as she's on the phone in the office next to the sitting room.

"Those bolts are a nightmare," Sandy calls out. "I need to get them fixed – they're so stiff. They're meant to keep burglars and troublemakers out, but just now, they're keeping us all in!"

As Aisha walks up the hall with me on my way out, I'm trying to think of the right word to describe this girl. I feel that I'm no nearer getting to know her than I was when I came though this hallway over an hour ago.

Impermeable. That's the word. Like a medieval castle fortified with granite walls ten feet deep.

Aisha reaches up to the top of the door to loosen the bolt. As she stretches up her left arm, her sleeve is pulled down an inch or two to reveal her wrist. I recoil with sudden shock. On the inside of her pale, slender wrist there are ugly red slashes, which have recently scabbed over, but still look raw and angry.

I look away. Trying to stop my hands trembling, I pull the heavy door open and step outside. When I turn back to say goodbye, Aisha has already shut the door firmly. I hear her putting the heavy bolts back into place.

Friday, 26th March. I'm pacing back and forth in Belview's sitting room, fuming. The grandfather clock chimes the half-hour. It's half-past nine and Aisha just cannot seem to get herself out of bed.

She knows I'm here. The carer on duty, Yvonne, has marched into her room four times and shouted at her. Even if Aisha gets up now, by the time she's washed and dressed we'll have lost almost half the session. With three subjects to get through this morning, this is not good news.

I gaze blankly out into the garden, trying to think up an alternative plan. I'd been thinking about the timetable we put together on Monday. It gave an equal amount of time to all Aisha's subjects, except for French and I.T., which she'd told me she can manage on her own. This timetable might still need adjusting. Perhaps we should concentrate on the subjects which Aisha's struggling with. Or where she is falling behind because of lack of guidance. Today, I'd planned to spend forty minutes on each subject – maths, science and English. This would establish Aisha's strengths and weaknesses. Then I could adjust the work plan accordingly.

At least we'll have some books to work from today. Seeing the urgency of the situation, Sandy, the Manager, sent Aisha into school by taxi yesterday afternoon to collect her English set books. I'm hoping she's also remembered her science textbook, and the instructions for her coursework. Last night, I was studying science until 2 a.m. – chemistry, to be precise – trying to get my head round covalent bonding (something to do with atoms sticking together). I think I've just about cracked it. But I need to teach the topic immediately, if I'm to anchor it into my brain. Otherwise, all the atoms will just vaporise and disappear off into the ether again.

I'm beginning to feel anger and frustration welling up. I'm tempted to storm upstairs and haul Aisha out of bed. Apart from being against the rules, this course of action would ultimately prove self-defeating. Aisha needs to take responsibility for herself. I don't want to become a nagging mother figure on whom Aisha relies to get her up in the mornings. On the other hand, given her history, she might not yet be capable of even small acts of self-empowerment.

While I'm wondering, and agonising, Yvonne comes running into the room.

"She's up! She says she'll be down in a minute."

Five minutes later, we're sitting at the table, Aisha half-asleep and totally unrepentant.

"Aisha, this is not good enough. I've been waiting nearly forty minutes. This is a complete waste of my time and yours."

Aisha shrugs. "Sorry."

She doesn't sound in the least sorry. I look at her sharply. She's somehow found time to 'put on her face'. Full eye make-up, lipstick, blusher – the lot. She's taken care with her clothes, too. A different long-sleeved *kurta*. Pale yellow, and even more figure-hugging than the last. How can I instil even the tiniest scrap of urgency into her? Make her as interested in her education as in her appearance?

"Aisha, I'm here to help you with your GCSE subjects. You have two months in which to do seven subjects, including your coursework. And you will lose two weeks because of the Easter holidays, two weeks from now. Can't you see how much time we've lost today?"

Aisha is silent. She looks down, twirling her hair around finger and thumb.

Then, with set lips, she says icily, "Look, I'm knackered. I just don't do mornings, right? Can't you come later?"

"No, I have another pupil at eleven o'clock."

"Can't you swap us around?"

"*No*, Aisha."

"Why not?"

I suck in a sharp breath. One of my golden rules is never to discuss one pupil with another. Yet…I glance at her. There's genuine curiosity on her face. She's not just being bloody-minded. Nor am I, in refusing her request. She needs to know that.

"Because I'm trying to reintegrate this pupil into school, and we're tied to the school timetable."

"You could come in the afternoon, then," Aisha persists.

"I have a commitment in the afternoons."

I've organised Aisha's sessions as though my former pupil still existed. Afternoons, until only this week, were for Thomas. Now, hollow and empty, they are a space for mourning. I can still feel his essence, filling the hours between one-thirty and three-thirty with his indomitable spirit. For the moment, afternoons are sacrosanct. I blink hard and clear my throat.

"So we'll begin, shall we? I'd like you to make a start on the anthology. There are a lot of poems in there to read – and enjoy!"

"I left it at school."

"WHAT? But you went in to school yesterday to get all your work!"

"Yes. And I did go round all the different teachers collecting my stuff. I remember carrying a whole pile of it in my arms. But afterwards I went into the art room because my friends were in there doing some work, and I wanted to talk to them, and I somehow forgot my English books."

I clutch my hair. "Aisha, you need your English set books *now*. Most of the exam questions are based on them."

"I'll ask Sandy if I can go next week," says Aisha, blinking at me with a calm insouciance that makes me want to scream. "I'll sort it, okay?"

She folds her arms across her chest and leans back in her chair with a bored expression. My sense of urgency is entirely wasted on her. I try again.

"Right. Well, maybe we'll start with science, instead…"

I manage to remember the chemistry from my midnight cramming session. The covalent bonds are still just about bonded to my brain cells, but this could soon change.

"I'm dropping science." Aisha glances up at me briefly beneath heavily mascaraed eyelashes.

"Dropping…!" I can hardly get my words out. "But why?"

"I haven't done the coursework. But, *basically*, because I can't be arsed. I told the science teacher, yesterday."

"Oh *Aisha*…" I'm not sure if my disappointment is more about me than about Aisha. The hard-earned covalent bonds are free at last. Floating out of my brain cells into space, never to return.

"I'm still doing five subjects," says Aisha, defensively.

I shake my head. "I just think it's a shame. Science is such a useful subject, and you're quite capable of passing it. Any chance of you changing your mind?"

"No."

"Well, let's do maths, then, shall we? I know you said you could work on your own quite a lot, but I've brought along some past examination papers. If you work through these, it's a very good way for you to find out your strengths and weaknesses."

"Whatever."

I select a sample paper and place it in front of Aisha. Languidly she reaches into her bag and finds her pencil case. She gets out a biro. I bite back my impatience.

"Can I make a suggestion? Biro is very messy for maths. There are loads of things – for example compass work and drawing angles - where you can easily make mistakes. You don't want to do that on the exam paper. Use a pencil so you can rub out."

At last, Aisha's ready. She flicks through the questions in the paper.

"I can do that…and that…this one's easy."

She comes to a question on angles, and hesitates.

"Can't do that. I could never get my head round them. I don't see why this angle *here* and that one *there* are exactly the same. I don't believe it." She jabs her finger at the diagram, crossly.

"Okay. I'll explain. It's easy. You see those lines? They're parallel lines."

"How do you know?" says Aisha, doubtfully.

"See that little symbol, on the lines? That tells you. Now, do you remember how many degrees a straight line has?"

"180°," Aisha says promptly. She gives me a look which plainly says: 'Stop asking me this kindergarten stuff'.

"So if the angle on *this* parallel line is 60°, then this one, on the other line, must be the same."

Aisha studies the diagram for a minute or two, frowning suspiciously. Just now, she reminds me of Cassie, as she gazed in horror at the top row of noughts in a subtraction sum. Cassie would look at the little '**1**' I'd carried along the row to the units column, as if it were a bomb about to explode. 'Where on earth did *that* come from?' she'd asked, peevishly.

But for Aisha, maths holds no terrors.

"Oh I see. I get it." She nods. "Right. I can do that now."

"Go on then. See if you can do the whole question."

Aisha works steadily. She certainly has a flair for this subject. Thank goodness it's geometry. I've always liked its elegance and form. It gives a visual image. I can see what I'm up against.

Aisha has finished the question and for the first time she's looking pleased with herself. She wants to continue with the next question, but I want to move on to English.

"I'll leave you the exam paper. You can do it for homework. You've got the whole weekend. Do you think you could complete it by Monday? Give me a lovely surprise!"

Aisha smiles faintly, as if humouring an idiot.

English next. In the absence of any set books, all I can do is concentrate on the language exam. In this, one of the questions always involves 'writing to explain, inform, or persuade'. Persuasion seems to be the theme of today.

I place a wad of worksheets on the table, each with a different subject for debate. There's genetic engineering, scientific experiments on animals, euthanasia – as well as other hardy perennials such as fox-hunting, and the death penalty. There's an interesting one with the headline from a newspaper: "*'Housewife gets life sentence for knifing burglar'*. Is this fair? Discuss." There's one on abortion, I notice, as I flip through the sheets. Quickly I cover it up with another worksheet. There was no mention in Aisha's file of her ever having had an abortion, but this might be a sensitive subject.

Each worksheet has imaginary scenarios to help pupils think about the topic. The worksheet on euthanasia depicts four people in varying states of debilitating or terminal disease. A seventy-year-old woman who is paralysed from the neck down. She's not in pain but wants to die. A man of fifty who has cancer. He's in pain some of the time and can only walk a few steps. A brain-damaged sixteen-year-old girl cannot communicate with anyone, or perform even basic functions. And lastly – poignantly for me – there's a seven-year-old boy suffering from the final stages of leukaemia.

Praying that Aisha will choose another worksheet, I wave a couple of other subjects in front of her. But for the first time, her eyes are alight with interest.

"I'll do this one," she says, and picks the very one that will be most difficult for me.

"Right." My heart sinks like a stone. I give her a piece of paper, with a line down the middle. One column is headed 'Arguments for' and the other 'Arguments against'. I keep a similar one for myself.

Aisha glances at the paper, and flicks it aside.

"I'm not writing it. You said we were going to talk about it."

"I thought we'd discuss it first. Then write it down. You have to write in the exam."

Aisha tuts. I hold my breath. There's a pause, then she pulls the worksheet towards her with an impatient gesture. She looks intently at the illustrations. I can see she's really concentrating. After a minute or two she puts down the worksheet and sits back in her chair.

"Well," she says, with the considered air and tone of voice of a judge summing up a precedent-creating court case, "what I think is – well, *basically*, I'm against euthanasia. Because, like, life is God-given. But also because as long as people are alive, there's always some hope. You know, like the man with cancer? *He* might get better. And so might the boy with leukaemia. I'm not sure about the paralysed woman, whether she might get better too. I don't think she will, or the brain-damaged girl. But…" She pauses.

"But…?"

Aisha searches for words. "But the fifty-year-old man is only in pain *some* of the time," she says slowly. "So some of the time he isn't. And so what, if he can only walk a few steps? Like, he can do other things? He could read, see his friends, have a laugh with his children…" Aisha stops suddenly and swallows. She takes a tremulous breath.

"So how could we sum up that ability to do other things?" I prompt her, gently.

"Well, it's like – he can still enjoy his life…?"

"Yes! Excellent. We can call that 'quality of life'. That's something very precious. It's also a medical term doctors use when they're considering medical conditions. Anything else?"

Aisha frowns, and looks at the pictures. "I think there's something wrong with these pictures. I mean, like they're not really good examples."

"Oh?"

"Like they're all so different. You can't really use one argument for all of them. Some are worse than others. I think the brain-damaged sixteen-year-old girl is the worst. That must be terrible!"

"But could we apply the same arguments you've just discovered, to her as well as to the others? Can she have quality of life, too, even if she won't get better?"

"Well yes, I s'pose. She can still enjoy her food, even if someone has to feed her. And she might like pop music. And being hugged by her mum." Aisha checks herself, suddenly. There's a glint of tears in her eyes. She looks down into her lap. "I mean, every day little things. But we don't *know* exactly what she can enjoy, do we?"

She jabs at the worksheet, then stares into space. "I suppose that's the point. With some people, who can't talk, or tell us what they need or enjoy – well that doesn't mean they're not having, like, quality of life. So it's not up to other people to decide, is it? For doctors to switch off their life-support machines. So that's an argument against."

I stare at Aisha, fascinated. It's like watching a very beautiful old painting being oiled and restored after years of neglect. Suddenly it springs to life, all its colours glowing. After five minutes, she's covered all the arguments against euthanasia that I can think of and added a couple of her own.

"So, Aisha, what about some arguments *for* euthanasia?"

Aisha looks mystified. "There aren't any."

"In your opinion, no. But in the examiner's mind – yes. And there are always two sides to every argument. Even if you don't agree with them. We need to fill in this half of the paper." I point to the column headed 'Arguments For'."

Aisha shakes her head. "I'm telling you, there aren't any."

"Tell you what, let's play a game. Without telling each other as we go along, we'll each think up some arguments *for* euthanasia, just for the exercise. However much we disagree with them and however ridiculous they seem. I bet you can get more than me. Let's see how many we can write down in ten minutes. Ready?"

I pull my piece of paper towards me. For a heart-stopping moment, Aisha looks as if she's either going to tear hers up or fling it to the floor. Quickly I start writing: 'NHS budget – Can't keep *everyone* alive'.

Aisha glances down and reads what I've written, then pretends she hasn't. She chews the end of her pen and looks out of the window. Suddenly, she starts writing. After ten minutes, we compare notes.

Aisha reads out: "Expensive machinery needed to keep paralysed woman alive. Lots of nurses needed to look after her and the little boy. Boy is in pain and suffering. You can see the drip in the picture – in the olden days there weren't any drips. He would have died and suffered less."

"But Aisha," I interrupt, "his quality of life could still be very good, even in the last two months."

There's a silence. Aisha looks confused *and* alarmed. "But…" her voice trails away.

I realise that I've just jumped sides.

"Sorry, Aisha. My mistake."

I should have taken this week off. I can see Thomas's face as clearly as if he were sitting next to me, his presence surrounding me like a rosy mist. With an effort, I gather my wits.

"I'm sorry, Aisha," I repeat. "For a moment I got completely muddled. I forgot which side I was arguing on. I confused you. Please carry on."

"Well, the man of fifty can't work so he isn't being useful. He's not pulling his weight. Other people have to pay for him to live. Give him money and maybe a nurse. So he's costing the country money. Some people might say they don't want to spend this money on him, they might want to use it for schools or building hospitals or houses…" She frowns and thinks hard for a moment.

"Another thing is that this man's wife might be worn out looking after him. So it's her quality of life, too."

"That's fantastic, Aisha! You've really thought out those arguments so well – considering you're on the other side!"

Aisha flushes. She doesn't acknowledge the compliment in any way, but fiddles with her pencil-case and looks away. I wonder if I've overdone my enthusiastic praise.

"It would be great if you would choose another subject for homework. For when I come on Monday. This time, do a full piece of argumentative writing. But make notes first for your arguments, for and against, just like we've just done. Suppose in an exam you didn't manage to finish the question? You might be able to hand in the notes and they could gain you marks. Also it's easy to forget your ideas in the heat of trying to get them into some kind of order…"

Aisha's looking mutinous. I need to create some space. I stand up.

"I'm just going to the loo. While I'm gone, choose a worksheet. Remember, you've got two weeks to do it!"

I need to have a minute or two to myself. In the mysterious, synchronistic way the universe often moves, today's English subject-matter, intended to be a routine exam question, has brought up a lot of emotions. For both of us. My pride in my ability to act professionally at all times, by putting personal feelings to one side, has taken a huge dent this morning. And Aisha too, for a moment, let her guard down.

When I get back, I see that she's chosen the worksheet on prison for the 'have-a-go' housewife. I give her a few suggestions on how she can fruitfully use the two weeks' Easter break which begins the week after next. We'll do as much as we can before the holidays, of course, once she's collected her work from school. Meanwhile, in the holidays she could read through the anthology, choosing five poems from one of the set poets, and make notes which we'll go through after Easter. She could also read through poems from other cultures and traditions. And, if time permits, revise the other set books, including the Shakespeare. Plus, I shall leave her some specimen maths papers.

"I won't be able to do all that!" Aisha glares at me, balefully.

"I don't expect you to. I'm just suggesting things you *could* do. Honestly Aisha, I can't emphasise enough how important it is to use the Easter holidays for revision. All your classmates will be revising hard, I bet…"

I babble on. Aisha doesn't appear to be listening. She's leaning forward, her elbows on the table. With her left hand, she's rolling a biro back and forth on the polished surface. At first these movements are small and unhurried, but now she's gradually lengthening the distance of her forward reach. There's an urgency, a frenetic quality to the way she's stretching her arm. Her face is cool, but her body has tensed up.

Now her sleeve is dragging back, revealing the cuts on her wrist. Thin ribbons of dark-red scar tissue.

My pep talk grinds to a halt. A shiver runs through me. Is Aisha deliberately revealing her cuts? She's looking down at the table, her face obscured by the mass of curls. Yet her movements alone are saying something, I'm sure. Is she demonstrating – graphically – that I'm pushing her too far? Unless she looks at me directly, I won't know how to respond. I wait. There seem to be minutes rather than seconds between each tick of the grandfather clock.

Suddenly Aisha stops rolling the pen and sits back in her chair. The scars are hidden again. She gives me a brief glance – cool and appraising.

"Is it time to stop yet?"

"Yes." I check the clock. "You've done well today, Aisha. You've completed some excellent oral work, and done some writing, even though you don't like doing it. And though you might think I'm pushing you, I'd still like you to do at least some of the work I suggested."

Aisha stands up and puts her things away. If there was an actual brick wall between us at this moment, it couldn't feel any more solid than Aisha's silence. I gather my notes together.

"Bye, Aisha. I'll see you on Monday. Have a good weekend!"

"Bye." Her tone isn't hostile, or angry. There's just that chilling politeness which reveals nothing. She opens the door into the hall, and I hear her running upstairs to her room.

I go to find Sandy, the Manager, in her office. She's busy on the computer, but says she'll see me out. Those heavy bolts are a Health and Safety issue – I could dislocate my shoulder trying to shift them.

I mention the strange way in which Aisha let me glimpse her scars – accidentally-on-purpose. Should I have said that I'd seen them?

"No," says Sandy. "Unless she actually mentions them herself, it's best not to say anything."

"Right."

This has shaken me. What depths of despair can drive a youngster to inflict such savagery on her own body? Yet what a potentially brilliant mind she has. All her arguments in our practice debate were articulate, intelligent, and consistent. She thought laterally, making connections and comparisons as she went along. With that kind of mind, and that gift for verbal reasoning, she could be a lawyer.

Yes. *This* is the image of Aisha I must keep in mind. Not just the damaged, self-harming teenager. I must hold the image of what she will *become* – one day.

Friday, 2nd April. Once again, I'm chewing my nails waiting for Aisha. Her persistent refusal to get out of bed in the morning has suddenly leapt to the top of my mental list entitled: 'Aisha – Problems to Solve'.

I can now cross off Getting Work from School. After last Friday's session, I'd telephoned her class tutor, who'd promised to locate the work and send it on. I'd also had a brief chat with the science teacher. She too was disappointed that her brightest pupil wanted to drop the subject, but she confirmed that Aisha wasn't particularly interested in science. In addition, she hadn't even started her coursework. And, she would have to come into school to do a practical exam, which might prove difficult, as she hadn't done the latest experiments.

I'd managed to talk to her other teachers too. Her I.T. tutor predicted that Aisha would sail through this subject. She's completed her coursework before she dropped out. Mme Lamont, Aisha's ebullient French teacher, exclaimed that her work had been *'magnifique',* and that her sudden departure was a great loss to the class. Even so, she was sure that Aisha would pass French with flying colours.

Thank goodness the English textbooks arrived in the post on Wednesday. We'd immediately made a start on *Macbeth*, Aisha's chosen Shakespeare play, and on the anthology, a collection of poems, old and new. However, the English teacher had enclosed a note with the dire warning that unless Aisha's coursework was handed in by the end of the Easter holidays, it wouldn't be marked.

But Aisha is not yet up.

I go in search of someone to help. Carly, the carer on duty, a quiet, passive girl, looks as if she wouldn't say boo to a goose. She tells me breathlessly that she's twice knocked on Aisha's door and called her – with no response. I bite back a sarcastic reply. Aisha needs to be fork-lifted out of bed and downstairs into her chair. But who can do this?

Luckily, reinforcements arrive through the front door in the form of Sandy, the manager, and Carol, her deputy. Carol is built like a tank and has a matching brook-no-nonsense face. Together, they march upstairs to Aisha's room. I hear stern warnings and muffled groans. I sigh with relief.

Opening the AQA English Examination Specification (oral work), I look through the requirements for coursework. One of the activities we can do is based on the speaking and listening section: 'Discuss, Argue, Persuade' in a group situation. This would normally take place with classmates as a participating audience. Today, however, our 'class' will consist of Aisha, Sandy, Carol, Carly and me. Under Aisha's guidance we'll be discussing whether the housewife who had a go at a burglar and accidentally killed him should be put in prison.

Well, this was the plan we had yesterday, but unless Aisha makes a start in the next five minutes, there won't be enough time.

At the eleventh hour I hear heavy footsteps on the stairs. The door opens. Aisha is being escorted on either side by Carol and Sandy. Wearing her full make-up and a red crushed-velvet top, she sweeps into the room with the haughty air of Elizabeth I being led to the Tower of London, victim of a treacherous plot.

"I'm starving! You can't deny me breakfast. It's against my human rights!"

Sandy raises her eyebrows at me, and I nod. Carol asks Yvonne to make some toast and a drink and to bring it in – quickly. No monarch could get better service than this, incarcerated or not. This is all highly irregular, I think, full of misgivings. At best it's a short-term solution to the problem of Aisha's tardiness. But – desperate times, etc.

Five minutes later, the session starts. Yesterday, Aisha decided that she was going to be a lawyer acting on behalf of the deceased burglar. His family are baying for justice – and compensation. A shrewd move on Aisha's part, as our sympathies tend more towards the housewife. If she can present a good case, I can mark her accordingly.

She's remembered to address her audience correctly: 'M'lud, Members of the Jury', etc. At last, I relax and begin to enjoy the show. I soon see that Aisha's fully in charge. Her arguments are carefully thought out and succinctly put. She hasn't even made notes. Her reasoning is all in her head, flowing into words as effortlessly as a waterfall into a stream. You'd think she'd been rehearsing for hours. She uses variation in tone and pace, humour, and engages us by looking at each of us in turn. It's an amazing performance. Suddenly, she's morphed into a top barrister. Now, the discussion is thrown open. We, the jury, are giving our views.

"Well!" explodes Carol. "I'd have had a go at him, that's for sure. Coming into my house, bold as brass, and making off with all my best stuff!"

"I'm not sure," says Sandy, doubtfully, "that I'd risk my life for the sake of my telly and my mobile phone. It's only possessions after all. They can be replaced."

"And the police do warn us not to have a go at burglars," I put in, primly.

"He could have been armed!" squeaks Carly, wide-eyed, from her corner of the room. The argument rolls merrily along, with Aisha still in command. At the end I give her the highest possible marks.

Before I leave, I remind her for the umpteenth time that there is still much more coursework to be done over the Easter holidays. Her chosen texts involve a lot of written work. With a sinking feeling, I realise that even if she were to spend the entire two weeks on writing these three essays – which is highly unlikely anyway – she still needs to revise the set books for the written examination. As well as do revision for all the other subjects.

It's too much. She won't do it.

I take a deep breath. She *can* do it and she will. This past week has been fruitful. We've made a start on the collections of poems in the anthology, and on the post-1914 drama. And she's just wowed us with her brilliant oral work.

"You've done really well this morning, Aisha!" I say enthusiastically, as she unbolts the front door for me. "Have a good break. I'm looking forward to seeing you in two weeks."

"Bye," she says, in a flat voice.

"I should make a start on the Arthur Miller. You told me you really enjoyed the first act of *All My Sons*. It's always best to start off with what you like most…"

I'm halfway across the gravelled parking area in front of the house before I realise that I'm still wittering on and that Aisha's closed the door behind me.

I really must let go, I think ruefully, as I drive away. I'm becoming obsessed. I've got my own holiday to look forward to. No kids, no hassle. Ten blissful days, starting tomorrow, stepping with a light heart along the beautiful Norfolk coastline. Yet how much heavier my footsteps would have felt had I realised exactly how fragile and precarious Aisha's confidence was. If I'd known that her spirits would once again plummet to rock-bottom, I'd probably have taken the first train home.

In fact, I doubt whether I'd have gone away at all.

Monday, 19th April. I breezed home from Norfolk last Wednesday, with calf muscles bulging from walking every day, and a rucksack twice as heavy as when I started out – packed with souvenirs and local folklore. The remainder of my time at home passed pleasantly, seeing friends and pottering round my garden. On Saturday, Thomas's mother came round for a cup of tea, bringing me some of his books. Her visit in itself was a gift, giving me comfort and I suppose in a way providing some measure of closure to my grieving process. Comparing my loss to hers, my grief seemed self-indulgent and almost intrusive – as if I were trespassing into the private garden of her own sorrow.

So, as I walk up the steps to Belview, I'm feeling relaxed and at one with the world, ready to cope with anything. Even with Aisha never being up in time. Carol opens the door. Immediately she puts her finger to her lips and beckons me into the office. Her broad, homely face is distressed and anxious.

"Aisha's up: she's ready for her session."

This is extraordinary.

"Is she all right? Has something happened?"

"She's okay now," says Carol, "but she hasn't been. She's had another self-harming episode."

I stare at Carol, horrified.

"She's okay now. You can start right away."

"But no, hang on…" Stupefied, I'm trying to take this in. "She seemed fine before the holidays, quite positive and…When did this happen?"

"Last Sunday. A week ago yesterday. About ten o'clock at night it was. I remember, because I was on duty then, and found her…"

"*Found* her? What do you mean?" A horrible fear contracts my stomach.

"She cut her arm again, and then swallowed some aspirins in vodka. She was out for the count."

"My God!"

"Gave us all a shock, I can tell you."

"What triggered this off? Something must have happened…"

"We're not sure exactly. Though we've a pretty good idea. She seemed to be struggling with the coursework you set her." Carol gives me a direct look, and then says bluntly. "There was something she didn't understand. We tried to ring you in the week, and then again on Sunday afternoon, but you were out. Then we tried again about six o'clock that evening."

"I was on holiday."

"Yes, we realised that afterwards. Sandy said you'd told her you were going."

Carol is making this sound like an accusation. I gather all my forces to staunch the waves of self-blame beginning to course through me.

"There must have been something else," I say faintly. "She didn't seem too fussed about her coursework. And I remember leaving her very clear written instructions. She just had to follow them…" I can feel myself going into defensive mode, and check myself. "But how is she now?"

"They kept her in overnight. It wasn't an overdose. Just a few aspirins, not enough to… Thank goodness it wasn't paracetamol. But combined with the vodka, it knocked her out. She might have taken it to stop the pain of the cuts, rather than a suicide attempt. And the cutting itself was clearly a cry for help."

"This is terrible, *terrible*…poor Aisha! I'm so sorry that this has happened to her."

"Yes, it was totally unexpected, really." Carol goes to the office door, listens, and then shuts it firmly. "I thought she might be listening. She seemed fine for the first two or three days of the holidays. She got down to the coursework you set her, as I said. She spent a lot of time typing on the computer. Said it was easier than writing, and that you'd said it was okay to do that."

"That's right."

"She showed me what she'd done after she'd printed it out – something about *Macbeth*? I think she'd finished it."

"When was this?"

"Tuesday or Wednesday. But after that, something seemed to change. She stopped working. She seemed to get depressed. She started drinking again, secretly. Alone in her room."

I collapse into a chair and bury my head in my hands. Carol looks at me suddenly as if noticing my stricken expression for the first time.

"It wasn't just the coursework, I'm sure," she says, awkwardly.

She goes on to say that on Thursday, Yvonne, the carer on duty, had found an empty bottle of vodka under Aisha's bed. She'd hunted round for more booze, but there didn't seem to be any hidden anywhere. On Friday, Aisha had tried to do some more essay writing, but wasn't sure how to go about it. She must have stashed away another bottle somewhere, because on Sunday evening, she'd got drunk. Before that, in the afternoon, she'd told Yvonne that she'd just had another go at the coursework, but she just couldn't get her head round it.

"Oh, my God," I wail again. "Poor, poor Aisha. She must have been feeling really wretched. But I did explain it to her, I *know* I did!"

"Now, dear, you mustn't be thinking it's all your fault." Carol gives me a hearty slap on the shoulder which nearly knocks me off the chair. I catch hold of the filing cabinet for support. "All this was probably brewing up behind the scenes for a long time."

"What do you mean?" I take a long, shuddering breath.

"Well now. It's a bad situation with her parents, isn't it? Terrible thing, that is. Her father not speaking to her. In fact, we think that's what triggered the self-harming incident."

"But you said she was upset about her coursework."

"Yes, she was. But there was something else. On Sunday morning, Aisha rang home and tried to speak to her mother, but her father wouldn't let her. Then he said something to her which really upset her. We don't know what. She couldn't even speak when she came off the phone. I know, because I was here. I let her phone from the office. She was as white as a sheet. She wouldn't tell me what he'd said – just ran upstairs to her room."

And then on that Sunday afternoon…she'd tried to do some coursework! A knife twists inside my gut.

"Luckily," says Carol, matter-of-factly, "I went up to her about ten o'clock to ask if she wanted a night-cap. She was lying on the floor…"

The office begins to swim around and go grey. When I come to, my head is between my knees and Carol is thumping me on the back.

Aisha's at the computer when I finally stagger into the sitting room. Under all the make-up, she's pale and drawn. And very subdued. I draw up a chair next to her.

"Aisha, I'm so sorry I wasn't there to help you with your coursework. I thought I'd written it all down for you."

"I lost the notes." Aisha's voice is flat and lifeless. "I hunted everywhere for them. I couldn't remember what they said."

"Never mind. We can go through them again now. What was it you wanted help with?"

"Just…just what to write about."

"Well, once you have decided what set book you are going to start with, you can choose your own topic. Do you remember that we talked about the main components of a play or a novel – style, characterisation, plot, structure, atmosphere and setting? Then there's also underlying themes and issues and the historical background…"

"Oh. Yes." Aisha blinks, as if trying to capture an elusive dream.

"And you decided that, as you were going to write about Macbeth's character, you'd probably choose a different angle on the Arthur Miller play."

Her eyes widen. She sighs. "Yes. It's all coming back to me now. I decided I'd write about whether the father should have been making those aeroplane parts in his factory in the first place."

"That's right. The moral issue."

"I do remember now, but I didn't then. Anyway, I didn't know how to start. Like the first thing I have to write. It was in the notes I lost."

"Yes. I suggested that you start with an introductory paragraph with a very brief outline of the plot and characters, with particular reference to the war background."

"I couldn't start," Aisha repeats, dully. She stares at the computer screen, her shoulders slumped. "I didn't know where to begin."

And how would anyone know where to begin, I think angrily, with a family like hers? I want to hug her and comfort her as if she were my own daughter. I put my arm lightly round her shoulders.

"Let's make a start now, shall we?"

And we'll start again…and again. For as long as it takes.

Tuesday, 20th April. "Well done, Aisha! You're up and ready – this is amazing. I'm very impressed."

"I couldn't sleep."

Aisha, slumped in front of the computer, glances at me briefly. Her voice sounds flat and far away.

"What are you doing? Still working on *All My Sons*?"

"I did a bit yesterday after you'd left. Then I felt like a rest. I slept all afternoon."

"That probably did you a lot of good."

I draw up a chair next to her. I'm feeling more relaxed this morning. Yesterday, I'd rung the school and told them what had happened. Thankfully, the teacher in charge of the exam entries has given a time extension for Aisha's coursework. We now have till the end of next week before it has to be handed in, but that is the final deadline.

"I'll just close this down," says Aisha.

"Ah, you're not doing coursework then?" I squint at the screen. "Were you looking something up?" I catch a glimpse of a Google search before she clicks out of all the links.

"It wasn't anything. Just something I wanted to know about."

"Oh? What was it? Maybe I might be able to help."

"It doesn't matter. It's stupid."

"I bet it isn't. Tell me."

Aisha leans back in her chair and winds a strand of hair round and round into a ringlet.

"Well, it was just…Oh, this is stupid."

"Tell me."

"It was just, when I was in primary school, I used to like history. You know, the Tudors and stuff? And Elizabeth I? And one day the teacher was telling us about their funny customs, like first thing in the mornings the ministers or whatever – the people who used to advise the King – used to march into their bedchamber with all the documents they wanted him to sign…"

Aisha's voice tails off. She looks at me uncertainly, as if gauging whether I'm really listening or interested.

"I think I remember reading about this too. There was a special word for it, wasn't there?"

Aisha nods. "'The Reveille'. I *think* that's what it was called. I remember it because it was French. And I thought it was funny, when I was little. So I was trying to find something about the ministers and the royal bedchamber. But maybe I was mixing up *that* waking-up thingy – in the bedchamber – with a different 'Reveille'."

"Wasn't that Louis XIV? The Sun King? I thought that was where the word came from."

"I don't know," sighs Aisha. She looks crushed, as if some important mission has just failed.

"Let's have another go shall we?" I suggest. "Try looking up Louis XIV."

Twenty minutes later and we've trawled through half a million sites on politics, book-titles, bugle wake-up calls for soldiers, and Versailles. Louis XIV features as a very colourful character, but there's no reference to his waking-up habits.

"Did you know that Louis XIV only had one bath in his whole life?" I say brightly, trying to cheer Aisha up.

She turns towards me. Her face is distraught. This really means something to her.

"I think we'll have to stop now," I tell her, regretfully. "But I'll keep trying, and you keep trying too. I'll ask in my library. There's a very helpful librarian there who finds out all kinds of odd things for me."

Reluctantly, Aisha settles down to *All My Sons*. Half-heartedly, she makes a few notes. I make encouraging noises and restrain myself from being too helpful. This is *her* coursework after all, but she's struggling hard to concentrate. I suggest she has a break.

"Have you had breakfast, Aisha?"

"No. I wasn't hungry."

"How about a slice of toast and a drink? You can't work on an empty stomach."

Aisha sighs again and stands up. I watch her drag herself listlessly out of the room. She's not herself. Although I'm not yet sure what Aisha's 'self' really is. However, this grey lassitude, her fretful searching for something lost long ago, is even harder to be with than her icy aloofness two weeks ago.

A few moments later, I hear her talking to Carol in the kitchen and smell the tantalising smell of buttered toast. I settle myself on the settee and think about what to do next. Aisha still has two more tasks to do for the speaking and listening component of the exam. For one of these, she must discuss one of her set books critically and analytically. That shouldn't be a problem – she can do this as we work on the books together; but she also has to give a talk on a subject that interests her. And she hasn't even thought about the written work – a piece of original writing. Depressed and lacklustre as she is just now, I'm wondering how she'll manage any of these tasks.

On the long pine coffee table in front of me there are some books written for children. Idly, I pick one up and glance through it. It's about the Elizabethans. One of the *Horrible History* series. I'm soon absorbed in it, and chuckling to myself.

Aisha comes in. She sits at our worktable next to the settee with her cup of coffee, watching me read.

"They're good, aren't they?" she says, yawning.

"Yes, they are. They're very funny. Have you been reading them?"

"Sort of. They were in the other room. There's loads of books in there, on the shelves."

"You used to enjoy history, then, Aisha?"

"Yes. When I was younger. I used to like it when we dressed up like Elizabethans. We did a play once. To the whole school. I was Elizabeth."

"That was some part!"

"Do you think I look like her?" Aisha suddenly lifts her curls from her shoulders and piles them up on top of her head. I study her, appraisingly. There's a passing resemblance, but I'm sure Elizabeth was much paler and without Aisha's stunning looks and hourglass figure.

"Well…your hair is very similar. And it's *almost* the right colour." I can hear the doubt in my own voice. Also," I add, suddenly inspired, "Elizabeth loved her make-up, didn't she? Just like you do!"

"Yes, look!" Aisha jumps up and grabs the *Horrible History* book. She leafs through it rapidly, and waves an illustration at me. "See all the stuff she used to put on her face every day of her life. Loads of it!"

"Bucketfuls, I imagine. And a lot of it was poisonous, wasn't it?" I crane sideways to read the list of nasty ingredients. "Poor Elizabeth. She never realised how much she was ruining her skin."

"She had rotten teeth, too," adds Aisha, "because of all the sugar the rich people ate. I remember that from school. Our teacher kept on about it all the time, trying to scare us off sweets!" She flicks through the pages of the book. She's perked up a bit. I have an idea.

"You know your talk, Aisha? The one you have to give as part of your oral coursework?"

"Mmm?" Aisha's only half-listening.

"Well, you could use the Elizabethans – or Elizabeth – as your subject."

"Like, how?" Aisha frowns, still turning the pages.

"Well, you could talk about Elizabeth herself, or the Tudors in general, or you could even tell us about the play you performed at school. It really doesn't matter what you talk about, as long as it's a subject that interests you. Perhaps there were some funny moments in your school play…?"

Aisha shuts the book and yawns again.

"When do I have to do this talk?"

"I've told you lots of times. As soon as possible. We need to set a date, when there are the most staff on duty. Do you know when this might be?"

Aisha stretches and half shuts her eyes. "Um. On Friday there's more staff. They have meetings on Fridays."

"Right. I'll ask Sandy if she can spare twenty minutes for everyone on duty to be your audience!"

"Whatever."

"So, does Elizabeth appeal to you as a subject?"

Aisha sits still, her hands in her lap. She opens the book again. I can feel that familiar tension rising in my chest. Deadlines.

"I *could* talk about her, I suppose. Yes, I might do something about her make-up – and maybe her clothes."

"Good. Think about it today. Make some notes. If you need any guidance, you can ask me tomorrow. But I'm sure you'll have lots of good ideas of your own. I don't know *anything* about make up. I bet you could teach me a thing or two about the subject!"

This raises a ghost of a smile.

For the rest of the session, we work on the anthology. I cast surreptitious looks at Aisha. She's still far away, barely concentrating on the rich text of the poems we're reading together. I'm worried. She's had a serious setback. My absence over the holidays didn't help. How can I get her back on track?

Wednesday, 28th April. "Did you like *All My Sons*, Aisha? After you'd read right through to the end of the play?" This play, by Arthur Miller, deals with all the family dynamics Aisha would understand.

"I didn't think it would be so hard," says Aisha, staring morosely at her copy of the play, open in the middle of act II.

"What's hard? Tell me."

I draw up a chair next to her at the table. I'm worried. Things haven't been going well for the past week. Last Friday, Aisha reverted to her dormouse mode. By the time she was up and dressed it was too late to give her talk on Elizabeth. She hasn't managed to do any more of her coursework, all of which has to be handed in to the school by Friday this week. It's twenty to ten and she's only just come downstairs. This is in spite of dire warnings from the staff, who've threatened to withdraw privileges such as her allowance and evenings out. And she ignores all my entreaties. How will she pass her exams? Why is she jeopardising her chances of doing A-levels, or getting a job?

The bottom line is that Aisha, just now, doesn't *care*.

Now she stares moodily down at the polished surface of the table, making little circular movements with her fingers.

I try again. "What are you finding difficult?"

"Writing about the moral issues," sighs Aisha.

"What are you finding so hard about it?"

Aisha leans back in her chair and frowns, chewing the end of her pen. I have a sense of foreboding. I'm thinking that, of all the aspects of the play she could have chosen, the moral issues and themes are probably the most challenging to write about. They're abstract and elusive. Responding to them requires a level of maturity and wisdom that Aisha – or indeed any youngster aged fifteen – can't be expected to possess. They haven't yet made the connections, haven't *lived* enough. I wish she'd chosen an easier topic. The setting, for example. More graphic, less nebulous. Aisha has been working on this essay for weeks now, and getting absolutely nowhere.

All My Sons is a powerful drama about an affluent American family. As the play opens, the Keller family seems almost too perfect. They are affectionate towards each other and Joe Keller, the *pater familias*, is affable and kind, and apparently well-loved and respected. As the play unfolds, however, we learn that Joe Keller has a dark past. During World War Two, the munitions factory he owned was responsible for shipping out faulty aeroplane parts. Joe's son, Larry, a pilot, went missing in the war, though the family have never given up hope that he will return. The play becomes heavy with family secrets and shocking revelations.

"What I find hard about it," says Aisha, slowly, "is that when I started doing this, I was just going to say about whether or not Joe Keller *did* ship out those cracked thingies…"

"Cylinder heads."

"Whatever. Anyway, I was going to give Joe's point of view. You know, like he had to support his family somehow. He's spent years building up his business…and then I was going to give the other bloke's point of view – Steve, his business partner, the one who was sent to prison, because he took all the blame? Like, if Joe wasn't there to ask, because he said he was ill in bed, what was Steve supposed to do? Because Joe was his boss…" Her voice tails off.

"That's good, Aisha. A good clear start!"

"But then I got on to something else. You know, the whole thing about responsibility. Like exactly *who* is responsible. And, like, when do you blame others and when don't you?"

"*Yes!* Another good point."

"Well, then I started thinking that the mother – Joe's wife – was responsible too. Because she kept her mouth shut though she suspected something…" Aisha swallows and looks down. She clears her throat before adding: "And even Chris, their other son, had a sneaking feeling…"

"Excellent!"

I glance at Aisha. Something seems to have touched a raw nerve here. She takes a deep breath and changes tack.

"And then at the end, Joe says…wait there…" Aisha flicks through the pages. "Yes, *here*." She reads out a piece of dialogue in which Joe challenges the moral superiority of those questioning his actions. He argues that in the war, everyone had their price and that each person did something for something – no altruistic moral high ground, just "dollars and cents".

"Well," Aisha concludes, sombrely, "that's true today, isn't it? Like the Americans bomb Iraq, right? And before they've even finished destroying the cities and the electricity stations and the beautiful museums, you get people bidding to see who's going to be the first to build them up again! It's *obscene*."

My jaw drops. Aisha gives me a searing look, hot with suppressed anger.

"I *am* Muslim, you know. Or I was. I've got an uncle working in Iraq. But," she concludes bitterly, "I bet I couldn't write *that* down."

"Of course you can! It's *your* response to the text that counts. Quite apart from that, this is a free country. Every citizen's opinion matters."

"Yeah, right." Aisha relapses into a moody silence.

My head spins. Something has been stirred up in Aisha. I've never seen her so passionate – or eloquent.

"The points you've made are very perceptive, Aisha. Have you made notes?"

"No. I told you. I hate writing. They're in my head. I'll remember them as soon as I go on the computer."

"Mmm." Risky. Writing notes is as important to me as a safety-net to a trapeze artiste. "Did anything else strike you as you were reading?"

"Yes, loads," says Aisha, curtly. She gives me a hostile look. (Now what is *that* about?) "There is also the whole thing about what you do for your children. Like, how far do you go for them? Like Joe was building the business up for Chris, his son, and he said he'd do anything for him. So that's why he lied about the whatsits…"

"Cylinder heads."

"Yes, and they just got shipped out anyway. And so…" Aisha's voice falters. "I can't think of what I was going to say."

"Your point was about the father doing *anything* for his son."

"Yes!" Aisha's eyes widen. "I can't…I keep forgetting what I'm trying to say. It was to do with the moral issue…."

"You were saying that Joe would do anything for Chris…"

"Yes. Just because he's Joe's son. For no other reason. Because he loved Chris. So…" Aisha's voice quavers.

"So…?" I persist gently.

"So, it all comes down to a choice. If Joe had had a conscience, maybe if he'd been religious and believed in God, he'd have thought to himself: 'To hell with the business. I can't risk soldiers' lives. Even if I go bust – even if I…'" Aisha takes a deep breath… "'even if I have to let my son down'. Because then Chris wouldn't get his dad's money. They'd all be broke, the whole family."

"So what all this boils down to is…?"

"It's like, Joe has to make a choice between God – like, between his conscience – and his love for his son." Aisha's voice has become a whisper. She fiddles with her notepaper.

"That's very well observed, Aisha. Well done. Joe does have to make a choice. But what Chris will lose, if Joe follows his conscience, is only the business. Only money. Not his life."

"But in the way it turns out afterwards, it's the same, don't you see?" Aisha doodles moodily round the margins of her notepad. "Because if Chris ever found out what his dad had done, he might never speak to him again. He'd probably leave home. His dad would be dead to *him*. And Chris would be dead to his dad. Then his mum would be upset. The whole family would be ruined!"

Aisha's hand is shaking. Her pen drops to the floor, and she scrambles around under the table. She keeps her face turned away.

"It's a very complex issue," I say, when her head reappears, "and I think you've expressed it extremely well."

"There's another issue. Wait there."

I stare at her while she thumbs through the pages of the play.

"Look – there, on page 163," she says urgently, tapping her pen impatiently on the table while I hurriedly find the right page in my copy.

"Chris's mum says that maybe if Joe offered to go to prison, Chris would forgive him. And then – look there – his mother says that there's something much bigger than the family. And – and – Joe says: '*Nothing is bigger.*' Aisha looks at me expectantly. "Don't you see?"

"I'm not sure. Are you emphasising what you've just said about the family versus individual conscience?"

"*No!* Well, I suppose yes, in a way. But I've already made that point. This is something else. This is about forgiving people. This is what Joe says." In a voice that trembles, Aisha reads out Joe's poignant speech in which he declares there is nothing Chris could ever do that would cause him to judge or reject him, because he is his son and that outweighed everything. This is what it means to be a father.

She stops suddenly. There's a haunted expression on her face. The silence in the room hangs around us like a shroud.

I swallow. "This is powerful stuff. It can bring up a lot of emotion in us. It can touch on our own lives... Maybe on yours...?"

I hold my breath. Aisha gives the faintest of nods, and seems about to say something, but changes her mind. The silence closes in again.

Suddenly she makes an impatient gesture. "Anyway, I can't think of anything else to say about it."

"This issue of forgiveness is an important one, Aisha. In the play, and in life. You've got to the heart of it, the way you've just explored it. It comes up in other Miller plays, just like all the other issues you've mentioned. You've done exceptionally well to sort them all out the way you've done. I just hope you can remember them when you come to do your essay."

"I will."

"Couldn't you make just a few mini-notes?" I ask, wistfully. "Just enough to see your brain through from the table to the computer?"

Aisha raises a ghost of a smile. She lets out a long, sighing breath.

"So, a while ago I asked you whether you liked the play. Can I take it, that's a 'Yes'?"

"I loved it."

I blink at her. This is the first time I've heard her express a like or dislike with such strong feeling.

"That's great," I say. "I love Arthur Miller, too. In fact, I think he's my very favourite playwright – apart from Shakespeare."

"I'd like to read some of his other plays. Have you read many of them?"

"Nearly all of them. And you should see them performed on the stage, Aisha! Now, that's something. You get the full impact, of the language, the setting, the characters…I remember seeing *Broken Glass* a few years ago, and feeling *electrified*. There's no other word to describe it. And then I was thinking about it for days afterwards."

"The way he writes," muses Aisha, wonderingly. "He's kind of – he gets to you, somehow."

"He reaches into your soul, Aisha," I say, smiling. "Like Shakespeare does."

"Yes." Aisha nods. She puts her head on one side, and gazes thoughtfully into space. "Yes." She nods again. "He's okay, Miller. He's good."

As she goes off to the kitchen to make herself a drink, I gaze after her in amazement. Not for the first time, I'm having to eat my words – or my thoughts. Fancy thinking Aisha couldn't tackle such a difficult subject as the moral issues in *All My Sons*. This girl could do anything she set her mind to do. But, unless she believes this…

Somehow, we need to build up her confidence – and her self-esteem.

Thursday, 29th April. "I'm not going to bother," says Aisha, stubbornly. "It's too much hassle just for a few extra marks." She leans back in her chair, and folds her arms.

"But your coursework can make all the difference between a pass and a fail! It's 40% of the total marks." I try to keep my voice calm and matter of fact, though I want to scream with frustration. Aisha is even more switched off than usual this morning.

"I don't want to do a piece of original writing. It just doesn't appeal, okay? Anyway, I can't think of anything."

"But – Aisha, look!" I point to the AQA English Specification. "This invites you to write in order to 'imagine, explore or entertain'. That covers just about every conceivable kind of writing. It could be a story, a holiday account – anything! It's just got to be original. And it's not just a few marks – you could get up to twenty."

Aisha hesitates. "I just said, I don't know what to write about. I never write anything – except letters. To friends, when I go on holiday."

"What about doing that, then? You could write to a friend from an imaginary – or real – holiday place."

"That's boring. Like, 'Dear Lizzie, I am having a great time in Spain? The weather is nice and sunny…'" Aisha's lip curls. She's not impressed.

I feel as if I'm plummeting downwards in a broken lift.

Things are not going well. For a start, yesterday evening the New Hope computer crashed, fortunately just *after* Aisha had managed, at last, to finish her writing on *All My Sons*. But it looks as if, because of her reluctance to put pen to paper – literally – she's now gone on strike.

She's reverted to being the Snow Queen, with a chilling white aloofness which keeps me firmly at arm's length. Perhaps I – or Arthur Miller – got too close yesterday. She let her guard down, revealing hidden depths of feeling, and past hurts, leaving her feeling exposed and vulnerable. So once again, she's wrapped herself in her icy cloak.

I draw my tried-and-trusted spider-gram. On one of the radials I write: 'Letter home from soldier in the war'.

Aisha continues to stare moodily out of the window.

This is frustrating, and disappointing. The only coursework that remains for Aisha to do now is her talk on Elizabeth and this piece of original writing. But it's plain that she's taking a long time to recover from her latest self-harming episode. Sandy told me that Aisha's stopped going out in the evening with the other two girls. They're all allowed out twice a week if they've behaved themselves, and they usually go to a popular café frequented by teenagers. Before Easter, Aisha had just started to enjoy these visits out. Now, she doesn't even want to go shopping during the day, spending the time mooching about in her room.

And once again, she was late getting up.

I'm at a complete loss as to what to do. Coaxing, threatening, even brisk jollying along – none of these work with Aisha.

What is this nonsense about not wanting to write? I stare at her, mystified, as she studies, in turn, each of her carefully manicured blue nails. It's not as if she's dyslexic. I've seen her write. True, it hasn't happened often. Just occasional notes in the margins of the text in the anthology – a few words, squeezed out of her reluctantly, like juice out of a lemon. But there wasn't any problem there, with the actual writing, as far as I could gather.

"Can I ask you something, Aisha? Something is puzzling me."

Aisha frowns, and gives me a wary look.

"What?"

"I'm just curious about why you don't like writing – I mean pen-on-paper writing. I've seen how fluent you are on the computer, so…so, it's not that you can't think up words and sentences…"

"So? What's the problem, then?"

I bite my lip, unsure how to express myself. "I'm not making a judgement, Aisha. Not criticising you in any way. The work you've done on the computer has been very good indeed. I'm just wondering, that's all. Is it the act of writing? Does it make your wrist ache?"

Aisha's face relaxes a little. She looks relieved at the harmlessness of the question – it's simply about the mechanics of writing. Maybe, she seems to be thinking, I'm not trying to dig out hidden truths from the depths of her psyche.

She shrugs. "A little, I suppose. I'm left-handed."

"I've noticed, Aisha," I say, smiling, " but that shouldn't be a problem."

"But I do write sometimes. You've seen me do it."

"I've only seen you write *occasionally*. And that in itself is puzzling. Because – do you remember, before Easter, when we were thinking up arguments against euthanasia, and I gave you just ten minutes to write as much as you could? Well, you wrote very quickly, and fluently. You didn't seem to be struggling at all!"

"I was drunk."

My jaw drops. *"What!"*

"I'd had a drink. Of vodka. To get me up."

"But – but – in the *morning?*" Sounding like a character in a Noël Coward play, my voice rises to an incredulous squeak.

Aisha's lip curves upwards in a sardonic smile. "So, it's okay to get pissed in the evening, then?"

"No, I didn't mean that at all. If one drinks, it should be in moderation at all times," I say, primly.

"Well then, what's the difference whether it's morning, or evening?"

"There's a world of difference, Aisha! For one thing, you were drinking alone in your room! That can't be good. And for another, you shouldn't need to drink in order to get yourself up for your tuition session. Why do you need to? Am I such an ogre? Do I make you so fearful?"

"No, but…"

"But what? Tell me. Maybe I'm not going about your tuition in the best possible way…"

"It's not you. It's the whole thing…the tuition…the exams…look, I can't explain, right?" Aisha relapses into a moody silence.

"It's okay, Aisha. You don't have to explain if it's too difficult. For me, it's just helpful to know that there *is* something there…something that maybe can be sorted out, given time."

"The drink helps me face the morning. No..." Seeing my expression, Aisha adds quickly. "It's all right. You don't have to look so horrified. It *helped* me face the morning. I'm not drinking first thing now. Not since they confiscated my bottle of vodka. Well tight, that was. But it's hard to get up. I have to force myself."

"But *why*? Your work is so good."

"*Good?*" Aisha spits the word back at me. Her eyes flash suddenly. "That's not what my father thinks. He doesn't think I'm *good*." She clenches her hands, digging her long fingernails into her palms. She bites her lip.

"Well, I'm sorry to have to disagree with your father, but *I* think you're good. And so do lots of other people. Your teachers at school for example. And all the staff here at New Hope. And not just because of your work. You're fine, just as you are. *You* are fine, as a person. I know – I can see – that you're doing the very best you can – now, and every day. You can't do any more than that! And in a way, I feel I shouldn't be pushing you any further than you're ready to go. You don't have to prove yourself to anyone…"

"But I want to pass these exams. I really do. Just to show…" Aisha stops suddenly.

"But you must do it for *yourself*, Aisha. Because *you* want to pass them. You're the important person in all this."

Aisha's face is flushed. Her eyes have widened, and she's staring straight ahead. Then she makes a dismissive gesture. "Okay, okay. Let's drop it, shall we?" The subject, as far as she is concerned, is closed. There's a long pause, during which we both gather our forces together.

I make a last-ditch attempt. "Look, if you don't feel like doing any writing just now, that's fine. You don't have to. But don't just abandon the idea of doing some original writing – perhaps later today? You said you might like to write a letter. Does that idea still grab you?"

"S'pose so. Can't think of anything else."

"Well then, I've had an idea. It's just a suggestion. You don't have to follow it, but it might spark off some ideas in you, for writing *when you're ready*. How about a letter to the future?"

"How do you mean?" Aisha's eyes flicker towards me briefly.

"I'm going to read you a letter that's never been read before today. You're the very first person, apart from me, to know about this."

I'm flagging this up for all it's worth, but at least I've caught Aisha's attention. Abandoning her nails, she's looking at me curiously.

"This is a letter from one of my ex-pupils," I intone, theatrically solemn. "I got his permission, after he'd finished tuition, to keep this letter and to show it to other pupils. But first I had to promise that I would wait ten whole years before I did so. And I kept my promise, almost to the day."

"Does he live round here? Do I know him?"

"No. He moved up north a couple of years ago. I know that for a fact, because he still keeps in contact with me. And also, I've changed his name to protect his identity. For the present purpose, he can be known only as…" I pause for dramatic effect, "…'Keith'."

Aisha stares at me. Then she gives me what my old granny used to call 'an old-fashioned look'. Roughly, this translates into: 'What the hell is she up to/thinking/plotting *now*?'

"So do you want to read this letter?"

Aisha tuts. "Oh, go on then."

With a flourish, I extract some printed sheets of A4 paper from my folder.

"Actually, there are two letters. The first letter is from Keith, aged 15 to his imaginary self in ten years' time, aged 25. The second is his reply, from his imagined future, to his younger self. Do you get the picture?"

Aisha rolls her eyes skywards. "Let's just get on with it."

I place a copy of the first letter in front of her and begin reading:

<u>Letter to Keith aged 25</u>

Dear Keith, I don't know what to say to you, I can't believe you will ever get to age 25 – or do I mean I can't believe I will never be that age?

Well I hope you are doing a lot better than I am. Have you heard what a dick-head I am? Got myself into trouble AGAIN last week: I got drunk and then tried to drive this car away. It was my mate's brother's friend's car. Well, how was I to know he was in the police? He got really heavy. Like REALLY MAD. I spent the night in the nick. I'll be lucky to get off with probation. My case comes up next week.

You know what I'm like around cars, and you know what I'm like around drink. Put the two together and you get dynamite.

I'd like to think you've got a steady job by now: if you have, you'll not only be the first one in the family to have one, you'll also be the first one to have ANY job, full stop! Mum says Dad was always on the dole, even before he left us. I wish he was back, even though he knocked me about. When he was sober, he was a really good dad. He let me help him work on the car. I helped him change the wheel once. Another time he was welding a rusty wing and I learned what you do and how to spray the paint on to match up to the main car colour.

Have you got a girlfriend? I used to fancy this girl in my class but since I dropped out of school I haven't seen her. My mates all seem to have steady girlfriends, but I think that is a bit sad at 15. Get a life, I say.

I want to get back to school and yet I don't really want to. Does that sound stupid? I am stupid, don't you think? I must have been to be in the bottom maths group. I never seem to have caught up after Year 7. Decimals and percentages and long division - Ugh! They do my head in.

Mum says I'm good at English, she likes the way I say things. Well, she would say that, wouldn't she, she's my mum. She's stuck by me, though I'm sure her patience is wearing thin by now. She said last night that I'm a bad example to Simon and Garry. Who wants to be a good example to two nerdy younger brothers? Mum says that one day, when Garry goes to school, she's going to get a job. She's always fancied working in a shoe shop. (Not surprising when you see all the pairs of shoes she has in her wardrobe.)

Anyway, I'll stop now as my arm is aching. I hope my home tutor appreciates this piece of work as it's the first time I've picked up a pen for 4 months. Do write back to me and tell me your news. Love from shit-head younger self. Keith.

When I've finished reading, there's a long silence. Aisha's head is bent over her copy of the letter, her face hidden by curls. Suddenly she looks up.

"Go on then! Read the other one – where he replies."

"Right. But I forgot to warn you about the language. Apart from correcting the spelling, Keith made me promise that I would only print the letter exactly as it was, unexpurgated."

"As if I care," says Aisha, sarcastically.

"Here goes, then:"

Dear Keith, aged 15.

No I'm not going to call you shit-head! Why are you being so hard on yourself? Anyway you'll understand what I mean soon.

Yes, I do have a job. Guess what? I'm working in a garage on the Industrial estate. It's a really well-equipped workshop. I do all the repairs, bodywork, welding, spraying – everything! I've been here for two years now. Before that I was in another garage, but I didn't get on too well with the boss, he didn't give me enough responsibility, just all the crappy jobs. It's really good money. I have my own car, it's a merc. Cost loads of money.

I don't live at home anymore. I live with my girlfriend Tanya. We rent a really posh flat on the seafront. She's working too, in an estate agent's office. We can afford the rent, great clothes, whatever we want in the world to eat, and best of all, holidays. You know you always wanted to go to Australia? Well, Tanya and I are going there in the summer. If we like it we might stay there and get a job and go surfing.

Don't beat yourself up because you can't do maths. You said you didn't catch up after Year 7. Well, haven't you made the connection yet, dick-head? That was when Dad left Mum. You were twelve at the time. And do you know what? You thought it was YOUR FAULT. You'd had a big row with him just before he walked out. You'd told him he was a piss-head. Well, good for you. He WAS a piss-head. What you didn't realise at the time that Mum and he also had a big row (well, another row because they were always rowing), and Mum told him that she couldn't stand him drinking any longer and said some other things to him that I can't remember but I know it made him furious. SO IT WASN'T YOUR FAULT!!!! it would have happened anyway. It took me a long time to realise this for myself.

I like the way you write. Keep up the English. It comes in useful for things. When I finished Home Tuition I went into college. I got some G.C.S.E's and then I did a Car Mechanics Course. I bet you can't believe all this, can you. The first one in the family to get education and a job!

I still feel angry at Dad. He made our life crap. I don't want to see him though I know he lives in town. If I saw him I'd get really mad at him. Yet in a way I do want to see him, I want to know why he drank and got out of control. I want to know if he still remembers me. One day I'll see him. But not yet.

You look after yourself, little one. Love from BIG KEITH.

When I've finished reading, there's another long pause. Aisha picks up the first letter and reads it through silently. Her face is impassive. She takes even longer to re-read the second letter.

I watch her lingering over the words, trying to take in the sense of it all – yet still trying to look as if she doesn't really care.

Suddenly I'm transported back ten years. I'm watching 'Keith' write these letters. He'd just been sent on an anger-management course. But his anger seemed to be getting worse, not better – he was still getting into trouble, and sudden insights were bursting into his consciousness, making him volatile and unpredictable. While writing, he couldn't get the words down fast enough. I can picture the hurried scrawl, all the spelling errors that for the first time didn't worry him, the hole he tore in the paper when he wrote the word 'piss-head'. And suddenly I remember how awesome it felt to be part of all this. And how I cried for an hour when I got home.

Keith – and now Aisha. Two of the brightest pupils I've ever taught, with the most potential. Things have worked out well for Keith. But for Aisha – what will her future life be like?

Aisha glances up at me briefly.

"I'm going to make myself some toast. I'm starving. Is that okay?" she adds as an afterthought, a token acknowledgement of my insistence on keeping to time boundaries.

"Yes, I suppose so." There are still five minutes before our agreed break time, but it's not worth having a dispute over it.

I cross my fingers under the table. "So, how about doing a similar letter for your coursework? To yourself, in ten years' time?"

Aisha stands up and moves towards the door.

"Mmm. Don't know. I'll think about it. I'll decide while I'm having my coffee. Would you like a cup of tea?"

This is a first. I take this offer as a good sign, even if it simply means she's taken pity on me. My burning desire for her to complete her coursework must be clinging to me like a fiery aura. Not to mention my hidden agenda – sneaking in some inspirational thinking – which Aisha no doubt spotted a mile away.

I sit down on the settee, feeling like a limp rag, and try to relax.

Face down on the coffee table in front of me, open on pages 40 and 41 is a book entitled *Betrayal*. It's one of the Lady Grace Mysteries, by Grace Cavendish, Maid of Honour to the Court of Queen Elizabeth I. The real author, in tiny, modest sub-text, is Patricia Finney. A clever device. Intrigued, I start reading the part where Queen Elizabeth, heralded by trumpets and much pomp and ceremony, and clothed in sumptuous black velvet, imperiously sweeps into Court.

Aisha has padded in silently and placed a cup of tea in front of me.

"Were you reading this, Aisha? It's good, isn't it?"

"It's okay. Elizabeth is well bossy. She orders her ladies-in-waiting about. And she treats Raleigh and the Earl of Essex like shit."

"Were those her admirers?"

"She had loads of them, but she kept them all, like, *off*. You know?"

"I can imagine."

Aisha sits down at the worktable and cups her chin in her hand. She stares down at her folder, making a big point of not looking at Keith's letters. The unspoken question hangs between us: what, if anything, will she write about?

"I think I'll write a letter about…" Aisha pauses for dramatic effect, like those dreadful TV shows where a smirking presenter waits, working the audience up for half a minute before announcing first, second and third place…"Elizabeth I!"

"Oh."

"Yes, I'll be Elizabeth writing to her lady-in-waiting, Grace. I'll pretend Grace has gone away to see her family, and Elizabeth is telling her all the things going on at court. And she misses Grace, and wants her back. Something like that, anyway." Aisha stops, abruptly.

"That's a great idea! Make a start now, while the idea is still in your head!"

I heave a sigh of relief. Lose some, win some. I was hoping Keith's letters might trigger off some insightful and cathartic writing, but Aisha simply isn't ready. Deep down, I knew this. It may be years before she can even begin to look back at the events that have shaped her life. But the good news is that the letters have at least given her some ideas.

"I'll do it later," says Aisha, yawning. "Maybe this afternoon."

"But it's got to be handed in by the end of tomorrow. I've promised your exam coordinator that I will be bringing all your work down to the school personally, at four o'clock – on the dot!" My voice tails off into a strangled yelp of frustration.

"I'll do it, right? I've got all tomorrow morning, anyway."

"Aisha, you're giving your talk on Elizabeth tomorrow morning, first thing. Remember? And Carly and Yvonne are coming on duty especially early to be your audience – it's all been arranged!"

"It'll get done, keep your hair on. Anyway, I'm not in the mood. I can't think of anything to write." Aisha gives me a sleepy, bored look.

So near and yet so far. I gaze down glumly at the cover of the 'Lady Grace' book. This session is going nowhere. Might as well call it a day.

Suddenly, drawn deep from some hidden reserve-tank of energy, I have a brainwave.

"It sounds as if you need some visual aids for both your talk and your letter, Aisha. What we're going to do now, is go off to the Museum. It's got an excellent Elizabethan section. You can see all the costumes the ladies wore… and the make-up!"

Aisha blinks. A gleam comes into her eyes.

"The museum's only just five minutes' walk away! We can be back in an hour. We'll see things that will spark off ideas, buy some postcards…and maybe there'll be a poster that you can hang on the wall for your talk…"

"Might as well, I suppose," yawns Aisha. She uncurls herself from her chair, and stretches her arms above her head.

I start gathering up the papers on the table. My fingers are on the bottom corner of Keith's letters, ready to whisk them away into my folder. Aisha puts her hand down on the opposite corner.

"I might…um…borrow them for a while," she says, casually. "I don't want them for myself, but I could show them to Abigail and Lily. They'd be quite interested."

"Sure," I say, equally nonchalant. "They're on my computer. Let your housemates keep them for as long as they like."

Aisha nods, and stares down at the letters on the table.

"What's he doing now – Keith? After ten years?"

"He's doing a degree at Manchester University," I say airily, as I stuff the last of my books into their holdall. "Mechanical Engineering. He'll be in his second year by now."

Aisha's jaw drops. I reckon that look of amazement on her face is worth all the aggro of the last hour. As she goes off to get her jacket, I can hardly wipe the grin off my face.

Friday, 30th April. "Are you ready?" I whisper.

Carol and Sandy, lined up behind me, nod.

"Why are we whispering?" asks Carol, puzzled. "The louder we are, the better, I would have thought."

"We're creating dramatic effect!" I hiss back to her.

As we file silently upstairs, the grandfather clock in the sitting-room strikes the hour – nine o'clock.

I knock on Aisha's door. No reply. Aisha, after being woken several times by Carly, the carer on duty, and by Sandy, has gone back to sleep yet again.

I knock once more and fling open the door. We make our grand entrance.

Sandy, who belongs to a choir and has a fine soprano voice, counts us in to the first line of Greensleeves, Carol joins in with a deep contralto verging on baritone. I hum along as best I can, having never learnt the words.

One behind the other, we move towards Aisha's bed, bearing tasselled cushions, each with one of Aisha's subject folders perched on top.

"What the fuck…!" Aisha startled face pops up from beneath the duvet.

"Your Majesty," I say gravely. "Urgent affairs await your attention. Your trusted ministers are at your service."

Solemnly, we all bow.

"Bloody hell!" Aisha struggles into a sitting position, pulling the duvet up to her chin. "What *is* this? Some kind of sick joke?"

"We can't proceed without you, Your Majesty," I tell her, regretfully. From under my arm I extract a large rolled-up parchment. Ceremoniously, I unfurl a poster of Elizabeth I and display it in front of her.

"We await your discourse, my liege. Will it take place here, in the bedchamber, as is the royal custom? We would all gladly give audience to your royal proclamations, while you rest in your bed. Or would you perchance care to repair to the meeting chamber downstairs?"

Aisha's jaw drops.

"Bloody hell," she says again. "I don't believe this." She stares at each of us in turn, aghast. For a moment she looks as if she's about to cry. She draws the duvet even closer around her ears. "Why are you giving me this grief?"

This phrasing – the idiom of twenty-first century youth – has a comically authentic sixteenth-century ring about it. Aisha catches its resonance, and suddenly bursts out laughing.

"We are here because YOU are important, Your Majesty." I sit down on the edge of her bed, at a respectful distance. "You are far too important to allow you to sleep the morning away."

"So where's it to be then?" asks Carol, suddenly deserting her role of minister, and plonking herself heavily down on the other side of the bed. Queen Elizabeth topples sideways, then struggles upright, trying to maintain her dignity. "So? Here or downstairs, where it's all set up for your talk?"

"With your ladies-in-waiting, Yvonne and Carly, ready in their seats, Your Majesty," I add, reluctant to relinquish my part.

"But we can get them up here, if you prefer – Your Majesty," says Sandy, helpfully.

Aisha giggles. In spite of herself, she's enjoying this. And so am I. I'm relieved it hasn't turned out to be a complete disaster. But what could I do? Aisha, at this most crucial point in her coursework, was not up – yet again – when I arrived. Desperate measures were called for. And luckily, I've had the full support of Sandy and Carol, who I must say have played along brilliantly.

Aisha stares at us all in turn, with an expression I can't quite fathom. She's half-smiling, half-angry. She blinks rapidly and puts her hands up to her cheeks. Without her make-up she looks much younger. Her hair is tousled, face flushed with sleep and embarrassment, eyes wide. In the big bed she looks tiny, like Alice in Wonderland after she'd swallowed the mixture that makes her shrink.

For a moment, it looks as if she's going to dive under the duvet again, but then she capitulates.

"All right, *all right*. I'll get up. But I need the loo. Can you all just get out, for Godssake?"

"The ministers will retire and await your pleasure, Ma'am." I incline my head, solemnly, and get to my feet.

Backing away towards the door, I keep bowing. The others follow suit.

"But if you're not bloody well up in five minutes, ready or not, we'll all be piling in here together – plus any other staff we can find." Carol lobs her parting shot as her head disappears round the door. "Like Mike. He's outside, mowing the lawn. Been here since 7.30, he has. He could do with a break. *Your Majesty.*"

"Okay, okay! I said I was getting up, didn't I?"

Aisha flings aside the duvet, as we retreat. We bow our way through the doorway back on to the landing. Then we run downstairs, stuffing our fists into our mouths like children.

"Don't I get any privacy in this place?" calls out Aisha, as she pads along to the bathroom.

Downstairs in the office, Sandy hands me Aisha's latest piece of coursework, hot from the press. The sitting room computer was still out of action, so Sandy let Aisha use the office computer yesterday evening. She'd needed some persuasion, but I'm impressed that she has, at last, got round to it. I scan through the single sheet of A4 print. Hmm. Not bad, though a bit short and sketchy. I'm relieved that she avoided plagiarism by abandoning Grace, the lady-in-waiting. Instead there's a sweetly romantic letter from the Earl of Leicester to Elizabeth, declaring his undying love and loyalty.

I'm struck by the innocence of the writing – and by the longing and hope nestling between the lines. Aisha the romantic is very much alive and undamaged. This *must* be a good thing.

Tuesday, 11th May – (11p.m. - at home in bed.) The list of suggested texts for the English exam depresses me more and more each year. They always seem to include *Lord of the Flies*, *A Kestrel for a Knave*, and *Of Mice and Men*. These are great novels, but the subject matter is heavy, focussing on the dark side of human nature. After reading them, I experience overwhelming despair and helplessness. I've read them many times, always failing in my quest to find light and redemption within the pages. Maybe I'm not looking in the right place. But I wonder how fifteen and sixteen-year-olds are affected by such reading matter.

I wonder who chooses the texts, and on what basis. Looking through this year's anthology – with selected collections from well-known poets – I'm struck by the number of poems which flag up the violent side of life. They present a dismal picture, often portraying gratuitous violence. And I wonder, by this choice of material, if we are simply reflecting society as it is – or are we colluding with it?

There's a poem here about a motorist who picks up a hitchhiker:

'I let him have it

on the road out of Harrogate – once

with the head, then six times with the krooklok

on the face – and didn't even swerve

I dropped it into third...'

I'm not judging the poet, only the selectors. *Why?* When there's already enough violence on TV and on the cinema screen, in video games and on the streets. Youngsters find it hard enough to escape from it, without piling yet more on top. How can they fail to be influenced by such stuff? It seems that many film- and video game makers are trying to jump on the 'entertainment' bandwagon, dragging it down to the lowest possible denominator. And each time something really horrific is screened or written, someone else has to up the stakes and produce something even more gorily sick and shocking.

We're *all* responsible. We watch the carnival parading before our eyes, seeing the naked emperor go past, afraid to speak out. We don't want to be the party pooper, the lone voice in the crowd. We want to be liked and accepted by our young people – not thought old-fashioned or prudish. So we soften what we see with euphemisms and silken words which slide over the problem and thus compound it. We talk about the 'gun *culture*,' the '*culture*' of violence.' A soft word, associated until recent times with intellectual and artistic enlightenment – and now debased. By doing so, we are colluding in a sick society. We are all guilty.

Of course, we mustn't blind our youngsters to the 'real world', but how much of our entertainment is actually helping to *create* this so-called reality? While not denying the darkest elements of life, why focus on them *ad nauseam?* Why not redeem them now and again with tales of courage and endurance, love and laughter and hope?

For children to get the most out of studying these GCSE texts, certain conditions need to be in place. Firstly, there must be a teacher who is prepared to spend enough time on discussing each poem, or book, in order to tease out from his or her class all the various points of view. This demands a lot – energy, time, commitment, sensitivity, good debating skills and class-management. Plus a good rapport with the pupils so that they feel free to speak their minds and to trust that their opinion will be heard and valued. Secondly, the selectors of texts do so – presumably – on the assumption that all the pupils will be mature enough to understand the moral and ethical issues involved, to judge them within the context of a wide spectrum of human behaviour. They assume that all students will devote a lot of time and thought to the texts. Sadly, there will be many youngsters who lack the maturity and good study skills; and who do not have adequate teaching. (How many hard-pressed teachers rely on handing out copious notes, but don't have time for discussion?) I can imagine many disaffected students reading their set book – in a rush for the first time – the night before the exam. What on earth will they make of it?

How about a different choice for a change? Let's find some literature with light, love, humour, courage, compassion and faith. A novel or biography that energises and inspires our young people to emulate the hero or heroine. Or maybe something that's simply hilariously funny. What's wrong with just having a laugh? Don't they deserve it, these youngsters stuck inside revising on a glorious day in June, when the rest of the world seems to be on holiday!

I shift around, trying to get comfortable. Doing preparation in bed is never a good idea. Pens and papers disappear under the covers and under the bed, never to be seen again. I'm tired – it's time to stop.

Let's hope Aisha finds some meaning in it all. If anyone's experienced the dark side of life, she certainly has. Sometimes, I have the feeling that she's way ahead of me in her understanding of the set texts.

Wednesday, 12th May. Maybe the prospect of waking up every day to our less-than-tuneful rendition of Greensleeves tipped the balance. Since her dramatic 'reveille' eleven days ago, Aisha has been getting up on time.

By nine o'clock, when I arrive, Aisha is sitting down at our worktable, reading through the poems of Carol Ann Duffy in the anthology. There are exactly two weeks before her English Literature exam and we've only just made a start on these. At last, Aisha is beginning to see the urgency of the situation. And she still has all her other subjects to revise, particularly maths. Over the last month, it's become clear that she hasn't covered the whole syllabus in this subject. Even Aisha, capable though she is, is finding some topics very difficult.

So reluctantly, professional integrity has compelled me to give three of my ten hours with Aisha to a colleague, Amy, who teaches maths at GCSE level. She has been helping Aisha with algebra, probability, trigonometry and other mathematical mysteries.

Aisha looks up from her reading. Her eyes are bright.

"It's my mum's birthday next week!"

"That's nice!" I say, absently, my mind still preoccupied with our heavy workload today.

"Yes. I might be seeing her. My social worker's trying to arrange something. We might go out somewhere."

I glance at her while I unpack my bag. She's trying so hard to sound casual, but the raw longing in her voice is painful to hear. This meeting is far more important to her than her GCSEs.

I sit down next to her. "Have you any ideas about where you'd like to go?"

"That depends on what Mum wants to do, really."

"Have you asked her?"

Aisha's face clouds over. "Not yet. The social worker's been talking to my mum, trying to increase the contact time between us. But it's – well, it's complicated…it's not just up to Mum…" Her voice tails off.

Too right it isn't, I think angrily. Aisha's father, Nasser Mansur, has to give his permission to a meeting between his wife and daughter. It's unbelievable all the hoops Aisha has to go through just to see her mother. My most recent conversation with Sandy revealed that, while Mrs Mansur was only too happy to increase the contact, her husband was putting every possible obstacle in the way.

Aisha's looking down, frowning, rolling her pen along the table top. Suddenly her face lights up again.

"I'm going to take her shopping, get her to choose her own birthday present!"

"That sounds like a great idea!"

"Only, if we do, it'll most likely be in the morning, so I won't be able to have tuition."

"Don't worry, Aisha. Your mum's birthday is important. We'll work around it, somehow."

"Because I woke up suddenly last night with this idea. Mum and I could go to Russell's – you know, the department store in town? – and like, browse around. Mum likes it there because there's loads of different things to buy and they're all in one shop. Like scarves and handbags and household stuff…" Aisha pauses, tumbling through her thoughts. "Mum hates being out in public, having to keep on going into different shops, all crowded and that…"

"I'm sure that would be a real treat for her."

"And while we're there, we could go in the restaurant for a snack. Mum likes it there, because it's quiet. She says you get a nicer class of people in there!" Aisha smiles indulgently. "We wouldn't need to go out of the store to find a busy café somewhere, so we could spend longer, shopping…"

"A good idea…"

"…and I bet she'd like a scarf, a long, wide, floaty one…"

"Aisha, we really need to begin now."

"…or maybe a handbag. I've been saving up for ages. I could easily…"

Gradually, Aisha runs out of steam. I try to draw her attention back to the anthology.

"What did you think of Carol Ann Duffy's poetry?" I ask her.

"Hmm?" Aisha's attention is still elsewhere. "Oh... The poems. I think they're weird. I mean, they're good. Well written and that. But they're all about death and stuff."

"Not all of them," I say, amused.

"Well, most of them. Look. This one – 'Havisham'. It's about her dead lover who she was going to marry. And this one's well sick – 'Salome'. She's cutting off the heads of all the blokes she sleeps with – just for fun! Weird, or what?"

"The poem's based on a well-known story..." I launch into the derivations of the poem, with difficulty persuading Aisha to make a few notes in the margin. "Did you notice anything else about the poems, apart from death?"

"Yes, she bases them on real people's lives. Like Elvis, or Shakespeare. Or on characters in novels, like Miss Havisham."

"Good! And how does she do this?"

"She sort of – elaborates on them. Imagines what they're thinking and feeling. So you get more than you get in the original story. I bet Dickens's Miss Havisham didn't express her feelings in the same way."

"No? How is it different, then?"

"It's deeper, more gutsy," says Aisha promptly.

"So maybe the poems aren't just about death? What else could they be about?"

"Well, for example in 'Anne Hathaway'. It's about her dead husband, Shakespeare, but it's also about, like, love."

"What phrases tell you that it's about love?"

Aisha pores over the text, and reads out:

"*'My lover's words were shooting stars which fell to earth as kisses on these lips...'*"

She pauses, uncertainly. Her face is expressionless.

I hesitate. Any observations from now on must come from her. So far, she's been engaging in quite an animated way. But this is sensitive material – the imagery is very erotic. I don't want to push her. Yet I don't want to over-protect her, either. I compromise:

"Can you find any other striking similes or metaphors on the theme of love?"

Aisha scans the poem. Her face has suddenly become impassive, almost business-like.

"Yes, there's this one:

'The bed we loved in was a spinning world

of forests, castles, torchlight, cliff tops, seas
there he would dive for pearls...'

and there's this one:

'Some nights I dreamed he'd written me the
bed a page beneath his writer's hands...'"

Aisha stops and stares at the text. "I don't know what that means. Oh, hang on a minute, I see what the poet's doing. She's making Anne Hathaway compare the bed to a page. And she's comparing Anne and Shakespeare, when they're together, to his writing. Like all the rhymes and romance and drama."

"That's right! Well observed."

"This bit about the second-best bed. I don't get it. Oh, yes – I do, now. So although it's only Shakespeare's second-best bed that he's left to his wife, actually it's much better than the best bed, the one the guests sleep in. Because Shakespeare and Anne have a real romp. It's quite full-on. But the guests just 'dozed on, dribbling their prose'. The point is – well, what I think, is that he and his wife really love each other."

"*Excellent*, Aisha!"

Wow! I'm bowled over by her keen observation and understanding of the meaning. And I'm also struck by her apparently mature handling of the sexual imagery, which is quite graphic and doesn't need too great a leap of imagination to get the full picture.

In a class full of GCSE students, – even from kids with trouble-free backgrounds – the poem could have provoked some sniggers and lewd comments. But any youngster in a one-to-one situation such as ours might have found the poem embarrassingly cringe-making. In fact, with some kids, I wouldn't even attempt it. I'd chicken out. And how many youngsters would, without prompting, have seen beyond the sexual innuendo, realised how the sensuality of the metaphors shows the tenderness, the strong emotional bond between the lovers?

Yet Aisha, in spite of our one-to-one, and her damaged childhood, spotted the links right away, and was willing to point them out! Amazing. Her mature response to the text, her willingness to share her ideas, without any apparent embarrassment, surely indicates that she has somehow transcended her earlier traumatic experiences.

Or has she? Something in Aisha's demeanour and tone of voice niggled uneasily at the back of my mind while she was reading out the quotations. There was a detachment, a flatness about the way she read which was totally out of keeping with the passionate language of the poem. She might as well have been reading out extracts from *The Financial Times*. I get the strange feeling that Aisha is functioning on two entirely separate levels – or rather on just one, for the other, for the moment, has gone underground.

Many teenagers who have been sexually abused want desperately to be part of the crowd. So they laugh and boast and joke about sex with their peer group. Some become promiscuous, acting out the sex without the emotion. But others react differently. They long to feel *normal*. Yet there's often, lurking deep inside them, a haunting fear about their own – and others'– sexuality. In effect, the whole area becomes a no-no. 'Don't go there,' warns their subconscious mind. Any feelings, emotional resonances, about the subject become split off, sometimes buried deep in other parts of the whole organism – the *soma*. Sex becomes theoretical, lodging in that part of the brain where it can be retrieved for academic purposes such as analysing a poem. But in truth, sex has now become about other people – to be observed, from a safe distance, in literature and in the lives of friends. Disowned.

Yet by doing this, by shutting down one part of our being, by stifling our passion and sensuality that so hungers for expression – 'Life's longing for itself' – we become less than ourselves. Our very essence withers and atrophies – all our emotions, our creativity, our Life Force.

Just now, Aisha's survival instinct is showing her how she must cope. For the moment, her inner wisdom has conjured up a protective cloak, swaddling her vulnerability. But how tragic if, in the future, this cloak were to become her straitjacket. If Aisha were to lose her verve for life.

She's flicking back and forth through the pages in a desultory fashion. She seems to have lost interest in the anthology.

"Have you read through all the poems, now?" I ask her.

Aisha hesitates for a fraction of a second.

"Yes, I think so."

"What about this one, the one called 'We Remember Your Childhood Well.'?"

"I'm not sure. I can't remember. I might have missed that one." Aisha shifts uneasily in her seat.

"Shall we read one verse each?" I suggest. This is our usual way of approaching a new poem. It gets into the rhythm and meaning very quickly in a companionable kind of way.

I read a few lines. When it's her turn, Aisha seems to be rousing herself from a deep slumber. She pulls the poem towards her very slowly. She reads out in an expressionless voice:

" *'Your questions were answered fully. No. That didn't occur.*

'You couldn't sing anyway, cared less. The moment's a blur, a Film Fun,

Laughing itself to death in the coal fire. Anyone's guess.

Nobody forced you. You wanted to go that day. Begged. You chose

The dress. Here are the pictures, look at you. Look at us all,

Smiling and waving, younger. The whole thing is inside your head'. "

After Aisha stops reading, there's another long silence. It's filled with sadness and grief.

"Can we just leave it?" says Aisha suddenly. "I'm tired. I don't have to do *all* the poems, do I?"

"Not if you don't want to. I'm sure you can get by on the ones you've studied."

"I need a break." Aisha stands up suddenly, tossing her copy of the anthology aside like a Frisbee, sending it skimming halfway across the table.

"Okay."

"Can we do something different afterwards?"

"Sure. We'll revise *Lord of the Flies*."

That book isn't exactly a laugh a minute, but it will provide a change of scene – and of theme. With a sinking feeling, I pull the anthology towards me and read the last verse of the poem:

'What does it matter now? No no, nobody left the skidmarks of sin

on your soul and laid you wide open for Hell. You were loved.

Always. We did what was best. We remember your childhood well.'

Friday, 14th May – 8.30 a.m. "She's on a waiting list to see a psychiatrist," Sandy tells me, moving her coffee carefully away from the computer keyboard, "but we've been waiting for three months now, almost as long as she's been with us."

"Couldn't she see a counsellor, privately? Surely New Hope would pay?"

"Unfortunately, that's not company policy. New Hope have got homes all over the country. Every one of their residents is disturbed in some way, in need of extra help. It wouldn't be financially viable."

"But cost-effective in terms of happier residents. And they would be contributing to a more stable society," I say drily.

"I'm afraid that New Hope relies heavily on us utilising National Health and social services provision. The irony is that if Aisha were rampaging round the town wrecking nightclubs or assaulting the police, she'd get on an anger management course right away. And once there, she'd most likely be with a whole lot of other kids who'd been sexually abused, so she'd get some real insights into her own problems. But" – Sandy sighs and spreads her hands out wide – "that's not going to happen, is it? Not that we want her to behave like that, but…"

"I see what you mean," I say. "Aisha's problems are far more internal. Hidden. In fact, she's almost in denial."

I've arrived half an hour earlier for this informal meeting with Sandy in her office. Many issues have suddenly come to the fore. Apart from Aisha's urgent need for counselling, there's the question of this birthday outing with her mother. It's heart-rending to watch how much expectation and hope she's investing into it.

"What are the chances of this outing actually happening?" I ask Sandy.

"Your guess is as good as mine." Sandy bites her lip and shrugs. "Aisha's social worker is beginning to get through to her mother, but Aisha's father is a really hard nut to crack. As far as he's concerned, he no longer has a daughter."

"That's awful!"

"Of course it is. According to his beliefs, she's disgraced herself. She has defiled her body. She has dishonoured her family and her religion."

"But it wasn't her fault! She was a child!"

I choke on the last word.

"She still is a child," says Sandy, quietly, "in many ways."

I nod. "She needs mothering so desperately. Casting her out of her home is so unjust, so cruel!"

"It's disgusting." Clearly Sandy is upset as I am. "And as traumatising for her as the original abuse, I would have thought."

For a moment, we both lapse into silence. I'm thinking that there's often a month or more between appointments with a National Health psychiatrist. Aisha needs to see someone at least once a week.

"Isn't there anyone else?" I ask. "Or a support group especially for teenagers like Aisha?"

"I don't know of anything round here," says Sandy. "There's a real gap in the market, isn't there?"

For a moment, we both sit in silence again. Then I remember something.

"Last night, I was looking through some stuff that a mental health organisation sent me. I found this." I hold out a small booklet produced for teenagers entitled: 'Dealing with Abuse'.

Sandy takes it from me.

"This is good," she says, flicking through the pages. "It goes into what sexual abuse actually *is*. Many of our children are confused about this. And it lists the signs." Sandy holds the booklet open at a particular page. "How you can tell if someone might have been abused. This is really helpful. It goes on to say what the *effects* of being abused are. This is just what Aisha should be reading. If anyone needed a counsellor, that poor kid certainly does."

"Does she open up to you at all, Sandy?"

"Sometimes. If I'm on duty at night, and we get talking over a bed-time drink, she sometimes lets her guard down a little."

"I've had the same experience. A lot has come up for Aisha through the reading material we've been doing for her exams. It's resonated with her in many different ways, but it's like treading on egg-shells. And I don't want to step beyond my role of tutor, by probing too deep. In the end she wouldn't trust me and that would affect her work. Anything she talks about has to come from her. Yet, until she gets more insight into her own problems, she's unlikely to open up."

"Yes, that's right. And I'm so busy just keeping this place ticking over smoothly that I rarely have the chance to sit down and talk to the residents. The last time, when Aisha was on the point of telling me something that was on her mind, the phone rang and interrupted us."

"I think the ideal would be for all youngsters like Aisha to have ready access to a counsellor especially trained in abuse issues," I say. "Somewhere to go which is set apart from their home situation. And then, when they come back to the safety of their living-space – and it's got to be a *really* safe space – well, if someone happens to be around whom they like and trust…"

"…And when and if they feel ready to talk about something on their minds – then that's different!" Sandy nods thoughtfully.

"Yes. Because it's *their* choice. They're in control of the conversation, how it proceeds. They're the ones calling the shots."

Sandy holds the little booklet in the palm of her hand and stares down at it, as if deliberating.

"I'm on duty tonight," she says. "I usually have a night-cap with Aisha. The other two girls are allowed out on the town, but Aisha's become such a recluse that she never joins them now. Keeps her out of mischief, I suppose. Anyway, would you like to leave this with me?"

"Yes! That would be great!"

"I could just hand it to her, kind of casually," muses Sandy, "if she's in the right mood. I'll tell her it's for her information. Mind you, I can't promise anything. But I'll do my best…"

Monday, 17th May. Sandy greets me at the door. She puts her finger to her lips. Silently, she motions me into her office.

"Just a quick word before Aisha comes downstairs. We've managed to arrange the outing on her mother's birthday. It's on Friday."

"That's good news! So Mr Mansur relented, did he?"

"In the end, the social worker insisted. She threatened that social services would take the matter to court – on the grounds that it's Aisha's human right to have contact with her mother, if her mother wants to see Aisha, which apparently she does."

"What a relief. Will they have more contact now, Sandy?"

"It will have to be increased gradually. At the moment, it's only about once a month, but we want to increase this to regular weekly meetings. And another victory is that Aisha will have regular telephone contact with her mother – at a set time each week."

"Aisha must be feeling so pleased! This is going to make a real difference for her."

"Ye-es," says Sandy, cautiously, "though we've still got a problem with Mr Mansur. He's not budging one inch on his position. He's still on his high horse. He won't see Aisha. That's making things very difficult for his wife. The danger is that he'll exert moral pressure – or emotional blackmail, call it what you will – on her. If that should happen, things might well slide backwards again."

"That would be awful. Is she that much under his thumb?"

"Under his thumb?" snorts Sandy. "Under his *feet*, more like. A complete doormat, if you ask me. Though that's just my opinion, you didn't hear me say that, right?"

"But I totally agree with you. So what's the timetable for Friday's outing?"

"Ah. There's a slight problem. Mrs Mansur doesn't drive, so her husband will have to take her into town. He's got a meeting at 10.30 a.m. in his work place and so wants to get his wife into town by 10.15. Aisha's going to meet her mother in the entrance to Russell's."

"How will she get there?"

"One of us will take her," says Sandy. "Depending on who's free here. The thing is, if Aisha and her mum have lunch out, she won't be back until at least two o'clock. Can you do a split session?"

"Yes, if I juggle another pupil around. I'll do an hour first thing and another when she gets back in the afternoon."

"Good. That's sorted then." Sandy sighs with relief as she sits down at her desk. As I go towards the door, she says:

"Oh, I just remembered. You know that little booklet you left me to give to Aisha – about abuse? On Friday night I did have a quick word with her. Nothing really heavy – Aisha wasn't in the mood to open up. But I did say to her that we – you and me, and all of us here at New Hope – realise how much her experiences must have impacted on her life, and how it was natural if she felt rotten at times."

"How did she respond?" I ask eagerly.

"It's curious," says Sandy, reflectively. "I've been trying to get exactly the same message through to her for weeks, but up till now, my words have seemed to just slide off her, somehow."

I nod. "It's as if she doesn't want to hear."

"Exactly. But this time, Aisha heard me through without walking away or shrugging it all off. She looked at me as if she were really listening, making eye-contact for a change. Then, as if I'd just thought of it, I said that I'd just been given this booklet, and that she might like to read it some time. I held it out to her, and she kind of hesitated, but took it eventually and went off with it somewhere."

The phone rings on Sandy's desk, making us both jump. As she reaches towards it, she adds, "I haven't a clue where it is now, or whether she's even looked at it."

Aisha isn't in the sitting room. She calls out from upstairs:

"I'm nearly ready. For God's sake don't come up and get me. Just keep out of my room!"

I chuckle. Although I've been waiting an extra five minutes, Aisha seems at last to be getting the message that being late for her session will no longer be tolerated. And I can't expect perfection every time.

In the sitting room I begin to spread the morning's work on the table: Aisha's set books, my notes and some practice exam papers. Her English folder is in the way. I move it along to make more room on my side of the table. There, underneath, is the little booklet I'd left for Sandy. Has she read it? There's no way of knowing. I pick it up, curious to see if the bookmark is still marking the same page. On this page there's a list of twenty signs of sexual abuse in children from age twelve upwards.

A knife twists in my stomach. I see that Aisha has put a tick against nearly all of them.

Shocked, I skim down Aisha's list:

'Is chronically depressed.

'Is suicidal.

'Self-mutilates.

'Shows self-hatred.

'Runs away frequently.

'Experiences memory loss.

'Is fearful about certain people, like relatives.

'Finds excuses not to go to a particular place.

'Has recurring nightmares.

'Is unable to concentrate.

'Seems to be in a world of his or her own.

'Exhibits a sudden change in school habits.

'Becomes truant.

'Becomes withdrawn, isolated, excessively worried…'

This is a formidable list, but there's more. In the next section – the impact of sexual abuse on children – Aisha has underlined, with a black felt-tip pen: **'Disturbed behaviour including self-harm, depression and loss of self-esteem.'**

Suddenly I feel icy cold. Here, laid bare in black and white, is the hidden core of Aisha's being – all that makes her who she is, just now. This is so disturbing to see that I almost wish I hadn't peeped inside. Maybe it was a bad idea in the first place. I should never have brought the booklet in. It might tip her over the edge, into a deep depression, or another self-harming episode.

Yet – I'm also struck by Aisha's insight into her own condition, and by her courage in reading the booklet. Many teenagers who have been abused recoil from self-analysis until years, even decades later – if at all. Aisha is facing her demons, now. That must be a good thing.

I can hear her padding down the carpeted stairs. Quickly, I replace the booklet where I found it. By the time she comes into the room, I'm sitting down ready to begin the session.

Yes, I do still feel like a spy, and it isn't a comfortable feeling, but now I'm glad that I left her the booklet. All that ticking – the action – in contrast to the dark horror of the list itself, gives me hope. A conviction that one day, Aisha *will* recover.

One day. But alas, her problems aren't over and done with, allowing her to move forward with her life. There's the added dimension of her family. In effect, she has been abandoned by those she loves most dearly. How can Aisha begin to heal while she's bearing such a heavy burden?

Will this birthday outing be a chance for the family to get together at last?

Thursday, 20th May. As soon as I step inside Belview's front door, I sense a lightening in the atmosphere. Aisha's on her way downstairs, her feet almost flying through the air.

"Guess what?" she cries, as soon as she sees me. "It's all been fixed up – you know – for my mum's birthday?"

"That's fantastic, Aisha!"

"I'm meeting her at half-past ten in Russell's. Just her and me. No minging social worker hovering in the background. Making it into some big deal, us being together. We're going to be like, normal. Shopping and having lunch and stuff."

"I'm so pleased for you."

"But I won't be back till about two o'clock. Can you come later?"

"Of course. We'll have a split session."

Aisha sits down, her hands clasped in her lap, smiling. She inhales deeply, a series of small quivering in-breaths, and sighs the breath out again. The sigh of a well-fed baby falling asleep at her mother's breast. I've never seen her so relaxed.

She wants to talk about what she'll wear for the occasion. She's found just the right outfit, which she describes in detail. Then there's the subject of her mother's present - a scarf. She wants me to guess how much it cost. I'm delighted to see her so ebullient, and loath to dampen her spirits with a load of dry old exam papers.

"Have you read the *Koran*?" Aisha suddenly fixes me with sharp, enquiring eyes.

"The *Koran*? Well, no actually," I admit, shamefaced. "I'm always meaning to read it, but I'm so busy, what with one thing or another…I did take it on holiday, once, but…." The hot, Cornish beach in August wasn't quite the right setting, I remember.

"You should read it. See if it says anything about women covered from top to toe in black. Or kids not being allowed to see their mothers. He's well out of order there, my dad is."

"It must be very hard for you, Aisha. I wish there was some way we could all help…"

"He was just the same when we were all younger! Laying down the law, making me go to the mosque every Friday after school, when my friends wanted me to play round their houses. Coming down on me like a ton of bricks if I tried to take my headscarf off when we were getting into the car to drive there. It was well embarrassing. I dreaded any of my friends seeing me, all covered up like that."

Suddenly I'm transported back to my own childhood.

"I can understand a little of what you felt like, Aisha. When I was five, my mother insisted that I have piano lessons twice a week after school. And then do half an hour's practice every day, in between. I just wanted to play with my friends, too!"

"Piano lessons!" Aisha glares at me as if I've completely missed the plot.

"I was just agreeing with you, but shifting the emphasis a bit – to parental expectations. My mother put great store by 'accomplishments' – to use an old-fashioned word. My parents – and yours – had certain goals and expectations for us, according to their belief system, and tried to make us adhere to them. But I could hear the other kids playing outside when I was stuck indoors – and I hated my piano lessons."

"I don't think that's the same at all!" sniffs Aisha. "I'm talking about my father being a religious zealot and you're going on about your piano lessons!"

I laugh. I'm enjoying this. Our first real sparring match. Aisha's suddenly become alive. And that word 'zealot' allows me yet another glimpse into her talents. What other riches lie beneath the surface? It's like discovering seams of gold in all the dross.

Seizing the moment, I ask, "Have you thought about what you want to do after your exams, Aisha? Would you like to go to sixth-form college and do some A-levels, or get a job…or…?"

"Don't know," she shrugs.

I wish I hadn't asked the question. In the space of a few seconds, Aisha's cheerful mood has gone.

"No ideas at all?"

Aisha puts her elbows on the table and props her chin on her hand. She gazes gloomily out of the window.

"All I want is to see my mum and – and my dad."

"I can see how difficult it is for you to think ahead just now. But it would be good if you could start making a few enquiries and gathering information. Without committing yourself to anything…"

"I don't care about anything else," says Aisha, dully.

"But you must care!" I exclaim. "You owe it to yourself. You've got so many different talents. You could do anything – *anything* – you set your mind to. No – just let me finish. Don't block up your ears like that, please…"

Aisha lowers her hands from her ears and gazes at me with huge, troubled eyes.

"I want you to think about all the things you enjoy doing. And what you're good at. That's all. There are loads of things – I've seen them for myself. Like your talk on Elizabeth. That was brilliant! You're a natural public speaker. Have you ever thought about going to drama college, for example?"

Aisha's eyes widen. She shakes her head, doubtfully.

"You love clothes, and make-up. It's all part of the theatre – putting on a dramatic production. You don't have to be an actress if that doesn't appeal. You could be the costume designer, or the make-up artist."

For a split second, reflected in Aisha's eyes, I catch the glint of possibilities. She hesitates.

"What would I have to do to get into a course like that?"

"An A-level in drama would be a good start. Or in English literature. Then you could go on to do Theatre Studies at university. Or drama college, as I just said."

Aisha bites her lip and frowns.

"I don't know. I haven't thought about it."

"Of course you haven't – yet. All I'm doing is just exploring the options with you. You're so capable, Aisha. Probably one of the most able students I've ever had in thirty-five years…Okay, okay. Sorry to embarrass you. But it's true. I have to say it. I've also heard your debating skills, putting all the different points of view, even when you don't agree with them. You've got a fine, clear-thinking mind. A lawyer's mind. You could easily get a degree in Law."

"Law!" Aisha pulls a face. "Like divorces and claims and that? I'd die of boredom."

"Lawyers do other stuff. Like fighting for people's rights. Do you remember how passionately you argued for the rights of asylum seekers when we had that practice debate last week? Why not fight for people like that – for the dispossessed, the downtrodden. And," I add cunningly, "for the oppressed, for women who haven't the right to vote, or work, or inherit…"

"You mean, not in this country?"

Ah, I've hooked her in, now. "Anywhere in the world, Aisha."

"So I could be, like head of the United Nations, and go around to different countries, sorting them out, getting their governments to talk to each other!" There's a sparkle of mischief in Aisha's eyes.

"You could indeed. You could change the world, Aisha!"

Aisha's silent for a while, her head on one side, thinking. Then her shoulders slump.

"I don't know."

"Or …" Once I'm on a roll, there's no stopping me. "How about doing history at A-level? In primary school you loved the Elizabethan age, and that love has stayed with you right up to this moment."

"Yeah. I like the costumes and learning how they lived and their customs and that. But I hate battles and treaties. And writing essays. I'd have to do all that, wouldn't I?"

"I'm sure you'd have choices. There are lots of historians who specialise in costumes, and social history. You could work in a museum – a really splendid one like the British Museum, or the V & A. You loved our visit to the local museum!"

Aisha sighs deeply. "I just can't think about anything like that."

"I'm just throwing you ideas. You don't have to catch them all at once. Another idea is doing English at A-level – English literature would really suit you. That's another subject you really seem to enjoy."

"Do I?"

"Do you what?"

"Do I enjoy it? How do I know if I do?"

I burst out laughing. "Don't you mean, 'how do *I* know that you enjoy literature?' Well, *I* know because I've listened to you discuss, and argue, persuade and analyse. And quite honestly, I've been very impressed by the depth of understanding, and the maturity that you've brought to the subject… and—"

"No," Aisha interrupts abruptly. "I meant just what I said. How do *I* know if I enjoy it?"

"Enjoy what?" I've completely lost the plot – again. "English, or history?"

"Any of it. Anything. How do I know if I enjoy anything at all?"

I stare at her. "You just know! There's a huge difference between doing something that gives you a buzz, and doing something that bores you out of your mind or that you hate. Surely you can sense that?"

"No. I can't sense it." Aisha stares back at me, a terrible desperation in her eyes.

"But – surely – when we were going round the museum last Thursday you could sense it then, your enjoyment? I could see it. It was obvious."

"But – was it real? How do I know if it was real enjoyment, or if I was kind of…acting?"

This is like a Pinter play. I'm beginning to lose my grip.

"Well…You must have felt something inside yourself that gave you the message. Like – 'This is fun!' or 'I'd like to do this again!'"

"*Where* do I feel it? Where inside?" Aisha points to her ribcage, her throat, the top of her head, her knees.

I can feel hysterical laughter bubbling up inside me, but Aisha's intense expression shows that she is deadly serious.

"It depends," I say. "If I'm enjoying something, I can usually sense it in my whole body and mind. It's a kind of lightness of mood. But often I don't even sense it at all, because I'm so busy being in the moment, all my attention is on what I'm doing. I'm absorbed in it. For me, it's gardening…"

Aisha gives me a pitying look.

"…But often it's only afterwards, when I suddenly think: 'Hey! That was really good. All that fresh air, the scent of newly mown grass and young tomato plants, the feel of damp earth on my hands…the sound of the bees…all my new bedding plants just opening up'. And I can feel the healthy ache in my muscles when I sit down with a cup of tea... It's *then* I know I've enjoyed myself..." I finish, lamely, watching Aisha's face. She looks lost.

"I don't know what you mean." Her shoulders slump. And suddenly, I can feel a knot in my stomach, because, at last, I do understand.

"Aisha, I'm so sorry. I do know exactly what's going on for you. You said you weren't sure what was real and what wasn't, in terms of enjoying yourself. I'm afraid I missed the point. I should have picked that up sooner. That must be very confusing for you, not knowing when a feeling is real or not."

"It's me. I know it is. I'm just different." There are tears in Aisha's eyes. "When I was at my last school I was the odd one out. It was awful. I used to see the other kids doing all these things. Like being in the school orchestra, or in the swimming team, and I used to wonder: *Why* do they all do the things they do? What makes them choose this thing and not that? What makes them like something or not like it? And how do they know it's *real?*"

I swallow hard. I'm grappling with what Aisha's telling me, trying to get the sense of it. And what I'm sensing is very dark indeed. Thoughts tumble through my mind and I struggle to sort them out.

Aisha's rushing on, "And I used to think, that if I joined in with them, with whatever they were doing, I could stop myself being different. And then I'd *know* if I was real, and if my friends were being real, or maybe they were all just pretending, like me. So when they were all going mad about a rap concert, waiting outside just to get a glimpse of some group or other, I'd be there with them. Shouting and screaming and dancing about – but I didn't feel anything. It didn't feel real."

"Then maybe it wasn't real, Aisha. Maybe it wasn't *fun*. You'd have known if it was. You'd feel the rhythm of the music throbbing in your ears and in your bones. Vibrating through your whole body right down into your feet..."

"I didn't feel that. I felt – nothing."

"Then maybe rap wasn't your thing. What else did your friends do that you tried to join in with?"

"There was a computer club in the dinner hour. All these geeks used to gather together and surf the net and spend the whole time comparing their computers and all the different things they could do on them. But I couldn't join in. I thought I should, because I like using the computer. But I felt – nothing."

"So? You were bored, that was all."

"But was I really bored? Was the boredom *real?*"

"I can't say. But it sounds to me as if you've been doing what every young person does. You've tried out different activities, hoping to find one that fires you, one that gives you a buzz. People try lots of different things before they find something that really makes them tick, makes them want to get out of bed in the morning!"

"That's exactly what my last foster-mother said. She didn't understand, either." Aisha gazes at me, tragically.

"Hang on. I'm sure I do understand. You're saying that you were trying different activities but you didn't enjoy them. Right? Well, that seems clear enough. It could be, then, that it just wasn't your thing. We've all got different interests, haven't we? And it would be boring if we all liked the same thing…"

"I know all that..."

"Hang on. The point is, Aisha, that somehow, you doubted that feeling of not enjoying something. And you weren't sure if that doubt was real or not."

"That's right."

"I think," I say slowly," that what you're describing – this not knowing what feels real – happens when you haven't yet developed a sense of self. Do you know what I mean by that?"

"I've heard about it," says Aisha, touchingly.

Her odd phrasing brings tears to my eyes.

"It's a knowledge of exactly who we are, Aisha. Where we fit into the world, into the society we were born into, what we like or dislike – and ultimately this sense of self helps us find our true path in life. But it often takes ages to get to know our *real* self. It can take years and years."

"But all the people in my year at school seemed to know!"

"I expect some did. The lucky ones, that is. But I bet there were others, like you, who were trying out different things, as well as different personas."

"What do you mean?"

"I mean trying out being different kinds of people. It's a bit like an actor taking on different roles, according to which play he's acting in. Did you feel like that, sometimes?"

"Yes, a little. I nearly joined the school drama group. I put my name down for *Salad Days*. I was going to audition for the choir. But..."

"But?"

"I looked at them all – the drama kids – when they were all together, talking about which part they were going to try for. And I just didn't know if I'd fit in with them."

"Fit in?"

"Belong. In the drama group. I used to watch them. They'd all gang up in the lunch hour, talking about drama. About different plays they'd been in or seen, or wanted to act in. They were so sure of themselves, and so sure that they were really interested in it all. And – and – they were so – *easy* with each other. And I didn't feel I belonged with them."

"You wouldn't know till you tried!"

"But it was more than just belonging." Aisha looks distraught. "Like I said, I didn't know if my wanting to do drama in the first place was *real*... You just don't get it, do you?"

Before I can reply, Aisha says suddenly. "This is doing my head in. I need the loo." Her face has gone blank.

"All right."

As she leaves the room, I can feel my heart thumping. This is difficult stuff for Aisha to grapple with. I'm desperately trying to find the words which will prove to Aisha that I do understand how she feels.

Aisha seems to be referring to two distinct aspects of herself. That feeling she has of not belonging is normal for teenagers. So they join some group or other, not so much because they love drama or whatever the group represents, but simply to get that feeling of belonging. And teenagers are critical and wary and exacting. They don't tolerate differences in each other gladly. So they often scrutinise their peers closely before they decide whether they'll feel at home in their company. At this stage in their lives, most youngsters are drawn towards their peer group, rather than towards an interest. The minority – those who already have found their passion, whether it's computers or music – tend to be thought of as 'odd' by their more group-hungry classmates. In fact, the odd ones are the lucky ones. They, whether by nature or nurture or both, have already found their path in life. They've found their true selves.

So in wanting to belong, to be one of the crowd, Aisha is behaving quite normally. But, tragically, she has another problem. Just now, she doesn't, in effect, belong to a family – to a real one, her family of origin. She doesn't have that firm base from which to spread her wings and fly out into new territory. To find a new 'family' of friends or kindred spirits. And she also needs that firm base to explore her own inner territory, to find her passion, her reality. Her true self.

Aisha's description of not knowing if her enjoyment is real is very worrying. This is a problem deeply embedded in children who've been abused. Their feelings are there, but often buried deep inside, where they no longer have the power to disturb. Children like Aisha who have been betrayed by those they trust, learn not to trust. Friends, feelings, opinions – and enjoyment – what *is* trustworthy? What is real, and what is merely one of many masks or personas donned by the abused child as they desperately search for a base – a safe space in which they can feel at home, can *belong*?

No wonder Aisha feels like an outsider. For just now, that's exactly what she is.

My heart lurches. This is enormous. Aisha has a monumental task ahead of her, and I don't know how to begin to answer her questions. But I must at least try.

Aisha comes back and plonks herself back in her chair. "What are we going to do now?" she asks, warily.

"We're going to look at some of these prospectuses in a minute. But first, Aisha, I just want to finish our conversation. No…please just listen to me for a minute more. I know this is difficult for you, but I just need to say one more thing – and then we'll change the subject. I promise."

"What?" Aisha lowers her head and looks up at me through narrowed eyes.

"Aisha, do you know what I think? I firmly believe that anything you're feeling just now is okay. Right? However weird or puzzling it seems to you."

"You're just copping out of giving me a proper answer," sulks Aisha.

"No. This is a proper answer. I think you're expecting too much of yourself, too soon. You've been through one hell of a time."

Aisha swallows hard and looks away.

"You've been trying to cope with your family, with different foster homes AND your school work. All at the same time. Your poor brain's on overload. So isn't it natural that practically all of your energy has been spent just trying to keep afloat? I'm not doubting that there is a problem still to be resolved – I mean, you not being sure what is real or unreal. Yes, that's a real puzzle for you, a confusion that's worrying you. And I can hear that you really want to understand it. To know if your enjoyment is real or not. I think the very fact that you *want* to know is a good thing – a very positive thing! It shows that you're trying to find out more about yourself. But understanding ourselves can take a long time…"

Aisha's sitting very still. Though her head is turned away, I can tell she's listening.

"I think it might take a little while for you to know which of your feelings is real, if your enjoyment is real."

"Why? Why will it take a while? Why can't I see it now?"

"Because, as I said, you've been through a rough time. Your whole *being* needs a while to recover. Just now, you need to be easy on yourself. Take life one step at a time. And while you're recovering, don't spend all the energy that's essential for rest and recuperation on trying to work things out. If you'd had double pneumonia, you would rest, wouldn't you?"

"Yes, but…"

"What you've been through needs an equal amount of rest, a quiet period of not-thinking-about-yourself-too-hard. There's plenty of time for that. One day soon, you'll know if your feelings, your likes and your dislikes or likes are real. What you can do now is get out there and try things out. Whatever you *think* appeals to you, just do it! Don't wait to find out if it's real first. After a while, you'll just know!

"How will I know?"

"Because you'll recognise the buzz, the tingling in your fingers and toes. The lightness in your body and in your spirits. You'll suddenly catch yourself laughing out loud. Your feet tapping to the music. You'll start looking forward. You'll want more of this – drama, music – whatever it is. And then, you'll feel real. But you've got to start now, by chasing every tiny inkling of enjoyment you can sense stirring inside you! Try to catch it. Don't worry whether for the moment it feels real or not…Would Shakespeare have ever got round to writing his first play, if he'd spent his life agonising whether his love for drama was real, or not?"

"Shakespeare started writing for money. I saw the film *Shakespeare in Love*."

I burst out laughing. "Yes, but if it were just the money, he might have chosen something that paid a lot more than play-writing."

Aisha sighs. "I don't know. I don't think I'll ever change."

"One day – and I think this will be soon – you'll feel ready to talk to a trained counsellor, someone who has heard a story like yours many times. Talking to this person will help you a lot. You'll be able to ask all the questions you've just asked me. I can guarantee that he or she will tell you exactly what I've told you. So you won't just have to take my word for it. And this person will keep telling you these things, until you feel them in your bones. Until the words ring true for you."

Aisha shakes her head. "I just don't know."

"For the moment, Aisha," I say slowly, "I think you need a witness."

"A what?"

"A witness. Someone who you know and trust, who can reflect back to you that what you're thinking and feeling *is* most probably real. Sometimes we all need others to remind us."

"What do you mean?"

"For example, someone to remind you that yes, you *were* enjoying the museum. And the *Horrible History* book and dressing up as Elizabeth, when you gave your talk. Discussing *All My Sons*. Perhaps you need someone to point out how they can see that you're enjoying yourself."

"So, how do you know I was?"

"I was watching you. I saw your face as you skipped around the museum, looking at all the display cabinets with the jewellery and artefacts. As you admired the costumes and exclaimed how beautifully they'd been made, without sewing machines. Your eyes were sparkling. You weren't even thinking whether anything was real or unreal. You were captivated, delighted by everything you saw. At that moment, you became real. Do you remember how you felt back then?"

"Sort of…"

"Well, that's true enjoyment. That's your reality!"

Aisha rubs her forehead. "This is bursting my brains. Can we just change the subject?"

"I think you need a break. And – would you mind very much making me a cup of tea?"

Aisha escapes to the kitchen.

If anyone needed a break, in every sense of the word, she does. The path ahead of her – leading to her true self – is a difficult and stony one, but she's made the first steps. In fact, she's doing brilliantly. She's shown unusual insight. She's taken that risk – to look inside herself. A scary process at any age. Many far less damaged adults go through a whole lifetime without ever trying.

Yet that elusive prize, one's true self, is like the Holy Grail. A prize worth striving for. It won't be easy for Aisha. But today she's given me great hope.

Tomorrow's meeting with her mother *must* go well. If it does, it will boost her confidence and her spirits. Just what she needs to become real again.

Friday, 21st May. "What did you think of this course, Aisha?"

I point to the International Baccalauréat prospectus. This particular course, run by Exeter Community College, is one of only a few in the country. It is a much broader version of A-levels. It looks right up Aisha's street.

"I haven't had time to look at it yet – or the others," says Aisha. There's a rare lightness, a jauntiness, in her voice.

I'm hardly surprised. I reckon that nothing could be further from her mind just now than next year's study programme. Her happy mood is not just about her mother's birthday – there's been an unexpected development.

At Belview, an emergency situation has arisen. Aisha's two housemates, Abigail and Lily, have been found in possession of drugs at school. They've both been suspended. Sandy has to take the pair of them in to school for a meeting at 2.00 p.m. with the headteacher and governors. Abigail and Lily are at home until then, and all three remaining duty staff are needed here at Belview to keep an eye on them, and to work in the office. So after Aisha's outing, Mr Mansur has been persuaded to pick up his daughter as well as his wife. He didn't sound too pleased, Sandy told me. He protested that Belview is in the opposite direction from the Mansurs' home, but we both know the real reason for his reluctance. He's determined not to be diverted from his moral stand: Aisha, he considers, is no longer his daughter.

But Aisha's excitement is as palpable as an electric current. It's heart-rending to see all the longing and expectation she's investing in this brief encounter with her father. And worrying. For nearly two years there's been a yearning gulf between them. Yet now Aisha's hoping that within the space of a ten minute car journey, their rift will miraculously heal.

Aisha gazes out of the window, tapping her feet, drumming her fingers on the table. Her inability to concentrate isn't helped by the noise coming from above our heads. The ceiling sounds as if it's coming down. Upstairs, Abigail and Lily are stomping about, swearing. We can hear Carol's booming voice, as she tries to calm them. Out of consideration for Aisha's tuition session, Carol's trying to keep the two girls in their rooms, with instructions to tidy up. Judging by the racket going on upstairs, they're not taking kindly to what they consider house arrest.

"Shall we have a quick look through the prospectus now?" I ask Aisha, desperately trying to salvage something out of a rapidly deteriorating situation.

"Yeah, okay," says Aisha, with a faraway, dreamy smile.

I soldier on. "I think it will suit you down to the ground. Most sixth-form courses consist of five or six AS level subjects, which narrow down the following year to just three A-levels. The International Baccalauréat course is much broader. There are six subjects. And the best thing is that students also have to learn a new skill – like public speaking – or typing. Anything! And they can try out different sports. Someone I know tried paragliding. And they also encourage you to do something creative. You could do your drama! I think you'd love it all."

Aisha picks up the I.B. prospectus, and flicks through it, mildly interested.

"Some universities are beginning to value the International Baccalauréat as much as the usual A-levels," I rattle on, "because of its broader curriculum."

Aisha studies the prospectus silently for a minute or two.

"It does look quite interesting," she says, finally. "I like the idea of not having to choose just three subjects. And look – here it says you have to learn a language. That's easy! I could do French."

"Yes – that's one of your subjects taken care of right away," I say eagerly. "That would cut down on your workload. I know many students who find languages really difficult."

Aisha puts the prospectus to one side. "I don't know. I'll think about it. I might just get a job when I leave."

"Of course you don't know yet. Just keep your options open."

"How *do* people decide?" sighs Aisha reflectively, "When there's so many different things that they can choose? Like jobs, and different training courses. How do people just *know* what they want to do?"

"I suppose many people have to take what comes along. They might need the money right away. But others are luckier. They can follow their passion, their star, whatever that is. Do you know the old saying, Aisha?"

"Oh, no, here we go again!" Aisha rolls her eyes at me.

"It goes: 'The happiest people are those whose passion is also their work!'"

"I think I'll get a job," says Aisha, her expression suddenly mutinous. "I'll have my own money – lots of it. I'll be able to get out of here and get a room. That'll show my dad."

I sigh. "Aisha, don't rush into anything, please. Think it through carefully. Whatever you decide, do it for *yourself*. Not just to prove something to somebody else… You like algebra, don't you?"

Aisha blinks at this sudden switch of topic. "Ye-es…but…"

"Well," I say triumphantly, "there's a special formula for success. You won't have heard of it, because I've just made it up this minute. I'm going to patent it. And I'm going use it as the basis of a best-selling self-help book! It goes like this:

'LIFE-PURPOSE + PASSION = FULFILLMENT + HAPPINESS.'

"…How about that, Aisha?"

"Right. Whatever." Aisha is unimpressed.

Sandy pokes her head round the door. "I'd like to leave in five minutes, Aisha. Will you be ready?" Sandy's face is tense and strained. This latest episode with the drugs could reflect badly on her management of Belview.

I watch Aisha spring to her feet, scattering prospectuses far and wide. She heaps up her folders and worksheets into a rough pile and heads for the door. Suddenly she spins round to face me.

"Do I look all right?"

Anxiously, she pats her hair, and makes little smoothing movements down the side of her skirt. In fact, Aisha looks like a star dressed up for the BAFTA awards. She's taken endless care with her appearance, achieving an effect that's modestly restrained – yet stunningly attractive. She's wearing one of her long-sleeved *kurtas*, but this one, in deep cream cotton with *broderie anglaise* round the neckline, is very loose-fitting, worn over a long, navy skirt.

Now Aisha places around her shoulders the turquoise chiffon headscarf which had been resting on her lap. She gathers it up and arranges it round her head, pulling it forward so it hides her hair. She drapes it across the front of her throat and down her back.

"Will my mum think I look okay?" Aisha twirls around in front of me.

"You look a picture, Aisha," I say, admiringly. "Any mother would be proud of you." *And*, I'm thinking, *any father, too*.

I place all our work in neat piles in the centre of the table, ready for the second half of our session this afternoon. I follow Aisha into the hall. Sandy comes out of the office, rattling her keys abstractedly.

"Right, Aisha," she says. "I'll just drop you off quickly by the entrance to Russell's. I won't park. I need to get back here quickly."

As if in confirmation, we hear more chaos upstairs. Loud voices raised in heated argument. A CD player blares out mega-decibels of thumping rhythm. I block up my ears.

"Hang on," says Aisha suddenly. "I'll take my English and my maths folder to show my mum." She dashes back into the sitting room, waving the two folders at me as she comes out. She runs after Sandy.

Standing at the front door, I watch as Aisha climbs into the car.

"I'll see you later," she calls and waves regally as the car disappears round the end of the drive.

2.00 p.m. I'm chatting to Carol in the office, waiting for Aisha to return. Sandy left for the school half-an hour ago, with the two troublemakers. Poor Sandy has the unenviable task of facing an irate headteacher, plus the governors, at a full emergency meeting. She won't be back until at least four o'clock.

Carol is holding the fort. Taking advantage of the unusual lull, she's sent the two young carers, Yvonne and Carly, off to do the weekend shopping. After this morning, the house is eerily silent.

"How do you think she's doing, then?" asks Carol, giving me one of her blunt, direct looks.

"I think she's doing very well, considering all her problems." I reply, guardedly.

"Hmm. Well, I have to say this, but don't get your hopes up about her passing these exams. Or even taking them in the first place. I never see her doing any work in the evenings."

"She works very well in our tuition sessions," I protest, staunchly loyal to Aisha. I know it's her nature, but Carol always seems to be unnecessarily pessimistic where Aisha's concerned. Or, is she simply being realistic, I wonder, uneasily. Am I the one in cloud-cuckoo land? "And," I rush on, "she really does seem to be facing some of her problems…"

There's a frantic banging on the front door. Carol and I jump and gaze at each other in alarm. Carol rushes to the door.

"Who's that?" she calls, without opening it.

I can hear a car revving up as it reverses and turns round in the drive.

"Just let me in, will you? LET ME IN, QUICK!" Aisha's distraught voice reaches us through the heavy door.

Carol releases the bolts. Aisha half-falls through the entrance. Her face is white as a sheet. For a moment she stares at both of us.

"Aisha – what on earth…?" I begin, my voice trembling.

"My dad," chokes Aisha. "He didn't speak to me. Not once. I sat in his bloody car for ten minutes and HE – DIDN'T – SAY – A – FUCKING – WORD!" Aisha thumps her fist on the wall next to her. "And he didn't even want to look at my work folders! BASTARD!" She ends on a gut-wrenching sob.

Aisha rushes upstairs. We hear her bedroom door slam shut.

Carol and I stare at each other, horrified.

"I'll go after her," says Carol. "Hold the fort here for a moment. Someone's supposed to be ringing me in a minute. If he does, would you say that I'll call back?"

I stand at the bottom of the stairs, wringing my hands.

The doorbell shrills, and I break out into a sudden sweat. I'm expecting Carol's phone call, and for a moment I stand still, disorientated. Dazedly, hardly knowing what I'm doing, I move towards the door. Carol's forgotten to redo the bolts. I open it.

Standing on the doorstep is a short, stocky man.

"Aisha forgot these," he says, coldly. He places Aisha's folders in my hands, and turns to go.

So this is Aisha's father!

He's walking briskly back to his car, his feet scrunching on the gravel.

"Mr Mansur!" I cry out. "Wait! Please…just a minute…"

He's reached the car, and is just about to open the door. He stops and swings round.

"Yes? Who are you?"

My mind has gone completely blank. I acted without any plan at all. My feet seemed to have propelled me into this situation. Now I'm hopelessly tongue-tied.

In the passenger seat I can see a slender woman in her forties. She stares at me, startled, and draws her veil closer round her shoulders. Before she turns her face away, I glimpse Aisha's reflection – the same fine bone structure and large, beautiful eyes.

"What do you want?" asks Mr Mansur, sharply.

"I – I – er…" I stare back at him, dumbstruck.

I was prepared to hate this man. In my mind, I'd built up a picture of a huge ogre, a fairy-tale giant who ate little children for breakfast. But Mr Mansur is small, hardly taller than me. Crinkly grey hair springs back from a high forehead. Soft brown eyes, set in a lined, care-worn face, stare back at me. His gaze is not hostile, just puzzled, questioning.

"I'm – er – I'm Aisha's tutor," I stammer. "I just wanted to say…" My voice tails off. To say – what? What is there to say to this man? What am I trying to *do*?

His gaze is mesmerising. I'm drawn into those eyes. In them, I see such pain – the pain of a wounded animal. And the hurt pride of one who senses that somehow he has failed, yet knows no other way to be.

I can't hate this man. Something akin to compassion stirs inside me. How terrible it must be to be in his shoes. Forced by his beliefs, by the dictates of his conscience, to choose between his daughter and his God.

"I just wanted to say that Aisha's doing very well – with her studies. She's working hard. I think she'll pass her GCSEs."

A silence. Mr Mansur frowns. His gaze, wary and defensive, scans my face.

"Well, goodbye," I say, awkwardly. "Thanks for remembering Aisha's folders."

I hold out my hand. Mr Mansur hesitates. My heart thuds in my ears. Then he takes it. Though brief, the clasp is firm. His hand feels slightly rough, and warm.

He nods at me curtly, and gets into his car. I stand still, rooted to the spot, watching him drive away.

Back again in the house, I stand at the foot of the stairs, listening. Aisha's sobs rend the air, touching me through the closed door of her bedroom, grabbing at my heartstrings. I can hear her thumping the pillow and throwing herself from one side of the bed to the other. Her anguished wailing has reached Biblical proportions. I run upstairs.

Half way along the landing, I bump into Carol, coming from Aisha's room. She's clutching something in her hand.

"Aisha doesn't want me near her," says Carol, her face crumpled with distress. "I went in to ask her if she wanted anything. She's just lying on the bed, throwing herself about. Hysterical, like. She screamed at me to keep away from her."

"Is there anything I can do?" I ask, helplessly. "Bring her up some water, or…something?" A sudden fear grips my stomach. "Should I go in anyway, in case she tries to harm herself?"

"Unlikely," says Carol. "I've just picked up her wash-bag – with her scissors and razor in it. There's nothing else in there she can do any damage with. Best to leave her. But stay outside her door for a little while, if you don't mind. I need to ring Carly and Yvonne and get them to come home right away. They can go back and finish the shopping later. And I'll try to get a message through to Sandy. If she can leave her meeting a bit earlier, that would help things here."

I pace outside Aisha's door, biting my thumbnail. I wait for some let-up in her sobbing, a breathing space in which I can put my head round the door. Just to let her know I'm here, that I haven't abandoned her. After a few minutes, there's a quieter sound – a muffled, strangled mewling. Somehow, this is even worse than her sobbing. I open the door quietly and peer round. Aisha's lying face down on top of the duvet, the corner of it stuffed into her mouth. I can just see the side of her face, beneath a tangled mass of wet curls. Her cheeks are red and blotchy.

"Aisha," I call, softly. "Is there anything you need?"

Aisha dives further down into the duvet. She thumps her feet angrily.

"Go away!" she sobs. "Just leave me alone."

"Okay. But I'll be nearby. Just call me if you want some water. Or some coffee."

I close the door, and sink down to the floor, leaning my back against the wall. Thank goodness none of Belview's internal doors have locks on. And all the windows are set to open no more than a few inches. The house is holding her safe. Just as we are, by the precautions we're taking to protect her. And by holding her in our thoughts.

I shut my eyes, and stretch my legs out flat in front of me. I can hear Carol's voice in the office, talking to the school secretary. The grandfather clock strikes two-forty-five, then three o'clock. Aisha's snuffling cries are more intermittent. At last they stop, and all is quiet.

I creep downstairs to the office.

"I think she's asleep," I tell Carol.

"Thank God!" says Carol. "I've never heard her carry on like that. Sobbing as if her heart would break."

"Perhaps it's a good thing? Maybe she's letting it all out at last. Should I peep round the door again in a few minutes…just to make sure she really is asleep?"

"No, I'll go up in a minute. I've just got to ring Lily's social worker. We've been trying to get hold of each other all day. I'll leave some biscuits and juice by the bed for when she wakes up…You might as well go. Sandy will be home soon, and Yvonne and Carly. I'll manage till then."

"Poor Sandy," I murmur. "Some day she's having!"

"Yes – and she'll be bringing the girls home. They'll be crashing around, disturbing Aisha. I'll try and get a message through to Sandy. She needs to tell those two scatterbrains exactly what Aisha's been through, ask them to consider how someone else feels for once in their lives." Carol sniffs and picks up the phone.

I drive round to the local corner shop and search for something that will cheer Aisha up, to remind her that we're thinking of her. There's a poor selection. I end up buying a box of chocolate liqueurs – not the best choice in view of Aisha's drink problem, and probably something I desperately want for myself just now. But there's nothing else, only chocolates with nuts in. Now for a card. The same problem – all I can see are Get Well cards with roses on. Ah, this is more like it. Here's a teddy, ill in bed, medicating himself with a huge box of chocolates. The message inside reads: 'Hugs are fine – but so is chocolate!' It doesn't quite hit the spot, but it will have to do.

Carol's in the kitchen with Carly and Yvonne, unloading carrier bags of food into cupboards and fridge. I ask them to sign Aisha's card and to write their own messages. Mine is: 'Chocolates are fine, but hugs are the best medicine.' Carol peers over my shoulder and nods approvingly.

"We'll make sure she gets plenty of those – whether she pushes us away or not! I'll leave the card and the chocolates by her bed so they're the first thing she sees when she wakes up."

I drive away with a heavy heart. Surely, no amount of chocolates or even hugs can ease Aisha's pain at present. The very best medicine – unconditional love from her real family – seems beyond her reach.

I make straight for the Pier Café. For once, cake – even chocolate cake – would stick in my throat. I drink a cup of tea and wait, gazing out of the window at the turquoise sea dotted with the bright sails of windsurfers, at the early holidaymakers huddling against their windbreaks on the beach. At last, the soothing whish-slosh of the waves crashing against the pier supports, and the cry of the gulls, give me the strength to drive home.

Later, I ring Belview to ask how Aisha is doing. Sandy answers, her voice cheerful. She reassures me that Aisha is coping well. In fact, at this very moment, she's sitting at the kitchen table with Lily and Abigail. They're all munching their way through the box of chocolate liqueurs, while complaining bitterly what a hard blow life has dealt them. Especially having to come and live in a place like Belview. In the background I can hear shrieks of laughter from Abigail and Lily. They've even managed to raise a few smiles from Aisha, Sandy tells me.

I ask about her meeting at the school. The girls have been lucky. Their version of the story – that the drugs had only just been passed to them in the playground by another pupil – turns out to be the truth. It's been corroborated by two other girls who also received drugs at the same time. All four swore they were just on the point of reporting the drugs to their teachers. Lily and Abigail have been given the benefit of the doubt and let off with a severe warning – next time, the police will be informed. I can almost feel the relief in Sandy's voice as she tells me all this. Her good management of Belview is no longer in question.

There's also a silver lining to all the hair-raising and traumatic events of the day. Their individual dramas have drawn Aisha, Lily and Abigail closer together. Aisha, hitherto perceived by her housemates as remote and aloof, now has their full sympathy. As soon as Sandy had told the girls how much grief Aisha's father had caused her, they'd immediately made their own cards for her. Inside, they'd written funny messages – quite unrepeatable, Sandy says – and had persuaded her to get up and to face the world again.

"So will she be all right?" I ask. Stupidly. Knowing that Sandy is no more clairvoyant than I am.

"Who knows? She seems okay at the moment, but you can never tell with Aisha. She might just be putting on a front – like she often does. She goes up and down like a yo-yo."

"I just hope she lasts out until her exams," I sigh.

I say goodbye to Sandy and that I'll see Aisha as usual after the weekend.

I'm worried. For now, Aisha seems to have rallied magnificently from what must have been a crushing blow to all her expectations. She's had the loving care and support of all those around her. But tomorrow, or the next day, when she begins to really think about what's happened – when the reality of her situation hits her – what then?

And yet – and yet – there's also hope. Though terrible to hear, there was catharsis in those sobs. As if, with such full-bodied anguish, Aisha was finally bringing some internal cleansing process to fruition.

Maybe, at last, she is beginning to let go of any expectation that her father might change. Coming to terms with such a loss will be painful. Her situation is truly tragic. Many more tears will be shed. But today, I sensed a shift. Aisha has moved forward a little towards acceptance.

Thursday, 27th May. "I'm not going to take the exams," says Aisha. "What's the point?"

My stomach contracts. "Aisha! Of course you must do the exams!"

"Why? What good will it do? What's it all for?"

Aisha's shoulders are slumped, eyes dull and downcast. Her whole body seems to have collapsed.

"It's for you, of course. So that you can move forward – towards A-levels, the International Baccalauréat, further training – we've been through all this!"

"I'm not interested in any of that now."

"And why not, when you've done all your coursework and most of your revision?"

"Because…" Aisha shrugs. "Because…I just don't care about all that crap. A-levels, training. I'm going to get a job, anyway. In August I'll be sixteen. I can move out of here. No one can stop me."

My heart sinks. This is awful. We've gone right back to square one. After last Friday's disastrous outcome, I'd half-expected this, but the timing couldn't be worse.

Tomorrow is Aisha's first exam, English literature. Her English language exam is not until after half term, on the Wednesday. In between, she has other subjects. I would dearly love to coach her right up to the very last minute, in the gaps between her other exams. However, the Education Department has made it a new policy that tuition with GCSE students must finish just before their first exam. After that, they're on their own, to do their revision in their own time.

Today will be my very last day with Aisha.

Since the dramatic events of last Friday, Aisha has been very subdued. This week, she's been up in time for all our session, she's gone through the motions of doing last-minute revision, but she's on automatic pilot. Some of that fight, the spirit that had just begun to surface before her mother's birthday, seems to have drained out of her.

But I can't give up. If she can't fight, then I have to do it for her. Suddenly I feel furious.

"Aisha, this won't do! I just won't have it!"

"What?" Aisha looks up.

"This defeatist attitude. It doesn't do you justice. I'd expected more of you. And what about me? How do you think I feel? For two whole months I've worked with you, encouraged you, willed you – yes *willed* you – not to give up. I've felt for you when things have gone badly. I've even…even cried for you. Now, at the last moment, just when you've reached the culmination of all your work, you're going to cop out. Sabotage your chances. And throw all my support right back in my face! So how do you think *I* feel?"

I catch my breath. I've said more than I meant to. In all my years working with disturbed children, I've never spoken in this way to a pupil, never made myself so vulnerable. I feel as if I've crossed over some line. My tightly held professionalism has collapsed around my ears – just as, before my eyes, Aisha's confidence is crumbling now.

Aisha stares at me. She flushes. "I…I…"

"I feel let down, that's how I feel. And more important, I think you're letting yourself down. You could sail through these exams. You've done the revision. The only thing that's stopping you is *you*."

"But you just don't understand…" Aisha looks at me with huge eyes, filled with pain. "I don't care anymore. About anything. Anything at all."

A knife twists in my stomach. "Aisha, you *must* care. Because *I* care. And so does everyone at New Hope – Sandy, Carol, Yvonne, Carly…even Mike, the gardener! He often asks how you're getting on. We're all rooting for you, honestly!"

Aisha's silent, looking down, twisting her hands in her lap.

"Look," I continue, more gently, "I know you've been through a very rough time, especially recently – on Friday. That was a terrible blow for you. I can understand how it has made you feel, but you mustn't just cave in now, Aisha. You can't give up, without a fight. Running away isn't the answer. And that's what you'll be doing. That's the coward's way out…"

"Maybe I'm a coward then," says Aisha, crushed.

I catch my breath. This conversation has suddenly taken a wrong turn.

"No, Aisha. You're not. You've just, for the moment, lost your fighting spirit. That's natural. But you can get it back again, I promise…Look. Supposing, just supposing, you do your exams anyway. Do them *as if* things are going to work out well for you in the end. Even if you can't imagine this being a reality just now, even if it means doing them as a kind of exercise."

Aisha shakes her head, her eyes haunted. "I'll feel like a robot."

"So? Maybe sometimes in life we have to act like robots…" Ah. Suddenly, that look in her eyes hits me like a blow in the solar-plexus. I realise that Aisha must have had to become robot-like – to switch off her emotions – when enduring the sexual abuse. "But these would be good, sensible robots, Aisha, not frozen, fearful ones. These robots are friends we can trust, who can get us through situations that, deep down, we know are best for us. *These* robots are our inner wisdom. They recognise our true needs even though we can't quite understand them just now. But if you don't like the word 'robot,' why not think of another? I'm just trying to find a word for the power – the force – that is always there inside us all. It often acts like a kind of robotic energy. I'm trying to describe this sense of *rightness*, a steadiness deep within us, which can override all the fear, the doubt and the anger…We need to take a deep breath, and act *as if* it will all come right in the end. *'As if,'* Aisha! Two little words, with so much power in them!"

Aisha sits very still. The seconds tick by. I hold my breath. I squeeze my fingers together so tightly in my lap that I can feel the shock waves all up my arm. And suddenly I realise why, with every fibre of my being, I'm *willing* Aisha to take these exams. For by doing so, she won't only be acting for herself. Nor even for me. This brave step, this leap of faith, will be for ALL my children. The abused, the abandoned. Kids who are so unhappy that they can't even imagine a future. For every single one of the courageous children I've taught in the past, and sadly, for those who are still to come. Somehow, over the last two months, Aisha's story – and her struggle – have come to encapsulate all the pain I've witnessed over the years. The tears. And also, all the hope.

Aisha sighs, a long shuddering sigh. "I don't know…I'll think about it."

"Great! That's the spirit! So, do you feel ready to tackle *Of Mice and Men*?"

I heave a huge sigh of relief. But we're not out of the woods yet. There's nothing in today's revision programme today that's going to cheer Aisha up. *Of Mice and Men* makes a gruelling read. This book, by John Steinbeck, follows the fortunes of George and Lennie. George, by force of circumstances, has become the carer, as well as the friend, of Lennie, who has learning difficulties. Lennie's a huge giant of a man, a friendly simple soul, whose great physical strength is barely under control, and gets him into constant trouble. George is fond of Lennie and wants to take care of him, although Lennie puts an almost impossible strain on their friendship. Even so, George remains loyal to Lennie almost to the last.

The men have no permanent jobs and the story follows them to yet another farm where they are taken on as casual labour. Because of Lennie's misdeeds, life for George is a struggle. During their time on the farm, John Steinbeck depicts the dreadful conditions of the poor, the black and the disadvantaged.

In the end, because the ranch hands are going to kill Lennie, George has no choice but to shoot his friend.

Not exactly a bundle of laughs.

Now, I feel anything would be more suitable material for Aisha than this book. I find it heavy going, even when I'm in a good mood. But this is the one book we haven't spent much time on. Today will be Aisha's last chance to revise it.

Thursday evening, after Aisha had been so happy and up-beat that day, I'd dug out some old exam papers and found a question that seemed challenging, but interesting: '*Of Mice and Men* is a depressing book, about depressing events, with a tragic end. There is no light in it at all. Discuss.' Just the right question, I'd thought.

Just now, this seems a bad idea. I'm worried that simply reading through this book could tip Aisha back into the slough of despond. But my notes have been prepared and there's no time to think up new questions.

"Shall we discuss this question, Aisha?" I ask, tentatively. "It's a favourite that often comes up. And just re-reading parts of the book will help refresh your memory about the events and the characters."

"I don't mind," says Aisha, flatly.

She drags her copy of the book towards her and flicks through the pages in a desultory fashion. I pull my pad of A4 towards me and, with pen poised above paper, prepare to take notes, hoping Aisha will follow suit. Which of course she won't. Notes are anathema to Aisha, whereas to me they are the very stuff of life. Today, in my anxious mood, Aisha's refusal to write anything down is worrying me more than usual. How on earth will she fill up at least two sides of the exam paper for each question?

"So, any ideas, Aisha? Can you see any redeeming quality in the book? Anything that lightens the darkness?"

Aisha stares down at the book in her hands, her face expressionless. During the two months I've been tutoring her, I've learnt that she often needs a long time to think, before she replies. She needs to have the words all ready in her head before she expresses an opinion. But today, I'm not sure whether she's even concentrating.

This is hard going. And disheartening. We've covered all the work. This is the final hurdle.

I wait. The grandfather clock ticks away solemnly as if each second marks the end of something. I remember that today is the last time I'll hear it chime. There's a lump in my throat as I gaze out into the garden. Mike has just put all the summer bedding out - petunias, busy lizzies, African marigolds. All ready to unfold. In two weeks the garden will be a blaze of colour and I won't be here to see it all. I swallow hard. I know full well what's going on inside me. It's far easier to grieve about a stupid old clock and a bunch of marigolds than to acknowledge my real sadness. That deep sense of loss that I feel with all my pupils, when my journey with them is ended.

Aisha's turning the pages of the book, almost synchronising to the rhythm of the clock. I feel as if we're both suspended in time. Her face is hidden by her hair. I don't know if she's even reading the words. Maybe she's just gone off somewhere in her head – into some dark, inaccessible place. Perhaps I should prompt her a little…

But Aisha suddenly straightens up. She rests her elbows on the table.

"What I think," she says deliberately, like a judge summing up all the evidence for a high-profile court case, "is that there *is* some light in the book."

"Ah! And what makes you think that?"

"I think…what I think…"Aisha frowns, grappling with her thoughts… "is that the light isn't like, *obvious*. Like a happy ending? It's sort of hidden, in all the words."

"In the words? Can you give an example?"

"I don't know if it's in the words so much as in what happens," says Aisha slowly. "Like the events. I know they're gloomy and horrible and that. But running through them there's something else that isn't dark. And it's not just the plot. It's in some of the people in the book, too…oh, I can't explain." She tuts and sighs, impatiently.

"That something that isn't dark, Aisha. Try to describe it."

"I don't know how to. It's like a feeling…"

"A quality?"

"Yes!" Aisha's face clears for a minute. "That's it. A quality. And George has got it. And Crooks, the one who's the only black man on the ranch. You know how they're all horrible to him – all the other ranch hands? But he just keeps going and makes the best of things." She stops and takes a deep breath.

"That's good, Aisha. Very good."

"And George, sticking by Lennie even when he crushes the mouse in his huge hands and does horrible things like that."

I ask gently, "Is there a name for this quality that George and Crooks show?"

"Well, it's like I said. They just keep going somehow. It's like, I saw this programme once. There was this woman, right? And she had this child who had problems and he used to scream all night and bang his head and she never got any sleep. She could have put him in a home, but she loved him too much. So every day, she'd keep going and clean up his mess. Every single day of her life. And she didn't know when it would end. It was awful for her."

"That's amazing. That woman certainly had a lot of courage."

"Yes!" says Aisha. "That's the word I was looking for. Courage."

"I've known many other examples of that," I say, reflectively "Like the man with terminal cancer who just carries on with his life, even though he knows he will soon die. He plays with his grandchildren on Sundays, and on his better days, he'll go out into his vegetable patch and potter around a little. He'll sow seeds in his greenhouse to come up next spring, though in his heart he knows full well he won't be around to see them grow."

"That's well sad," says Aisha.

"It is sad, but it's also courageous. The same sort of courage that George shows. And Crooks."

"It's strange, that..." Aisha's brow furrows. She gazes into space, working something out. "Because when you say that word – 'courage' – I think of, like, a fireman who rescues people from a burning building? Or an explorer who has to fight off cannibals who are just about to put him in a pot and cook him..."

"Or a soldier who runs out under fire into the battlefield to drag his wounded friend back into the trenches..." I add, triumphantly.

I'm enjoying myself now. Aisha's back into battle. Her face is more animated, her eyes alert with interest.

We spend a few minutes thinking up extreme courage stories. But it's time to get down to the heart of the matter.

"So what we're discovering is that there are two kinds of courage, Aisha. There's the spectacular courage that wins medals for bravery and gets reported in the papers – like the soldier and the fireman. And there's also this other kind – the *quiet* courage that doesn't get medals. That often doesn't get recognised at all. Like the cancer patient and the exhausted mother. And like George, who just keeps going even when he can't see the end of all his troubles..."

"But he can see the end of all his troubles in a way!" interrupts Aisha. "You know that bit, where George suddenly thinks of buying a little plot of land with the money he's going to make on the farm. And he tells Lennie about it. And they both get excited about it?"

"And…?"

"Yes – yes. I see!" Aisha's eyes open wide. "*That's* the light. Like the hope. It's only a dream, but it keeps him going when it's so awful at the ranch…"

"Yes. It keeps his courage going. It stops him giving up."

Aisha's silent. I'd love to know what she's thinking just now.

"So," I say, very carefully, "this quality of just keeping on, not giving up. This quiet courage. Some people don't have it. They just give up, they let life toss them about like corks on the waves. But the lucky ones, who do have it – these people are life's survivors. Like George. And like you, Aisha. Because I think you have this very special quality too."

There! I've said it. Something I've been thinking for a very long time has just burst forth, bubbling out of me before I could stop it.

Aisha starts, and makes a choked sound. She flushes deep red. Then she puts both arms across her face and twists her body away.

"I'm sorry, Aisha. I've embarrassed you, I know. But I'm not the only one who can see your courage. Everyone here at Belview has witnessed it. We're *all* impressed. Someone has to tell you what we've seen, so it might as well be me."

Aisha twists back round to face me. She peeps through her crossed arms. For a moment she reminds me of a very small child playing 'Peek-a-Boo.'

There's a very long silence. I wonder whether I've gone too far this morning, pushed my luck well beyond the call of duty. Yet…it's as if I'm compelled to encourage Aisha by all means possible. To make each word a rallying cry – to buoy her up with every ounce of energy I can muster. Because tomorrow will be too late.

Aisha unwraps her arms. She looks straight at me.

"For God's sake," she says, accusingly. "First of all you say I'm a coward. Then you say I'm courageous. Make up your bloody mind!" I catch a glint of mischief in her eyes.

"No, Aisha, what I meant was…"

Aisha pushes back her chair. "This is doing my head in. I need a coffee. I'll be back in a minute, right?"

"Right…And …and would you mind very much making me a cup of tea?"

Suddenly, *Of Mice and Men* seems less of a drudge. Thank you, Aisha, for helping *me* see the light in it.

It's the end of the session. We've done all we can. *I've* done all I can. Aisha's on her own now, as far as her GCSEs are concerned.

For the last time, Aisha unbolts the front door. The bolts have been replaced and slide back easily.

On the doorstep, I hold out my hand.

"Good luck, Aisha. I'll be thinking of you tomorrow, keeping my fingers crossed. But I know you'll do well! I can feel it in my bones."

Aisha takes my hand shyly. She watches me as I go down the steps. Just before I get to my car, I remember something important. I turn, and call out to her:

"Oh, and Aisha… Make some NOTES on the spare sheet of paper they'll give you. Then if you run out of time you can hand the notes in. And it will help you organise your ideas…"

"Yeah. In your dreams," says Aisha, grinning.

"Goodbye then, Aisha. Good luck!"

"Bye."

As I turn round the bend in the drive, I look back. Aisha's still standing in the doorway, waving.

'IVAN THE TERRIBLE'

∽

Thursday, 17th June 2004. Last night, Sally, my line-manager, rang me. She was desperate for help. Would I take on Ryan Ivanovich, a fourteen-year-old boy excluded from school for challenging behaviour? Ryan has been out of school for the last three months. The Education Department are keen to get him into a new school by the end of the summer term.

I'm on the way to Ryan's house – and I'm stuck in a traffic jam on the hottest day of the year. Fortunately I won't actually be seeing him today. Ryan and his mother have a meeting this afternoon with the Educational Welfare officer to discuss possible new schools. Today's mission is a recce. I need to know exactly how long it will take me – bang in the middle of the holiday season – to drive from Bethany's house, two miles away, to Ryan's home. Getting to this part of the town is always tricky at the best of times.

Ryan lives at the eastern end of town – the extreme opposite to the docks and the harbour. The coast, where most of the traffic is aiming for, is tantalisingly near but so difficult to reach by car it might as well be in the Outer Hebrides. As many of the hapless grockles, now furiously beeping their horns in frustration, are just about to discover. For this road does not lead to the sea.

The traffic has ground to a halt. Red-faced families sweat in over-heated cars. A steamy mirage rises from the tarmac in hazy swirls, while the tempers of the drivers rise to boiling point. I, too, break into a hot sweat, but this is not due to the scorching sun streaming through the window. I'm remembering what Sally told me yesterday.

"I have to warn you," she'd said, "that Ryan can be violent. Unpredictably so. He was excluded for bullying. Always small boys, never girls or kids his own age. He picks on the puniest, weakest ones in year 7. And you should also know that his last tuition placement didn't work out. A few days ago, Ryan attacked Tim on two separate occasions. Once with a pair of scissors and the next day with a knife."

This was extraordinary. Tim, a colleague, is a big, burly man – a Rugby prop forward, who has the knack of dealing with disaffected teenage boys with firmness mixed with charm. He's never had any problem with them before. Hearing this, I'd felt weak at the knees and had to sit down.

"So, why me, Sally?" I'd squeaked, panic rising.

"Because Ryan won't perceive you as a threat," Sally replied, confidently. "You're female. That's a good start. And you're small, and slight, and…sort of…flimsy-looking… In retrospect, it was not a good idea for Ryan to have a male tutor. Tim must have somehow represented his father, who was a violent alcoholic."

With a shaking hand, I gripped the phone. "Sally, I'm not sure if I'm the right…"

"You'll be fine!" said Sally, breezily. "You're one of our most experienced tutors. You have a kind, gentle way with you…"

"Thanks a billion, Sally, but I still think…"

"Sleep on it. Then pop in and look through Ryan's file tomorrow morning. Okay?"

With a sinking heart, I heard the smug sound of *fait accompli* in Sally's voice. Somehow, she always gets round me, even though I can see through her buttering-up techniques. And what did she mean by calling me 'flimsy'?

The traffic's on the move again. We crawl through an area which is grey with concrete buildings. Along the dusty road, on the right, the urban sprawl of bungalows gives way to the council estate where Jack lives. I wonder how he's getting on? Then there's a short parade of shops, and a garage. Beyond these, two ugly tower blocks of flats rear up. On the seaward side of the road, opposite the council houses, there's a huge industrial estate. The road finishes at the quarries, with all the attendant works for producing clay and related products. There are tall rectangular structures with steel towers, hoppers, and long hangar-like sheds.

There is no through way. This road ends in big barrier gates and a warning KEEP OUT notice. And this is what causes the chaos, every day – especially in the summer. Holiday makers, heading for the beaches beyond the town at the eastern end drive along here, on what they believe to be a coastal road. They're lulled into a false sense of security by an occasional glimpse of a turquoise sea between the buildings on the industrial estate. It's always the same. At some point, they realise their mistake. They try to turn round. Not a good idea, with heavy trucks coming the other way.

This timed journey was a good idea, though. It's taken me forty minutes so far. I haven't even had time for lunch. Next time, I'll bring a snack with me.

We're moving a little faster – positively speeding along at twenty miles per hour. Past the industrial estate, past the high-rise flats. But now the fun really starts. Cars grind to a halt again. I'm about two hundred yards away from the barrier gates of the quarries. Beach-seekers, peering ahead, suddenly realise they're about to reach a dead-end.

Two young children watch me out of the rear window of the car in front. They wave. I wave back. They roll their eyes and make monster faces. We spend a pleasant few minutes having a 'horrible face' competition. Suddenly they both turn towards the front. The driver – presumably their dad – is thumping his fist on the steering wheel. In his mirror, I see the shape of colourful oaths. Without warning, he reverses, nearly colliding with my front bumper. He executes a noisy three-point turn. As he draws level, he leans out of his window, fuming.

"How the hell do I get to the beach?" He glowers at me as if it's all my fault.

"You have to drive back the way you came until you reach the roundabout. Turn left. Go straight ahead until you reach the T-junction. Turn left into the main road out of town. Follow the railway line on your left for a half a mile until you come to the bridge. Soon after, you'll see a sign which says Puffin Bay and Shell Beach."

With an angry jerk of the gears, without even a 'thank-you', the man drives off. His children stick out their tongues at me.

I sigh. This happens all the time. People are too busy navigating the roundabout to see the sign, partly hidden with trees, which says No Beach Access.

Now the quarries and the clay factory buildings are looming large in front of us. To the summer visitors who have unwittingly ended up here, the clay works are ugly. But to their employees, the place undoubtedly has its own beauty. It employs much of the town's working population. Sadly, there are rumours that it might soon close down.

Some distance ahead, I can just see the gates being opened to let some big trucks through. Then there's the usual skirmish by the barrier as those tourists who've been a bit slower on the uptake suddenly start to panic.

Luckily, I'm not going as far as the quarry gates. Unexpectedly, there are more houses along here. I turn right into a dark, narrow road.

Huddling up against the high perimeter fence of the quarries are two drab, mean streets, running parallel with each other. Tumbledown terraced houses, brick-built and soot-begrimed, stand forlorn – remnants of another era. These are the battle-scarred survivors of the bulldozers. Once, there were more streets here, but in the 1960s, in the name of progress, whole neighbourhoods, close-knit communities, were swept away to make room for the high-rise flats nearby. Yet for some reason, these two streets were left intact. I check the broken sign at the beginning of the road nearest the perimeter fence: Jubilee Road. This is where Ryan lives.

I drive along slowly, looking for Number 32. The street looks neglected. And forbidding. The houses are overshadowed by the tower blocks on one side and the quarry factories on the other. It's a swelteringly hot day, yet little sunlight reaches the scrubby patches of ground that were once front gardens. Jubilee Road seems to have thrown up its hands and given up on itself.

I stop the car and get out, looking for house-numbers. Here's Number 24. I'll walk from here. Not a good idea to park just outside a pupil's front door, anyway. It attracts too much attention from the neighbours. And if it's a first visit, the pupil often does a runner out the back. But in this area, any car – even my ancient Fiesta – parked in a regular spot each day would be a prime target for theft or vandalism.

Depressed, I glance up and down the street. *This* is the environment in which my new pupil – a violent pupil – has to live.

I walk along the cracked pavement. On closer inspection, the houses don't look so bad after all. True, there are roof-tiles missing and the brickwork needs repointing, but these homes were solidly built. The poor things are simply suffering from fifty years of neglect. In Islington, even in this condition, they'd sell for half a million pounds. All they need is some tender loving care. Suddenly I want them to stay, to escape the next wave of bulldozers. When did it all start, I wonder – the idea that houses are commodities rather than homes; of profit-making at the expense of communities?

Number 32 looks more neglected than the other houses. Peeling blue paintwork on crumbling wooden windowsills, wet and flaky with rot. There's a deep crack in a small, frosted-glass window upstairs. In the narrow strip of front garden an old washing machine lies on its side, next to rusty paint tins. Gulls swoop down pecking open the black plastic bin bags piled up against the front wall.

Quickly I return to the car. I sit a while, gazing at the run-down street, feeling increasingly despondent.

First thing this morning, before seeing Bethany, I'd popped into the office to look at Ryan's file. The information was brief – and stark. Ryan's full name is Ryan Ivanovich. His father, Sergei, is Russian. In the early 1980s, Sergei came to London to study economics and politics. Ryan's mother, Catherine, is English. She'd just got a degree in Russian, and had landed a plum job at the Russian Embassy as a bilingual secretary. Sergei and Catherine met at a Russian Club. In 1985, they married, and their first son, Karl, was born soon afterwards.

In 1990, the couple moved to Bristol. Sergei had obtained a good job in an export firm. He had also started on his thesis, which would gain him an M.A. By this time, Ryan had been born. House prices were cheaper in Bristol – another good reason for moving out of London.

So far, so good. While reading all this I gained the impression of a high-flying, well-educated couple, comfortably off in their own home. But what happened next was unexpected.

Subsequent information given in the file was sketchy and factual. Mostly, it consisted of a series of dates, but it soon became obvious that, for the Ivanoviches, things were changing for the worse. In fact, the dramatic downturn in the family fortunes read like the plot of a Dostoevsky novel.

In 1995, Sergei's job with the export firm was abruptly terminated. In 1996 he was hospitalised for two months. A psychologist's report at this time stated that Karl, the eldest son, was showing disturbed behaviour at school.

In 1997, the family was suddenly made homeless. Social services became involved. The youngest child, Nina, aged three, was deemed at risk.

By 1999, Sergei had started drinking heavily and had periodic episodes of violence towards his wife. Now Ryan, aged nine, was beginning to show aggression at school. By now, the whole family was considered at risk. Catherine and the children were moved to a safe house. At the end of 1999, the couple were no longer in contact with each other. Yet Sergei was trying to see his wife, to get her back. Catherine lived in fear for her life.

In 2000, Catherine became ill, and had three months in hospital. The children were found foster homes near the hospital and saw their mother frequently during this period. After Catherine came out of hospital, she managed to keep the family together, though she was very weak. She found a small, privately-rented one bedroom flat for herself and the children. However, as long as her husband was in the same city, she felt unsafe.

Six months ago, Catherine, now divorced, moved with the children to Jubilee Road. The whole family, stated the report, were hoping to make a 'fresh start'.

I sit still, gazing out at the gloomy street – at homes as dismal and bleak as the Ivanoviches' story. Is *this* their new start? How can someone like Catherine, highly intelligent with such good prospects, have fallen on such hard times?

Soberly, I turn the car round and drive away, thinking hard. I want to understand Ryan. I need to work out a strategy that will engage him right from the start, to catch him unawares with the element of surprise. I'm hoping to make his tuition – at least to begin with – as unlike school as possible. I want Ryan to have a chance to reinvent himself.

Oops! Did I just call him '*Ryan?*' Think again – quickly!

His file had left out one crucial piece of information. Luckily, I'd had the sense, last night, to ring Tim. To ask *why* Tim thought Ryan had attacked him.

And I learnt that for the last two years Ryan has refused to answer to anything but the name 'Ivan'.

"Forget this at your peril," warned Tim, ominously. "He'll have a go at *you* if you do."

As Tim found out, to his cost, last week.

It seems that my newest pupil has adopted a new identity. Ryan Ivanovich has become Ivan the Terrible.

I turn into the main road towards the roundabout, nudging the car between two noisy trucks belching out exhaust fumes. I'm feeling tired. It's almost the end of the school year, and mentally I've been winding down from tuition, sure that there'd be no more work until September. Yet, just when I thought it was all over, I've been presented with a new pupil. But not one I would have chosen. Tomorrow I'll be meeting him. And I'm scared.

Perhaps I should ring Sally when I get home – refuse to take him on?

Yet, since when has my work been about picking and choosing the children I teach? Somehow, Ivan has come into my life. Somehow, whatever happens, we'll find a way of working together.

Ivan, welcome.

Monday, 18th June. I'm back at 32 Jubilee Road. I knock. A few seconds later the door is opened just a fraction. A small face with freckles and bright blue eyes peers through the narrow gap. This must be Ivan's sister.

"Are you the new tutor?" The eyes stare at me with curious disbelief.

I admit that, yes, I am. I introduce myself.

The door closes while a chain is detached, then opened wide.

"Come in." A young girl of about ten, with bobbed red hair cut in a fringe, looks at me shyly.

I step inside while she closes the door.

The hallway is dark and narrow, typically Victorian. I'm already feeling anxious, and the scarlet flock wallpaper reminds me of *Dracula*, and Victorian melodramas. It hangs, peeling, from the corners near the ceiling. There's also a chilling dampness in the air. I shiver.

"You must be Nina." I hold out my hand, solemnly. "That's a pretty name. Quite unusual, too."

"I'm the only Nina in the whole school," she answers, proudly. Then she looks at me speculatively.

"How long are you staying?"

I hear doubt in her voice. It verges on incredulity that I should be here at all.

"Well," I reply, "normally, I'll be staying for two hours. But today I'll just be here for an hour. It's quarter to two now, so I'll be here until…"

"Till quarter to three?" Nina's eyes grow even rounder. "Ivan won't last that long!"

Nina seems to have all the composure and self-assurance of someone twice her age.

"We'll see," I say, with a brisk confidence I don't feel. "Is he in this room, here?"

I point to the first door on the right.

"No, don't go in there! That's Mum's room. She's asleep. You have to come this way. Follow me."

Bustling ahead like a tour guide, Nina leads me towards a door at the end of the passage. She reaches for the handle, then stops suddenly, swinging round to face me.

"If he starts playing up, Mum says you're to call me first, and I'll wake Mum up if I judge that there's a problem. Right?"

I can't get over how mature she sounds. She stands there, squaring her shoulders, a small, slightly built child. At the tender age of ten, she seems to have taken on heavy responsibilities.

"Right. But there won't be a problem, Nina."

Nina looks at me sceptically as she pushes open the door. I step inside a small living room. Through an open door opposite, I can see a small galley kitchen which juts out into the garden. On the right of this door, a sash window overlooks a long, narrow patch of ground. There's a table under the window, with three chairs. But – no Ivan.

Nina nods silently towards the right of the room, and like a wraith in the night, glides out of the room.

On the settee, piled high with blankets, I spot movement. A shock of black hair slowly emerges. Then Ivan's face – pale, with Slavic cheekbones. Dark brown eyes glower at me incredulously.

"What the fuck…! Which graveyard did they dig you out of?"

"And good afternoon to you too, Ivan." I place my workbag on the table. "Where are we going to work? Here, at the table, or on the settee?"

Ivan stares at me, not moving.

"My considered opinion," I say, conversationally, "is that it's always better to work at a table. However, as this is just an initial visit, we can do the main business at the settee, if you prefer."

I grab a chair and swivel it over towards Ivan, so that I'm sitting next to him, level with his head. He's half sitting up, propped up on one elbow, glaring at me. I open my folder.

"This, Ivan, is your page, which is already prepared. I have a points system. You get points for work done in our session, for good behaviour, and for being ready to begin when I arrive. Being ready also includes keeping to agreed break times, which last about five minutes. This last thing is important. You can gain up to four points for this alone. Now..."

I narrow my eyes and gaze at him thoughtfully.

"...I think it's only fair to give you one point for being ready. Just for this morning, I'll count you as being ready, as you are actually in the room, and as I hadn't yet explained my system. However, in future, starting on Monday, points will be given only if you are sitting at the table when I arrive."

"Bloody hell! What *is* this – boot camp?"

"If you can manage to get thirty points, Ivan, you get a small prize. If you get ten lots of thirty points I give you a large prize – or money of equivalent value."

Ivan stares at me, mouth agape.

I continue, "You might like to see examples of how my points system works…"

I lean over his semi-prostrate body, propping the folder up against his raised knees. I show him Jack's column, thick with points on every page. Then I turn to Cassie's – keeping her name covered.

"This pupil," I say, sadly, "didn't manage to gain points as quickly as Jack. It took her three weeks before she got her first prize. But as you see, Jack managed to get thirty points almost every week."

Ivan gawps at me as if I've just landed from outer space. I can see him trying to decide whether I'm just harmlessly batty – or if I'm a force to be reckoned with. This uncertainty throws him. He's plainly flummoxed, wondering where he fits into these two extremes. Trying desperately to get the measure of me, so he knows how to operate. Just now, I'm an unknown quantity.

"So, for now, you have gained your first point, Ivan. Well done!"

With a flourish, I enter it in his 'Ready' column.

"What we're going to do now, is draw up a work plan. My aim – *our* aim, Ivan, is to get you back on track. I'm here to help you sort yourself out."

"Bloody hell!" mutters Ivan, shifting uneasily. "Who do you think you are?"

"Someone who's been doing this job a very long time. I've worked with children and teenagers of all ages who've had all kinds of problems. In all, I've supported hundreds of them. And at least 95% of them have successfully got back on track, sooner or later."

Ivan swallows, hard. For a moment his eyes meet mine, then flicker away to the side, but not before I've glimpsed a very faint spark. Of hope. Then, trying hard to look as if he couldn't give a damn, he surreptitiously peeks to see how many points other children have gained. He asks why some points have been crossed out. I explain that I deduct points for bad behaviour. He wants to know if anyone has ever reached the magic number of three hundred. I tell him, as I have told so many others before, that very few pupils have, because if they're doing that well, they're usually back in school by then. Ivan listens, his mouth half-open. He's still not quite sure if I'm sane.

"So let's make a start, shall we?" I say, at last. "It would be good if we could sit at the table, so I can rest on something while I write."

"Go on then," says Ivan, truculently. "*You* can. I'm not moving."

"Fine," I reply, as I decamp to the table.

Judging when to make an issue of something is a fine art. I've never managed to crack it completely. Today, I'll play safe.

"So what do you enjoy doing most of all, Ivan?"

"Nothing," says Ivan, predictably.

"And when you're not doing 'nothing'? Do you like maths, English...?"

"Fucking boring. Don't like any of it."

"Other subjects? I.T., languages...?"

"Sport," says Ivan, sulkily. "That's all I liked. And we hardly ever did it."

"Any sport in particular?"

"Athletics. But it stopped because the teacher who did it left."

"Do you like football?"

"Don't like football."

Unusual. "What else?"

"Nothing. Look – they didn't do the sport I liked at school. Right? I hate team games. I like surfing, and rock climbing. And bombing."

"*Bombing...?*" My stomach lurches, sickeningly.

"Yes. Jumping off high cliffs into the sea." Ivan levers himself up a little and for the first time, looks at me directly. "You know Puffin Bay? There's that bit of cliff that juts out – at the very end of the beach? Well, there's a huge rock you can climb down on to. Then you just bomb off."

"Not Puffin Rock?" My heart's thudding.

"Yes. That's where we go, me and my mates."

Ivan's sitting up now. He swings his legs to the floor, and swivels round to face me.

"It's ace..." He leans forward, his eyes shining. "But we have to do it when we know the coastguards aren't around."

Because it's been banned, I think grimly.

Two years ago, there was a terrible accident off Puffin Rock. A young lad, Ivan's age, misjudged the depth of water all around the bottom of the cliff. He plummeted to his death on the lower submerged rocks. After that, all 'bombing' stopped for a while. However, in the last month or two, it's been slowly creeping back again. For many teenage boys, a successful leap from the rocks into the swirling waters far below is a local rite of passage.

"Did you know that there have been accidents off Puffin Rock, Ivan?"

"Yeah...so? That bloke that killed himself, right? He was well stupid. He didn't judge the jump properly. You've got to know when the tide's coming in and where the rocks are in the water. You have to find the gap between the rocks."

My imagination boggles with horrible images.

"Ivan, you do realise that what you're doing is highly dangerous, don't you?"

"So?" Ivan shrugs. Then he narrows his eyes. "You'd better not stitch us up. You weren't planning to, were you? Because, if you were…" He clenches his fist and draws back his arm, menacingly.

"What I'm concerned about is your safety. My job is to support you. To help you get yourself into a new school by the end of this term. What good is it if, instead of bringing one healthy teenager to meet your new headteacher, I – or your mother – have to deliver a bag of broken bones?"

Ivan blinks at me. One side of his mouth suddenly twitches into a grin. The he squares his shoulders.

"I can take care of myself, right? I'll be careful, Okay? I shouldn't have said anything…just drop it, will you."

I drop it.

I ask if he likes science. Ivan says he did like it in the first year of secondary school. The teacher was good. He allowed the pupils to set up their own experiments, and Ivan enjoyed doing this, and watching demonstrations. But the next year, the science teacher was 'crap'. The discipline in the class was bad, children couldn't see the demonstrations properly because the teacher let the pushier ones get to the front. Ivan scowls, this injustice still very much fresh in his memory.

"Well," I say, brightly. "I suggest we draw up a timetable, together."

Ivan yawns, and affects a complete lack of interest. It looks as if he's just about to curl up and go back to sleep. I take a new sheet of paper and divide the page into columns headed by the days of the week. I tell Ivan that we have to do English and maths, but apart from these two subjects I'd love to hear his own suggestions.

"Dunno," says Ivan. "Don't give a toss." His eyes are firmly shut.

"I think we should start with science on Monday," I say firmly. "And I've also got some ideas for sport. Individual sporting activities, not team games. Rock-climbing for example. But that will come later, depending on how well you behave in our sessions together."

Ivan opens his eyes. He sits up again.

"Can we go bombing?" he asks eagerly.

"Bombing is off the menu, I'm afraid. But there are other sports that involve an equal amount of daring. Do you know what I think, Ivan?"

"No, what?" – truculently.

"Some kids, especially boys of your age, need to move about a lot. I mean, move their bodies. It doesn't seem natural for them to be sitting still at a table or desk, writing. It makes them fidget. Do you feel like that sometimes?"

"Yeah…s'pose."

"So, before I arrive on Monday, I'd like you to make a list – or at least think about – some activities you'd like to do. Maybe a new one you'd like to try for the first time. I'll make enquiries – find out which centres or organisations have them on offer."

Ivan stares at me warily. Suspicion, interest, curiosity chase each other across his features.

"It's time to stop now. Well done, Ivan. You've managed to concentrate for a whole hour. That deserves another point."

I write down: 'Good concentration. Managed almost an hour. Engaged well with subject matter'.

"What are you writing about me?" asks Ivan, suspiciously.

I show him. He blinks. "You haven't said anything bad, then?"

"No. Only good things this afternoon."

"And those – there. Are those my points? Have I got two?"

"Yes. You'd have had more if you'd sat at the table. Maybe next time…"

I stand up and begin to pack my folder and pencil case away. Ivan watches me for a moment. Then his swings his legs down to the floor and stands up.

"Is that it?" he says.

"That's it," I reply, smiling. "Until Monday."

Ivan stretches his arms above his head. Then he walks into the kitchen. He moves with an easy unhurried pace. But it's like watching the lazy movement of the lions at Longleat. I sense pent-up energy ready to spring out at any second.

I watch as he reaches up to one of the wall-cupboards in the kitchen. He's tall for a fourteen-year-old, five-foot-seven or -eight. Six or seven inches taller than I am. His dark brown eyes are deeply set beneath straight black eyebrows, giving him a sombre, brooding look. His cheekbones are high and well-defined. A wide, expressive mouth seems to be set in a permanent scowl. He reminds me of Nureyev, the legendary Russian ballet dancer. Yet his physique is still boyish – narrow-shouldered, straight-backed. And his voice, though husky, hasn't fully broken. His journey into full manhood has barely begun.

I open the door into the hall. Nina, bent over the keyhole, nearly falls into the room.

"Was he good?" she whispers, eyes round with curiosity.

"Very good. You can tell your mother that when she wakes up. In fact, I'll tell her myself when I see her on Monday."

"She *might* be up then," says Nina, solemnly. "We never know how she's going to be from one day to the next. She never knows, either. We just have to take it day by day."

She sounds just like a doctor reassuring anxious relatives about the progress of their loved one.

"I see." I nod, gravely, trying to stop my lips twitching with amusement. Yet, it's not really funny. Nina's talking more like a thirty-five year old than a child. And shouldn't she be at school?

I call back to Ivan: "I'll see you on Monday. We'll do a science experiment. I'll expect you to be up and ready though – or we won't have time."

Ivan grunts from the kitchen – I can't tell whether in agreement or disagreement.

I let myself quietly out of the front door. A great sense of relief floods over me. I'm not quite sure what I was expecting, but suddenly I feel lucky to be all in one piece.

Monday, 21st June. "I'm not doing it," says Ivan, mutinously, flinging down his pen. "I told you. I hate English. I hate worksheets. You said it wasn't going to be like school. Liar! And you promised we were going to do science."

"Just one worksheet, Ivan. And *then* we'll do science."

I'm trying desperately not to back down, but that horrible, gnawing feeling in the pit of my stomach tells me firmly that I've bungled – badly. I curse the protestant work ethic that dogged my youth. It insisted: 'Work Before Pleasure,' and exhorted us all to 'Postpone Gratification'. Whatever that might mean.

"I said, I'm not doing it,' sulks Ivan. "Commas and stuff. You deaf, or what?"

'*Or what*', I think ruefully. In fact, I'm still not sure how I got myself into this pickle. I'd sworn that I'd wow Ivan with the surprise element. I'd make our sessions cool and fun and not the least bit like school. It's that doubting Thomas inside me that's the problem. The small guilty voice that insists that I should be instilling *some* education, however little – even into the most intractable of pupils. Now I've dug myself into a hole, and I've no exit strategy.

Ivan folds his arms and lolls back in his chair. We lock gazes across the table. At least he's sitting at the table today. Thank heavens for small mercies.

"All right, Ivan. I hear what you're telling me. And you've expressed your feelings clearly. That's good. You didn't throw a wobbly." (Well, not quite…) "Nor did you 'act out'. So to show that I acknowledge your feelings, we'll leave English for today. Right?"

Ivan's mouth drops open at this rather pompous speech. He grunts, eying me suspiciously.

"However," I continue, "I'd love to give you some more points. And the quickest way to get them is simply to do a bit of English or maths. But if you're determined not to, there's a maths game I'd like you to try out. Okay?"

"Depends," says Ivan, sourly.

There's a new decimal game I found in one of my catalogues. It explains the mysteries of decimal points and place value very clearly. It's also colourful and attractive. I get it out of my bag and place it on the table.

Ivan sees it and swears under his breath.

"Do me a favour. That's a baby game."

Yet, with a gleam in his eyes, he's reaching out for the game board and the cards that go with it.

"Will you shuffle, Ivan? I'd just drop them all over the floor."

Ivan shuffles with the dexterity of a card shark. We read the rules and the game rolls along merrily. I breathe more easily. Ivan wins and looks touchingly pleased with himself.

"Can we play again?" he asks, trying to look as if he couldn't care less. But he's already shuffling the cards and dealing them out. The young child is very much in evidence – and a child, perhaps, who hasn't played many games, or even had much fun in his life.

"Well done," I say, at the finish. "You played that very well. No cheating – and you were very quick at getting the idea."

Am I talking down to him? I've noticed that I've started speaking to him as if he were still at primary school. I bet he thinks I'm patronising him. I hold my breath, expecting some blistering retort. But Ivan's leaning over me, squinting sideways at my folder, open at his page.

"Go on then, put the point down!"

"Did I say you get one for playing games?"

Ivan looks angry and disappointed.

I capitulate – again. "On the other hand, I didn't say you couldn't, and as you were doing something really important – helping me to try out a new game – I'll give you one *this* time."

I enter it ceremoniously in the column headed: 'Work achieved'.

"Can we do science now?" he asks.

"Don't you want a break first?" I ask, surprised.

"Nah. Afterwards."

If Ivan were still at his old school, his class (Year 9) would be doing Energy, with particular emphasis on 'Renewables'. This topic has been gradually gathering momentum over the last ten years. Now, it's exploded into the curriculum with a vengeance. With good reason. If there's any hope of saving this poor planet of ours, it must rest with our children, whose greater enthusiasm and awareness will surely change their parents' ways more quickly and effectively than any government initiatives.

Last night I was hard pressed to find the right experiment. It needed a) to spark off Ivan's enthusiasm and interest, b) be age-appropriate, c) be quick and simple d) use basic inexpensive household materials, and e) comply with Health and Safety. A tall order.

Making a waterwheel seemed to meet all these requirements. On the table, I place two grey cardboard egg cartons, a sheet of thick card, an old wooden ruler, a nail and some string.

Ivan watches me silently as I lay them all out.

"Let's read the science behind the experiment," I say.

Before he can make a fuss about this, I place the book in front of him and launch straight in, reading out loud from a photocopy of the same page:

"The energy from moving water is one of the most widely used of the energy sources. It supplies 20% of the world's electricity through the use of hydro-electric power stations…"

I read on. I'm expecting Ivan to be fidgety or bored. I'm reluctant to even look at him in case he interprets this as confrontational or checking up his listening/concentration ability. If he begins to see everything we do as a challenge – a battle of wills – then we're both lost.

Yet after a short while, I find the silence next to me unnerving. I glance up briefly. Ivan's eyes are darting from one illustration to another, his expression rapt with fascination. There's a picture-diagram of a hydro-electric power station. His finger traces the direction of the arrows showing how it works. He turns the page. His eyes light up at the energy efficient, charcoal stove.

"That's ace!"

He flicks back a couple of pages and pounces on a picture of a wind pump.

"Wow!" he exclaims. "I could make one of those!"

I can feel the familiar frisson of excitement. He's come alive, his eyes sparkling. Plus he's way ahead of me, reading stuff I'd planned to spend at least two more sessions on.

"Shall we read on?" I say, at last.

While I read, he's uncannily quiet. We go back to my original mission: the waterwheel experiment. Suddenly Ivan glares at me.

"Where's the paint for the egg cartons, then?" he asks accusingly.

"I didn't bring any. I thought we'd just cut out the 'buckets' for the water wheel first of all, and glue them on to the cardboard. Then we can test it out. There's no point in going to all the bother of painting it if it's not going to work. Paint takes ages to dry. But I could bring some tomorrow…"

Ivan makes 'idiot' faces at me.

"You thick or something?" He jabs his finger at the egg cartons. "See those? They're made of cardboard...*Card...board?* Like, absorbent? Like, not waterproof? Dur!"

I blink at him, then glance at the illustration. Somehow, I'd managed to miss this crucial snippet of information in the instructions, i.e. waterproofing.

"And the paint has to be gloss. Or varnish might be best," adds Ivan.

Last night, the experiment had looked easy, so I hadn't followed my usual rule of always trying it out first, in the privacy of my own kitchen.

"Well, perhaps we'd better leave it for today, Ivan. Yes, it was stupid of me to forget the paint. Let's read the next section – on wind energy..."

"Wait!" interrupts Ivan. "I've got some modelling paint upstairs. That dries quickly. If we paint the buckets first, they can be drying while we cut out the cardboard circles and measure the string..."

Before I can say a word, Ivan vanishes. His footsteps clatter upstairs on a bare wooden staircase. A bedroom door is flung open with a crash. Floorboards creak above my head, and I hear cupboards and drawers being opened.

Nina sidles round the door, her eyes like saucers.

"I woke Mum up," she says. "I judged that there was a problem, 'cos Ivan shouldn't be going upstairs in the middle of his lesson."

"Actually, Nina, everything's fine. Ivan's just gone upstairs to find some paint."

"Oh," says Nina, crestfallen. "I thought he was being bad again."

"That's all right – you weren't to know. You were only..."

I stop. In the doorway, behind Nina, stands Mrs Ivanovich.

"Nina says Ivan's playing up," says his mother. Her eyes search my face, anxiously.

"No, he's fine. He's behaving himself perfectly. I've just told Nina – he's gone upstairs to get some paint. She didn't know that."

Nina's looking at her mother guiltily. She's close to tears.

Mrs Ivanovich crosses the room and sits down suddenly on the settee, as if her legs are just about to collapse beneath her. Her features, which had been set in a worried frown, soften with relief.

"Thank God for that. I thought he was giving you the runaround."

"No, on the contrary, he's very interested in what we're doing just now. He was so keen to get on with the experiment that he didn't think..."

I find myself wittering on – partly to reassure Mrs Ivanovich, but also, if I stop talking, I'm in danger of being rude by staring at her. I catch my breath, trying to disguise my shock. I can't remember ever seeing anyone – outside a hospital ward – who looks as ill as this. *Grey* is the only way to describe this apparition. Everything about her is grey: the drab shapeless clothes, the ginger-grey, straggly shoulder-length hair, tousled from sleep. But most disturbing to look at is Mrs Ivanovich's complexion – a sallow, yellowish grey. There are dark rings under her eyes. Even her lips seem to have all the colour sucked out of them.

I introduce myself, and say how sorry I am that I'd disturbed her rest.

"Don't worry," says Mrs Ivanovich. "I'd planned to get up to meet you today. In fact, I'd intended to do so on Friday, but I'd had a really bad night and just needed to catch up on my sleep. And – I'm not 'Ivanovich' any longer. I've reverted to my maiden name, Jones. But please call me Catherine."

Her voice is cultured, well-modulated, with Home Counties vowels. But her little speech seems to have exhausted her.

"If you don't mind, I'll have to get back to bed. I'd love to talk more – perhaps at the end of the session. I'll just get myself a cup of tea before I disappear again. This is the problem with M.E. One's energy level can change, almost minute by minute…"

"I'll get your tea, Mum!" says Nina, importantly. "You go and lie down. I'll bring it in to you."

"Thank you, dear." Her mother gets unsteadily to her feet, and walks towards the door. "And there's a bowl of cold rice in the fridge. Would you bring that in, too?"

Nina runs into the kitchen and puts the kettle on. I'm just about to offer to help her, when Ivan clatters downstairs again. He crosses over to the table, placing down some tiny pots of paint.

"There!" he says. "Silver and gold. This paint dries really quick. And I found some brushes. Come on then!" he yells at me.

I'm standing, dithering, by the settee. I can still feel the presence of Catherine, and her illness, pervading the room with a cloud of negative energy.

"You were supposed to be cutting out the cardboard circles, and the string…"

"I was talking to your mother," I excuse myself, feebly. "And I thought it would be easier to paint the egg boxes all in one piece, then cut them up afterwards."

Ivan stops in the middle of prising open a tin of paint. His jaw drops.

"You special needs or what? If you cut out the buckets *after* you've painted them, the water will get into the edges where you've cut." He gives me a scathing glance. "I might as well do this myself…"

"You're welcome to, Ivan. But I'll help with whatever you want."

Ivan grunts and finishes opening the paint-pot lids. Then he neatly arranges all the materials in preparation for the experiment. Now and then he refers to the instructions. His movements are swift and sure. Purposeful. There's a lightness in his step as he moves around. He hums, a few fragments of a pop song.

Suddenly he stops and looks at me.

"Why are we doing *this* experiment? This is baby stuff. Can't we do something…" he frowns, searching for the words. "Something more…*real*."

"Let's see how this one goes, first," I say, smiling at him. "Then, *you* can choose the next experiment."

The water wheel, when finished, is a miniature version of any successful 'Going Green' project. And though I haven't lifted a finger towards its construction, I feel as proud and satisfied as if I'd just built my own eco-house.

Thursday, 24th June. "He's out the back," says Catherine, opening the door. "He's in a hole. You can go straight round – it's quicker."

A *hole?* Mystified, I make my way through the small alleyway that divides No. 32 from next door.

Whether or not we're in what is known as the 'honeymoon period' of tuition, I can't be sure, but since Monday, Ivan has been doing better than I expected. He sailed through a few easy decimal worksheets, saying – predictably – that they were 'baby stuff'.

For English, I told him he could do a description of anything he wanted: his room, a member of his family, or an activity. I wanted to check his writing ability. At first, he refused, saying he hated writing. I bribed him with the promise of more science experiments, extra points, and, when I could arrange it, a visit to an activity centre. I was rewarded with a bone-chilling account of Ivan's latest 'bombing' expedition. His handwriting was all-over-the-place, with little concept of punctuation and many spelling mistakes. However, his love of his subject gave his finished piece of work verve and colour, and he showed real feeling for atmosphere and action words: 'I bombed down through the air, and cut between the rocks, sleek as a seal'. Delightful! There's talent here which I'm dying to develop. I reckon he's just switched off from English.

How can I get his literary juices flowing again? A good start would be a visit to the local library. Ivan says he 'doesn't read'. Maybe he needs a nudge in the direction of teenage fiction – there are some excellent adventure books for boys around just now. Yes, that's what we'll do today.

At the end, the passage ends in two tall rickety gates. The one on the right leads into Ivan's back garden. I click open the latch and go in.

At first, I don't see Ivan. Then, at the bottom of the garden, flying shovelfuls of red earth draw me to the spot. Ivan is indeed in a hole. A deep one, up to his waist. He barely acknowledges my arrival. Stripped to the waist, he's panting, red and sweating. The temperature today must be almost 30° Celsius – or, if you still think in Fahrenheit, like I do, almost 90 degrees.

"Ivan! What on earth are you doing?"

Ivan stops for a brief moment and wipes his forehead with a grimy hand.

"I'm building a wind pump."

"A *what?*"

"Wind pump. Like in there." He nods towards the science book I left with him on Monday. It's lying a few feet away, open at page 30, and patterned with red-soil fingerprints.

"My precious book," I wail, grabbing it.

"Sorry," says Ivan, returning with a will to his digging. "But you did say I could choose my next experiment. This is it."

I shake off some of the loose earth and study the page entitled 'Wind Energy'.

"Ivan, this looks incredibly complicated. When I said you could choose, I didn't mean anything on such a grand scale as this!"

"It's for real, that's why," pants Ivan. "I'm not messing around with any more kiddy stuff."

"But why does the hole have to be so *deep?*"

"To get as far down as I can to the water table, of course. Then I'll know how much piping I need."

For once, I'm quite speechless. I study the picture. This is indeed no piddling kitchen experiment, but a diagram of a bona fide wind pump. A pump shaped like a windmill, with a long pipe going into the rock below. There's pipework which connects the pump with a water storage tank. More pipes from this lead down to a sink, or bath. It would be an ambitious design for the most extreme and experienced Eco-Builder. But here's a fourteen-year-old throwing himself into it – literally – heart and soul.

I feel totally redundant. And useless. How can I, with my 'soft' feminine energy, match this incredible display of male force? Just now, I think with a gut-wrenching stab of recognition, he needs a father. A dad, who'll match his vigour and enthusiasm. Who'll work and sweat by his side – suggesting, encouraging, ironing out problems. A buddy.

I sit down at a safe distance on a shaded patch of grass and watch him. Now and then he looks up and grins at me, but he never slackens his pace for a moment.

"I'd offer to join you in the hole," I say feebly, "but I'm not dressed for digging."

"You can get me a drink," says Ivan. "A cold one. There's squash somewhere in the kitchen."

I run into the kitchen through the open back door, his willing slave. The house feels damp and cold, even on this hottest of mid-summer days. What must it be like in the winter? No one's about. Catherine's gone back to bed. Nina, for once, seems to be at school.

I open the fridge, expecting to see orange squash, but the fridge is bare, except for a tub of margarine and some vegetables. There's a large bottle of spring water in the door-shelf, but that's all. No cheeses or meat or sandwiches for Ivan's lunch.

I shut the fridge and open cupboards. All the kitchen units are old – yellow-painted chipboard, scratched and peeling. I'm hoping that, as well as the squash, I can find some biscuits: Ivan needs some boost of energy, working at this pace. However, the cupboards are also bare. Just a few tins of baked beans and tomato soup. Does this family ever *eat*? In the last cupboard I find the squash and hunt around for a mug or beaker. There's a glass tumbler in a sink which reminds me of my grandmother's – deep and square and made of white enamel, next to a wooden draining board. These houses, I marvel, are museum pieces. One day these sinks will be dug up from people's gardens where they've been relegated to plant containers, and restored to their rightful place as kitchen centrepieces.

There's no ice in the freezer compartment. I run the water till it turns cold. Then I take out Ivan's drink to the garden.

Ivan's run out of steam. He sits at the edge of his pit, gazing into it, reflectively. I crouch down next to him. Why choose this particular project, I ask him. Why not something easier?

"To save water, of course," says Ivan, still squinting into the hole. Suddenly he turns to me and barks, "You didn't run the tap cold, did you?"

"Yes. To get the water cold enough for your drink."

Ivan swears. "Idiot. You should have used the water in the fridge. We always use that."

"In that spring water bottle? I thought that was maybe for your mother only."

Ivan grits his teeth and tuts. I apologise, and say I'll know for next time.

"But Ivan, you still haven't told me why you've chosen this project. As I said, it's very ambitious."

"I just said, to save water." Ivan gives me one of his most potent 'Are-you-thick?' looks. "Mum says we can't afford the next water bill if it's as high as the last one."

"But..." I stare at him uncomprehendingly.

"We're on a meter, see." Ivan stabs the hard earth viciously with his spade. "All the houses in this street and the next are. Mum says we've got to save where we can, otherwise she can't have baths. So I'm getting us our own supply. Then Mum can have as many baths as she wants."

Ivan downs his squash in one gulp and jumps down into the hole.

I stare down at him. What an extraordinary family – and what a struggle they're having just to survive day by day.

One thing's for sure. The library is definitely off the agenda today. For the rest of the session, it *has* to be Grand Designs!

Friday, 25th June. Rain is falling – an insistent, misty cloud of tiny droplets. It sticks to my thin cagoule like a second skin, making me feel damp and clammy. The pavements are thronged with shoppers trying to sidestep the streams of water pouring down from the awnings.

Ivan lopes along, a few paces ahead of me. He's trying hard to give the impression that he's not with me. His eyes dart from side to side, warily. If his friends should spot him out with me, this would seriously damage his street cred. I notice a damp patch all round his shoulders and upper back – of course, he's left his waterproof jacket in the car, saying he wouldn't need it. Luckily, the library is only a short walk from the car park.

The good thing about today's weather is that it has, for the moment, stopped Ivan digging. Yesterday, I could see that he was in danger of becoming obsessive. But the heavy clay soaks up the water and even Ivan could see that today, he'd be fighting a losing battle. In any case, he's almost hit rock. His reaction to this impasse is interesting. Rather than seeing it as a block – literally and logistically – Ivan is ecstatic about having reached this stage in his project. It means he's reached his Holy Grail – the water table. He's not the least bothered about how exactly he'll ever get through this layer of stone. I've noticed that he crosses each bridge as he comes to it.

"I'll sort it," he says, confidently, each time there's a hiccup in one of the experiments we've been doing all week.

Where I can only see problems, Ivan sees possibilities and potential solutions. I'm full of admiration for his way of thinking and working. Ivan, I'm beginning to realise, has the mind of an inventor.

I glance at my watch. We've got about an hour and a half in town. Forty minutes in the library, half an hour to do an English exercise, (an unusual one which I hope will tickle Ivan's imagination), and twenty minutes of spare time.

Ivan's walking too fast now, trying to shake me off. I'm in danger of losing him in the crowd. I quicken my pace and catch him up. I ask him to slow down a bit. 'Remember our agreement?' I remind him. Ivan curses under his breath. He sticks his hands in his pockets and hunches his shoulders defiantly. But he does slow down. I heave a sigh of relief.

"This trip will be a trial run," I told him yesterday. "I've found a leisure centre that has a climbing wall, and taster sessions in all kinds of exciting activities."

Ivan's eyes had gleamed when I showed him the brochure. If he behaves himself today, I'd promised, I'll take him there next week. But one false move, and the deal is off.

We hurry past a greengrocer's and a café and numerous estate agents. I catch up with Ivan on the corner of a side road. There's a pedestrian crossing and Ivan fidgets while we wait for the lights to change. On the opposite corner, I notice three teenage girls about Ivan's age – obviously 'mitching' off school. All wearing skimpy tops and bare midriffs, they're huddled together against the wall of the Bank, chattering non-stop. They shriek with glee when one of them gets a soaking from rain dripping down from an over-hanging ledge.

The lights are green and we cross over to their side. Suddenly the girls fall silent. Nudging each other, they eye Ivan up and down.

"Want to come out tonight?" calls one of them, with a suggestive wriggle.

Her friends collapse in a heap of giggles.

I blush on Ivan's behalf. Yet to my amazement, he doesn't even seem to notice them. His eyes, wary, uneasy, scan the pavements on the other side of the road. On the lookout for his mates, in case they should catch him behaving himself for once. The shame of it!

I glance back at the girls. They're still staring after Ivan, open-mouthed. Not surprising. He's very striking, with his dark, brooding eyes and chiselled features. Yet Ivan seems totally unaware of the effect he's just had on these three admirers.

In this respect, Ivan is still a boy. Just now, proving himself to his friends by daring deeds, being accepted by them – this is what drives him. Thank goodness. Give him a few more months and testosterone will kick in. Once he realises his charms… From this point of view alone, it's a race against time to get him back into school with some sense of direction and purpose. Before all the parents of the town start locking up their daughters.

In the library, I suggest to Ivan that he browse around on his own for a while. I'm curious to see what kind of reading matter attracts him. He gazes around, looking like a fish out of water. In the end, I steer him gently towards the children's non-fiction section. Perhaps there's something on water pumps? Ivan's face lights up when he sees a row of construction and engineering books. He sinks down on to the floor, his back propped up against the shelves, and reads – avidly.

While he's thus engrossed, I wander over to the fiction section. Louis Sachar's *Holes* almost jumps out at me. This story, about a Boot Camp in America, where boys are made to dig holes all day – five feet across and five feet deep – will surely resonate with Ivan's hole-digging experience.

And also, I hope, with his own feelings about having been booted out of school. Children who have been excluded, whether deservedly or not, often harbour deep resentments and a sense of hurt and rejection, which they find hard to express, or even acknowledge to themselves. This is a little-addressed problem. These youngsters need counselling. They need to confront the fact that – yes, this *was* an awful thing to happen to them. And that they are, understandably, left with a deep sense of failure.

A perfect choice, this book. As a bonus, it happens to be on the Year 9 reading list this year.

Before we go, I ask Ivan to choose another fiction book, as well as the four science and construction books he's clutching in his hands. He grumbles – but I insist. He chooses a novel almost at random – by its title alone. He doesn't read the blurb on the back. The book's called *Tough Guy*. Incredibly, it's about a bully – but more significantly, it describes the effects of this child's bullying on one particular victim. Synchronicity at work again!

Five minutes later, having put the books back in the car, Ivan's 'doing his English'. His brief: to imagine that he's a blind person, walking down the High Street. I was so impressed with the way he wrote about 'bombing' that I want to capitalise on his good use of descriptive words. This time, however, he is not allowed to use any adverb or adjective pertaining to sight. All his other senses will be heightened, I tell him, if he were blind. Can he find some words to describe what he experiences?

So that Ivan doesn't appear to be a 'complete nerd', as he puts it, I make unobtrusive notes for him, writing down his observations as we walk along. He has to imagine all the obstacles and difficulties a blind person might encounter. No, I say, I don't expect him to shut his eyes. I'm not *that* batty. "Just *imagine*, Ivan," I encourage him.

"Can I have a dog?" says Ivan, rolling his eyes at me in disgust.

"Yes. But don't make the dog do all the work."

Ivan walks along slowly. The pavement narrows now and then with scaffolding. Ivan bumps into one of the poles and curses. Then grins. He discovers protruding window ledges. Pushchairs and dogs wrap themselves around his feet. Crossing the road is a major operation – how will he know when it's safe? Where does he need to shop? How will he know which shop is which?

I scribble down words and phrases as he says them. 'Shuffle, trip over, uneven pavement, people bump into me, they force me into the road, loose dangerous paving stones, rough bricks on a low wall. Scratch myself. Deafening motorbikes, silent bicycles – what's coming next when I'm trying to cross. Is this a crossing for blind people, will it have a comforting bleep?'

He's getting into his stride, enjoying the exercise, in spite of himself, but after ten minutes he runs out of steam. The unaccustomed mental activity has worn him out. We pass a café, and I suggest we have a break.

"I'm not being bloody blind in *there*," scowls Ivan, his eyes scanning the packed tables.

"Your dog might enjoy it though!" I joke, trying to jolly him along. But I tell him he can choose whether or not he continues with the exercise.

At the counter, Ivan's eyes round like saucers when he sees all the goodies on display.

"I'll buy you a drink and a biscuit or cake," I offer. "You deserve it. I was really impressed by the way you stuck at that last exercise."

Ivan chooses a milkshake and a sticky bun. We carry a tray with his snack and my cup of tea to the one empty table at the back of the café.

He scoffs his bun as if he hasn't eaten for a week.

"What do you like eating at home, Ivan?" I ask, diplomatically.

"Everything. But Mum's on this diet, see. She can't have bread or dairy products. And not much other stuff really. She mainly eats just rice and vegetables and a little bit of meat. It's the M.E. She's got some kind of allergy from it."

"I see. But does Mum buy – I mean, what do you eat? You and Nina?"

"Oh, Mum gets stuff for us too. All the normal stuff – potatoes and cheese and sausages and bread. But she only goes shopping when she's well. Sometimes the neighbours do it for us. Or I do. If Mum's too tired that day, I cook for me and Nina, and we have huge helpings. We eat all the bread in one day. The food soon goes!"

Ivan gulps down half his strawberry milkshake and wipes the froth off his mouth with his wrist.

"This is good," he says. "Sometimes Mum forgets to get milk for us, because she's on soya milk, and milk is heavy to carry."

"What about the milkman delivering?" I ask.

"Too expensive," retorts Ivan. "It costs much less at the supermarket."

I sigh, and then feel angry. With consumerism. With globalisation rearing its ugly head in yet another guise.

Ivan's beginning to relax. He's stopped peering towards the door of the café, in case his mates should suddenly appear. I ask him about his brother, Kurt. Does Ivan ever see him? Does he have a job?"

It's as if a storm cloud has descended over our table. Ivan's face darkens.

"He's a loser. Can't stand him."

No brotherly love here, obviously. I wait, to see if there's more on the subject of Kurt.

"He doesn't work," scowls Ivan. "Just bums around, sponging off people. Like off Mum. He's coming next weekend, worse luck. Staying till Monday. He only comes because we've got a washing machine. And to scrounge money…"

"Does he come home often?"

"About, like, once a month maybe? I always make sure I'm out."

Ivan bangs his empty glass down and glares at me. The subject is plainly closed. It's time to get back home, anyway.

Once back in the car, I heave a sigh of relief. This trip into town has gone well. So far, apart from the expected surliness, Ivan hasn't put a foot wrong.

I drive out of the car park, and nose our way into the stream of traffic crawling along the High Street. It's a bad time to be at the wheel of a car. Both the hour and the weather are against us. The town is bursting at the seams with holidaymakers who would normally be sunning themselves on the beach. The rain has driven them towards retail therapy. They drive slowly and erratically, not knowing the lie of the land. And locals who would usually do their shopping on foot have taken to their cars. It's not a good mix. There's far too much sudden braking, tooting of horns and general irritation.

Ivan too looks irritable. He seemed fine, until we got into the car. Then he started complaining – about the 'grockles', the busy road; about the fact we've gone over our session time by twenty minutes and I've still got to get him back home. I guess the effort of behaving himself for two hours has caught up with him. He's sitting beside me, glaring out at the traffic.

"We'll be here all bloody night," he snaps.

"It'll be clearer once we're out of town," I say, calmly.

At the bottom of the high street, we turn right on to the main road which runs along the sea-front and eventually out of town. The traffic has eased a little and Ivan slumps back in his seat.

Halfway along the sea-front, I suddenly remember that I've advertised a chest of drawers and a book-case for sale – a last-ditch attempt to feng-shui my cluttered home. I need to buy the newspaper to check that these items have been listed. There's a newsagent halfway along, next to the pier. I ask Ivan to look out for a parking space.

"There's one!" shouts Ivan. "Look, just in front of that red van."

The van is parked a little way ahead. I indicate left and begin to slow down. At the same moment, another car – a sports convertible – with hood down and music blaring out, flashes past us. It cuts me up and zooms into *my* parking space. Four grinning faces turn towards me – youths of eighteen or nineteen at most. I pull up alongside the car and prepare to remonstrate. Politely.

But I'm not prepared for what happens next. Ivan suddenly winds down his windscreen. He makes an obscene gesture at the youths. A stream of unrepeatable swearwords pour from his mouth and blister the air. His face is purple with rage. Ivan has lost it entirely. At one point, he's just about to wrench open the door and leap out.

Quickly, I put the car into gear and drive off. Forget the newspaper. Let's just get Ivan home. I can feel my hands trembling on the steering wheel. My legs are shaky and I can hardly locate the clutch.

Next to me, Ivan stares ahead, stonily. He grits his teeth, breathing heavily. His fists clench and unclench.

In silence, I concentrate on my driving, trying to calm my thoughts and my nerves. At the end of the seafront, the main road veers to the right, past the entrance to the caravan park. Finally the road is clear.

After a couple of miles, we turn left, then right at the roundabout into the road leading to the quarry. Thank goodness all the traffic is coming in the opposite direction at this time of day. We're almost at Jubilee Road. Ivan hasn't uttered a word since his outburst. Nor have I. It's as if neither of us wants to break the fragile silence.

At last, Ivan says, "He was well out of order, that bloody creep."

I swallow, to weary to argue. "Let's just say that it's hardly worth getting het up about, Ivan. It's *his* problem. That young fellow's. He's the one who'll end up with no driving licence one day."

I pull up outside Ivan's house.

"See you Monday, Ivan," I say, evenly. And coolly. "Have a good weekend."

Ivan gets out and slams the door. He disappears into the alleyway without a goodbye or a thank-you. Not even a backward glance.

I drive away with a heavy heart. It was all going so well. What went wrong? If only I hadn't remembered that wretched advert. At that particular moment. Or maybe it was just far too soon even to consider taking Ivan out. After all, just as two swallows don't make a summer, nor do a few days' trouble-free sessions make a model pupil.

Ivan's shown me a side of himself I was hoping not to see. A side that is unpredictable and potentially violent. How can he flip so easily? One minute, he's touchingly childlike, guzzling his milkshake and bun so appreciatively. And the next – well, he almost provoked a major road-rage incident. Tim had said that Ivan was a Jekyll and Hyde character. Privately, I'd scoffed at this, and thought it wild exaggeration. But now…

I'll go straight home and have a cup of tea. My universal panacea for all ills. *Then* I'll think about Ivan. Something is still bugging him. I need to find out what it is. Otherwise going back to school too soon could be a disaster.

Saturday, 26th June. "More shepherd's pie, Colin?"

"Um – why not? Yes, please."

I dish up another large helping – one of his many favourite meals.

However, this lunch date is not about Colin, an old friend. I'm doing it for Ivan. My mission is to pick his brains and enlist his help with Ivan's wind-pump project.

Colin and I go back a long way – to our university days. In my final year, I was sharing a house with four other girls. One evening, Colin, a third-year Geography student, turned up on our doorstep, desperate for digs. He'd just been let down on a house-share arrangement. Though we were all doubtful about letting a man into our cosy female enclave, Colin proved to be a congenial house-mate. He willingly took his turn with the washing up and cooking. He was easy-going and good at fixing the things the landlord never got round to. And for a few weeks, he reduced our expenses, sleeping (illegally) on the downstairs settee while paying us for the privilege. I remember hiding him under the stairs when the landlord came to collect the rent. Eventually, one of the girls left and Colin became a fixture for the rest of the year.

Even back then, he was eccentric. He would build strange contraptions and household gadgets which sometimes worked but usually didn't.

Colin and I lost contact with each other until four years ago, when I literally bumped into him in town. He'd moved down here and now works for the Town Planning Department. But in the evening he does his Real Thing. He disappears into his huge, hangar-like shed at the bottom of his garden. For the last few years, he's been into steam engines. He also has a particular passion for vintage lawn mowers – the older and more decrepit the better. These he takes to bits and lovingly restores their parts, before putting them back together again.

We meet up from time to time for lunch. Colin loves his food and is also a good cook. But sharing his kitchen table with a load of greasy bolts and other mysterious bits of dirty metal is not my cup of tea, so usually he comes round to my house.

We chat for a while about his work and mine. Soothed by his voice, by normality, I wait for a chance to tell him about Ivan, but suddenly he wants to talk about Maggie.

Colin has a history of disastrous relationships. Maggie lasted out three years before the strain of sharing her man with four lawn mowers proved too much. A few months ago, she scarpered off to Thailand to 'find herself'. She took very little, other than her toothbrush and a rucksack full of self-help books. Colin is devastated. Where did he go wrong?

I listen sympathetically till he runs out of steam and looks a bit happier, saying that at least he won't feel so guilty now when he disappears for hours on end into his shed.

I tell Colin that I've just discovered the next Isambard Kingdom Brunel. It's our patriotic duty to foster Ivan's amazing talent. All he needs is a little guidance from an old hand, someone whose genius for problem-solving and creative thinking is…

Colin leans forward, arms folded on the table. His eyes sparkle with interest.

"How big is this wind-pump?" he asks.

"Oh, I don't know. I'll get the book, Colin."

I find the text-book and show him the illustration. Colin studies it in silence, still as a statue. I hardly dare breathe. Here, in front of my eyes, is a genius at work.

"Got any paper?" he asks.

I place a notepad and pencil in front of him. Rapidly, Colin covers a page with a tangle of diagrams – all completely meaningless to me.

"There!" he says, triumphantly.

"What do you mean, *'There'?* You know I won't be able to explain any of this to Ivan."

"I mean, it's doable," says Colin, smugly. "A bit unorthodox in a back garden, though."

"Does it need planning permission?"

Colin chuckles. "Doubt it. It'll be hardly more than a model, really."

"Will it work?"

"Yes, with the right parts."

"But where can he find the parts? The family don't appear to have much spare cash."

Colin studies his diagram. "I've got a lot of this stuff at home." He points to the frame, a mini-pylon which supports the wind-sails. "I've got just the right material for this. It needs to be strong but light. And you could look in recycling centres for the rest of it."

"Colin," I say, "I wonder if you…" I look at him pleadingly. In the way we used to in our college days, when we wanted another shelf for our books, or when the sink needed unblocking. "Could you…*would* you go and look at what Ivan's done so far? He just needs some encouragement. It's really too ambitious a project for him But he's so enthusiastic. Even if it doesn't work out, he'll learn so much from just doing it."

"Even if it doesn't work out? Of course it will work out!" snorts Colin.

Unwittingly, I've pressed the one button guaranteed to catapult Colin over to my side. He drums his fingers on the table, and stares thoughtfully at his scribbles again.

"Okay. I don't see why not. I could pop round to see Ivan one evening after work. You free on Monday evening?"

"Monday will be perfect. I'll have to ring his mother and ask her first. But I know she'll be grateful for any help with Ivan. Thank you so much."

I've a hunch that as soon as Colin sees Ivan's excavations, he'll be hooked. He'll want to get involved. In fact, there'll be no stopping him. The danger is that he'll try to take over. I'll need to be vigilant, to make sure that he works *with* Ivan, lets him do most of the donkey work. I'll have to feed Colin, either before or afterwards. But I'll enjoy cooking my way through Colin's long repertoire of favourite dishes. Eating together means I can spend more time with him.

Monday, 28th June. Catherine opens the door, looking much better. She's brushed her hair and arranged it high on her head, with a comb either side. It looks quaintly 1940s, but it suits her. There's also more colour in her cheeks.

"Are you feeling better?" I ask.

"Quite a bit better today, thank you. I think it's the sunshine. And the warm weather generally. It's drying out all the damp in the house."

The ghostly chill in the house does indeed seem to have gone, replaced by a pleasant coolness that's in welcome contrast to the sweltering heat outside.

Catherine puts her finger to her lips and lowers her voice.

"I talked to him about his behaviour on Friday," she says, glancing anxiously over her shoulder towards the open door of the living room, "when he was out with you. I said if he carried on like this, no school would ever take him. And I said he should apologise to you."

Last night I'd had a long talk with Catherine, mainly about Ivan's wind pump project. I'd said how impressed I was at her son's technical ability, and asked if she would mind if Colin helped him a little. I wanted to emphasise the positive. Poor Catherine already has enough to worry about. It was only in passing that I mentioned Ivan's outburst. I added that I had to take my share of the responsibility for it happening at all – we'd gone over time, Ivan was tired, etc. But Catherine was shocked, and worried. Ivan had been so much calmer for the last three weeks, she said. She'd hoped he was 'growing out of' that kind of behaviour.

"He'll be fine," I say, with a confidence I didn't really feel. "I'm sure it was just a blip."

Ivan is at the table. He looks subdued, and doesn't meet my eye. I sit down at right angles to him and unpack my bag. I'm playing for time. Not just to give him a chance to bring up Friday's incident and to apologise for it – or at least to explain his behaviour. I'm still feeling unsure about my part in it, so I'm not sure how to proceed. I'm hoping that divine inspiration will pierce the fog in my brain.

I get out my folder and *Holes*, our reading book. And then I notice the sheet of A4 file paper that Ivan has placed on the table in front of me. With *two* pages of writing!

"Go on then," says Ivan. "Read it! To *yourself*," he adds, self-consciously. He picks up one of his library books and ostentatiously studies some of the pictures, as if he couldn't care less what I think of his work.

I start reading:

'Going out with Mitch.

I'm walking down the High Street with my dog, Mitchell. I call him Mitch for short. He's a kind of sandy colour with a white tail, that's what the Guide Dog trainer told me anyway because I cant see him, I'm blind. It's a rainy day my worst kind of weather because my feet skid on the wet pavements and rain drips all down my neck and I can't see where the puddles are, I always come back with wet feet. Sometimes I trip up over uneven paving stones. Once I fell over. I was well shocked. Also there is too much traffic when it's raining. Traffic is what I'm most scared of because cars and lorries just expect me to get out of the way. Motorbikes are the worst they zoom out of nowhere and make me jump out of my skin. When I cross the road I cross at a crossing with a bleep for blind people. But I still listen out with my ears on stalks. I can tell the different traffic by their sounds buses are low and steady and have a nice throbbing sound and I know the drivers are safe and won't run me over. But vans are bad, they are always in a rush. They toot their horns at me as if its all my fault I'm slow. They just don't care that I'm blind…'

Ivan has filled two whole pages of A4 file paper.

"This is a great piece of work, Ivan," I say appreciatively.

Of course, there's a lot to work on. Paragraphs, for example. How a youngster can get to the age of fourteen without putting a single paragraph in his work, is forever a mystery. But I come across it so often that it doesn't surprise me. Paragraphs don't have to be boring. I remember how I learnt about them, at school. An inspired English teacher stood before the blackboard and asked for the beginning of a story, which she wrote down. 'What happens next?' she would say, and we'd all wave our hands frantically, wanting to be the next one to add to the narrative. Each child who wanted to could have a turn, each had her own paragraph – and could choose her own colour of chalk. I always chose yellow. 'See how the paragraphs are like stepping stones across a river!' said the teacher. 'Separate, but they move you on. They take you to the next part in the story…' In my mind's eye, I can still see the blackboard, shafts of sunshine highlighting the colours. And my words, *my* bit of the story, dancing out at me like golden sparks.

Apart from his punctuation, I'm excited by Ivan's piece of writing. This by itself counts as an apology, in terms of the effort he's put into it. And then I notice the little scribble at the end of the page. Almost indecipherable, it says: *'Sorry for losing it. Signed Ivan'.*

"And I accept your apology, too," I add, smiling at him.

"So we're going out this week – to that Leisure Place?" demands Ivan, getting down to business straight away.

"Yes. I think you just about deserve it. Especially after this." I point to his writing. "Do you realise that this is your very first piece of homework, Ivan? That deserves some points – three at least."

Ivan cranes his neck towards his Record of Work page.

"Hey, I must have thirty by now. I get a prize, don't I?"

"You would have, but I had to take three points off last Friday."

Ivan jumps up and stares disbelievingly at the three points I've crossed out – with the comment 'For unacceptable behaviour'. His face is like thunder. For a moment I'm sure he's going to thump me. Then he sits down again. He looks close to tears. I feel mean as hell, but some instinct makes me stick to my guns.

I pick up *Holes* and find where we last left off, at chapter 5. I start reading out loud. After a few minutes, Ivan is engrossed in the story.

I heave a sigh of relief. The crisis is over. Until the next time.

Wednesday, 30th June. "Left foot down a bit – that's it! No, *down* a bit. No, much further than that. Further! And *don't* look down."

All Ivan's commands fall on deaf ears. I'm a blob of terrified, shaking jelly, trying to find my next foothold. I'm jammed flat against this damned climbing wall, spread-eagled like a swatted mosquito. I freeze. How did Ivan do it? Before I had a go, he'd shimmied up and down in about ten seconds flat.

"You're doing fine!" yells Ivan, encouragingly. His voice spirals upwards as if from the lower slopes of Mount Everest. "Just reach down two more inches with your left foot..."

Two inches. It might as well be two miles. My whole life flashes before me.

It seemed a good idea at the time, showing Ivan that I still had some mettle left in me. That I wasn't just a boring old fuddy-duddy. After all, heights don't usually worry me. I've walked along more cliff tops than most people have had hot dinners. And wasn't I, aged ten, the second best tree-climber in my class? But walking along the top of a cliff is not the same as clinging to the cliff-face. Which is what this wall feels like – even though I'm only about eight feet above the ground.

"There, that's it," says Ivan. "Now – the next foothold. Right foot down. *Right* one, stupid. Down a bit..."

Our roles have suddenly reversed. Ivan's definitely in charge here. And even in the midst of my terror, I realise that he is, in fact, successfully guiding me down to safety. He could so easily have run away, laughing.

"There you are!" he says, as I reach *terra firma* at last, shaking all over like a leaf. "That wasn't so bad, was it? Do you want to have another go?

You should, you know – now you've got the hang of it. You just need to keep practising."

"I think I need a cup of tea, Ivan, but thank you for guiding me down. I'd still be up there tomorrow morning if you hadn't."

Ivan grins and swaggers a little. Any praise boosts his confidence one little bit more, and he does deserve it.

We find the café. Ivan dives into his doughnut and strawberry milkshake, starving as usual. For once, he looks exhausted. The wall climbing was the last item in a whole raft of exciting activities. Scuba diving in the pool, roller-blading, trampolining. Now he's eagerly scanning the brochures for what he can do next time we come.

"I want to do caving," he says. "And rock-climbing. And canoeing…"

"Those are longer courses, Ivan. You can't just do them as tasters, like today. You have to sign up for several weeks on a regular basis."

Ivan's face falls.

"You'll have to earn yourself some money," I say, cheerfully. "Maybe do some digging for the neighbours? A few holes?"

On Monday evening Colin had picked me up and we'd driven round to Jubilee Road in his van. He'd brought a few of his tools. Maybe it was the pneumatic drilling that did it, but Ivan's excavations have suddenly attracted quite a bit of attention from the neighbours on either side. Word is spreading that something is afoot at number 32. Fortunately, no one in the road seems particularly bothered. The few residents who own their houses are elderly. They've lived there most of their lives, and seen too many changes to worry about a mere hole in a garden. The other neighbours are, like Catherine, tenants of the absentee landlord. They too find life a struggle and have far too many other things to worry about.

This is all just as well, as it looks as if Ivan's wind pump is a viable project. As I'd expected, as soon as Colin saw what Ivan was doing, he was immediately hooked. He'd hardly been there ten minutes before he'd drilled a hole deep down into the rock to take the pipe-work. He's also found an old tank which will store the water. Colin has given Ivan the task of making a platform for it, out of the dug-out earth.

This is all very gratifying for me, yet what delights me most of all is that Colin and Ivan have hit it off right away. Colin is just the right buddy for Ivan. Practical, good-natured, straight-down-the-line, there's no 'side' to him. With Colin, what you see is what you get. And like Ivan, he has ideas spilling out of him. Ideas just waiting to materialise. Colin, too, sees all problems as challenges. They'll spark off each other, those two. I can feel it in my bones.

Now, Ivan's still thumbing through all the leaflets I've spread over the table.

"When can we come here again?" he asks. "I want another scuba-diving lesson. It's ace!"

"Depends," I reply, cautiously, "on whether you continue to behave yourself."

Ivan looks uncomfortable. He knows that today, he's here only by the skin of his teeth.

I pick up one of the leaflets.

"Look at this, Ivan! There's a six-month, full-time course here. An Outward Bound course. It trains you to be a Youth Leader. If you did this course, you could do all these activities – rock-climbing, canoeing, horse-riding, all for free!"

Ivan grabs the leaflet. His eyes shine, as he reads. Then he looks crushed. "You have to be eighteen. It says, here." He jabs at the print.

"I didn't mean it for now, Ivan." I look at his crestfallen face and wish I'd kept my mouth shut. "You could do it in your gap year."

"What's that?"

"You mean you haven't heard of a gap year? It's what young people do before going to university or college. Some go travelling, some do work, either paid or voluntary. This course would be ideal, just right for you. You'd be good at instructing youngsters. Think how you got me down from that wall!"

Ivan stares at me uncertainly. I can see that, on one level, he hasn't connected with what I'm saying. After all, I'm talking about his life when he's *eighteen*! To Ivan, such an age might just as well be forty or fifty or one-foot-in-the-grave. He can't project himself that far into the future.

"But is it just for people who are going to university?" he asks.

I laugh. "No – it's for anyone. Anyone who wants to do it and is suitable, that is. I just mentioned university because – well, because I think you're bright enough to go to college or university one day. Maybe do a course in science, or engineering. Or how about sports science? Now, *there's* an idea for you…"

Ivan blinks at me. He pulls one of his 'what's-she-on-about-*now*' faces. I can see he's still trying to decide whether or not I'm batty. Or…

Or whether maybe – just *maybe* – I'm being authentic. That I can see something in him that he hasn't yet recognised for himself. And that I'm giving him information that he might want to act on – one day.

Thursday, 1st July. I'm twenty minutes early today – for once, the roads were relatively traffic-free. I knock on Ivan's door, but there's no answer. After a minute or two, I walk through the side alley into the back garden, expecting to see Ivan up to his waist in Hole Number Two.

Just outside the back door, reclining in an old striped deckchair, Catherine is reading the local newspaper. The sun has settled on this little patch of the garden and encased the deckchair in a pool of light. The scene reminds me of one of those old seaside postcards.

Catherine looks up and greets me, smiling.

"Good afternoon," I say. "It's good to see you relaxing. How are you feeling?"

"Rather tired – but better, compared to how I was feeling a week or two ago," says Catherine. "The sun makes such a difference. What do you think of my deckchair? I found it in the shed."

"I haven't seen one of these for ages, except on beaches of course." I pat the wooden frame. "Do you know, I prefer them to these square nylon things you get nowadays. They're much more comfortable."

"Yes, there's something very civilised about deckchairs, even if they are impossible to put up and down."

We both laugh. I ask if Ivan's around. Catherine says she doesn't know where he is. Mid-morning, he'd gone out, promising to be back in time for his lesson. He'd said something about going to meet some friends in the next road.

I ask her if she'd like me to make a cup of tea.

"Thank you, that would be very kind," says Catherine. "Do make one for yourself as well…" she calls after me as I go into the kitchen. "And bring out one of the chairs from the living room and join me for a while."

I take out a chair, then the drinks, and settle down next to Catherine. The sun filters through the branches of the trees, creating dappled patches of light and shade. Apart from Ivan's efforts, I reckon no one's touched the ground for years. Overgrown buddleia and lilacs straggle along what were once borders. Their branches lean out towards the rough grass down the middle of the garden, encroaching on the narrow space. This tapers to an end in a tangle of nettles and brambles, and a tumbledown shed. Just enough of the brambles have been cleared away to allow access to a wooden gate. This leads out into the foot- and cycle-path that runs along the back, between the gardens and the perimeter fence of the quarry works. The path eventually leads to a footbridge across the railway line, and out on to the main road.

On the back wall, Catherine has placed a couple of hanging baskets filled with lobelia and petunias. The heady aroma of a scented geranium wafts up from a flowerpot next to the kitchen door. Bees drone, dipping in and out of a honeysuckle which has gone haywire against the right-hand fence. On the other side, I can hear young children laughing as they splash in and out of a paddling pool.

I feel peaceful and contented. If I'm honest, I'm in no hurry for Ivan to return.

"Ivan tells me that your eldest son is coming home for a visit soon," I say, to pass the time. "I expect he'll enjoy seeing his family again."

Catherine pulls a face. "Enjoy? I think that would be going too far for Kurt. He's usually got some particular reason for coming back – something to suit himself."

"Like getting his washing done?" I say, lightly. "That's the classic reason for youngsters to come home to Mother."

"That – and other things."

Catherine's expression has darkened. I've just decided to change the subject, when she adds:

"I don't look forward to his visits. He's not easy. He was the one most affected by my husband's drinking – and by the violence."

Her voice is even, but intense. She's sitting up now, leaning forward and looking at me searchingly, as if gauging whether I'm ready to hear what she's about to tell me. My heart misses a beat. I feel a sudden shock at this change in the tone and tempo of our conversation. But here's my chance to find out more.

I take a deep breath and ask, "Did he – I mean, was your ex-husband ever violent towards Ivan – or Kurt?"

"I'm fairly sure he never hit the boys. Ivan was always in bed when Sergei came home drunk. But Kurt saw him hitting me on several occasions."

I swallow. I don't know what to say.

"I can see you're shocked," says Catherine.

Her face has gone even paler than usual as she continues, "The drink changed his personality. But it was the gambling that caused him to drink in the first place. He got into debt. He had a good job with this export firm – in charge of a project with a budget to manage. He stole some of the funds."

Catherine stops, watching my expression. I don't want to hear this – yet somehow I must. This is Ivan's story, too.

"Sergei was sacked," continues Catherine, in the same even, expressionless voice. "And he owed thousands of pounds. *Tens* of thousands. Our home was repossessed."

"How awful it must have been for you!" I exclaim. "No wonder you got ill."

"Yes. You've made the connection," says Catherine, sounding surprised. "I'm sure the M.E. was caused by stress. Though it didn't start as M.E. I got a very severe bout of flu which developed into pneumonia. I had to go into hospital, and for months I couldn't even get out of bed. Then for a few years after that I was almost housebound. Gradually I got some of my strength back. I suppose I must have been about three-quarters recovered just before we moved six months ago. But the move itself seems to have taken its toll. I've felt completely wiped out since then."

"That's understandable. What do they say about moving house? That it's the third most stressful life event?"

Catherine nods. She lets out a huge sigh and sinks back into the deckchair. "Yes, I found it utterly exhausting – wondering if Sergei would come looking for me, trying to find accommodation…"

"How did you find this house?"

"It was a last resort," says Catherine. "I tried to get something through the council, but you have to have lived here for three years. I was renting privately up in Bristol and though I get Disability Allowance and Income Support, I couldn't do a house-swap or anything like that. I just happened to see an advert in the paper one day and came along to have a look. But I would have taken anything by that stage."

"And do you like it, now you're here?"

"It's not so bad now. But I hated it at first – all the cold. The only way I could get warm was to have a hot bath. Sometimes I'd have one twice a day! But it was making for massive water bills."

"Ah – Ivan told me about the water meter. That's why he's so keen to get you your own water supply!"

Catherine smiles. "Yes, he's good lad underneath all his bravado. And quite gentle, really."

Hang on a minute, I'm thinking. *I can't let this go.*

"But the bullying at school!" I exclaim. "Do you know what that was about? I was just wondering why he always picked on the smaller boys – not girls, or kids in his own class."

"I think that was because..." begins Catherine. She checks herself, suddenly.

My cheeks flush. I'm hounding poor Catherine with my questions and it's making me feel uncomfortable. Yet instinct is telling me if I can find out the answer to this puzzle, Ivan's behaviour will be much more understandable. But Catherine's following some thought process of her own.

"You'd imagine, wouldn't you, that of the two boys, Kurt would be the one to hate his father the most. But Kurt still visits him from time to time. Sergei's got a flat somewhere in Bristol, not far from where Kurt lives – dossing down with his friends." Catherine wrinkles her nose in disgust. "That's why, after we'd been here only a couple of months, Kurt went back to Bristol. I do believe he's missing Sergei. Isn't that the oddest thing?"

"It is," I agree. "How does Ivan get on with his dad?"

"Hates him. Hates his guts," retorts Catherine with a vehemence that startles me.

There's a long silence.

"I suppose that would explain his bullying," I say at last.

Sally had been right, I reflect. When Ivan attacked Tim, this was a projection of Ivan's anger against his father. I'm thinking about this, when Catherine says suddenly:

"Ivan's never, *ever* raised a hand to me."

Her eyes suddenly fix on my face, anxious and watchful. There's something about her sudden change of tack, her tone of voice that makes me wonder. It's as if her remark is infused with hidden meaning.

"No, I can see that," I tell her at once. "He's very protective towards you."

Catherine nods.

"Yes. As I said, he's as helpful as one might expect, given what's happened to all of us. Unlike Kurt, who's the complete opposite. He…"

At the end of the garden, the gate clicks open. Ivan saunters in and wanders up the garden towards us.

"Ivan – you're late," says Catherine, sharply. "By twenty minutes. Your tutor's been here over half an hour."

Ivan glances down at his watch. He seems genuinely surprised when he sees what time it is.

"Sor…ry," he says, nonchalantly. "I was – with my mates. Anyway, I'm here now. I'm starving, Mum. Got any food?"

"There's bread and cheese," says Catherine, wearily. "But you need to start your lesson first. It's very rude to be so late."

"Okay," says Ivan, unexpectedly compliant. He darts me a wary look, then walks straight into the living room and sits down at the table.

"Can we carry on reading that book about holes?" he asks. "I'll find the place where we left off, okay?"

Ivan opens the book at chapter 5, and sits quietly, waiting for me to join him. He's taken the wind out of my sails – I was prepared for a row. I'd planned to tell him off for his lateness. But he's far, far too amenable, I haven't the heart. Yet there's also a shiftiness in his manner which makes me uneasy.

"Right, Ivan," I say at last. "We'll read for ten minutes, but I'm afraid I'll have to take another two points off your score. You agreed that you would start all the sessions on time. But you were very late."

I hold my breath, waiting for the explosion. The fist banging down on the table, the foul language.

"Okay," says Ivan calmly. "That's fair, I suppose. Shall I read first?"

He draws the book towards him, looking as if butter wouldn't melt in his mouth. I stare at his bent head, as he reads out the first paragraph.

Then, I notice his hair. It's wet. Not obviously, but there are damp clumps of it around his ears and at the back of his neck.

My mind races. Suddenly it all clicks into place. Didn't Ivan just come in the back way? That means he hasn't come in from the direction of town, or from the shop a little way along. Or even from his mates in the next street. The path behind the gardens in Jubilee Road leads to the main road. And where does that lead to? Why, to the beaches of course. To Puffin Beach. And Puffin Rock.

I fume, inwardly. There's no doubt in my mind that Ivan has been bombing again. How dare he? After all the accidents, and that tragedy of a boy's death. Only today, in the very newspaper Catherine was reading when I arrived, the local coastguard has written yet another warning article. I open my mouth, ready to burst out with accusations and blame.

Just in time, I stop. I inhale deeply and count to ten. There's another way. A means of stopping Ivan more effectively than anything I could say to him.

I don't feel good about it. But if, ultimately, it saves his life, or the lives of other kids…

It just has to be done.

Friday, 2nd July. July is always the 'Silly Season'. For me, it's that time of the school year when I begin to forget dates and times and appointments. I'm not sure whether it's due to the heat or to winding down. Or, most likely, to the effects of a whole year's roller-coaster of non-stop emotional output. Every summer term I swear it won't happen, but it always does. And just now, I've done it again.

Yesterday, before I left, Catherine reminded me that she and Ivan would be visiting a possible new school this afternoon, so the session would have to be cancelled. I'd made a mental note of it, but on the way home, I'd been so preoccupied thinking about Ivan's latest bombing exploit, that the school visit had gone clean out of my head. I've just driven all the way to Jubilee Road for nothing.

Having found myself over on this side of town, I decide to make best of it and treat myself to my long-awaited afternoon on the beach. It's a universal phenomenon: people who live in or near tourist attractions hardly ever visit them. In my case, it's more a lack of time and opportunity. Now, I can't wait to get down on to the sands.

In the boot of my car, I keep a canvas beach bag packed with books, my costume and a towel – just in case. Clutching this under my arm, I make my way from the car park down the long slope leading to the beach café. I buy a cup of tea and a doughnut and find a pitch on the sand. I'm surrounded by flying beach balls and small children rushing back and forth from the sea edge with buckets of seawater to fill their moats. But this is all part of the fun. Having been a visitor to these parts for many, many years, I'm very aware of my own good fortune in actually living here. Now I delight in being an honorary grockle for the afternoon.

With a deep sigh of utter bliss, I gaze out towards the sea. Today, the waves are gentle swirls of white foam that curl towards the shore with barely a splash. Toddlers paddle at the edge, next to big brothers and sisters who protectively hold their hands tight. Fathers carry small boys aloft on their shoulders, and bear them, shrieking, into the deeper water. It's a joyful scene that can't have changed over aeons of years. And just for that reason, it's beautiful and precious and it moves me to tears every time.

After an hour I stretch, and look at my watch. Three fifteen. I get up and wander over to the beach shop. There's a wonderful display of shells. I choose a couple to remind me of this afternoon. Then something catches my eye. It's one of those sand-surfing boards. *I could do that, I reckon.*

I buy one. The shop lady smiles indulgently.

"For your grandchildren, is it? They'll enjoy that!"

I hurry back to my pitch on the sand. There are far too many people about at this end of the beach even to contemplate having a practice session with my new toy.

I cover the board up with my towel, and, self-consciously, walk away from the café and the shop towards the other end of the beach. It's a long way – about a third of a mile – but that end is always less crowded. If the worst comes to the worst and there are teenagers, or worse, serious sand-surfers, I shall simply pretend that my towel-wrapped board is a superior sunbathing mat.

On the way, I pass a couple of seasoned sand-surfers: two boys of about ten who are skimming along as if they were born to it. I stop and watch them. Simple, I decide. You just have to put one foot on the thing and scoot it along a bit, then bring the other foot to join the first one…

I wander further down, barefoot, relishing the sensation of soft sand under my feet. But as I feared, there are four teenagers in wetsuits out in the sea. They're actually surfing the waves, which are always bigger and fiercer here than at the café end. I'll have a stroll, instead. Maybe they'll be gone soon.

At the very end of the beach, the cliff juts out into the sea for about fifty yards. The last part of the cliff, right on top, is formed of grey, slippery granite, and slopes towards the sea, forming an overhang. This is Puffin Rock.

The tide is going out now, probably at the halfway mark, leaving a glimmering carpet of wet sand. But sticking up from the sand, blackened and jagged like the teeth of giant witches, are other smaller rocks – between four and twelve feet high. They're tall and narrow, spaced out at intervals. These are the rocks Ivan and his friends have to avoid when they bomb down from the cliff-top.

I squelch my way between them. The sand covers my feet and ankles with a sucking sound. I walk a little way round the cliff. You can walk round to Shell

Beach this way. Lots of holidaymakers do it every year, and forget the tide times. They suddenly wake up from a snooze to find that they'll either have to walk back along the road to their cars, or wait for the tide to turn. Now and then, they make a dash for it, back the way they came. Risky. The tide gushes in quickly, and the waves are fierce and powerful.

I'll turn back – I've been to Shell Beach many times before. As I round the cliff, I look up again at Puffin Rock. There is no one up there. And I can be pretty sure that there was no one there this morning. Yesterday, I imagine, Ivan and his friends would have timed their bombing carefully. They would have caught the high tide, when at least thirty feet of water lap round the base of the Rock. But they won't be doing it again tomorrow, or the next day, or at any time in the foreseeable future.

Early this morning, after a restless night, I rang the coastguard. I told the duty officer that I had reason to believe that a group of young teenagers were regularly risking their lives. I said that if he would guarantee my anonymity, I could tell them where these youngsters lived.

The coastguard was most understanding. What they'd do, he said, was to call round at Jubilee Road and Victoria Road, where Ivan's mates live, maybe this evening or over the weekend. They'd make some 'routine' house-to-house enquiries at the addresses I mentioned. They'd say that 'someone had seen boys answering to their description' jumping from the Rock. They'd give severe warnings to the boys in front of their parents. From now on, the miscreants would be told, the coastguards will be on the lookout for them. And if they were ever caught again…

If Ivan and his mates ever find out that it was me who snitched on them… But hopefully, by that time, they'll all have moved on to other things. Or I'll have left the country.

The surfers have gone and at last this part of the beach is clear. I unwrap my board and march towards the sea edge where a faint line of froth marks the best place to practise. The sand has to be wet, but you don't want the waves to lift the board.

Cautiously, I place my right foot on the end of the surfboard and give it a gentle push. Nothing moves. I give it a shove. It skims along and I jump on the end with both feet. It tips up, smacking me in the face. Next, I attempt scooting along, with one foot in the middle and hopping along with the other, trying to keep up with the damn thing.

Maybe I should, like, get it going first? I give a hefty push then run after it and jump right into the middle. It stops suddenly and I fall flat on my face.

As I bite the sand, I hear maniacal laughter above me. I lift my head. There, doubled up, *creased* up, splitting his sides, is Ivan.

"Oh my… Jeez…for fuck's sake…" Tears stream down his cheeks as he clutches his stomach.

"It's not that funny, Ivan," I say, spitting out sand, and hauling myself to my feet.

"Look, you're doing it all wrong. Shall I give you a demo?"

Without waiting for a reply, he bends over the board, holding it by the sides and whooshes it along. When it's got up some speed, he jumps on it, kneeling at first, then balancing upright. He gives me a nonchalant wave as he whizzes by.

"There!" he says. "That's just one way of getting on. The easiest way. *You* have a go now. Before you lose your nerve."

"I haven't any nerve to lose, Ivan. I didn't even get that far."

"Look, I know what!" says Ivan helpfully. "Don't even try to stand up. Just kneel on it. Run along with it, get it going, and jump on with your knees. It's no different from wave-surfing, really." He looks at me as if I'm already an expert in this area at least.

Oh well. In for a penny…I follow Ivan's instructions to the letter and succeed in moving the stupid object at least six inches along. Ivan hoots with mirth.

"Try again!" he commands.

"And again!" he shouts, as this time, the infernal machine runs ahead of me so fast I'm left clinging to the end of it with my knees tracing interesting skid marks in the sand.

"Ivan," I gasp. "I can't." Every sinew in my body is crying out for rest.

"You shouldn't give up so easily," says Ivan, looking at me sorrowfully. "You have to *practise*, if you want to get good at something."

Suddenly, I have a flash of understanding. But this is no ordinary realisation – no 'Aha' moment that plops into your brain and goes no further. This is a whole-body insight that surges through me with the intensity of an electric shock.

What I'm experiencing in this moment is how some of my pupils have been feeling for years. Those children who find English or maths alien and scary. And those who have missed so much practice that even the simplest exercise seems like climbing a mountain. Or kids who just aren't wired up that way, and will never really bond with the subject. Being urged to 'have one more' go, at a piece of writing, or a sum, or whatever it is – do they feel like I do now? Exhausted, inadequate, stupid, hopeless…?

I suppose I've always known about this in an academic, cerebral way. But never, before now, has it hit me in the face like this.

And the way Ivan is looking at me now…Disappointment written all over him.

"Okay, Ivan. I'll try again."

And so I do. For ten more minutes I put everything I've got into getting myself and that sand-board moving together. At the sixth attempt I just about manage to whoosh, kneeling, along a stretch of about twenty feet.

"You're getting it," says Ivan, approvingly. "You know what? You need to come down here every day for the whole of the summer. And just practise. Don't do anything else…"

"Can we stop now?" I pant, sweat pouring off me. "I'll buy you an ice-cream at the café. In return for the lesson."

"Okay. Yeah. Thanks."

"Unless you had any other plans? Where were you going when you saw me?"

"Oh, nowhere. Just for a walk."

Ivan gives an involuntary glance towards Puffin Rock. His face has taken on that shifty look again. But, I reflect, he can't have been planning any more bombing today. The tide's out and by the time it comes in again, it will be late evening.

We walk towards the café. Ivan bounds along beside me like a young gazelle. There's a spring in his step and he seems in a good mood.

"Oh!" I stop suddenly and stare at him. "I forgot! You had an interview, didn't you? How did you get on – did you like the school?"

"Yeah. It was okay. Better than my last crap school, anyway."

"What did you like about this one?"

"Dunno, really. I just liked it a bit more. They do…hey, you know what? It's well good. You can do canoeing and sailing and stuff. They have after-school clubs. And the older kids go up on the moor and do rock-climbing and that thing like, when you have to find your way…"

"Orienteering?"

"Whatever…and I saw the science labs and they're ace…"

"So I take that as a 'yes', Ivan! You did like the school!"

"S'pose."

I'm really pleased. This school, in the next town along the coast, has a reputation for sports – particularly for the individual type of sports that Ivan's so keen on. Last year, his school did very well in the Ten Tors Event, a gruelling two-day hike over Dartmoor that stretches the young people to the utmost of their ability. I can see Ivan doing that.

If only he can get himself together on time. With a pang of anxiety, I realise that there's only three weeks till the end of term – and no doubt the school will want to take him 'on trial' for the last week.

We sit on a low wall at the edge of the terrace outside the café, licking our ice creams, and tickling our toes in the sand. Clouds have suddenly appeared, and shade sweeps across the beach like the wing of a giant bird. Families begin to dismantle their beach tents and windbreaks and gather their things together.

Something occurs to me, something I've been wondering about for ages.

"Ivan," I venture, tentatively, "what made you become 'Ivan', instead of…I mean, why did you change your name?"

Ivan shrugs. "Because. Because of my surname: Ivanovich. They started calling me Ivan."

"Who did? When?"

"The kids in my class. Well, a few of them, anyway. Then it sort of spread round the class. In the end the whole school started calling me Ivan."

"But just because of your surname?"

"No. We were doing Russian history, and I was interested because I'm half-Russian. I think the teacher did it especially for me, because to start with it was all about Europe. And she told us about Ivan IV. He was the first king of Russia…"

"Tsar…"

"Yeah. That's the one. And he made it all one country for the first time, like with one government. But if people mucked him about, even the slightest bit – he'd..." Ivan makes a slitting movement across his throat. "He murdered them. About three thousand of them. That's why he was called Ivan the Terrible." Ivan finishes with a little swagger.

"So, did you mind when everyone started calling you that, too? Ivan IV isn't exactly a good role model, is he?"

"I minded at first. I used to fight the kids who said it. But then, I thought, what the hell, if they're going to call me that, I'll act like it. So I started, you know, getting into trouble and stuff…and it wasn't *just* that. It was because, well, because…"

Ivan's clammed up suddenly.

"Because?" I persist.

"Oh, I dunno." Ivan shifts uneasily. "I just got fed up with being Ryan. With that name. Got it?"

"Right."

The subject is firmly closed. But I've got my answer, sort of. Anyway, I'm glad I asked the question. It was one of those things I'd always wanted to know but never dared to ask. I expect Ivan IV's subjects felt pretty much the same.

"I have to get back now, Ivan," I say, reluctantly. "Thank you so much for teaching me sand-boarding. I will practise, I promise."

"I'll carry the board out to your car, shall I?" says Ivan, unexpectedly.

"Thanks."

Ivan places the board carefully on the back seat. He pats it lovingly.

"I'd like one of those. But I can't afford it."

My first impulse is to give it to him straight away. After all, he'll get so much more fun out of it. But wait… I harden my heart. Ivan's got to earn it. He's still got to prove himself. Just now, he's still unpredictable. Though today he was charm itself, the circumstances were more relaxed. There was no pressure. We weren't in a tuition session, and he wasn't in school. Let's wait and see…

"Bye, then, Ivan. I'll see you on Monday morning, as usual."

"Bye," he says.

He watches while I get in the car. And he's looking at me in a new way. I can't describe his expression. Respect? Acknowledgement? Partly – yet there's something more. *Connection.* Yes, that's the word.

And it feels good.

Monday, 5th July. Catherine opens the door. She's dressed, but looks tense and haggard. That sallow look has come back, and there are dark rings under her eyes. Behind her stands Nina, with her thumb in her mouth.

"Hi, Nina. Not at school? Is it one of those Baker Days?"

My voice has an edge to it, though I'd meant to make it light and jocular. Really, it's not right that Nina should have so many days away from school. She seems to have a semi-permanent role as Catherine's young carer. And today, she doesn't look too happy about it, either.

Catherine clears her throat, "Um, my elder son, Kurt, is staying, as you know. He was supposed to be going back to Bristol early this morning, but he suddenly changed his mind. He said he wanted to see a couple of his friends in town first." Catherine hesitates for a moment. "I don't think he'll be back while you're here."

"It wouldn't matter at all. He wouldn't be in the way," I reassure her. "And I'll be sorry to miss him. I'd like to have met him."

"You wouldn't really," pipes up Nina suddenly. "He's—"

Her mother shushes her and tells her to go upstairs and pick up her clothes from her bedroom floor. I ask Catherine if it will be all right to use the kitchen for a science experiment, promising to clear up afterwards.

"Go ahead," she says, approvingly. "Ivan's science has really taken off since you got him interested again. *And* his engineering. He spent half Saturday building some kind of platform with the dug-out earth. Anyway, I won't need the kitchen today. I'm going to have a general cleaning session today, starting with Nina's room. It's a pigsty in there!"

Catherine follows Nina upstairs, and I go into the living room. Ivan is already at the table, but his face is like a thundercloud.

"Guess what!" he bursts out as soon as he sees me. "This guy from the coastguards came round yesterday and said they knew we'd been bombing off Puffin Rock!"

Ivan quivers with indignation. My heart lurches with fear.

"And had you, Ivan? Been bombing again?" I ask, as if I'm not really interested one way or the other.

"Might have. Can't remember. Anyway, the point is, *someone* snitched on us. Wait till we find out who it was!"

Ivan grits his teeth and glares round the room. I keep my head down, and concentrate on finding Ivan's page in my folder.

"I suppose the coastguards are only doing their duty," I say, noncommittally.

"Yeah, right. Spoiling our fun. Like, we're not harming anyone for fucksake. Why don't they go down the docks and pick on the crack-heads down there? Anyway, the coastguard said this couple were walking their dog along the clifftop when they saw us. They rang the station. They'd *described* us, he said. That was well out of order. They should mind their own fucking business."

I offer up thanks to the universe. "And when exactly was this, Ivan?" I ask, innocently.

Ivan goes red and looks away. "Can't remember."

"Anyway," I breathe deeply again, "we must make a start. Let's see if we can finish *Tough Guy* today. It's due back at the library…"

I cajole Ivan into getting down to work. He's really liked this book – far more than I expected. In fact, for the first time in his life, he's been reading a few chapters in his own time. He's enjoying the storyline but, alas, completely missing the message behind it, i.e. that bullies can ruin their victims' lives. At the start of the novel, he identified far more with Joe, the bullying anti-hero, than with William, his eleven-year-old victim.

"It's his own fault," Ivan kept saying. "If William wasn't such a wimp… William should fight back more, really thump him…he's so weak, he deserves what he gets."

This attitude of Ivan's was worrying me a lot. Unless he learns to see the victim's point of view, he's likely to carry on with his bullying behaviour at his next school. However, last week, I saw a crack in Ivan's armour, a little glimmer of hope.

We'd been reading about Joe's latest bullying episode. Joe and his cronies tied poor William to a tree, saying they were going to shoot arrows at him. (This involved a digression into the William Tell story, which Ivan had never heard, so I suppose the book did have some added value.) In the end, 'all' the bullies do is run away laughing and leave him there for hours, sobbing and terrified. But William is also worried about his disabled mother who is in a wheelchair. There is no food in the house, because William is a young carer and does all the family shopping. As if this weren't enough to cope with, his Labrador, Rusty, will be whimpering at home, waiting for his master to take him for a walk.

While we were reading this, I noticed that Ivan's sympathy was, for the very first time, swinging round towards the victim. Did the disabled mother resonate with him? Or was it Rusty? In my experience, bring a four-footed friend into any story and you've won over the most hardened offender. Whatever it was, it gave me some hope.

Today, in the penultimate chapter, Joe is upping the ante and shutting William in the cellar of an empty house. It's dark and cold and yet again William's been there for hours. And once more his poor mum and dog are missing him.

It's my turn to read first. I put all the emotion I can muster into making this part of the story come alive. I look up, expecting to see – not exactly tears streaming down Ivan's face, but at least a flicker of empathy.

Ivan is stony-faced, mouth turned down. He's taken his compass out of his geometry set and is jabbing holes in the cover of his folder. I thought he was listening, following the story, but...

"This is boring," he says.

I wonder. Does Ivan mean 'boring' as in 'intrinsically uninteresting'? If so, this is surprising, given that up to now he's been captivated by the story. Or is the subject matter making him feel uncomfortable?

I look at him, puzzled. He's very agitated this morning. And edgy. He keeps looking up, first towards the open door of the living room, and then through the window into the garden. I reckon the coastguard's visit is still nettling him. Maybe he thinks the police will be coming after him next.

"Let's do science, then, Ivan. We can read the rest of the book tomorrow. And come to think of it, we're going to need at least an hour if we're to do both experiments. Are you ready to begin?"

Ivan nods, still looking preoccupied and surly.

I've brought all the items needed for the experiment, and I lay them out on the work-surface in the kitchen: bicarbonate of soda, salt, lemon juice, bleach, milk, vinegar. I can't use Catherine's stuff – it wouldn't be fair, even if she had them in stock, which I doubt. We're going to do some PH testing – a perennially favourite chemistry experiment. Ivan tells me that he missed this when they did it at school. He's by my side now, his mood suddenly buoyant. His eyes sparkle as we prepare the 'indicator' – a messy job involving red cabbage.

Ivan works neatly and methodically, recording the PH value of each substance on a chart. He's quick, too. It takes him no time at all to match the colour of the litmus testing strip to the PH colour chart, whereas I tend to dither indecisively for ages.

"Get a move on! You're not choosing paint for your bathroom walls, are you?" says Ivan, scathingly.

Just for fun, halfway through our experiments, we break off to do some secret writing, using up the rest of the lemon juice. We both write invisible messages in lemon juice with the end of a feather, and put our pieces of paper in the oven on a low heat. It's a primary-age experiment, and I'm hoping Ivan won't think it's beneath his dignity. But no, he's hovering by the oven door, looking at his watch, impatient for the messages to be 'cooked'. It reminds me yet again that Ivan has probably missed out on a lot of fun. Children who are around violence – or even potential violence – are often in a semi-permanent state of fear or anxiety. So even if the opportunities for learning, play and enjoyment are there, these children don't always make the most of them. It's as if that ever-fearful part of their psyche acts as a filter to prevent them throwing themselves whole-heartedly into whatever's going on. In the worst cases they switch off completely and don't even try. I've seen such children in the playground, hanging back on the outside of a group of carefree, laughing children. They're in a permanent state of frozen watchfulness. It's heartbreaking to see.

Yet there's a way forward with these kids, even with those who are older and most damaged. If they can be taken back to an earlier stage of development and have the chance to enjoy all the things they missed – play, learning, stories – *at that level* – this process can be enormously healing. This is the thinking that lies behind many 'hands-on' therapies, including play therapy. It's incredibly moving to see such a child blossom in this way. First, it's as if a hard block of ice in the core of his or her being begins to melt. Then, there's the gradual unfolding; the beginnings of curiosity, the hunger for self-expression. And finally, the magical realisation that WOW! There's a whole world out there!

Of course, it's plain that Ivan, luckily, has not been traumatised to this extent. But there's no harm, once in a while, in taking him back a few learning stages and finding an opportunity for play.

The secret messages are ready. We take them out of the oven. My message to Ivan reads: 'Colin will be calling round this evening, bringing a water storage tank. And to see if the platform is high enough. Be ready at 7 o'clock.'

Ivan reads it, grins and hands me his message. I'm just trying to decipher it, when there's a sudden interruption. The outside door opens with a crash. It's as if a tornado has burst into the kitchen, threatening to sweep up everything in its path and hurl us into space.

Kurt stands in the doorway, glowering.

"What are you doing in here, Ryan?" He moves into the kitchen, and stands close – too close – to Ivan, glaring down at the experiments, glaring at *me*.

He's tall, at least six foot two, and burly with it. In fact, he looks more like thirty-five than nineteen. His hair is dark, like Ivan's, but there the resemblance ends. Kurt's features are heavy, unappealing. A large nose and mouth, with loose, slack lips. Swarthy, unhealthy-looking skin. And his eyes! There's hostility – hate, even – in the way he looks at Ivan.

And Ivan has shrunk. Not just in size – he looks like a small child next to his brother – but in his body language. He's turned away from Kurt, busying himself with measuring out a spoonful of baking powder. But he's shrinking away, huddling against the corner of the work-surface, his back turned. With a shock, I realise he's shaking.

"We're doing some science experiments, as you can see," I say evenly. It's plain that Ivan can't bring himself to reply.

"*I* need to be in here. I want to make myself a sandwich." Kurt lolls against the work-surface, staring at me insolently.

"There's room for both of us, Kurt," I say, pleasantly "You won't be in our way."

"You *what?*" Kurt's jaw drops open. "Did you say *I* wouldn't be in *your* way?" He turns on his brother. "You're in *my* way, mate. This is a kitchen, not a friggin' laboratory."

"Kurt," I interject coolly, "I've already spoken to your mother, and she has given her permission for us to do some experiments here. As you can see, we're only using one side of the kitchen. There's plenty of room for you to make a sandwich. I'm sure we can work alongside each other."

Kurt stares back at me, narrowing his eyes, weighing me up. I can see him working out how far he's going to take this, whether it's worth having a stand-up fight over the making of a sandwich. He's edged close – uncomfortably close – to Ivan, who's pressing himself into the work-surface as if wishing that he could somehow melt into the chip-board.

Kurt swears under his breath – a particularly unpleasant oath.

"I'm going out," he snarls. "I'll get a sandwich at the shop. Carry on with your baby experiments, Ryan. I hope they explode in your face!"

With this parting shot to his brother, and giving me a murderous look, Kurt storms out of the door.

For a few moments we stand stock-still, as if not sure if the tornado really has passed over. I feel shell-shocked. God only knows what poor Ivan is feeling just now. He's white as a sheet. His hands tremble as he tries to carry on with the experiment, tries to pretend to me that he doesn't really care.

There can be no doubt about one thing: big brother Kurt terrifies poor Ivan out of his wits. And most probably has been doing so for a very long time.

Tuesday, 6th July – 1a.m. I'm on the floor of my living room, prostrated in front of my ancient printer. It's gone on strike – as usual, at the most inconvenient time. Red and green lights flash malevolently at me. I'll swear it deliberately chooses the worst possible moment to play up. Like now, when something really urgent needs printing. And when I'm feeling most exhausted.

Two hours ago, I'd just been dropping off to sleep when I'd remembered that I had to write a report for the headmaster of Ivan's new school. It should have been on Sally's desk yesterday morning, to be included in Ivan's file. I'd dragged myself off, bleary-eyed, to the computer, and typed up the report. But my printer has a mind of its own.

I wriggle along the floor clutching the printer manual and peer again at the flashing buttons.

"Please, Oh Mighty One," I mutter, "Don't die on me now."

I press 'Print' again.

"I am not printing," replies the printer sulkily, via the screen.

"I can see that. But what's wrong with you? I've fed you. Evenly, and with a wad of paper exactly the right thickness – I know you don't like too thin a slice. I've cleaned you. What more can I do?"

I press one of the buttons next to the flashing green light. In response, the printer intones three sonorous, solemn notes, like a cathedral organ at the end of a requiem.

"I – HAVE – SAID."

Then it sighs into a profound silence.

I give up, and go to bed. But sleep eludes me. I toss and turn, worrying about Ivan.

After Kurt's threatening behaviour this morning, Ivan just about managed to last out till the end of the science experiment. But his face was deathly pale, the skin around his eyes and mouth taut. As he went through the motions of writing up his results, I watched the anger building up inside him.

I gave him an opening, trying to make my voice as neutral as possible.

"It's a shame that Kurt wasn't able to share the kitchen with you. There was plenty of space for all of us."

I was unprepared for the force of the explosion. Ivan swung round to face me, eyes ablaze.

"HE'S A FUCKING PRICK!"

With a choking sound, he swept his file paper off the work-surface. Then he too dashed out of the house.

If only, instead of this, we'd been able to have a calm de-briefing session. But then I suppose Kurt could have come back at any moment. For this reason, I didn't feel able, just then, to tell Catherine what had happened. It wouldn't be good if Kurt should suddenly return and find me complaining about him. And all I wanted at that stage was to get out of the house – fast.

I felt I should warn Colin that Ivan might not be in the right mood to work on the wind pump that evening, and that he should check with Ivan's mother first before he went round. I rang him. He said not to worry, he might call round anyway; if Ivan was unavailable, he would ask Catherine if she needed any jobs doing in the house.

Wearily, I plump up my pillow and try to sleep. It's been a bad day. Just now, it seems as if almost nothing could be worse in this worst of all possible worlds.

I'm wrong. It could.

9 a.m. Afterwards, I told myself that what happened this morning wasn't my fault. Not all of it, anyway. It was simply due to a chain of unfortunate events. But with hindsight, I have to take responsibility for much it. I'd made three crucial errors of judgement.

I assumed, now Kurt had gone back to Bristol, that the storm would have passed over and that we could return to normal. My first mistake in was not reading Ivan's mood correctly.

My second was in wanting to get that damn report finished, come hell or high water. Sally wanted it by the end of the day. But my fixation on the report meant that only half my attention was on Ivan. Being goal- instead of pupil-orientated is always a recipe for disaster.

And my third mistake? Well – I could have chosen a much more suitable activity for Ivan while I was preoccupied with my writing…

For the moment, Ivan's very quiet as he works through the maths sheet I've given him. I'm pleased to see him – apparently – concentrating so well. Yet, if I'd only studied him more closely, I would have noticed his tension, like a tiger waiting to spring.

It's just in the last week that I've succeeded in coaxing Ivan into doing worksheets. His confidence has been very low. However, after sailing through several easy ones, he's graduated to graphs, percentages and equivalent fractions, and now, geometry. He no longer believes he'll be the 'thickest' in the class when he returns to school.

Today's worksheet involves compass practice. Ivan has to draw and cut out circles of various sizes – a preliminary exercise to help him understand diameter and circumference, and the relationship between the two. It's the type of practical activity that Ivan most enjoys. I'm hoping it will keep him occupied in time for me to finish his report.

Because it's handwritten, this is taking me much longer than I thought. I'm trying to make my writing as neat as possible. Handwritten reports seem to be considered *infra-dig* and unprofessional these days, but I actually prefer to do them in this way. I enjoy the act of writing, and it gives me longer to think. And anyway, handwriting was good enough for Shakespeare.

Opposite me, Ivan is fidgeting.

"I've done the circles," he says. "What do I do next?"

"Hold on, Ryan," I say, absently. "I just need to…"

"**WHAT** *did you call me?*"

It's as if a bolt of lightning has struck. Ivan's fist crashes down between us. He jumps up and grips the edge of the table. His lips are drawn back in a snarl.

My stomach lurches, sickeningly. Jekyll has just turned into Hyde.

"What's wrong, Ivan?" I stare at him, incredulously.

"You did it on purpose, didn't you? To wind me up…"

"I haven't a clue what you mean!"

Then, I suddenly twig. Throughout my report, I've been referring to Ivan as 'Ryan', his official name. I'd actually been writing the word just as Ivan was asking me what he should do next. I open my mouth to explain all this. But I'm too late.

With a bound, Ivan leaps to my side. He stands over me, his arm raised. In his hand – its point six inches away from my face – is the open compass.

"I could *stab* you – I could **KILL** you!"

There's a demented look in his eyes.

I freeze. I stare straight ahead. I can see Ivan's hand shaking, the compass point level with my eyes. I look down at my writing. Slowly, deliberately, I pick up my pen. I take a deep breath:

"You could, Ivan. You *could* stab me." I try to keep my voice level. "But you won't. And do you know why? Because you've far too much sense. And because you've got too much to lose. Much more importantly, it's wrong. And you know it."

I can hear and feel Ivan's heavy breathing, close to my ear.

"I'm sorry I called you Ryan," I say, coolly. "As you can see, I was writing a report for your new school. The file it will go into is entitled '*Ryan* Ivanovich'. So naturally I can't suddenly change your name for this report. It would confuse all your teachers. But it's entirely your decision what name you choose to be known by once you start there."

I keep my head bent as I carry on writing.

Next to me, I can sense Ivan's shoulders and hand shaking. There's a long silence. Electric sparks fly around the room. Then he steps away from me. His hand drops to his side.

My heartbeat gradually returns to normal.

I look up. "I wouldn't have expected that of you, Ivan. Not now. It wasn't worthy of you."

Ivan makes an odd, strangled noise in his throat. Suddenly, he hurls the compass across the room. It hits the wall and crashes down on to a bookcase. He swears. There's so much pent-up feeling in him that he doesn't know where to put himself. He kicks the wall, and flails with his fists, swearing. At last he flings himself face down on the settee and sobs.

I wait a while for the storm to pass.

"It's okay, Ivan," I say, quietly.

Gradually, Ivan calms down enough for me to say:

"I can see that it was a very bad idea for me to try and do your report during your session. Not while you were feeling so angry and upset from yesterday. This morning, you needed a chance to talk. About Kurt's behaviour and how it made you feel…"

Ivan doesn't reply, but there's a sudden stillness in him. I draw my chair a little closer to the settee.

"Do you know something, Ivan?" I say, softly. "Kurt was well out of order yesterday. I found his behaviour in the kitchen extremely rude and unacceptable."

Ivan buries his face deeper into the cushions.

"Tell me if I'm wrong. But I guess all this is about Kurt. There's nothing else, is there?"

Ivan mumbles something incomprehensible. I lean closer.

"I didn't hear that…"

Ivan suddenly stiffens. He pummels the cushions hard, grunting like a boxer on his winning bout.

"I – HATE – HIM! I – HATE – HIM!" He emphasises each word with a kick and another thump.

"Ivan, tell me – has this been going on for a long time? Kurt throwing his weight around. Shouting at you like he did yesterday. Trying to scare you?"

I jump out of my skin as Ivan suddenly leaps to his feet. His face is dark with rage.

"That's nothing!" he chokes. "*Nothing*, compared to what he did when I was little…"

Briefly, he catches my eye. It's a visceral, gut-wrenching look, full of pain and terror.

"…He used to get me up against the wall…"

With a choking cry, Ivan shields his face with his arms and shrinks back.

I watch, horrified, as Ivan relives his brother's cruelty. And suddenly, it's all too much for him. He thumps the wall again and dashes towards the kitchen, kicking the table leg as he goes. I hear the outer door slam shut. In a flash, he's gone. I just catch a glimpse of him as he squeezes through the brambles at the end of the garden and slips out through the gate.

I stare after him helplessly. For a minute I'm rooted to the spot. My heartbeat thuds in my ears. Where on earth do we go from here?

One thing is certain. This whole family needs help. Urgently. Catherine is a proud and independent woman, but she's not well. She shouldn't have to struggle along in this way. And I'm worried about Nina. It's not right to keep her off school so often. Catherine seems to be relying on her far too much for emotional and practical support. And even Kurt – his violence is as much a symptom as a cause of the deep malaise within this family.

But it's Ivan who concerns me most. His chances of reinventing himself in a new school will be ruined if his whole family remain stuck in the same patterns.

The door to the living room opens slowly. Catherine, sleepy-eyed, peers round. "Is everything all right? I was completely out for the count, when I heard some commotion in here."

"Actually, Catherine, there's a problem. A big one."

I tell her, as gently as possible, what has just happened. I include yesterday's incident with Kurt, and say how Ivan was terrified out of his wits.

Catherine slumps down on the settee.

"Did you know," I ask her, "that Kurt was hitting Ivan over a very long period when he was younger?"

The shock in Catherine's face is almost palpable. In fact, she looks so stricken that I get the feeling there's a whole history lurking behind this latest episode.

"I didn't know," she whispers, at last. "Of course, I could see that they didn't get on. It was clear that Kurt hated Ivan. He never played with him, he was always making snide remarks, winding him up. But I put it down to jealousy – normal sibling rivalry. But this – what you said – actually *hitting* him, not just once but often! It doesn't bear thinking about…"

Catherine wrings her hands, her knuckles showing white.

"…If only he'd told me…"

Suddenly, Catherine stops. Slowly, she lowers her hands into her lap. She stares fixedly ahead, wide-eyed, haunted by a memory. All the colour has drained from her face.

"Oh, *no!*"

"What? What is it?"

"*Of course* he didn't tell me. He wouldn't have dared!" Catherine clutches her throat as if covering up a secret.

"Wouldn't have…?

Catherine shakes her head very slowly. Pain and despair are etched in her face.

"This is a terrible thing to say about one's own son. But Kurt's gone too far – again. I can't ignore what's happening any longer. I think – I'm *convinced* now I think about it – that Kurt was threatening Ivan. Telling him that if he split on him he'd hit him even more. Or do something – something that would hurt Ivan more deeply than a beating. I'd no idea. Truly. I hadn't. But I should have guessed…" Catherine's staring straight ahead. Her face has become even more ashen.

Not a lot of this is making sense.

"What could Kurt possibly do to Ivan that would be worse than beating him up?" I burst out.

Catherine's whole body seems about to implode. Her lips are working, half-forming words with no sound. Then, in a tight little voice, she says:

"It was a few years ago, when he was about Ivan's age, maybe a year older. Kurt was a tall powerful boy even then. Heavily built. Much bigger than Ivan is now. And Ivan must have been nine or ten. Kurt's behaviour became very disruptive, both at home and at school. At that time I was still with Sergei, but things were getting so bad, I knew I'd have to leave him soon. Kurt started going out with his mates at night. He was drinking, I could smell it on his breath when he came in – often very late. And when I challenged him about it, he…he became quite violent. He'd smash things. He wrecked the kitchen once."

Catherine stares at me, hollowly.

"Did…did this happen often?"

"Maybe about half a dozen times. It was then I realised that I must leave Sergei quickly. We escaped. To a safe house."

"With Kurt? Did you take him, even after…?"

"What else could I do?" cries Catherine. "What would you do, if it was *your* son? I wanted to keep us all together. Yes, I realise, now, that I was making every excuse possible for him. I told myself that he was simply copying his father's behaviour. But I thought that if I got him away from Sergei, he'd calm down."

"And did he?"

"He seemed to – a little. But I think that's when Kurt must have started on Ivan. It was about this time that I became ill. I had to go to hospital, and the children had to go into temporary foster care. When I came out, after three months, I managed to get a tiny flat. We were all living on top of each other.

Kurt and Ivan shared a room, and Nina slept in with me. The boys quarrelled the whole time. About stupid things – whose shelf in the cupboard was whose. You know the sort of thing. Kurt was always shouting at Ivan…"

"Poor Ivan."

"If it were just the shouting," says Catherine, tremulously. "Several times I noticed that Ivan had bruises on his legs and arms. He swore that he'd been in a fight at school. And I believed him."

"Well, maybe it was true?"

"No." Catherine shakes her head, vehemently. "I'm convinced now that Kurt was bullying him and that this went on for a long time. And it's all my fault. If I'd only opened my eyes to what was happening. It's almost as if I didn't *want* to see it!"

"That's natural. You had enough to cope with already. You mustn't blame yourself."

"But I do!" Catherine swallows hard. "This is the most terrible mess."

She sits still for a few moments, her shoulders slumped, staring down into her lap. Then she gazes at me with eyes full of anguish.

"Ivan should have told me. I'm his mother – who else could he tell? If he had, I could have sought help for him – and for Kurt. I knew things were bad between them but I thought…I was so sure that once we'd made the break away from Sergei, it would all gradually get better." Catherine shakes her head, helplessly. "Why, *why*, didn't he tell me what was going on?"

My stomach churns. While I'm struggling to take in the magnitude of all this, Catherine suddenly sits up with a new expression on her face. A dawning, horrified realisation.

"Do you know something? I can hardly bear to think this, let alone to say this. But I've told you so much now, you might as well hear everything… I suspect that Kurt might have told Ivan that unless he kept his mouth shut…" Catherine inhales sharply, "…that Kurt would hit me, too."

My heart misses a beat. "Would he say that? Why?"

Catherine swallows hard. "It sounds crazy, I know. Listen, Kurt had a lot of problems. Far more that I've ever wanted to admit. And he'd seen his father… watched how Sergei behaved towards me…"

"But wouldn't that make him more…more protective towards you?"

Catherine lets out a long shuddering breath. "You'd imagine so, wouldn't you? But maybe, with Kurt, it worked in the opposite way. Kurt's got a lot of his father in him. He's unpredictable, and aggressive. Yet he's still my son. I – I love him. I've been trying to ignore this side of him for years. But I'm afraid, I'm beginning to see that Kurt's somehow identified himself with his father."

Catherine's voice trails away into silence.

"I see. You're saying that Kurt's taken on the 'aggressor' role. That it's become part of his personality."

Catherine stares at me with a haunted expression. "What I'm saying is that Kurt must have blackmailed Ivan. By telling him that if he told anyone, including me, about the bullying, he – Kurt – would beat *me* up too. Because that's what Kurt did. When he was drunk and violent, before I escaped to the safe house, before I got ill. He hit me several times. And I suspect – I can't be sure – that Ivan saw him do it."

I catch my breath, stunned into silence. I stare at her, hardly taking in what she's saying.

Catherine gazes back, and shakes her head helplessly. "It's a mess, isn't it? What can I do, now, to make it better?"

"I think you've done a lot already, Catherine. You've seen things for what they are. That's a fantastic start. The next step is for you and for the whole family to get all the help that you can."

I want to sound positive, encouraging, but inwardly, I shiver. Ivan looks as if he's going down the very same path as his brother. He's rapidly disassociating himself from what he perceives as his own weak helplessness. Splitting himself off from that small child who once 'allowed' himself to be knocked about by a vicious elder brother. In order to feel strong, Ivan too became a bully. His victims were the small defenceless boys in the playground who reminded him too painfully of his vulnerable, younger self.

And he also attacks anyone who, by inadvertently saying the wrong thing at the wrong time, reminds him of Kurt.

When this happens, Jekyll turns into Hyde.

Wednesday, 7th July – 7.30 a.m. The phone rings, jolting me out of a troubled sleep. It's Catherine. She tells me that Ivan has had a bad night. He's been sick and has a temperature. His tuition session this afternoon will have to be cancelled.

"And how are you managing?" I ask, concerned about her, too.

Yesterday, I'd stayed at Jubilee Road until nearly five o'clock. Catherine had talked non-stop about her marriage, and her fears for Ivan's future. It was as if a dam had burst, releasing a flood of painful memories. Gradually, she'd calmed down. She said that she understood that others would have to know about Ivan's threatened attack on me. But when it came to telling the world that her own son had beaten her, I could see her shrink back with the irrational shame that haunts victims of abuse for years afterwards.

Yet just now, at the other end of the line, Catherine sounds quite chirpy. There's a new lightness in her voice.

"I feel much better," she says. "I rang your line manager after you'd gone. I had a long talk with her, and told her – what we spoke about."

"That's great, Catherine!" I feel myself loosen and relax with relief.

"I had to. I had no choice. How can Ivan – or any of us – move on if we're still locked in the past?"

2.p.m. So, thank goodness, Sally now knows as much as I do. But sharing secrets in conversation is one thing. Setting them down starkly in Ivan's report is quite another. The words become immutable, like tablets of stone. This afternoon, I'm trying to get my head round this problem.

With Ivan's session cancelled, I'm in Sally's office, taking the chance to get that report done once and for all. Luckily, due to staff absence, there's a computer available next to Sally's desk. It feels good not to be working alone, for once. It takes moments of contrast, like this, to bring it home to me what a lonely job home tuition can be.

Just now, we're both trying to craft a report that will throw light on Ivan's past behaviour without causing his mother too much embarrassment.

"Perhaps you should just ring her?" Sally suggests at last. "Ask her if there's any information she doesn't feel comfortable with sharing at the moment."

"Good idea." I sigh with relief.

This is such an obvious solution, but I seem to be brain-dead just now.

I need a break before I ring Catherine. I offer to put the kettle on and escape into the adjoining kitchen. I've been hooked up to the phone almost non-stop since I got home yesterday. Many calls were not work-related, merely concerned with boring household matters. But at seven o'clock in the evening, I'd rung Colin. It was only fair to put him in the picture. I didn't want to be responsible if Ivan, in his present unpredictable mood, suddenly launched an attack on him, too. Tim's experience had been haunting me all yesterday.

Then, I'd rung Tim himself. During the last day or two a hunch had gradually worked its way into my brain. It lay there, simmering and smoking. Now, it's exploded in my gut as an absolute, known truth.

I'd asked Tim if he could remember if the scissors and knife attacks happened to coincide with one of Kurt's visits. At the other end of the line, I could almost hear the wheels turning in Tim's memory box.

"Well, now I come to think of it – it was on a Monday that Ivan attacked me. His brother – Kurt, is it? – had just left that same morning. Why do you ask?"

"I'll tell you another time, Tim. But thanks for the information."

I wait for the kettle to boil, pondering. Yes, my hunch had been correct, I'm thinking, uncomfortably. But that in itself doesn't help the situation. It doesn't change the fact that whenever Kurt comes to stay there are likely to be ructions between him and Ivan – and that Ivan will be the one who suffers most. Unless something can induce him to stand up to his brother once and for all. But this will only happen when Ivan sees Kurt's bullying for what it is – the behaviour of a very disturbed young man. To understand this, Ivan needs to understand himself. Just now, hiding inside Ivan's fourteen year old body there's a terrified nine year old. A small child who is still cowering in a corner, waiting for the blows to rain down on his head.

I carry a tray of tea and biscuits back into the office and phone Catherine. I ask how Ivan is. She tells me that he's made a remarkable recovery. He slept till half an hour ago and then wolfed down four rounds of cheese and tomato sandwiches. And he's also looking forward to Colin's visit this evening.

"Colin's coming round, is he?" I ask, surprised.

Colin said nothing of this to me when we spoke on the phone last night. Not that I need to be there any more, at Catherine's house. I've set the wind pump project rolling, and I'm happy for Colin and Ivan to sort their work sessions out between them from now on. I trust Colin in every way. In any case, Catherine will always be around. But, to be honest, I feel a bit hurt. Colin could have at least mentioned this visit.

"He rang about nine o'clock last night," says Catherine. "He asked if he could come round this evening."

"He'll be doing a bit more work on the wind pump, will he?"

"Well, no. I think from what Colin said on Monday when he was here, that the next stage will be a bit tricky. It might have to be done over in Colin's workshop, because he's got all the necessary tools there…"

"Oh, I see," I say. But actually, I don't. I've suddenly lost the plot.

"So…" I hear Catherine catch her breath. "Colin's actually coming round to help *me*. On Monday, he looked round the house – at the damp. He reckoned that if he could insulate the walls over the summer when they're dry, the house will be much warmer next winter. And he's also got this idea of lining the roof space with special woollen fleece…"

"Good idea," I say, wondering why Catherine sounds so flustered and light-headed. And kind of… *fluttery*.

"Colin thinks it will be a good project for Ivan and him to do when the wind pump is finished," continues Catherine in the same breathless voice. "Ivan will learn a lot about cutting and measuring…"

"Excellent! Anyway, Catherine, what I was mainly ringing you about was this report. How much of what you told me do you want included…?"

There's a long silence. When Catherine finally speaks, her voice is tremulous, but decisive.

"Don't leave *anything* out. I can't hide any more. It's time to move on. For Ivan's sake…" I hear a long, shaky intake of breath. "And for mine."

Monday, 12th July – 6.p.m. Ivan's project has reached a critical stage. He has to fashion the blades and the wind-vane for the pump out of some hard plastic material that Colin found in a scrap yard. This involves the special cutting tools that he keeps in his workshop.

I'm sitting in the back seat of Colin's beaten up estate car. Nina and Ivan both wanted to be by the window, so I'm squashed up between the two of them. I've let Catherine sit in the front passenger seat, as she's taller than I am and needs more room. We're on the way to Colin's house, and we're at the mercy of his driving technique, which tends to be somewhat erratic at the best of times. In the boot, the dishes of food that I'd placed in a cardboard box hurtle from one side to another as we spin round corners. I'm feeling distinctly queasy. To distract myself from the somersaults in my stomach, I watch Ivan as he leans forward, chattering in Colin's ear about wind-pumps, and marvel at the change in him.

Over the last few days, he seems to have already reinvented himself. For a start, he's abandoned his surname, 'Ivanovich', and from now on will adopt his mother's maiden name, 'Jones'. He's still undecided whether to ditch 'Ivan'. I reckon this name is still very much part of his present identity. 'Ryan' still brings back painful memories.

Therapeutic one-to-one counselling sessions have been set up for him at a Child and Family Guidance Centre, as a result of referral letters from the Education Department and Catherine's GP. We were lucky in getting emergency help for him. His first appointment will be next week. Ivan, Catherine and Nina will be invited to attend additional family therapy sessions, and it's hoped that Kurt, too, will eventually take advantage of these. Although Ivan hasn't even started on this programme, the effect on him has been remarkable. The thought that it will soon happen seems to have given him a new buoyancy. It's as if he feels 'held' simply by knowing that there are other people out there who are aware of his pain, and who are willing to help him – and his family. In addition, a place has been found for Ivan on a new anger-management course for teenagers, to start in the summer holidays. The last one hadn't worked for him. He wasn't ready for it, but much has changed since then. For the first time, Ivan is willing to make the first tentative moves towards self-determination.

And at last he's become motivated to work in our tuition sessions. In fact, for the last three days, he's been zipping through maths and English worksheets with lightning speed.

"To show my teachers," he announced, as he put yet another piece of work into his folder. "I don't want them to put me in with all the thickies." However dubious his motives for this sudden burst of zeal, doing such an impressive pile of work has given Ivan a great sense of achievement.

"Hey, teacher!" says Nina, sniffing the air, and then sniffing me, "you've put scenty stuff on." She looks down at my feet. "And posh shoes, *with heels!*

"It's a special occasion, Nina!" I say, feeling my face flush,

Catherine swivels round and beams at me.

"Yes, it is special, *very* special."

"I feel sick," says Nina.

Suddenly, so do I. Sitting in the middle of the rear seat, I have a fly-on-the-wall vantage view of Catherine and Colin's profiles. A dubious privilege. Colin is somehow managing to drive with his head inclined towards Catherine. As they talk, his eyes flicker towards her a tad too frequently. They linger over her face for much longer than warranted by their casual conversation – about a new one-way system and the closing of yet another post office.

Catherine's wearing her 1940s' hairstyle, locks swept up from the sides to the crown of her head, the rest falling in soft waves to between her shoulders. As she listens to Colin she half-turns towards him, with a coquettish sideways glance, and a twitch of her lips.

Yuk! How did this happen? I feel as if I've suddenly landed in the rear seat of the car scene in *Brief Encounter*. Colin's no Trevor Howard, but Catherine makes a passable Celia Johnson. And it's plain they have eyes only for each other.

Unwittingly, I've been playing Cupid. Sending love darts between Catherine and Colin. Or to be more precise, between Catherine and four lawn mowers. What on earth have I *done*? I just pray it won't all end in tears.

Just before Nina throws up, we arrive at Colin's house. Once out of the car, we head straight through the wilderness of his garden to the workshop at the bottom. This huge shed is home to a half-size steam-powered tractor that Colin built. It took over his entire life for three years. There's a couple of small model steam engines, and lined up along one wall is Colin's collection of lawn mowers. Now he proudly shows these creations to Ivan, who – wide-eyed with wonder – touches, prods, and asks intelligent questions.

Catherine and Nina soon become bored. I find some garden chairs and settle Catherine down in one of them, urging her to rest while I make a cup of tea for all of us. Nina skips around happily, exploring the large garden.

Quickly, I open the boot of the car and bring the food into the house. I carry it carefully into Colin's kitchen. With a sinking heart, I survey the scene.

As usual, the table is covered with greasy lawn mower parts. I sweep them up into sheets of old newspaper and stuff them into a corner. I give the old pine table a good scrub before setting out the food. The debris on the work-surfaces presents another challenge. Dirty crockery and cutlery are interspersed with model-making magazines and half-finished jars and tins of food. I pile all the dishes into the sink and wash up the more presentable plates. These I place on the table with some knives and forks. I'm hoping that my frenzy of extreme tidying-up will give Colin at least a sporting chance in his wooing of Catherine.

By the time the lady in question, smiling and relaxed, wanders into the kitchen to ask if she can help, the kettle is on. And the kitchen looks no worse than one might find in any bachelor pad.

We carry trays of drinks out into the garden. From the shed comes the deafening screech of an electric saw. Soon Colin and Ivan emerge, flushed and triumphant, Ivan clutching an armful of white plastic blades.

"Look!" he says, jubilantly. "We've done six of them already!"

"Only about another hundred to go," jokes Colin. "And be careful with the edges, Ivan. They're very rough and sharp. I'll get you sanding these down in a minute."

"Have a drink first, please, both of you," pleads Catherine.

"When do you want to eat, Colin?" I ask. "I need to know when to put the sausage rolls in the oven."

Colin looks at Ivan. "What do you think?"

"Let's finish the blades first. I want to have a go with the saw. You said I could. I'll be careful, honestly…"

"Right then," replies Colin. "You'll need goggles and gloves. I think I've got some spare ones somewhere."

Five minutes later, they both disappear into the shed again. They could be father and son. Catherine is obviously thinking along these lines, too. She gazes fondly after them, dewy-eyed.

We drink a toast to Ivan's future in his new school. Catherine is more-than-slightly tiddly, having drunk a small glass of white wine for the first time for years. Ivan eats enough for three, wolfing down his third helping of strawberries and ice cream, while Catherine, holding hands with Colin under the table, tastes bits of this and that, saying she'll suffer for it later. Nina grins round at us all, looking like a ten-year-old for once.

I look round at Ivan and Nina, Catherine and Colin as they eat, joke, laugh and I try to make some sense of it all. This, too, is all my doing. Unintentionally, I've somehow managed to bring them all together.

Another celebration, which may happen very soon, hangs unspoken in the air. On the journey home, the looks that pass between Colin and Catherine are even more *Brief Encounter*-like than before. Colin drops me off first, even though Catherine's house is nearer than mine and Colin will then have to drive back on himself. This means that they will have longer together.

As Colin pulls up outside my gate, I ask them all to wait for a moment while I fetch something from the house. I bring out a large sand-board.

"Your prize, Ivan," I tell him. "You deserve it. For a record number of points gained in three days!"

Ivan leaps out of the car, eyes agog.

"Cool!" he says. "Thanks."

"Yes, thank you for everything. *Everything!*" adds Catherine, leaning out of the window.

"Good luck then, Ivan!" I reach up and give him a quick hug, which he accepts with embarrassed grace.

Once in the car, the sand-board stretches from the boot to the front-seat, on its side between the two children. Ivan runs his hand along it, lovingly. He winds down the window.

"Thanks!" he says again.

"Enjoy it. Oh, and Ivan…"

"What?"

"No more bombing, right?"

Ivan grins. "I don't do that anymore. We've got a new game now, me and my mates. You know Puffin Cliff – that bit that sticks right out into the sea? Well, we all go round to Shell Beach when the tide's out, right? We wait until it starts coming in round the bottom of the cliff. Then we have to get round it, back to Puffin Bay. The last one to reach the other side is the winner. It's brilliant. Last time I won. I had to swim for it like crazy. The tide was coming in well fast…"

"*Ivan…!*" I say, aghast.

But Ivan, laughing, has wound the window up again. Well. It's not my problem anymore. It's Catherine's. And Colin's. As the car pulls away, they all wave: Catherine, Colin, Ivan and Nina. And somehow they all seem to meld together. They look comfortable with each other, as if they belong. I wave back until the car disappears round the corner at the end of the road.

I stand at my gate, watching night fall. Darkness wraps around the hills that enclose the town. There's comfort in those black, soft, rounded shapes that seem to hug me like strong arms. The air is balmy, warm, and sweet-scented with roses and evening primrose. I breathe it all in. For the briefest of moments, I feel content.

BETHANY

~

Tuesday, 24th February 2004. "Bethany! *Bethany!* Stop doing that – you'll hurt your head!"

Bethany either can't or won't hear. She's drowning out my voice with a low insistent moaning sound that rises and falls with each thump of her head. First against the wall and then on the cushion beneath. The thumps keep perfect rhythm, as if timed to a metronome. Wall, cushion, wall, cushion. The droning, nasal hum that accompanies each hit sounds like the old-style police car siren, changing into a lower register as it zooms past and roars off into the distance.

Bethany is my new pupil. She's nine years old, and 'borderline' autistic.

She's kept up the head-banging for ten minutes. It's an extraordinary performance. I'm horrified, fearful and fascinated all at once.

"Stop it, Bethany!"

I'm shouting and hating myself for it. Bethany's response is to hum louder and rock more violently.

This is not a good start to our first tuition session. And not what I expected after yesterday's initial visit. Yesterday, on this same settee where she is now crouched on all fours, busy bashing out her brains, Bethany sat demurely, hands folded on her lap, listening quietly to our discussion. When I'd asked her a direct question, she'd nod, or shake her head, or answer in monosyllables without eye contact. I could see she had problems, but I hadn't anticipated this bizarre behaviour.

I've got to distract her. Interest her in something – anything!

"Just look what I've got here, Bethany!"

In fact I haven't 'got anything here' at all – desperation has driven me to put mouth into gear before brain. I fish into my holdall, but all I can find is a game of Word Bingo, which is totally inadequate.

I needn't have bothered. Bethany hasn't heard me. Her rhythm never falters.

I lean over the arm of the settee so that she can see me, and wave the game in her face.

"Look! Let's have a game!"

Bethany turns her head away. Now she's banging with the side of her head, bashing her right ear. The hum becomes a shriek. I'm scared stiff – she'll damage her eardrum. Should I pull her away from the wall? But my touch might shock her. She's in some horrible trance. Yet she's not like a sleepwalker who can be gently led back to bed. She needs to be woken up somehow, but I haven't a clue how to do it.

Suddenly, the door connecting the living room with the hall opens with a crash. Mrs Webster, baby Joseph on her hip, stands in the doorway. Her black eyes snap and flash at Bethany, her ample body quivering as she struggles to contain the wriggling baby.

"Oh, she's at it again, is she? Hang on, I'll just put him down for a second."

She rushes back across the hallway into the kitchen, and plonks her little son down in a playpen on the floor. Joseph bawls lustily as she shuts the kitchen door and comes back into the living room.

Heaving herself up on to the settee behind Bethany, she pins her daughter's arms behind her back. She lifts her up away from the wall into a sitting position. She holds her very tightly.

"*No*, Bethany! You are *not* to do that. Your tutor's here. You've got to be good. Do you hear?"

Bethany can't move, but she can still hum – loudly. She's trying to block out her mother's voice. Mrs Webster brings her face close to Bethany's and yells in her daughter's ear:

"If you don't stop doing that at once you won't go to the shop. I won't let you. You'll have no money for chocolate!"

Gradually, the humming subsides, like the winding down of some infernal machine. Bethany's still facing the wall, but she's quiet at last. She turns round and looks at her mother.

"I want chocolate."

"Well then, you'd better behave," says Mrs Webster "You do your work with your tutor and we'll see – later. Sit round straight. Sit properly."

We both watch and wait. Slowly, deliberately, Bethany uncurls herself from her haunches and swivels round to face us. She swings her legs and looks past us, out of the window. I expected defiance, or sulks, but her expression is blank and indifferent.

"Will you be all right now?" asks Mrs Webster, hovering by the door. "I'd better see to Joseph. He's working himself up into a real paddy."

"Yes, thank you. We'll be fine."

She goes out, shutting the door firmly. There's a sudden silence as Joseph's angry yells subside.

I perch uneasily on the edge of an armchair opposite Bethany. We're anything but 'fine', I think. Not like this, not with Mum taking control rather than me and Bethany realising it. Knowing that every time she throws a wobbly I won't be able to cope. And her mother holding the trump card – chocolate! Because that's what Bethany gets for being good. But she only becomes good after she's made quite sure that there's chocolate being dangled in front of her. There's a fine line here between a reward for good behaviour – and a bribe. I'm not quite sure which side of this line Bethany's on, but either way, I don't fit into the picture. Yet it's vital that I establish my own authority, with *my* system of rewards and sanctions. And do it *now*.

I look hard at Bethany, willing her to make eye contact with me. Her head's down, her eyes slightly to one side, looking away from me. Not staring defiantly out of the window, or scowling like a teenager with attitude. She's started to rock, almost imperceptibly, backwards and forwards, her hands folded in her lap. Her face is blank, almost composed.

She's small and well-built without being overweight, with sturdy legs. She looks as if she could be good at games and gymnastics. She has olive skin, dark-brown hair in a ponytail, and her mother's black eyes. They're quite distinctive, large and slanting slightly upwards, almost oriental in appearance. But where her mother's flash and sparkle with a lively intelligence, Bethany's are lacklustre and vacant.

I sigh, and gaze at her helplessly. Maybe I should cut my losses and call it a day? She just isn't in the mood to cooperate. And if I push her too hard into engaging with me, in our first session, she might retreat even further into herself or throw another tantrum. I can't face another head-banging session.

Yet it's never a good idea to admit defeat and retire early from a session, however gracefully. The child feels, and becomes, far too powerful. Sometimes, with children like Bethany, it's best simply to play alongside – literally.

I sink down to the floor, apparently ignoring Bethany, and open one of my books. I flip through the pages, talking to myself.

"Just look at you, Tiger! What bright hungry eyes! I bet you could eat me for breakfast, dinner *and* tea! I won't get too near you. But I do love your stripes…" I turn the page, slowly, exaggerating my anticipation with much eyebrow-raising. "And now a cheetah! Hello, Mr Cheetah. You can run really fast – as fast as a car can go. Now that really *is* fast! Would you also eat me up, if I got too near you?"

Out of the corner of my eye, I can just see Bethany. She's as before, sitting quite still, her face turned away. But now, there's a different quality to the stillness – a listening attentiveness.

I carry on turning pages, exclaiming with pleasure at each picture: A panther, a lion, a snow-leopard. With my finger, I trace the outline of each animal, marvelling out loud at the design of these beautiful creatures, at their sleekness and grace, their bodies built for speed and power. Each muscle rippling as they spring up from a crouching position to stalk and catch their prey.

I'm nearly at the end of the book.

"I can hardly see you, Mrs Polar Bear, you're so white you don't show up against the snow. How do you find your babies if they get lost?"

A strange thing has happened to me. I'm in a world of my own – a world of wonder and delight. The book has completely taken me over. I don't care whether Bethany's listening or not. I'm doing this for *myself!*

"I know what you eat in the wild," I continue, "if you live in Canada, that is. But I bet you won't tell me if I ask you. I'd be so sad at what you gobble up for your dinner…"

"They eat seals."

Bethany's voice makes me jump. I glance at her briefly and smile at her. She's straining forward to see the picture. Her face is impassive. But in the empty depths of her eyes, there's a tiny spark.

"They eat seals," she says again, in a flat little voice.

"That's right, they do."

I carry on talking to the bears in the picture. "And I bet you get very hungry when all the ice breaks up after spring-time. Because then, you have to go ashore, where there are no seals…"

"I saw some polar bears at the zoo. And some seals." Bethany edges along the settee by an infinitesimal amount towards me.

"Yes, I've seen them too. I loved seeing the seals being fed. Now, I'd really like to draw a picture. Which animal shall I choose? Hmmm. This is so difficult. They're all so beautiful. Maybe I'll choose you, Mr Leopard, because then I can have fun counting all your spots."

I take a deep, steadying breath. This is the point at which I could crack. I long to scoop Bethany up with my enthusiasm and suggest she draws a picture, too. Laid out on the floor is an inviting kaleidoscope of coloured pencils and felt tips and paper. But I could go too far, and break the spell.

Slowly, deliberately, I open a sketchbook and copy the outline of a leopard. Bethany edges an inch closer. She points at my drawing.

"The body is too squashed up."

"So it is! I never noticed."

I rub out the haunches of the leopard and make them longer and sleeker.

"Thank you for telling me that. It looks much better now."

I carry on, adding a background to the leopard, and a running commentary to myself.

"See the long grass and the trees. They provide cover, a hiding place."

I'm hoping she'll join in now. Most nine-year-old fingers would be itching to do their own drawing, or perhaps fill in the leopard's spots. But not Bethany. She sits, watchful, silent. Then:

"Can I draw a spider?"

I feel thrown for a moment, like a rider whose horse has unexpectedly taken the wrong jump. *A spider*? I'm thinking wild and large and *Born Free*. I teleport myself down to the minuscule world of arachnids.

"Yes of course you can."

I tear off a sheet from the sketchpad. Bethany takes a pencil and carefully draws a spider in the middle of the page. It's tiny, but beautifully formed, with eight legs correctly in place.

"I'll draw the web now," she says, so quietly I can hardly hear her.

"I'm sorry, Bethany, but we've got to stop. It's time for me to go. Look, it's one o'clock." I point to the clock on the mantelpiece.

Do I detect the smallest flicker of disappointment brushing over Bethany's face? She sits, still staring down at her spider.

"But I'll be back tomorrow, at the same time, twenty past eleven." I keep my voice matter-of-fact, and begin to pack my things together. "You can finish drawing the spider's web then, if you like."

Her drawing is still on the floor. Absurdly, I feel a sudden pang, seeing it lying there on the brown tumble-twist carpet. A minute ago, it lay amid cheerful companions – the picture books and colouring pencils. Now it lies in splendid isolation, abandoned. I pick it up and hand it to her.

"It's a lovely drawing. Can you keep it somewhere safe until tomorrow?"

Bethany blinks rapidly and nods. She puts the drawing on the sideboard. I knock on the kitchen door and say goodbye to her mother. Mrs Webster's busy rocking Joseph asleep in her arms, so she just smiles and nods goodbye.

"See you tomorrow, Bethany. Goodbye."

She walks behind me as I walk along the hall towards the stairs that lead down to the front door of the first-floor maisonette. She stands at the top, watching me. I wave as I reach the bottom.

As I open the door I can just hear a very faint: "Bye".

1.10 p.m. My lunch break. I'll be lucky if I get half an hour: Thomas, my next pupil, lives way across town. The Pier Café, my usual haunt, is smoky and full-up. An unseasonably warm and sunny day has brought families to the seafront for a stroll along the promenade followed by fish and chips.

Instead of going to the café I find a bench and eat my sandwiches. I watch children walk past, carrying ice-creams in one hand, buckets and spades in the other. It must be half term. My half-term break was last week.

While I was off work, I'd had a phone call from Sally, my line manager. She sounded harassed and busy. There had been a sudden influx of excluded children, all urgently needing tuition. One of them had been Bethany.

As I ate my lunch, I remembered Sally's phone call telling me that Bethany was 'borderline' autistic – veering more towards Asperger's Syndrome. That it was difficult to gauge her educational level, because she'd missed so much school. She was a year or two behind in basic subjects. Sally had said that her main problem was school phobia. The last time Bethany attended school regularly was eighteen months ago.

That included three months she'd spent at a special assessment unit, attached to a hospital. This took place about a year ago. Then attempts were made to get her back into mainstream school, but she just refused to go. She wouldn't even go near the school gates. She'd scream and run away.

I finish my sandwich and think back to this morning's session. Now I've met Bethany, I know what I'm up against. I can still hear her thumping her head and that droning hum. I need some time to relax.

I take my shoes off and walk along the sand. Away from the kiosks and the screaming children. I pass the boat hire and the Krazy Golf, and the kiosk that sells beach balls and surfboards. At the more rugged and deserted end of the beach, rock pools invite exploration, and waves eddy and whirl around the jutting red cliffs.

I sit down on a flat rock and gaze into a rock pool. Purple anemones unfurl in the emerald depths, and tiny crabs peep out of crevices. I think about Bethany. I wonder if I can help pull her from her hiding place?

Last week, I'd called in at the education office to study Bethany's file. It had been interesting, but not very enlightening. Children with Asperger's syndrome display a range of autistic symptoms, such as obsessions, a dislike of bright lights and sudden noises, and bizarre phobias. But they can usually communicate by speech (though this is often stilted and unusual), and can often function, with support, in mainstream school, provided allowances are made for their sometimes solitary and odd behaviour. However, Bethany had been out of school for such a long time, she was becoming more and more isolated. One of the main problems for these children is making friends, as they can be very controlling. They can't seem to get the hang of sharing and taking turns, and because their understanding is so literal, the jokes and rough and tumble of the playground are a constant worry to them.

Bethany had attended school regularly until she was seven, but had always struggled with English and number work. She found it difficult to make friends, appearing to be very shy. She also hated changes of routine, bright lights and sudden loud noises. Barking dogs terrified her. So did the turmoil of the playground. She could often be found crouching in a corner with her hands over her ears.

At the assessment unit, she'd perked up a bit. The small group of mainly phobic children suited her, but when it ended, Bethany was devastated. She'd not understood that it was only a temporary placement. She withdrew into herself again, and refused to go back to school. Just to complicate matters, Joseph, her brother, was born during her time at the unit. Although Bethany loved the baby and liked helping her mum change and feed him, she was also very jealous of the time her mother needed to spend with him.

Bethany is the second of five children, and the only girl. Her elder brother, Callum, aged eleven, is doing very well – a confident, outgoing child, according to the report. Her two younger brothers, Pablo, eight, and Carlos, four, appear to have no problems. The psychologist reported that Bethany seemed fairly well-adjusted at the age of five, though she was very shy. The teacher's report at the time observed that she struggled with letter formations and number concepts, and might need remedial help later. However, very soon after this, about four years ago, Bethany gradually began to show signs of an autistic disorder. Almost imperceptibly at first, her shyness increased and she panicked when asked to read or write. Only with much coaxing could she be persuaded to do anything. Even then, she'd give up very easily.

I flipped through the more recent report from the psychologist, looking for clues. Unusually (because Mrs Webster was so willing to talk, the report noted), there was a lot of family history. Bethany's mother, Anita, was of Spanish origin, but had been born here to a family of immigrants who came over to England to find work in the catering industry in London, back in the fifties. Anita grew up in London, and became a waitress in her parents' café. That was how she met her husband Paul, and the father of all her children. Paul, originally from the West Country, was at that time working in London as an electrician, and they'd met while he was rewiring the café. Soon after, they came back to live down here, to be nearer Paul's family.

I read avidly. This background family information is so useful for possible clues into what makes pupils behave the way they do. The Websters were coping extremely well with their large family. Paul worked for a firm of electricians. Their only real difficulty, apart from Bethany, was that they were out-growing their three-bedroom council-rented maisonette.

Though Bethany's file was interesting, there was nothing here that gave me an insight into what made her tick. I'd closed the file, and sat back, tucked away in the corner of the very busy office. Computers flashed and flickered. Sally and her three assistants sat huddled over their emails, paper scattered all across their desks. Phones shrilled every two minutes. Who in their right mind would work in an office? I couldn't wait to get out.

And now, sitting on my rock, I gulp in draughts of fresh, early spring air, and taste the salt on my lips. For the umpteenth time, I'm filled with gratitude for the breadth and sheer variety of my work.

With Bethany, there's definitely a mystery to be solved. Is her autistic streak due to some innate neurological dysfunction? Or is there perhaps an emotional or psychological cause? Whatever it is, I find her intriguing. I can't put her into any category. She's not exactly 'in her own world' (one of the classic symptoms of autism). She can speak, and communicate non-verbally when she chooses to. And today, there's even been a bit of progress – a tentative opening through which Bethany allowed me a tiny glimpse into herself.

Wednesday, 25th February. Mrs Webster opens the door. She holds her finger to her lips.

"I've just put Joseph down for his nap," she whispers. "He was so restless last night. He's teething and he's all stuffed up with a cold."

"Right," I whisper back.

I take off my coat and hang it on the hall stand. There's a shoe rack next to it. The sky blue carpet is immaculate, unsullied by the tread of six pairs of feet. I wonder at Mrs Webster's awesome housekeeping skills.

"How old is Joseph?" I ask, as I slip off my shoes and add them to the neat rows of trainers and wellies.

"Eleven months. He's just started crawling. Not walking yet, thank goodness. I can never understand why people are so keen for their babies to walk early. They'll toddle off anywhere, you can't relax for an instant. As it is, I have to keep an eye on him."

"It must be very hard work for you."

"Nothing compared to Bethany. She's a handful."

An opening. Mrs Webster's in a chatty mood. I want to ask what she thinks is the cause of Bethany's problems. But just at that moment, a bedroom door opens and Bethany comes out. She sees me but doesn't acknowledge me. She stands still, gazing past my left shoulder, sucking her thumb.

"Hello Bethany! Are you ready to start?"

To my surprise, Bethany runs into the living room.

Bethany's mother lowers her voice.

"She had a good talking-to last night," she says. "No chocolates or treats or visits to the shops unless she behaves herself with you."

"Right," I say, hesitantly. I'm feeling uncertain about how much authority I've established with Bethany.

"If there's any trouble, just come and get me in the kitchen. I'll be ironing. I can only do it when Joseph's asleep. He grabs the flex otherwise." Mrs Webster disappears into the kitchen.

Bethany's sitting on the floor in the middle of the living room. I'm puzzled. I'd planned to read her a story, both of us sitting together on the settee.

"Come and sit here, Bethany, I've got a great story to read to you. About a zoo!"

Bethany's face freezes into complete immobility, like a mask. Her eyes, which a second ago glimmered with a faint spark, become dull and hooded.

"No."

"No?"

"No. No." Her lips are working. She's trying to say something, but can't formulate the words she needs. She's getting agitated and frustrated.

Then she looks towards the sideboard. I follow her gaze. Suddenly I understand. There, exactly where she placed it yesterday as I was leaving, is her spider picture.

"Oh, I see." Relief floods over me. "You want to finish your picture! You want to draw the spider's web. Well, why didn't you say so?"

I smile at her reassuringly, to show her I'm being encouraging, rather than telling her off.

Bethany nods and waits while I fetch the drawing for her. She watches me unpack my pencils, crayons and felt-tip pens.

"What would you like to draw the cobweb with?"

Bethany chooses a very fine HB pencil – so fine, I'm certain it won't even show up on the page. I watch her carefully spiral round the page. Yet her drawing is remarkably accurate and the more effective for being so faint, like a web speckled with dew on a winter morning.

Of course Bethany didn't want me to read to her. I understand now. In fact, she must have been completely thrown when I suggested it. When, at the end of yesterday's session, I'd told her she could finish the drawing today, she'd expected this activity to continue seamlessly as soon as I arrived. How was she to know that I always started my tuition sessions with a ten minute reading session, whether the pupil is six or sixteen, come hell or high water? I hadn't explained my system to her – well, to be fair on myself, she hadn't given me much of a chance yesterday. But today, I'll make sure she knows that tuition has a pattern, a routine. Just like school.

One hour later, and the morning's going well. Using my teaching clock, I explain the daily programme, and ask Bethany how often she wants to have breaks. Can she tell me on the clock? She can't yet tell the time, so this is a good chance to introduce the concept of half an hour, twenty minutes, and so on.

I also show how my points system works. Then we read a story and discuss the characters and the plot. Or rather, I talk, and Bethany listens. At least, I hope she does; her expression gives little away. But every now and then she looks at me directly, as if she's interested.

I'm careful not to push her. Reading and writing can wait a while, though I'm longing to know what she can actually do. Mostly I follow her lead. Now she wants to look through my books. She wants to find pictures of spiders and other creepy-crawlies. The session turns into nature studies and rolls along on oiled wheels.

Maybe the head banging was just a blip, and Bethany will prove easier to work with than I'd anticipated. Suddenly, I'm feeling supremely confident. At this rate of progress, I'll soon persuade her back into school.

Monday, 1st March. I've arrived late. There was an accident which snarled up the traffic. I feel shaky and flustered.

There's a long wait before Mrs Webster opens the door. She looks harassed, with a fractious Joseph straddled on her hip, and a ginger-haired, pale-faced little boy hanging on to her.

Ominous sounds come from Bethany's room. Bang. A muffled thud. Bang. My stomach tightens with a sickening sense of déjà-vu. There's also another sound – a creak. And that low nasal hum, the droning police siren. Once again, it's the theme tune from hell and it sends shivers down my spine.

"I feel sick," whines Carlos. "I'm going to be sick. It's coming up in my tummy!"

"Look..." Mrs Webster steers her son rapidly towards the bathroom. "It's not a good day. Bethany says she won't see you. She's in one of her moods. Oops! I think he's going to..." She thrusts Joseph into my arms. "Just hold him for a moment..."

Joseph, understandably enraged by this treatment, bawls loudly. I seek refuge in the living room, trying to blot out the disgusting sounds coming from the bathroom. I dance around the room with Joseph over my shoulder, singing 'The Wheels of the Bus Go Round and Round,' my voice harmonising nicely with Joseph's yells. After a minute the surprise element kicks in – Joseph stops in mid-howl. He twists around in my arms, his expression clearly saying: "Who on earth is this mad woman?"

The next verse: 'The people on the bus stand up, sit down,' reminds me painfully that my knees were many years younger when I last did the actions to this nursery rhyme. Bobbing up and down from sitting to standing proves a bridge too far. I haven't reckoned on the added weight of a twenty-two pound baby. My knees suddenly give way. Joseph and I collapse in a heap on the floor. Somehow I manage to hold on to him. Joseph thinks this is hilarious – part of the rhyme. He bounces up and down on my lap wanting more.

His mother comes in and rescues me. She takes the now smiling baby and puts him down on the carpet with some toys.

"It's been one of those mornings," she complains. "Nothing's gone right. Not one single thing. Carlos was sick in the night, so he's off nursery. I can't get Joseph down to sleep and I've got three loads of washing to do and the kitchen to clean. And Bethany's head-banging. You can hear her now. I can't manage her this morning, not with these two to cope with. It's really better if you go."

"I'd rather not," I say, abruptly. "I mean, it's not a good idea to let *Bethany* decide whether or not she's going to have tuition. If you don't mind, I'd like to stop her head-banging."

Mrs Webster's black-button eyes widen incredulously. Her whole body quivers with amazement.

"You'll never talk her out of it – she gets stuck in it. She can go on for hours."

"Please, let me at least try."

"Mum!" calls Carlos, frantically from the bathroom. "I've done a poo in my pants!"

His mother dashes off. I make my way to Bethany's room. I knock and open the door, leaving it open while I survey the scene. The bedroom is small, with bunk beds against the window wall. Everything is neat and organised, with toys ranged on the shelves, and Bethany's toiletries and little glass and china animals on the chest of drawers next to the beds. The orderliness of the room seems bizarrely out of kilter with what Bethany is doing, which resembles the behaviour of an inmate of Bedlam.

She's kneeling on all fours on the bottom bunk, her head to the wall, against which she's placed a pillow. Totally oblivious to my entry, she's in full flow. Her head moves up and down like a piston: pillow – thump – wall – bang. The bedsprings creak with a mournful, jarring cry.

"Bethany! Stop that!"

No reply. Instead, every sound intensifies.

"STOP IT!"

Now she's speeding up the action. The bed springs squeal and groan even louder.

Suddenly, I'm furious with Bethany. I want to throw a tantrum myself. I'd been looking forward to this session. In the boot of my car there's a surprise for her. I feel like a small child who's suddenly been told the party's been cancelled.

I breathe heavily, awash with anger and disappointment. But the last thing I must do is vent my fury on Bethany herself.

Before I fully realise what I'm doing, I'm down on all fours, next to her on the bed.

"You seem to be having a bad day, Bethany. Well, so am I. I'm having a TERRIBLE day. I'm fuming, cross, upset and disappointed. So can I join you?"

I imitate Bethany's actions, falling into rhythm with her, though I'm far too much of a coward to attempt the wall. I don't fancy bashing my brains out, and new glasses cost a fortune. Instead, I make feeble moves in the wall's direction, and concentrate my energies on a really good thump on the duvet. Each time I do this, I have to lower my neck into a crazy stork-like pose – and this hurts. I've always avoided extreme sports.

"I need a pillow," I mutter angrily into the duvet.

Bethany, without pausing for a split-second, obligingly shoves half of her pillow in my direction. We continue in tandem for a couple of minutes. I'm praying Mrs Webster won't poke her head round the door.

"Mmmm. This feels just right," I tell the wall. "I'm getting some of my anger out."

Briefly, Bethany turns her head just a smidgeon towards me. She doesn't make eye-contact, but after a minute, there's a change of pace. She's actually slowing down. I keep to her rhythm until, at last, she grinds to a halt, like an old steam train coming into the station. She raises her head and looks directly at me.

Now I feel silly.

Quickly, I swivel my legs round and stand up. "Thank you for letting me share your pillow," I say formally. "Now, can we make a start on your lesson?"

Bethany hesitates. "I don't want one today."

"Well, that's a shame, because I've got a surprise for you in the car. It's something I give to all my pupils if they work well, but I can easily give it to someone else...I'll be in the living room when you're ready, Bethany. I thought we'd start with a story about spiders."

To my relief, Bethany follows me. Maybe the word 'spiders' did the trick.

As I round the door into the living room, I nearly have a heart-attack. I'd completely forgotten Joseph, left on the floor with his toys. Now, having pulled out all the books from the bottom shelf of the bookcase, he's drawing himself up to a standing position, hell-bent on gutting the second shelf too. Books and case wobble dangerously.

"GRAB HIM, BETHANY!"

Bethany dives towards Joseph, as I hurl myself towards the bookcase and half fall against it to stop it toppling over. She wraps her arms around him, pulling him away to a safe distance.

"Is he all right?" I'm breathless and trembling.

Bethany nods, snuggling her face close to her baby brother's.

"Oh dear," I wail. "I shouldn't have left him in the living room at all. I bet your mum was expecting me to watch him for a minute while she saw to Carlos in the bathroom. I just didn't think. She'd put him down on the floor, and he seemed to be playing happily and then this happened!"

I look at Bethany and she looks back at me. Her expression, usually so deadpan, looks almost sympathetic. There's even a hint that she's finding this very funny.

"I forgot he can crawl," I say, lamely.

"He's never done that before."

"What, crawl?"

"No," says Bethany, proudly, "pull himself up. He's never stood up before."

"Ah." Trust me to get embroiled at the precise moment a baby makes a daring attempt to reach his next developmental milestone.

"Help me put these books back quickly, Bethany, please, before..." I don't actually say, "before your mother comes back in," but the implication is there. Bethany jumps up, and like conspirators we stack all the books back on the shelves as neatly as possible.

When Mrs Webster returns, Bethany and I are sitting side by side on the settee, looking like a pair of school children up to mischief. Bethany's giggling to herself. I haven't seen her so animated.

Poor Mrs Webster's too bogged down with housework and Carlos to notice our guilty looks. She whisks Joseph up from the floor for a nappy change and says she hopes to God that he'll sleep for an hour.

When she's left the room, I say, "We must tell Mum about this. She needs to know that Joseph can stand up, so that she can watch him, but we'll wait till she's less busy. Will you remind me, if I forget before I leave? And if I do forget, you can tell her about the bookcase, okay?"

There's a very faint, complicit gleam in Bethany's eyes. Otherwise, her face is quite expressionless as she nods.

At last things have simmered down sufficiently for me to read Bethany a story about Robert Bruce and the Spider. This is a classic tale, and I'm hoping it will have a subliminal message for her about not giving up. It's hard to tell what she thinks of the story, but she loves the illustrations. The web, especially, fascinates her for some reason.

I suggest that she makes up her own story about a spider and its web. Could she think of one, and tell me about it? I offer to do all the writing for her. Surely there can't be a fairer offer than that?

"No," says Bethany. "I don't want to."

That closed, mute look is back again.

"Oh." I feel thwarted.

Suddenly, she says: "Where's the surprise?"

"What?"

"You said you had a surprise in your car. For me, if I was good. And I have been good."

"Yes, you have. You've been a real star, helping me with Joseph, and listening well to the story, but it's a very *heavy* surprise. And I haven't yet asked your mum whether you can have it."

But Mrs Webster isn't around to ask. Bethany's mouth turns down.

"We can ask her afterwards," she says. "Can't I just see it?"

We tiptoe out to the car. I open the boot with a flourish.

"There!"

Bethany gives a little gasp of delight. "A fish tank!"

"Ye-es. But there aren't any fish in it. Just toad-spawn from my pond, and some other pond creatures. Look! Can you see these little things that zoom along the surface? They're pond-skaters. And I think there might be dragonfly larva at the bottom, but I'm not sure."

Bethany's fascinated. "Is that the toad-spawn?" She points to a long string of opaque, jelly-like beans with black dots in the middle.

"That's right. Frogs' spawn is all round, in a ball, but toads make a long string for their babies to hatch out of."

"There's Mum!" says Bethany, looking towards the front door.

Her mother is peering anxiously round. "I wondered where you were!"

I hurry up to the door to explain. I ask if Bethany can keep a tank full of toad-spawn.

Mrs Webster looks horrified. "Toads! I can't have them in the house!"

Bethany's face falls.

"No, you won't have to," I say, in a rush. "The moment they begin to grow out of the tadpole stage, I'll take them back. They're just on loan to Bethany for a short while. For her school work."

Mrs Webster frowns disapprovingly. "Where on earth will she keep it?"

"I'll make some room on the sideboard," calls Bethany. "Please, Mum. *Please!*"

Her mother hesitates. Then tuts and sighs. She spreads her arms out wide. "Put it on the floor for the moment then. I'll need to completely reorganise the living room." She turns, shaking her head, and goes back upstairs.

The tank, although only one third full of water, is extremely heavy. I can't face another disaster this morning Tired and slow-witted, I almost chicken out of attempting to carry it up the flight of steps to the front door, and then up yet another flight to the living room.

It's Bethany who thinks of the solution.

"If I get some bowls, we can put some of the water into them, and then we can put it all back together in the house."

"Perfect! Well done, Bethany!"

I'm struck by Bethany's quick thinking. She's demonstrating a natural flair for organisation when it comes to practical problems. I watch her dash round the side of the building to the back garden, and return with two old washing-up bowls and a child's bucket.

"Brilliant! You're a star, Bethany."

She scoops half the water from the tank into the two bowls and we carry them up into the living-room, placing them on the sideboard for the moment, out of Joseph's reach.

"Wait there," says Bethany. She finds some old newspaper and spreads it on the floor. We place the tank, now easy to manage, on top.

"We'd better wait before we put the water back into the tank," I say. "Mum wants to rearrange the sideboard first."

Carefully I move a few ornaments away from the sides of the bowls.

"Mum hates frogs and toads worse than anything," says Bethany. She peers into the water, and pokes the spawn gently with her finger.

"Oh no! Really?" I stop ornament-shuffling, and bite my lip. "I should have asked her before I brought it here. I'm in big trouble now. Mum will be very cross with me."

"No, she won't." Bethany looks at me in surprise, her mouth half-open, as if it hadn't occurred to her that teachers could get into trouble, too.

"Anyway, let's have a quick look at this pond book. There's a picture of some toad-spawn, and some other pond-creatures."

Bethany browses through the book. Totally absorbed in pictures, she's a different child. She gazes into the bowls, studying the creatures there with silent, rapt attention. She easily identifies them by the illustrations. Remarkably, Bethany spots minuscule differences between one creature and another. Somehow, she finds little larvae in the mud at the bottom the tank that I would never have noticed. She lifts them out, placing them delicately in the palm of her hand, with the air of a research scientist in a laboratory. She reminds me of Harriet and her tray of woodlice. Just watching Bethany now is a joy to me.

An invisible barrier between us seems to have been breached. Maybe all the ups and downs of the morning, and my reaction to them, enabled Bethany to see that I, too, have another side to me. One that's more human, more vulnerable than she'd expect in a teacher.

"I've got to go now, Bethany."

She's swirling her hands around in the water, trying to catch a pond-skater. She looks up briefly.

"Thank you for the tank."

"It's a real pleasure. See you tomorrow."

As I drive across town to see Thomas, I'm cautiously optimistic. This morning, Bethany has shown that she has definite gifts. She has advanced observational ability for fine detail and the capacity for quick, practical thinking and action. She helped save Joseph from being buried alive under the bookcase. Yet, she's been diagnosed as autistic or suffering from Asperger's Syndrome. Her report stated that her I.Q. was well below average, on the borderline with 'Special Needs'.

It hurts my brain to think any more. One thing is certain. The more I do this job, the less I understand about this extraordinary phenomenon we call 'intelligence'.

Friday, 5th March. With five lively children, it always amazes me how neat and organised Mrs Webster keeps her home. Even the baby paraphernalia has its proper place. The toys and play-mat are always in the same corner of the living room behind one of the two armchairs; and the kitchen, whenever I've had occasion to go into it, has clutter-free, freshly wiped-over work-surfaces. The whole place gleams with that special *hausfrau* look. It's the Midas touch, this special ability of Mrs Webster to create order out of chaos, to make wood, glass and china shimmer and sparkle. She also has a distinctive flair for arranging things. Ornaments and pictures are juxtaposed in such a way that the whole effect is artistic, warm and welcoming. It's a gift I notice in other people, and appreciate all the more, because I was born with the opposite of the Midas touch: I have a supreme ability to turn gold – as in household order – into chaos.

Bethany seems to have inherited her mother's talent. In the short time I've known her, I've been impressed by her ability to organise her own possessions and her own personal space. The room she shares with Carlos is small, yet every part of it is utilised, everything either tidily put away, or neatly on display. All Bethany's tuition things are kept in a special bright pink plastic bag. She tidies away pencils and felt-tips into their cases, and always files away new work in her folder. She even organises me, as I fumble through my large holdall for a particular teaching item.

"You put it in *there* yesterday. Look, in that bit with the zip," she says reproachfully, in the same tone of voice her mother might have used.

Just now, I'm sitting on the settee waiting for Bethany to return from a dentist appointment. Mrs Webster bustles into the living room with a cup of tea. She tells me that her husband, Paul, has taken half the morning off specially to take Bethany to the surgery in the van.

"He had to put off a customer who wanted some new sockets. His boss wasn't very pleased, nor was Paul." She says this with an air of satisfaction. I wonder whether this is a rare event, her husband getting involved with the children in this way. She continues, "I only remembered the appointment last night. It was important. Bethany's teeth stick out a bit and she may need a brace."

"I don't mind waiting," I say, contentedly sipping my tea in a rare moment of peace.

As I sink further down into the cushions, the door bursts open and Bethany storms in, followed by her dad, who looks as if he's just hiked twenty miles carrying a 60lb pack.

"Dad wouldn't buy me chocolate!" Bethany's voice is whining and peevish. Her face is quite immobile.

"There wasn't time to stop at the shop," says her father, tersely. "Anyway, it's crazy to go to the dentist and have your teeth cleaned by the hygienist, and then to ruin them with sweets."

This is a perfectly reasonable statement, yet there's no humour in the way he says it. I guess Mr Webster takes life rather seriously. He's a tall, sparely-built man, sandy-haired, with a long face and solemn expression. There doesn't seem to be much warmth, or even a spark of connection between his daughter and himself. He's not the least curious about the work Bethany is doing in her tuition sessions, though a couple of her drawings are spread out in front of me on the coffee table. Apart from a brief 'hello', he's hardly acknowledged my presence. He looks ill at ease in this company of females.

"Would you like some coffee?" asks his wife. "The kettle's just boiled."

"No, I'll be off. Got to catch up."

He nods at me, gives Mrs Webster a peck on the cheek, and bounds down the stairs taking them two at a time. The front door slams. He hasn't even said goodbye to Bethany, but she doesn't seem to mind, or even to have noticed.

"Mum, can I have a drink and something to eat? I'm starving!"

"What did the dentist say?" asks her mother.

"Can't remember," says Bethany.

Mrs Webster sighs and goes into the kitchen, returning with a glass of orange juice and two biscuits. Bethany wolfs these down. Since she's been in the room, she hasn't looked at me.

I'm feeling strangely blocked. And anxious. Every day is like starting afresh with Bethany. There never seems to be any carry-through from the momentum of the previous day. Maybe that isn't quite true, though. Overall, if I look back over the last two weeks, there has been definite progress in many directions.

Even so, it's hard to define this odd sinking sensation I get at the start of each session. It's like waiting on the platform for a train which may or may not arrive, depending on leaves or frost on the line, point failure or the driver not turning up for work.

Maybe that's what Bethany feels most of the time – blocked and anxious – and I'm picking up on this. If so, I need to know what's causing her to feel this way. I watch her wiping the last crumbs of biscuit from her mouth.

"I need to go to the toilet," she says.

"Be quick then. We need to start."

While I wait, I try to think positively. She has been trying hard this week. No head-banging, thank goodness. And we've established a routine whereby I read to her for ten to fifteen minutes at the start of each session, after which I attempt some basic number work, followed by an attempt to engage her in a word game or writing activity. We have two short breaks and finish with a 'choosing' period of fifteen to twenty minutes.

Bethany's adjusted fairly well to this routine, and is beginning to tell the time from an analogue clock. The problem is, the routine itself is a double-edged sword. It can become a trap: I've noticed that now, if I vary it, Bethany suddenly becomes anxious and freezes. That closed, mask-like expression returns and she downs tools. Several times, she's got up from her chair and disappeared under the table. This sudden switch from near-normality to showing classic signs of autism I find highly unnerving. It always catches me by surprise.

I need to keep to some kind of structure, because it makes Bethany feel secure – and up to a point, it's what she'll encounter at school and through life. At the same time, I must also establish a framework which is flexible. This flexibility also resembles school, with all its unexpected happenings and variations to the timetable. The tension between these two is creating problems for both of us.

I'd also love to discover what lies behind that blank impassive mask she wears most of the time. Only on rare occasions have I seen her face *move,* while she expresses a feeling. Once was when she saw the toad spawn in the tank for the first time. Another was that hair-raising occasion when Joseph was almost buried under the hailstorm of books. Strangely, she hadn't looked terrified when it was happening. Yet her face had registered genuine pride at Joseph's suddenly learning to stand. Whenever she cuddles him there's a softness, a lightness, in her expression. Mainly in the eyes. Yes, that's it! Any emotion only reaches her eyes. It rarely moves a muscle in her face. There's something disturbingly reptilian about her face, with the set expression and only the eyes that flash when she's upset or angry. And she has a habit of poking her tongue out of the side of her mouth. When she does that, she reminds me of a snake catching an insect.

When I think of the range of expressions that light up – or darken – children's faces, often within the space of a few seconds, Bethany's face registers barely 5% of them. Most children, particularly girls, of Bethany's age actually love to translate their feelings into their expressions. They have fun with it – they make it into a performance! They mime, act, make horrible faces at each other. They stick out their tongues, pout, roll their eyes while they stretch their lips with their fingers. Bethany does none of these. Odd.

Maybe I can kill two birds with one stone. I could vary the routine slightly by doing a bit of mime.

Bethany's back from the bathroom, and I jump straight in.

"We're going to play a game now, Bethany. Just for a few minutes. And then we'll have the story on the settee."

She looks at me uncertainly. Before she can object, I lead her out into the hall, where, at the top of the stairs opposite the coat-stand, there's a full-length mirror.

"Look, Bethany! Look at my face in the mirror. We're going to pretend to be different animals. I'm a monkey, and I'm feeling very cross. Someone's stolen my banana. Look!"

I screw up my face, purse my lips and frown. I was hoping that looking into a mirror would be less confrontational for Bethany than looking at me directly. But Bethany's face freezes – a sure sign of alarm. She peeps into the mirror as if a real monkey might suddenly jump out at her. Then, to my relief, she laughs. A low chuckle that lights her eyes and almost stretches to her lips.

"Can you be a cross monkey too? Let's do it together!"

It's almost impossible to keep a cross face while watching Bethany straining to imitate me. Soon I'm doubled up with hysterics. First she lifts her left eyebrow. Then lowers it. The same with the right one. Her lips press together. Her nose wrinkles. Yet none of this happens concurrently. Her features refuse to work together. She's like Waterloo station in a rail strike – there might be one train if you're lucky.

"Okay, let's do a happy monkey now. He's got his banana back again!"

I grin widely. I make my eyes like saucers. Bethany looks in the mirror.

"Monkeys don't do that," she says scathingly. "They look like this."

She bares her teeth in a genuine monkey grin, looking so uncannily monkey-like that I'm quite spooked.

"That's very realistic. Your monkey face is much better than mine." We stare at each other in the mirror. "I've got an idea. I'll be a little girl who's just been given her most favourite chocolate bar."

I make a delighted face, wildly exaggerated. Bethany tries to imitate me. Again, though the lips stretch and turn up, and the eyes widen, it's all disconnected.

"Think chocolate bars, Bethany! Think chocolate buttons, chocolate biscuits!"

"Dad wouldn't let me have one," she reminds me, with a stony stare.

"Wait there!"

In desperation, I extract a Kit-Kat from my handbag – my precious emergency rations. I break off two strips of biscuit, one for each of us.

"Yum, yum! I'm happy!" I mime extreme ecstasy. "Quick, look at *your* face now!"

Bethany's face has brightened considerably. For a second or two she catches her own expression. She giggles.

"There!" I say, triumphantly. "That's what I call a really happy face!"

"Can I eat my chocolate now?" she says.

"Yes, let's do yum-yum faces while we're eating it."

As we stand in front of the mirror, licking our lips and contorting our features into greed and delight, Mrs Webster comes out into the hall carrying Joseph. She almost drops him with shock.

"Look Bethany, look at your mum's shocked face," I imitate her for Bethany's benefit, completely carried away by now.

"What *are* you up to?" Mrs Webster's plainly worried about my sanity. I try to explain. In the telling it all sounds feeble and falls quite flat. And too late, I remember that Bethany has just had her teeth cleaned at the dentist's.

"Perhaps you'd better go and clean your teeth, now, Bethany," I say. I smile at her mother reassuringly, but she shakes her head disbelievingly. Her parting look as she goes into the kitchen shows she's having serious doubts about my credentials. Never mind, I'll have a word with her before I leave and explain everything.

It's a pity we were interrupted. I so want Bethany to express her feelings – in an appropriate way, not by head-bashing or withdrawing under the table, but by showing, and eventually by *telling* people how she feels.

This congruence – the linking up of facial expression with emotion – represents a healthy psyche. It's a vital ingredient in all human interactions. Some people who have personality disorders find it difficult. In extreme cases, someone might smile while talking about terrible things.

Not that I think Bethany has a personality disorder, but I wonder if, at some point, her emotions have been 'frozen'. Her blank expression could be the result of some trauma. But it's also the *cause* of some of her difficulties. It must be very frustrating for her, because it isolates her socially by making her look odd. It could be something she was just born with, like flat feet or short sight.

On Monday, if by then Mrs Webster hasn't rung Sally to get me sacked, I'll have a talk with her and find out more about Bethany's early development.

Wednesday, 10th March. Luckily, Mrs Webster's been too preoccupied with all the children to ring the education office about my quirky antics with Bethany, involving choc bars and the hall mirror, so my job seems safe so far.

This morning, I've turned up for duty as usual. However, I've been waiting for what seems an unusually long time for someone to open the door.

I put down my two heavy workbags and take gulps of fresh air. There's a wonderful melange of scents that refuse to separate into their component parts. Together, they linger tantalisingly all around, indefinable. Pools of sunlight dapple the neat front garden. There's a spider's web on the hedge by the gate, still partly veiled with filmy dew where the sun hasn't yet reached it. Spring wraps itself all around me like an invisible cloak. This would be a good day to take Bethany out for a walk.

Unfortunately, when Mrs Webster does at last open the door, she tells me that Bethany has a temperature and is in bed.

I try to disguise my annoyance. She should have rung me. The Websters live some distance from Cassie's house and it's always a rush to get here in time.

"I'm so sorry, I should have contacted you, but I've lost your telephone number." She looks contrite.

Slightly mollified, I ask if I can write it down again for her. Also, I've bought a book about spiders that I'd promised Bethany. Should I leave it for her to look through when she feels better?

"You'd better come in for a moment," says Mrs Webster, watching me scrabbling ineffectually in my handbag for a scrap of paper to write on.

She leads the way upstairs and into the living room, where she immediately locates a pad of paper and pen next to the phone.

"Would you like a cup of tea?" she asks. "You've come all this way for nothing. And if Bethany does wake up, you can give her the book yourself."

I hesitate. It's so quiet, I guess Joseph's asleep for once. Poor Mrs Webster's permanently weighed down with household chores – this might be her only chance of getting on with some essential task that can't be done when he's crawling under her feet. Or she may desperately need some time to herself. On the other hand, I'm longing to talk to her about Bethany's early childhood. When will I get another chance?

"I'll put the kettle on," she says, waddling into the kitchen and deciding the matter for me.

"Can I do anything?" I ask, following her.

"No, just take that basket off that stool and put it on the floor, then you can sit down. Do you mind if we have our tea in here? I've put Joseph down in his pram in the living room. I wanted to give our bedroom a good turn-out this morning. It's a right mess. It's hard to keep on top of things with a baby sharing our bedroom…and as I thought you weren't going to be here…"

Mrs Webster's definitely into multi-tasking. While we wait for the kettle to boil, and as she talks, she's putting out the tea mugs, washing out Joseph's beakers, loading the washing machine, wiping the work-surface, pricking some large potatoes with a fork, and taking plastic containers out of the freezer. Now she reaches for the basket and starts folding up what looks like an entire launderette of clean washing.

"Please let me do that. I like to keep busy," I say, lying through my teeth. But anything to stop this whirlwind of activity, which is making me feel dizzy.

Mrs Webster looks at me doubtfully, as if she doesn't think I'm quite up to the job.

"Well, if you don't mind..? Any cottons and cotton-mixes like shirts and T-shirts have to be ironed. Just fold them roughly and put them on the ironing board there. And baby things go in a separate pile – I don't iron those. Or towels."

"I always make tea in a proper tea pot," she says, putting two teabags in. "That way, it doesn't get cold so quickly and you can have a second cup. Excuse me a moment, I've just remembered, I need to soak Joseph's sheets."

Sitting down at the small, Formica-topped table, I start sorting clothes. The washing machine whirs away in a comfortable, homely fashion. I begin to place one pile of clothes on the sparkling work-surface, which is almost clear of objects – apart from some bright blue and white china canisters labelled Tea, Coffee, Sugar and Biscuits. A row of colourful mugs sits neatly on shelves above the draining board, along with pot-plants, egg cups, a sugar bowl, and china jugs of various sizes. All other kitchen accoutrements and gadgets have been neatly stashed away.

The kettle boils just as Mrs Webster comes back with a bundle of sheets. She stuffs these into a large bucket of sudsy water under the sink, and then fills the teapot. She places teapot, milk, mugs and the biscuit tin on the table and wedges herself with difficulty on to a stool opposite me, sinking down with a sigh of relief.

"First time I've stopped today. Just as well you're here! If I was left to myself I'd just go on and on. There's still the hoovering, but I can't do that while Joseph's asleep. And the windows need cleaning – I'll make a start on those today. So how Bethany doing?" she asks, giving me the opening I've been waiting for.

Briefly, I give her a quick résumé of all we've done, including an explanation of the choc-bar-and-mirror episode.

She laughs. "Ah, I did wonder what that was about. I thought you might be – well, I don't know. I didn't know what to think!"

"That's what I was hoping to talk to you about, if you don't mind."

Aware that I'm racing against time – Joseph might wake at any moment – I explain that I'm puzzled by Bethany's very limited range of facial mobility. The fact that she finds it hard to express her feelings verbally, or by using appropriate body language.

"Can you remember anything that might have happened when she was very little – something that might have given her a shock, for example?"

Mrs Webster scratches her head and looks puzzled. "Well, no – not really. Of course, her birth was a bit of a shock. I don't mean she wasn't planned. We both wanted a baby two years after Callum."

She tells me that Bethany arrived three and a half weeks early. It had been a very long labour followed by a difficult birth - a forceps delivery. Worryingly, Bethany did not cry immediately.

"She was quite blue," she remembers. "The nurse just whisked her away, saying that they wanted to do some tests on her. I didn't know it then, but afterwards I learned there's a danger that they haven't developed their lungs properly if they're born four weeks early or more, so I suppose they were checking for that."

And, I'm thinking, for brain damage if she hadn't cried.

"And was she all right?" I ask. "Did you see her then?"

"Not till the morning. The day nurse wheeled her cot in, and said she was fine."

"What a relief for you!"

"Yes. And the best thing was having her cot by my bed, just like the other mothers. Until then, I felt like I hadn't really got a baby. That it had all been a mistake. Perhaps I'd dreamt it all!"

We both laugh at this idea.

"Did she feed all right?"

"Well, she was a bit slow. She had a problem with her feeding. I was in there a week, as she was so early, though she was quite a good weight, just over six pounds. They wanted to be sure they hadn't missed any problem. They did some more tests, I'm not sure what for."

Mrs Webster suddenly puts her hand to the small of her back, and winces.

"Ouch, back-ache. Must sit down." She stops folding clothes and sits down heavily. She puts her elbows on the table and gazes into space, thoughtfully.

"Yet I do remember trying to feed her and that all the feed times were agony. Painful for me and she was so terribly slow at sucking and cried all the time. So they advised me to put her on to a bottle because she was losing weight. And so I did, and she sucked much better. But I sometimes wish I'd persevered with the breastfeeding because I'd fed Callum myself. It's much easier than messing around with bottles. I think I lost something because of it."

"Lost something?"

"Yes. Missed out. I never felt quite so close to her as I did to Callum. And she wasn't a naturally cuddly baby. She never...um...*snuggled* me."

"Ah."

"And then, three months after she was born, I fell for Pablo. That must have been a right shock for her, when he was born. Only a year between them, almost to the day."

"Were you in hospital long, after he was born?"

"No, only three days. He just popped out, no problem. Easy as pie. But when I brought him home, Bethany reacted quite badly. Of course she didn't understand – you can't prepare a one-year-old baby. And she – well, she went backwards for a while."

"How do you mean?"

"Well, she stopped doing the things she'd started to do. Like she was saying 'mum-mum-mum, dad-dad-dad' and trying to feed herself. She stopped making sounds. Went quiet. Except she cried a lot more, especially at night."

"And up to then, up to the time of Pablo's birth, had she developed normally?"

"She seemed to be fine." Mrs Webster inches herself up from the stool, and opens a cupboard. She takes an iron out and plugs it in by the ironing board. "I'll just make a start on these."

I'd love to offer to do it for her while she has a well-earned rest, but that might be overstepping the work boundary. Also, I haven't ironed anything for at least fifteen years and Mrs Webster would probably shudder at my efforts.

She seems to be thinking hard as she tests the temperature of the iron.

"Well, when I say she was fine," she says eventually, reaching for a white school shirt, "she was okay except for loud or sudden noises. She'd jump out of her skin. And sudden movements. We had to kind of warn her we were coming, if we were behind her. She was a very jumpy child."

"And did she start talking again? Babbling, and making different sounds?"

"She did, but much later. Not till she was nearly two. In fact, it was Pablo who brought her on. He'd started to babble by then and say a few words, so he kind of encouraged her. Strange really, as he stopped her in the first place!"

"And after that, did she catch up?"

"Sort of, but she was never a chatterbox. And she still hated loud noises. She couldn't cope with too much going on at once. If Pablo was crying, and then someone knocked at the front door, she'd run under the table and block up her ears. Actually..." Mrs Webster puts down the iron, and rests her hands on the side of the ironing board. Her eyes open wide with sudden recognition, "Now I come to think of it, that's when the head-banging started. When she was about two. She'd draw herself up on all fours and bang her head against the end of the cot. Used to keep it up for hours. Kept us awake. And the neighbours. It drove them mad!"

"So she's been doing it for seven years!" I exclaim, horrified.

"Well, yes. I suppose she has. Though not nearly so often now, and hardly ever at night. It's only when she's, like, stressed out or something."

Mrs Webster works steadily until half the clothes are expertly ironed and folded into a neat pile smelling deliciously of hot linen and good housekeeping. She gets up and goes to the fridge, then busies herself spooning helpings of some mysterious orange pureed mixture into tiny freezer containers.

"This is Joe's dinner," she says, catching my curious eye. "I puree everything we eat for tea. Like apple, or beef and mash, and he has it the next day. We can't afford those tins and jars. You never know what goes into them anyway. "So," she adds suddenly, "is there anything else you need to know?"

I can feel myself going hot with embarrassment. Have I been grilling her too much?

"No, you've been very helpful. I've so much enjoyed hearing all about Bethany when she was little." I stand up and take my cup over to the sink. I feel I've overstayed my welcome.

But Mrs Webster puts my fears at rest. She smiles at me with genuine warmth.

"It's been a pleasure. I've really enjoyed it. And it's made me remember things about Bethany that I'd forgotten. It might make me more patient with her when she's in one of her paddies!"

"Well, it's been very helpful for me, too. I can't think how you coped. It must have been hectic with three children under – what was it – three years old!"

"Under two and a half, when Pablo was born." She chuckles. "That's why I made sure there was a decent gap before Carlos. Nearly four years. And Bethany seemed to improve a lot, up to the time of his birth. Apart from finding it hard to make friends. She played by herself a lot."

Mrs Webster follows me along the hall, to the top of the stairs, where I reach for my jacket from the hallstand. She seems to want to keep me talking.

"Then Carlos was born, and, of course, I had less time for her as a result. That's when she started having real problems at school. She—"

Mrs Webster's interrupted by an angry screech from the living room.

"I must go," I say regretfully. "I'd love to hear more," – especially as Mrs Webster's now getting to what could be the heart of Bethany's problems – "but it sounds as if Joseph will be awake any moment now. I mustn't hold you up any more."

"That's all right, you're not. Not at all. I've been glad of the sit-down. I feel guilty if I stop too long when I'm on my own. Besides, I won't have the chance to sit down for much longer, even with company!"

"You won't…?" Puzzled, I stop halfway down the flight of stairs that leads to the front door. I look back up at her. And even before she speaks, I know the answer to my question.

From this angle, I have a vantage viewpoint of Mrs Webster's body that I wouldn't normally see. The skirt above her legs is riding upwards in a graceful inverted 'U' shape, revealing chubby knees. Her baggy skirt with its many folds is flattened and smooth over her abdomen, which bulges – prominently.

"I mean," she says, "that there's another one on the way. First of June. Then the fun will really start!"

Joseph yells suddenly. He sounds enraged and hungry.

"Well, nice talking to you," she says again. "I'll give Bethany the book when she wakes up. Thank goodness she's having a long sleep, at least. See you tomorrow."

I stand by the front door, my hand poised on the handle, unable to move, gobsmacked. How could I have been so blind! I'd assumed she was naturally buxom. In fact, Mrs Webster is very pregnant.

Exciting news that will have a huge impact on the family. How will Bethany be affected by the arrival of baby number six?

Thursday, 18th March. Bethany's head-banging again. I hear her as soon as I step inside the front door. Her mother shuts the door behind us, and sighs and puffs her way upstairs. She's holding Joseph, who's wriggling in her arms. His fretful grizzle, combined with the noise coming from Bethany's room, is harder on my nerves than his usual gusty yell.

"He won't settle," says Mrs Webster, as we reach the living room. "He's teething something terrible. Had us up most of the night."

Both mother and baby look the worse for wear. Mrs Webster's eyes, usually bright with alert inquisitiveness, are dull, with dark circles under them. Joseph clutches a teething ring in one hand, which he bangs angrily on top of his mother's head. He tries to shove his other fist into his mouth.

"Poor thing, he doesn't know what to do with himself, does he?" I murmur, stroking Joseph's red, angry-looking cheek.

"He's not in the mood for anything. I'm afraid you'll have to get Bethany out of her temper today."

"That's okay. I managed it before." I feign a confidence I don't feel.

"I'll give Joe a painkiller. It didn't work last night, but he's so tired, it might just knock him out now."

She sounds desperate. She hurries off into the kitchen. I hesitate outside Bethany's door, putting off the moment.

My heart's beating fast. I'm edgy today. I'm still feeling the angst of Cassie's sudden disappearance. The sudden end to our tuition sessions has left quite a hole in my day. I'm missing her – and Darren of course – more than I could ever have imagined. All this has dented my confidence somehow. And now Bethany's playing up again, just when I thought she was settling down.

I'm also feeling disappointed. I'd had great plans for Bethany. Today, I'd decided, was the day we were going to start the long journey back to school. Not all at once, of course. Just a few steps along the way, perhaps as far as the local park, half way to her school. We could combine this with a nature walk. I've brought along an old Ladybird book: *What To Look For In Spring*. Bethany loves flowers, I've discovered – wild and cultivated. She often puts a vase of daffodils or crocuses on the sideboard, (sometimes stolen from the next-door neighbour's garden). But apart from daffodils and crocuses, she doesn't know the names of plants. As we walk along, we could look into all the gardens along the road, seeing how each little patch varies from its neighbour in colour and style. I can teach her the names of any plants that catch her eye. I've also brought along a sketchpad, my *Reader's Digest Book of Wild Flowers*, and a disposable camera. I'm hoping all this will disguise the true motive behind the expedition.

If I wait long enough, will she stop of her own accord? Should I go in? Will I just make her worse? Perhaps it would be best to leave her alone until the storm passes, which, Mrs Webster's assured me, it eventually does. But after how long? I'm in an agony of indecision. I'm feeling tired and jangled, and not at my best. It's one of those days when I should have stayed in bed.

I can't go in to her when I'm feeling so negative myself.

I go into the living room, and sit down on the settee to calm myself down, and to think positively about Bethany. For the last couple of weeks, she's been doing really well. I've managed to get her to write a few simple words, and even to read a few lines out aloud from the *Puddle Lane* books. In my record book, under the grand heading of Emotional Intelligence I've been able to note that 'Bethany is beginning to extend her range of emotional responses'. Though I'm not sure whether Sally would approve of all my methods. Over the last week, in front of the mirror, we've 'done' fright, excitement, fear, grumpiness, anger, sadness, and finding something funny. We usually get stuck on this last one – Bethany's attempts to register 'amusement' on her face are so ludicrous that I spend most of my time doubled up with mirth. Bethany then tries to imitate me, thinking that this is part of the exercise. Yesterday I ended up, hysterical, on the floor.

Bethany can now 'do' some feelings quite well, but I wonder how much is pure imitation. She sometimes looks as if she's merely slapping on the appropriate mask, selected from some invisible shelf nearby, rather than expressing a genuine feeling welling up from within herself.

Still, at the very least, I tell myself – still determined to be positive – I'm teaching her that there are such things as feelings, and that feelings are connected to a stimulus such as an outside event, or to an internal emotional state. That we can express these in all sorts of ways: by what we do, by what we say, and by our body language. Most important, I want her to realise that people can understand us most easily by reading the expression on our face. Then, hopefully, they will know how to respond in the right way. I've often wondered how much of Bethany's isolation at school – her lack of friends – was partly due to her difficulty in this respect. Her classmates must have found her odd, and unapproachable at times. They must wonder what makes her tick.

Yet just now, hearing the cacophony coming from the bedroom, I wonder whether all our miming sessions have been a complete waste of time. Why couldn't Bethany have come to the front door to meet me, looking angry, for example, and been able to tell me what was bothering her? Deep down I know she's not able to do this. Not yet. I'm expecting too much, too soon.

Taking a deep breath, I go and knock on her door. I go in.

If Bethany realises I'm there, she doesn't give anything away, she just carries on – bang, creak, thump.

Grabbing a pillow from the top bunk, I join her and crouch on all fours next to her. Suddenly, all my disappointment and edginess bubbles up.

"I'm so upset," I tell the wall. "I'd planned to do all kinds of lovely things with Bethany today…"

Bethany carries on rocking. I continue:

"…like a walk in the sunshine along to the park, looking at the flowers growing in peoples' gardens. And taking some photographs, if Bethany can learn how to use a camera…but now we can't go. I feel really sad about that. And very disappointed…"

After less than a minute, far sooner than I'd expected, Bethany stops. Without looking at me, she sits up, tidies her pillow away, and gets down from the bed. She then marches off to the living room without a backward glance.

I feel like a suddenly-deflated balloon. I'd worked myself up for a long session. I straighten up, smooth the duvet and return the pillow. I'm relieved – but also puzzled. Why this sudden surrender? Maybe, not meeting any resistance on my part, she's lost half the fun of the battle. Like a teenager marching out the house, slamming the front door, and finding out that the whole family had suddenly turned into door-slammers! Where then would the shock-horror factor be? Or maybe – and I hope not – she feels I've hijacked some essential part of her identity.

Back in the living room, I find Bethany peering into the fish-tank. Some of the toad-spawn is still attached to the reed and twigs. The rest has separated into individual blobs. She's trying to lift these to the surface, breathing heavily and poking about with one of the twigs. Next to the tank is the pond book. I pick it up and glance through it, while Bethany fishes into the tank.

"Look! See that little thing there!" she exclaims. Before I can stop her, she shoves her arm, sleeve and all, right down to the bottom of the tank and comes up with the tiniest of creatures resembling a woodlouse. She places it carefully in the palm of her hand. "What's it called?"

"Um. Wait a moment…" I peer at the illustrations in the book for a long time. "Well, I think it's called a Stonefly nymph." I'm surprised at the number of creatures that have secretly been lurking in Bethany's tank.

"Let me see!" Bethany grabs the book from me and squints at it. "Which one, did you say?"

I point to the illustration. "I'm sure it's that one."

Bethany glances at the picture for a nanosecond. "No it's not. It's too big. And it's got different legs. And a different tail. It's that one, see?"

She points to a Mayfly nymph in the book, and then to the insect on her palm.

"They're the same, see? Mine's got three tails, like that one."

She's right! They still look alike to me – more or less the same size – but now she's pointed it out, I can see some very subtle differences. I didn't see them at first. Yet Bethany spotted them at a glance. I'm struck by her powers of observation. Once again, she reminds me of Harriet and her love of insects. I'm remembering the tray of woodlice Harriet kept in her room. If only Bethany had Harriet's academic intelligence and outgoing personality. Yet, one must never think in this way, comparing one child with another. Bethany is Bethany. All her sudden unexpected talents *and* her quirks are what make her who she is.

To my delight, Bethany agrees to draw five of the pond insects illustrated in the book, and label them.

"Shall we go out for a walk?" I suggest, when this activity comes to an end.

A shadow of suspicion furrows Bethany's brow.

"Where?"

"You choose. I don't know this area very well. You could show me your favourite places."

Bethany's face brightens. "The park! Can we go to the park?"

"Great idea!" *Couldn't be better*, I'm thinking. The park is halfway to her school. "But we must ask your mum first, so she knows exactly where we're going and also when we'll be back."

Mrs Webster emerges from her bedroom at this point, looking exhausted, and meets us as we go into the hall.

"He's asleep at last," she says. Her 'bump' seems to have grown prodigiously in the last ten days.

I explain our plans. Over Bethany's head, her mother and I exchange conspiratorial glances. We've already agreed that Bethany needs persuading out of the house, preferably in the direction of school. We have the full support of Mrs Bryce, Bethany's headteacher, who's complicit in the plot, and the approval of the higher echelons of the Education Department, who have authorised our unsupervised outings. Each day, between midday and one o'clock, Mrs Bryce will be watching out for Bethany. If, by some miracle, Bethany gets as far as the school gates, she'll come out to meet us and give her a small reward for taking such a big step forward.

"We'll be back in an hour," I promise.

Barely disguising her joy at having an hour to herself, Mrs Webster goes into the living room and lowers herself down on to the settee, clutching the small of her back. Gingerly, she lifts swollen ankles to the horizontal position and picks up the remote control of the TV.

"Be as long as you like," she says.

The park's almost deserted, except for two toddlers on the baby-swings and three boys on the slide. Surely they should be in school? The boys are having a rowdy argument about who should go first, and who whizzed down the fastest. Bethany takes a wary look at them, and seats herself next to the toddlers, on a big swing. She asks me to 'start her off'. Once she gets her momentum going, her legs fly back and forth until the swing bars are almost parallel to the ground. After a minute she seems to have gone into a trance. She doesn't want to come down. I'm worried that this might be another – milder – variation of the head-banging routine. And if she falls…?

Luckily, Bethany sees that the two boys have moved on to the climbing-frame. She slows down at last and gets off. She climbs up the steps of the slide two at a time, and whooshes down head first. Then, with a wary eye out for the boys, she has a go on the climbing frame, the parallel bars, and the climbing net. She's like a monkey, swinging through the high canopy of the jungle – graceful and fearless. It's the first time I've seen Bethany in full flow, physically, and with a sudden stab of regret I think about what she's missing, through not being at school. In most primary schools, games and gymnastics haven't yet been squeezed out of the curriculum in favour of academic work, as has happened at secondary level. Here's a way she could excel and express herself.

"May I take some photographs of you, Bethany?"

I should have remembered the camera earlier. Now Bethany wants to do the entire round of the equipment all over again, with even more extreme acrobatics. I take some action photos. She's curious to know how the camera works. I show her.

"*I'll* take some now," says Bethany. She snaps a clump of daffodils surrounded by primulas in a neatly dug bed along the side of the bowling green. Then she scans the grass surrounding the flowerbed. Her sharp eyes spot something crawling in the long stalks. Immediately she lies down flat in a wet patch on the path, and takes a photo at ground level. Then she peers into a puddle nearby.

"Bethany! Your coat – it's getting soaked. And muddy!"

"There's something there, in that puddle, but I don't know what it is," says Bethany, ignoring me completely. "But I might know, one day, if I photograph it…"

When she scrambles to her feet, there's a huge muddy stain on her jeans.

"Do try and keep clean, please. What's Mum going to say, when she sees you like this?"

"She won't mind," says Bethany. "She likes washing. She does it every day."

It's time to persuade her away from the park.

"Guess what?" I say. "I know where you can find the most beautiful garden. There are about a hundred tubs and hanging baskets filled with primroses, and red, yellow and blue primulas – some with stripes – and tiny baby daffodils. There are more colours, and more different types of spring flowers, in this garden than you could possibly imagine. Would you like to take some photos of it?"

Bethany nods, her eyes lighting up expectantly. I lead the way, feeling horribly like the wicked witch enticing Hansel and Gretel towards her house made of sweets. The house we're aiming for is at the beginning of the road which leads to Bethany's school.

"Tulips are my best flower of all," says Bethany as she skips along by my side. "Will we see any?"

"I'm not sure. It's a bit early. They don't usually come out until April."

Bethany looks disappointed. She has no idea of seasons, or for that matter of any time sequences whatsoever. She can't name the days of the week, or the months of the year. I'd better tackle this subject soon, I'm thinking… In fact, why not make a start on it right now?

I begin with a kind of stepping dance along the pavement. I chant the months of the year. If I step on a crack by mistake, I have to go right back to January again. Bethany soon joins in, the idea of not treading on the cracks appeals to her. We do the same with the days of the week. Our game does liven up what can be a repetitively boring exercise, but Bethany's paying a tad too much attention to the cracks, tiptoeing over them with wide eyes as though they were crevasses through which she might disappear forever. I hope I'm not feeding her mind with a new obsession.

Bethany takes some more photos. A robin chirruping on a fence post. Two gulls roosting on a chimneystack, cackling as if they're sharing a joke. We come to a garden with a pond, fringed with soft rush.

"See those long grasses, Bethany? In the olden days, before electricity, they used to dry those grasses to make lanterns. They've got a kind of oil in them. They used to call them rush lights."

Bethany peers over the garden gate at the pond. The she opens the gate and before I can stop her she's kneeling by the pond, trailing her hand in the water.

I pull on her arm. "What on earth are you doing? This is a private garden!"

"I only want to see if there's any toad spawn in there." Seeing my shocked expression, Bethany reluctantly allows herself to be hauled back to the gate. I shut it firmly behind us.

"Bethany, you can't just wander into other people's gardens! It's very rude."

"Not rude." Bethany stares at me.

"Well, not rude like saying a swear word, but not polite. It's something we just don't do!"

Bethany walks beside me in silence for a while, her mouth turned down. She clearly doesn't understand the concept of territorial boundaries, and feels I'm attacking her.

What a strange mixture she is! In the park, playing happily on the equipment, she seemed like any normal nine-year-old. Yet here she is, suddenly going into a stranger's garden, behaving in a way that most self-respecting four-year-olds would have grown out of.

We've reached the corner of Acacia Avenue, where the beautiful garden is situated. This road curves up the hill and to the right. Round the bend – and out of sight at the moment – is the school. The garden is halfway along, on the left, within full view of the school.

Bethany stops.

"My old school's up there!" Fear shadows her face.

"Really?" I say casually.

"I'm not going up there."

"We're only going as far as the beautiful garden, Then you can take a photo, and after that we'll go straight home, I promise. Have you got any more film left?"

Bethany hesitates, glancing down at the camera, and then along the road again. She's frozen in her tracks.

"Let's just have a quick look at the garden, take one photo, and then we'll turn round straight away. It's time to go home, anyway. Your mum will be waiting for you."

I'm not sure whether it's the photo-taking or the flowers that do the trick. But Bethany reluctantly follows behind me, dragging her feet. She looks like a prisoner being led to the gallows.

"How about that!" I exclaim triumphantly when we arrive at the gate. "Don't you think it was worth that extra distance to see all this?"

The south facing front wall of the house is a riot of colour. Baskets hang from hooks so close together that the brickwork is almost hidden. The baskets are packed with a glorious profusion of daffodils, primroses, primulas, ferns, and hanging foliage. Winter jasmine and clematis, in tubs on the ground, fill any remaining spaces on the wall. On the patio stand containers of all shapes and sizes filled with shrubs and miniature daffodils. Ranged in between all of these, looking like visitors at the Chelsea Flower show, stand little garden gnomes.

Bethany's entranced. Quickly she finishes the rest of the film, leaning over the gate. The gnomes fascinate her. She's dying to go in and have a closer look, but she's got the message. The gate remains firmly shut.

And then, a most felicitous happening. The front door opens. A rosy-cheeked, white haired couple come out into the garden towards us.

"We saw you through the window," chuckles the man, who looks remarkably like his gnomes. "Do you like our garden?"

Bethany blinks and nods, her mouth half-open. The man looks at her more closely, appraisingly.

"Do you like our gnomes?" smiles the lady. "There's some more round the back. Would you both like to come and have a look?"

"I'd love to," I say. "How about you, Bethany?"

Bethany looks at me for confirmation, then nods again. The couple lead the way through the trellis side-gate into a small, square back garden. Half its area is taken up by a large greenhouse. Trays of seedlings and geranium cuttings, neatly labelled, are stacked on wooden staging. The paved area next to the greenhouse is covered with yet more tubs – and rows upon rows of gnomes.

"They've all got names," says the man. "These here are Henry, Cyril, and Tony. They're named after my brothers. And see these, Bethany – do you know the story of the Seven Dwarfs?"

Bethany squirms uncomfortably at the direct question but rises to the occasion. She nods, whispers 'yes,' and half smiles.

"Well, these are all the dwarfs in the story." He chants all their names in a singsong voice.

I explain our situation, trying to be as tactful as possible to spare Bethany's feelings.

"Ah," says the lady, shrewdly. "Well, let me suggest something. We're in every morning. If you're ever passing by again, just wave from the gate. We watch everyone go by from out front window. We'll look out for you specially. You can come and say hello to the gnomes. By the way, I'm Annie, and my husband is Percy. Annie and Percy Holmes."

"Thank you, thank you so much."

I reckon the fates have conspired this morning to help Bethany on her way back into school. The next step will be to persuade her as far as the school gates. And that's not going to be easy.

Friday, 2nd April. For the last two weeks, progress towards the school gates has been disappointingly slow. Oh yes, Bethany will skip happily towards the Gnomes' Garden, as she has renamed it. And with good reason – Annie and Percy Holmes are there, waiting for us most days, as they weed, water and plant their garden. Occasionally there's a new gnome, which is celebrated like the arrival of a new baby.

Yet when we leave, and edge further along the road towards the school, Bethany's steps become slower and slower. Her face freezes with a look of genuine panic.

Last week, after teaching Bethany, I went to visit the school. I wanted to discuss Bethany's progress with Mrs Bryce, the headteacher.

First, I had a quick wander round the playground and the wide expanse of lawn and shrubs at the back of the school. If I could only persuade Bethany as far as the grounds! Swathes of daffodils, still in full bloom, made a golden carpet under the beech trees. In the flower beds bordering the car park, tulips – Bethany's favourite – were just coming into bud.

Mrs Bryce was in her study, which overlooked the playground. She was seated strategically by the window. She apologised for the fact that, while we were talking, she'd be looking out – literally – for a 'known trouble-maker', and hoped she didn't appear rude. I was impressed with Mrs Bryce. In her fifties, with springy grey hair and a small beaked nose, she had large, owl-like eyes that were constantly on the move as she scanned the playground for mischief.

I told her about the Gnomes' Garden.

"Ah, the Holmes," Mrs Bryce smiled. "A lovely couple. Their two youngest grandchildren are here. Neither of them are in Bethany's year, unfortunately, but they could be a link."

"I'm afraid Bethany seems to be stuck at their house," I sighed. "She won't go any further up the road."

Mrs Bryce looked thoughtful. "After the Easter holidays," she said slowly, "we've engaged the Prince's Trust to build a pond and a chicken run. Later, we've plans for an organic garden. I'm wondering if Bethany might be persuaded to just come and watch what they're doing."

This was a great idea, just the boost I needed to my flagging energy. Mrs Bryce asked me to contact her when Bethany wanted to visit, and she'd brief the Prince's Trust team to make a special fuss of her. I left the school feeling relieved that when Bethany does decide to return to school, she'll be in excellent hands. It's a rare headteacher who can spare time from a crushing load of administrative tasks, to give so much thought and attention to one pupil – especially to one as reluctant as Bethany.

Today, we're ambling wherever Bethany leads me, along the roads near her house. We're both carrying clipboards with a sheet of paper attached, playing a variation of I-Spy.

"My turn," I say, looking all around me. "I spy, with my little eye, something that's red." I write 'red post box' on my sheet of paper.

Bethany spots a red front door. She writes 'red dor' in large, uneven writing.

"Well done. Let's see if we can see anything else that's red. Then it will be your turn to choose a colour."

After a while, we change the game to normal I-Spy. It's Bethany's turn:

"I spy, with my little eye," she says carefully, "something beginning with P."

"Pavement?" No "Post box?" No. "Privet hedge?" No. "Parking space?" No.

"I give up. Tell me, Bethany."

"Pond!" she says, gleefully, leaning over a garden wall, and pointing. "P-o-n-d! I know how to spell it!"

"Well done! You get another go, because I didn't guess."

For now, I'm not too bothered that the school gates seem as elusive as the Gates of Heaven. Just wait till Bethany hears about the new pond being built in the school grounds! Then, nothing will keep her away.

Or will it? I could never have imagined that, behind the scenes, up in some ivory tower in the education department, plans were afoot for Bethany – plans that threatened to undo all the progress she's made so far.

Wednesday, 21st April. I can't believe this is happening! My stomach contracts with outrage and disbelief.

Bethany's review, in a bare, joyless room on the second floor of the education office, is in full flow. Present are: Bethany, Stanley Cotterill-Smith (Educational Welfare Officer), Mrs Bryce, sitting opposite me, Mrs Webster, next to me with Joseph on her lap and Bethany on her other side; and Julian Brown, a psychiatrist based at the local hospital, who has seen Bethany just once, a year ago. There's a quiet lady in the corner, taking notes. Unfortunately, Sally, my line manager, was not able to attend the meeting. This is a pity. She's had contact with the family, and understands Bethany's problems. In her place is another member of her department: Sam Jackson, a fresh-faced young man with a bemused expression. He looks as if he's straight out of college. He's never met Bethany before. Of all those present, only I, Mrs Bryce, and of course her mother, have any direct, recent knowledge of her progress. The purpose of the meeting is – ostensibly – to review Bethany's tuition and to set out a programme for a natural and gradual reintegration into school.

However, the meeting has been mysteriously hijacked by Cotterill-Smith. The agenda has suddenly become: Let's Get Bethany Back Into School A.S.A.P. Whether she's ready or not.

I'm ready to walk out. Any moment now I'll do so – after telling them all what a complete farce this meeting is. But that would be the end of my career – and it wouldn't help Bethany. I take enormous, deep breaths. I clench my fists together beneath the table, digging the nails of my right hand into my left palm so hard that tears spring to my eyes.

I glance up, through blurred vision. I catch Mrs Bryce's eye. She's giving me a significant look. Her eyes blink in a wise-owl way. She glances briefly at Bethany and makes an almost imperceptible, smoothing gesture with the palm of her hand. She smiles as she gazes vaguely round the table at the assembly of faces. As her gaze comes back to rest on me, she shakes her head, very slightly. The message is clear. Wait. Be cool. Don't rock the boat. Thank goodness she's on Bethany's side.

So far, Bethany has said hardly a word. Nor, for that matter, has anyone else. Cotterill-Smith seems to have appointed himself as Chair, and he's been doing most of the talking. He's a florid-faced, middle-aged man with fierce black eyebrows. Now he suddenly shoots a question at Bethany – he leans forward and stares at her hard.

"How do you feel your tuition is going, Bethany?"

Bethany jumps, and then shrinks back in her seat. Only someone who didn't know her – and who didn't understand children in the autistic spectrum – could have addressed her so abruptly, and asked such a useless, open-ended question. Bethany's face freezes, and takes on her most unintelligent expression. She looks down into her lap.

Cotterill-Smith tries again.

"Do you like what you're doing with your tutor? Or would you rather be at school with your friends? What do you miss most at school?"

Faced with this barrage of questions – just one would have been more than enough for her to cope with – Bethany simply retreats, literally. She puts her hands over her ears and begins to rock back and forth in her seat.

I daren't look at Bethany. I'm trying to let it be seen that I am totally unbiased (I wish) in any discussion about her future. Only that way will any recommendation I make carry weight. Not that anyone has yet asked me what I think, nor is it likely that they will.

Inwardly I'm fuming. This is a fiasco. In recent years, it's become politically correct to include the pupil, however young, in the full review. While well intentioned, the effect of this policy in most cases is that everyone pussyfoots around the main issue, desperate not to upset the child by some contentious remark. Often, as is happening now, the child is being subtly 'managed' in order to conform to some hidden agenda. Surely it would be best to divide any review into two parts. The first part, with the child present, would consist of hearing what he or she really wants, without prompting or judgement. The second part, without the child, would be a forum for everyone to put their agenda forward honestly and openly, so that everyone knows what they're up against. It might then be that there is no agreement at all about the best way forward for the child. Or, some consensus of opinion might be reached, which may, or may not coincide with the child's wishes. There might be a need for further meetings. But the child, at all costs, should be spared the ordeal of sitting through a lot of worrying and confusing – and often heated – discussion.

Poor Mrs Webster's completely out of her depth, hardly following the proceedings. With Joseph wriggling like mad, trying to get down from her lap towards the only thing of any interest in this starkly clinical room – the potted trailing *ficus* in the corner – who could blame her?

Wrapped in my own dark thoughts, I switch off for a moment. I switch back on with a sudden jump of alarm. Cotterill-Smith is speaking:

"So, what we're agreeing for Bethany is that a swift return to school is in her very best interests and in the interests of her family."

"What time span are we talking about here?" asks the psychiatrist. "It would be good to set a programme for this."

"I suggest four weeks. That would give Bethany time to visit the school perhaps next week, and then, the week after that she can go into class for a couple of hours each morning, gradually building up to full-time attendance at the end of the four-week period."

This is just what I feared most of all. Bethany is being pressured. Things are not happening at her pace. I want to stand up, and shout at them, to tell them about the Gnomes' Garden, and Annie and Percy's kindness, and that we've nearly reached the school gates. We haven't quite got there – but we will, thanks to the Princes Trust and the new pond. But all this sounds fanciful and airy-fairy. It doesn't fit with this other, non child-centred agenda, which is cold and budget-driven.

There's a long silence. No one asks Bethany what she thinks of this idea.

Mrs Bryce speaks, and her voice carries authority.

"I think we must acknowledge the steps that Bethany has taken so far. I know she has made progress educationally with her tutor, and that a programme has already been put in place to help Bethany feel more confident about going back to school. My personal view is that we mustn't rush Bethany, but rather encourage her and her tutor to carry on with the progress that's already been made in basic subjects, so that when she does return, she can feel more confident about keeping up academically with the rest of her class."

Cotterill-Smith frowns. "We must have some fixed time scale. We can't just be open-ended about this. We have a budget to keep to. The situation could just drag on and on…"

"Quite right," says the psychiatrist. "This collusion between mother and daughter is not healthy…"

"I agree," says Mrs Bryce. "That's why I suggest that, as soon as this meeting's over, I sit down with Bethany's tutor and work out a realistically timed programme of re-entry. This can then be approved by Sally – and by yourself, of course."

Nice one. Everyone suddenly remembers that Sally needs to be included in any decision. It's clear that the young man who is supposed to be representing her is totally out of his depth. And Clitheroe Primary is one of the most successful schools in the area. As headteacher, Mrs Bryce is highly regarded by parents, governors and by the LEA. She also has a steely reputation for getting her own way.

I'm wondering if anyone will ask my opinion. Most unlikely. Would they listen, anyway, if I pointed out that I may be draining the budget at the moment, but if Bethany goes back to school too soon, and can't cope, she might drop out permanently? Then how much will the LEA have to fork out, for long-term one-to-one tuition?

Cotterill-Smith wavers. Mrs Bryce switches tactics.

"Maybe," she says, with courteous charm, "we should ask Mrs Webster what she thinks is a realistically-timed programme for Bethany to return to school?"

"Humph!" Cotterill-Smith clearly doesn't like this turn of events. Reluctantly he addresses Mrs Webster. "What kind of timetable did you have in mind for Bethany? Surely you must be feeling under some pressure, having an extra child at home all day?"

Mrs Webster's struggling to keep Joseph on her lap. In fact, she hasn't got a lap any more. This is what's causing the problem. Joseph, after bouncing on his mother's bump in a way that makes me wince, is now using her legs as a slide towards freedom – and the potted plant.

I whip out my set of keys and place them on the table in front of Joseph. Distracted for a moment, he picks them up and examines them closely. He likes the little teddy bear they hang from. For a few seconds, there's a blissful silence.

"I'm sorry," says Mrs Webster. "Did someone say something?"

"I said…"

CRASH! go the keys on the table. The Educational Welfare Officer's words are drowned as Joseph discovers exciting new sounds.

Then all goes quiet again as Joseph inspects each key in turn.

"I said, I think we'd all like to know what you…"

BANG! The percussion section of the orchestra starts up again.

Another silence. Joseph pokes at the teddy's eyes. We all hold our breath. I'm enjoying this. My instinctive reaction to keep Joseph amused and quiet has suddenly turned into an all-out, one woman – plus baby – act of guerrilla warfare.

Mrs Webster grabs the keys and holds them out of Joseph's reach.

"What I'd like," she says, "is for Bethany to have longer. What with the baby due in just over a month, I don't want her to feel pushed out. She needs to do things at her own pace. That's how she is. You can't rush her. That's Bethany."

There's another long silence. Cotterill-Smith plainly wants a decisive conclusion to the meeting. But Joseph's restlessness – he's now crawling around under the table examining our shoes – and Mrs Bryce's firm stance, are making this difficult. He hesitates, trying to find a way of finishing the proceedings without losing face.

Suddenly, Bethany stands up and grips the edge of the table. Her cheeks are flushed, though her face is as impassive as ever. Only her eyes show her feelings. They glitter with a manic intensity.

"I'M NOT GOING TO SCHOOL! You can't make me. I won't go! So there!"

She grabs my keys from her mother's hand and flings them at Cotterill-Smith. They miss his left ear by two centimetres. Before anyone quite realises what's happening, Bethany runs out of the room, slamming the door. Her light footsteps clatter along the corridor and then down the stairs.

In the following silence, Joseph grabs a trailing branch of the *Ficus*. The heavy pot crashes on its side, covering Joseph with plant and compost. His shocked cries call an end to Bethany's review meeting.

Thursday, 6th May. The threat of having to go back to school has upset Bethany considerably, and set her back by several weeks.

For a week after her review, she refused even to go out of the house. I used all my wiles and ingenuity to entice her at least to the park, but Bethany was adamant:

"I'm not going anywhere near that school!"

There was no room for further negotiation. She'd made up her mind and that was that. I gave up trying to persuade her, and concentrated instead on improving her reading, writing and maths. At least she – and I – could feel satisfied that she was making strides in some direction.

Today, after teaching Bethany, I've driven down to the school to see how the Prince's Trust team is getting on. They started work two weeks ago, but a rainy spell had slowed progress. The heavy clay soil was a nightmare to dig out, and as the plan was to include the pupils in the project, the school was anxious not to antagonise the parents by sending the children home covered in mud.

Now, after a week of sunshine, work has resumed. A big heart-shaped pit has been half excavated. The earth is piled up nearby, ready to form a rockery. A group of rowdy and enthusiastic young men and women are standing round the pit, admiring their handiwork. It's their lunch break. They're laughing and chucking sandwiches at each other and trying to push one another into the hole. Bethany would have loved to be part of this. She'd have bonded right away with these young people.

After this, I stop further down the road at the Gnomes' Garden. I'm hoping Annie and Percy will be there. They must be wondering why we haven't called round for the last few weeks.

The hanging baskets have been removed, and the tubs emptied of their winter flowers. The garden looks quite bare. Only the gnomes remain, lining the path, looking like revellers waiting for the carnival to begin.

The front door opens. Percy Holmes, looking more than ever like a gnome with his bright twinkling eyes, greets me cheerfully.

"And where's your young lady, nowadays? We haven't seen her for a long time. Not ill, is she?"

I explain – as fully as I dare – about the plan to speed up Bethany's return to school. "I can't even get her as far as your house, now," I say, sadly.

"Well, that's a shame. Me and the wife, we're busy every day in the greenhouse, planting up the hanging baskets. We're putting in some of the seedlings we've grown. We've got Petunias, Surfinias, Busy Lizzies…She'd love them, your Bethany would. If you can get her along tomorrow, she can help Annie plant them in the baskets."

"If only I could! But she's refusing to leave the house."

"Well, just tell her that there are lots of spare seedlings. And a couple of spare baskets, too. She could make up a couple and take them home to her mum."

"Thank you! That might just change her mind. It might persuade her to leave the house."

I say goodbye, and walk thoughtfully to the car. Another idea is taking shape in my mind. So, Bethany won't go to school. Maybe, if Muhammad won't go to the mountain, then the mountain must come to Muhammad!

Friday, 14th May. Halfway through our session this morning, there's a loud knock on the front door. Bethany and I run down to open it.

A young man and woman stand on the doorstep, both wearing muddy jeans and jackets. The man points to the open van behind him, indicating a large pile of rocks inside.

"Where do you want these, love?"

They introduce themselves as Kirsty and Nick from the Prince's Trust. Nick's one of the team leaders. He has a kind, serious face, and long hair in a ponytail. Kirsty's a young trainee with mischievous eyes and a truculent expression. Both have been seconded from their work at the school, to help with Bethany's project. They're delivering a load of surplus-to-requirement rocks from the school rockery.

"Can you put them round the back?" says Bethany, taking charge with all the aplomb of director of the Eden Project. "I'll show you…"

She leads the way round the side of the house into a small square of rough ground. She paces up and down, importantly, selecting best place for her own rockery.

"Here." She stamps hard with her feet. "Wait there!"

She dashes towards the dense growth of brambles and shrub at the back of the garden, and finds a stick. This she plants firmly into her chosen spot with the triumphant air of an explorer putting up a flag at the South Pole.

"Right," says Nick. "We'll get the rocks out of the van."

There's a wheelbarrow in the shed. Kirsty complains about its rusty state. She's giving Nick a lot of lip. I guess she's trouble, but Nick seems to understand her.

"Let's all help Nick and Kirsty move the rocks, Bethany." I want her to be involved in every part of this whole operation. This must be *her* project, not ours.

We all unload the van and pile the rocks into the wheelbarrow. Bethany tries to pick up the biggest rock of all. It's the action of children who are much younger than Bethany. They want to be helpful – to carry the holiday luggage from the hall to the boot of the car. But it's always the biggest suitcase that they try to lift!

"They're heavy!" Bethany looks amazed, as her selected rock doesn't budge an inch.

"Try a smaller one," grins Kirsty.

We all wait patiently as Bethany tries several rocks, downsizing until she finds one she can manage. She staggers to the wheelbarrow, where she drops it with a clang.

"Well done!" says Nick. "You *are* a strong young lady!"

I feel an instant connection to Kirsty and Nick. They're both definitely on Bethany's wavelength. They tease her, yet take her seriously. They totally accept her odd behaviour. Kirsty has stopped arguing constantly with Nick and seems to be getting along well with Bethany, who is telling her about the Gnomes' Garden. Bethany takes Kirsty upstairs and shows her the hanging baskets, fruits of yesterday's expedition to see Annie and Percy. She's placed the baskets carefully in a sunny spot on the windowsill in the kitchen, waiting to be hung by the front door after the danger of frost has passed.

Kirsty comes down from upstairs with a tray of tea and biscuits. Some of her truculence has gone. She's been watching Bethany thoughtfully, as if trying to work out why she is as she is.

"Now," says Nick. "What we're going to do next, is to bring round some of our leftover earth. We've got far too much of it. This will save us trying to dig up your garden. We'd never get through all this tough grass and stones to find enough good soil."

I catch Nick's eye. I'm sending him a telepathic message. Luckily he receives it.

"Do you know, Bethany," he says, sighing and scratching his head, "we're going to need some help, from someone who's very strong, to help us load all the earth into the van. I wonder who that could be..?"

"Me!" says Bethany, flexing arms and legs in a bodybuilding pose. "I'm strong! I can do it!"

"That would be such a help!" I tell her, delighted by her enthusiasm. "We need some really strong people. So you get in the front of the van with Kirsty and Nick, and I'll follow in my car. First, I'll go and tell your mum we're just popping up to the school."

I nip upstairs and find Mrs Webster changing sheets in Pablo and Callum's room. We won't be long, I tell her, but we may have to make two or three journeys.

"Be as long as you like," she says, looking pleased to be rid of us all for a while.

I ask if I can phone the school, and then I dash back down to the van. With dismay, I realise there's a struggle going on inside. Bethany's trying to get out again, while Nick's hastily trying to start the car for a quick getaway. Wedged in between the two of them, Bethany looks as if she's just been arrested by the police.

Kirsty pokes her head out of the window. "She doesn't want to go now. She didn't understand that we were going to the school to get the earth."

It seems that Bethany, caught up in the excitement of a ride in the van, and a chance to show off her strong muscles, had forgotten that the rocks and the soil came from the school. Now she's sitting there, looking petrified.

So near, and yet so far! But I can't let this unusual opportunity slip away.

"Nick, turn off the engine for a moment. Thank you. Now, Bethany, it's entirely up to you whether or not you go with Nick and Kirsty to get the soil. No one will make you if you don't want to, I promise. But we'd love you to see the school rockery. It's almost finished. And Kirsty's told me there are some spare plants that you can have – isn't that so, Kirsty?"

Kirsty nods, her face lighting up with the fun of conspiracy. Bethany's calmed down a bit, she's sucking her thumb and looking at me with wide, fearful eyes.

"You can choose some of these plants for your rockery," I tell her. "You don't have to stay to help Nick and Kirsty put the soil in the van. You can just choose your plants, and come straight back with me in the car."

Bethany hesitates. I produce my trump card. "And guess what? Mr and Mrs Holmes are giving you one of their gnomes! As a thank you present for all the help you've given them this week in the greenhouse. But, they've had to go out today, so they've left it by the school rockery with the plants. Poor gnome – he just wants someone to give him a name, and he wants a new home. I think he'd be very happy living in your garden, Bethany!"

We all hold our breath for what seems an age.

"Okay," says Bethany, "but I'm not staying." She gives me a long look, as if she doesn't quite trust me.

I follow the van to the school. I cross my fingers as it turns into the entrance. Incredibly, we manage to pass the school gates and park in the car park. Bethany jumps out, looking around her like a frightened kitten. We go round the side of the school, and across the grass towards the fenced-off area in the corner of the grounds. Bethany walks between Nick and Kirsty, holding their hands.

The Prince's Trust team immediately welcome Bethany and show her what they've done so far. The rockery looks almost professional, planted with russet and purple heathers, sedums, white and yellow alyssum and cascading aubretia. Lined up next to the rockery is a surprise – a whole row of gnomes.

Tom, the other team leader, wastes no time with chitchat. He draws Bethany in right away.

"Ah, Bethany. I was hoping you'd come. We need someone to help us put these little people on the rockery. Where do you think they should all go?"

Bethany's so busy settling the gnomes into their new positions that she's forgotten she's at school The children aren't allowed in this part of the grounds, except with permission. Even though it's the lunch hour, and we can hear distant shouts coming from the tarmac playground on the other side of the building, Bethany seems unfazed, totally absorbed in her present task.

While Bethany chooses plants to take back, Mrs Bryce walks across the grass, casually. She says 'hello' to Bethany as if she sees her every day, and gives her a welcoming smile. She admires the rockery, and says how good the gnomes look, spaced out on the rocks like miniature mountaineers. She asks Bethany to show her what plants she's selected to take back home with her. Then she gives Bethany a small parcel, neatly wrapped with silver paper. Bethany holds it in her hands, and stares down at it, as if she's not sure what she's supposed to do with it. She seems overwhelmed. I'm suddenly worried that all this excitement will be too much for her. She looks up at Mrs Bryce uncertainly.

"You can open it now, or at home," smiles Mrs Bryce.

The gang of young trainees put down their trowels and spades. "Please open it now!" they chorus, crowding round.

"Go on, Bethany," I urge her.

She tears off the wrapping. Inside is a green china toad. Her face lights up. She holds it in her hand gently, as if it were alive.

"Do you know why I got you the present, Bethany?" asks Mrs Bryce.

Bethany shakes her head.

"Because you've been helping in such an important way to make our rockery!"

Bethany looks down at the ground.

"Look, I've got a 'Well Done' sticker for you. Can I put it on your sweater – where would you like it to go?"

Bethany shrinks back a little, but half-smiles as she allows the headteacher to place the sticker on her chest. Mrs Bryce produces a gold-wrapped chocolate coin from her pocket and hands it to Bethany.

"All my best pupils get one of these every week, if they do something special. And you have done something special today!"

As she turns to go back, she says, "And when you're ready to come into school, and sit in the library with your tutor, there might be another prize for you!"

She hurries back across the grass with a parting wave to Bethany.

Later, all the earth has been piled up in Bethany's garden. On Monday, we'll position the rocks and plant the alpines. Today's session is over.

I drive off, aiming for the Harbour Café. I'm in a happy daze. This calls for a celebration – a large slice of chocolate cake would fit the bill nicely. I can hardly believe it – Bethany's achieved more in one morning than I could have hoped for in a whole month!

Even so, I mustn't let myself hope for too much, too soon. Time is running out. In two weeks, the new baby is due. This could be a big setback for Bethany. She could regress. Cling on, once again, to her mother and to her home.

Tuesday, 25th May. After her dramatic entry into the school grounds the week before last, I'd somehow expected things to be plain sailing from now on. I'd imagined that, at first, we'd make cautious forays into the actual school building. Perhaps even as far as the classroom. Because the news has spread – Bethany is back! Several of her former classmates have made their way over to the pond and rockery area to say hello. They seem to have forgotten how odd and uncommunicative she was when she was in school. Children are very forgiving. I watch quietly as they come and go. They've been telling her about a class project – large papier-mâché models of mammals. Surely their enthusiasm and warm welcome will entice Bethany back into the classroom?

But Bethany remains steadfastly aloof, ever the outsider. She's happy to spend time digging out the new vegetable bed, or weeding the rockery. She'll kneel down for ages next to the now-completed pond, totally absorbed in watching the tiny frogs, decanted back from my own pond, as they make heroic efforts to climb up the sloping sides. However, as for going into the school building – that's a bridge too far.

It's not shyness. Of that I'm certain. Yet it's curious, the way Bethany relates to her peers. When they chatter away to her, she doesn't ignore them. I can see that she's listening. But she doesn't make eye contact – she'll be gazing off somewhere to the side of them, her mouth half-open. Her lack of response is maddening. I can see how it puts off potential friends. After a while they stop telling her things. One by one they fall silent. Then, with a 'Bye, Bethany!' they run off to the other side of the building to play on the tarmac, to initiate conversations on more fertile ground. Bethany doesn't mind. She seems quite unaware of the effect she creates.

I'm beginning to panic. Despite Mrs Bryce's charm offensive and persuasion, we've still got the Educational Welfare Officer breathing down our necks, pressing to know exactly when Bethany is planning to begin her four-week programmed re-entry into full-time school. And Cotterill-Smith wants her actually in the classroom. He's ignoring the fact that, for an hour a day, Bethany's in the school grounds. That she's learning so much about the natural world. About soil structure and its PH value, how to grow organic vegetables, the food-chain of mammals, as well as the nesting of our summer birds, their amazing journeys across continents to visit us – all this counts for nothing, apparently.

Plus, in exactly one week, the new baby is due. Another challenge. How Bethany will react to this event is an unknown quantity, but I suspect it might set her back. She could once again become Mum's Little Helper, and stick to her mum and the new baby like a bee to a honey-pot.

Yet, watching her now, I'm filled with a sudden glow of pleasure. Her face is flushed as she lifts spadefuls of red earth and places it in a ridge next to the trench she's hollowed out. Kirsty's shown her how to do double digging, and Bethany's frantically digging for victory like a World War Two Land Girl. With her small sturdy frame, broad back and strong shoulders, she's designed for the task.

"Phew. It's *hot*!" Kirsty, digging further along the patch, mops her brow. "Hey, Nick! This is slave labour. Can't we have a break?"

Nick, who's energetically hammering stakes into the ground for a new fence, looks round and grins.

"Weakling! No stamina, the young people of today. Not like when I was a youngster, way back in the year 2000. Keep at it, Kirsty. It'll get some of your weight off!"

"You b—." Glancing at Bethany, Kirsty stops herself just in time. Her ripe language has certainly become more muted since she's taken Bethany under her wing.

"Okay, gang!" calls Nick. "Time for a break!" He waves to the rest of the team. Strung out at intervals in a ragged line along the long boundary hedge, they're all busy with pruners and shears. The dark green of the privet forms a sombre background to their brightly-coloured T-shirts and peaked caps. Hearing Nick, they stop and look round. In unison, like seagulls spotting an unsuspecting holidaymaker with an open cone of chips, they down tools and flock towards us.

"Did you remember to pack your sandwiches, Bethany?" I ask.

"'Course. I always do," says Bethany, with an indignant toss of her head.

This midday break is the highlight of the day for Bethany. Just the thought of it keeps her going, as she struggles with the maths and English worksheets that we do at home for the first hour of the session. On the way to school, there's the bonus of our walk through the park to see what's growing. And that's the deal: no work, no park – and no Prince's Trust. Miraculously, Bethany accepts it.

What a delight it is, to see her now. She's munching her sandwiches, sitting up straight and proud. Covertly, she watches the others, imitating their mannerisms and gestures. Lazy, good-natured Ben slurps his lemonade and burps. Bethany giggles and does the same. Kirsty snaps her lunch-box shut and gives it an extra thump for good measure. Bethany bangs her lunch box even harder. Kirsty turns her peaked cap round and wears it American-style – Bethany immediately copies her. Such copying is the behaviour of a much younger child. Even so, for the first time, Bethany's learning how to interact in a group. She's observing them, learning their ways. These might not include the daintiest of table manners or conversation, but it's a start. The reward is that this bunch of young people accepts Bethany as one of themselves. In fact, she's become their mascot.

With Kirsty, a special bond is developing. Kirsty's extrovert personality, her irreverent humour, are the perfect antidote to Bethany's reserve. And Kirsty, initially the loud-mouthed troublemaker of the group, has changed since Bethany joined the gang. It's touching to see her trying to become Bethany's role model, to set a good example. For the first time in her life, Kirsty has to think before she acts. She literally has to rehearse a set of behaviours that are quite new to her. I've watched her leaning on her spade and frowning, her lips moving as if she's working out what to say to Bethany. Then she'll come out with some incongruous pearl of wisdom from her grandmother's generation.

"Bethany, you'll catch your death of cold if you don't put your sweater back on after all that heavy digging!"

"I'm boiling!"

"Well, you know the old saying, Bethany. Heck, I've forgotten. What the f—. Whoops – sorry. How does it go? 'Never something a clout till May is'… um. What the hell is a clout, anyway, when it's at home?"

"It's a piece of clothing. 'Ne'er cast a clout till May is out'." I try to keep a straight face.

"Oh that's it. I remember. Never cast a clout till May is out, Bethany."

"What?" Bethany gives us both her blankest stare.

"It means," explains Kirsty, triumphantly, "that you should never take off your winter clothes till May is finished. There might be a frost, and that. Like if you wait till June you won't catch cold."

Bethany looks even more mystified. She hasn't quite mastered all the months of the year in sequence. But obediently, for Kirsty's sake, she puts on her sweater.

"Kirsty, have you made any plans for when this project at the school is finished?"

As I ask the question, I feel a sudden sense of dread. For, at the end of the week, The Prince's Trust will be gone, their work completed. In fact, they've done so well that they're ahead of schedule. All they have to do now is to finish the fencing that will surround the pond, rockery and vegetable patch. For the last few days the school caretaker has been finding them extra jobs to do, such as pruning the boundary hedge. Without the company of this good-natured, boisterous bunch of young people, will Bethany still want to come to school?

"I dunno," Kirsty's saying. "I've never settled to anything so far."

"What did you do before you did this?"

Kirsty shifts uneasily. She glances at Bethany, but Bethany's now leapt out of earshot, trying to catch the tiny toads as they climb up the sides of the pond.

"Well, I was on the dole. I dropped out of school ages ago. I left home when I was fifteen. Then I got into a bit of trouble. Well, a lot of trouble."

"How old are you now, Kirsty?"

"Nineteen. I'm on probation, but it's nearly over."

"Did you like working here?"

"I loved it," Kirsty sighs. "Best thing I've ever done."

"Well then, why don't you get a job in a garden centre, or in the Parks department of the Council? Or, you could get some qualifications. How about an NVQ in Horticulture?"

"Oh, I dunno. I'm not sure if I really want to do gardening as a job. I mean, I like it. I'm interested in it. But I like it best here because of the others…" She nods her head towards her team mates, stretched out on the grass around us. "And because of that one, over there." She points to Bethany. "She's a one-off, she is. Never met anyone quite like her. I'll miss her, I will." Kirsty's trying to sound chirpy, but underneath the bravado, her vulnerability shows.

"You get on well with kids, don't you, Kirsty? I've seen how you talk to them…you explain things to them when they come over to watch us working."

"Yeah, well. I do like kids. Especially the young ones. Once I thought I'd like to…" She shrugs, "But I dunno."

"How about working with young children? In a nursery, or playgroup?"

"I've never had a job for more than two months. Like, work and me, we don't get on. You know?"

"But you've worked here! You've been brilliant."

"Here's different. We've got Nick with us. He knows how to treat us. And it's fun. Having a job isn't fun, it's just hard work and boring." She jumps up. "Nick's calling us." She waves back at Nick, who's standing by the hedge, brandishing shears.

"Time to go, Bethany!" I call. "Mum will be getting worried. We'll have to run really fast!"

Jumping over the pavement cracks, Bethany races home. I try to keep up with her, thoughts drumming through my brain. At the end of the week the half-term holidays start. A whole week's break for Bethany, during which we could easily lose all the momentum we've gained over the last month. A week during which her new baby sister or brother might be born. And after half term, there'll be no Prince's Trust to welcome Bethany back with open arms.

Bethany's return to school seems as elusive as ever. So near, and yet so far. What we need is an injection of new energy. Something totally different needs to happen at school. Something that Bethany can't resist.

Bethany's reached her gate, way ahead of me.

"Come on!" she shouts. "Why've you stopped?" You're not even moving!"

I've stopped because a crazy idea has just punched its way into my brain. My heart beat whooshes into my eardrums. Dizzily, I lean against a nearby fence.

It's crazy. And it's risky. But it might just work.

Monday, 7th June. This morning, Bethany's completely forgotten that Kirsty won't be at school anymore. Maybe she just doesn't want to believe it.

"You know Kirsty won't be there now," I remind her as gently as I can.

Suddenly Bethany bursts into tears.

"Then I won't go!" She stamps her foot.

"Oh, Bethany." I put my arm round her shoulders. "I know how you'll miss Kirsty. And I bet she's missing you too, just now, but all the work in the garden's finished. Kirsty's got to go and do another job, somewhere else."

I'm distressed to see her so upset. Yet there's hope, too, in these floods of tears. Kirsty's leaving has somehow broken through Bethany's armour of reserve.

"I won't go. So there!" sobs Bethany.

"That's a shame. Kirsty would be very disappointed if you didn't go. Because she's left a present for you in Mrs Bryce's office, and she wants you to ring her as soon as you've opened it. She's expecting a phone call. She's sitting down right now with the phone in her hands."

Like sunshine chasing rain clouds away, Bethany's face lights up. Without a word, she runs into the hall to put her shoes on.

Mrs Webster's in the kitchen. She's perched, perilously, on a thin strip of work-surface between the cooker and the fridge, deftly swiping almost-invisible grease stains off the ceiling. Her upper body moves with the awesome speed of a Chinese ping-pong champion. She has her back to me. I daren't say goodbye in case I cause her to topple.

I creep out and leave a note on the living-room table to say when we'll be back. I'm worried. Is it safe to leave her, in this flurry of extreme housework?

Bethany's calling me from the bottom of the stairs, eager to be off, however. It's a beautiful day, and we'd both rather be outside.

In the park, the summer bedding has just been put in. Stiff-and-starchy rows of salvia, lobelia and alyssum have yet to flower. The vast expanses of bare earth remind us that *real* summer is still to come. The tulips, however, still stand proudly centre stage. Bethany snaps a close-up of these, leaving a trail of footprints on the newly-dug earth.

"Bethany! What does that sign say? And just look at your trainers!"

Bethany glances down briefly at her mud-caked white trainers and kneels down to read the sign.

"Keep – off – the – flower – beds," she reads carefully.

"That means you," I say sternly.

"Well, I didn't know, did I?"

She skips off to the swings. I warn her that she's only got one minute. It's a shame to hurry her away, but it's essential that we get to school before the lunch hour starts. I want Bethany safely in the office before the children begin to spill out of the classrooms and mayhem reigns.

Over half-term, I'd called into see Mrs Bryce. We'd had a summit meeting about how to get Bethany back into school, (i.e. actually inside the building). It was then that I'd made my daring suggestion. To my delight, Mrs Bryce had listened attentively. She'd see what she could do, but it might take several weeks to organise. It might not even be feasible. In the meantime, we need some other carrot to tempt Bethany past the entrance

I think I've found the solution. After my meeting with the headteacher, I'd had a quick look round. To the right of the entrance hall, with its notice boards and stands of books and pamphlets, a short, wide corridor leads to an open sitting area, used as a library and to display the children's best work. On a long table, beautifully arranged on a white cloth, was a selection of the children's Show and Tell objects – a blackbird's nest, some unusually shaped beach pebbles, a dried-out starfish, a cockle shell…and best of all, a jar of stick insects. Next to each exhibit was a story card, describing it and giving the name of the exhibitor. A passing teacher, working over the holidays, told me that all the children up to Class 4 have their own classroom Show and Tell every morning. Recently the staff had felt that the older children were missing out, so the best items from each class were selected each day and displayed for the whole school to enjoy. What a great idea! I can't wait to show Bethany.

"Are you excited about the new baby?" I watch her closely.

Bethany nods in a resigned, matter-of-fact way, with a little sigh. As if she's seen it all before – too often.

"Well, I don't expect it will be long now," I say brightly. Probably in the next hour, I'm thinking, judging by her mother's frantic bout of activity earlier.

Bethany nods again, and says conversationally:

"The baby'll probably have to be made into juice, first."

I stop. I must have misheard.

"What did you say, Bethany?"

"The baby – it will have to be made into juice first. Before it gets born. I heard Mum talking to Auntie Mary."

Bethany runs ahead and then stops suddenly. She peers over a garden gate at a ginger cat sunbathing on a sunny doorstep.

I run after her. "Made into…?"

"So it can come out more easily," says Bethany matter-of-factly. She points at Ginger. "I want a cat. Just like that one."

My head spins. Bizarre images flash before my eyes. Of midwives – all Hattie Jacques look-alikes – brandishing liquidisers, and bearing down on a ward of mothers in labour.

"And where do you think that the baby comes out from, Bethany?"

"From her tummy button. That's why it has to be runny."

"And then what do you think happens?"

"Bethany shrugs. "Dunno. I 'spect it just gets put back together again somehow."

I'm speechless. I stare at Bethany. Is she having me on? But she looks perfectly serious. She tears herself away from the ginger cat, and hops-skips-jumps along the pavement, avoiding the cracks.

"Bethany! Stop a minute."

"What?"

She stands still, waiting for me to catch up. I struggle to keep a rising, hysterical note out of my voice.

"Bethany. Babies are NOT made into juice. And they do not come out of tummy buttons…"

Too late, I catch sight of a middle-aged couple on the other side of a garden wall. They've been bending over, weeding, but now they rise up, like phoenixes. They blink at us, wide-eyed, with pursed lips.

"They do. They have to. There's no other way out." Bethany treats the man and woman to one of her most gormless mouth-half-open stares.

"No, Bethany. They do not."

"Oh yes they do!" says Bethany, emphatically.

The couple are standing quite still, transfixed. This is turning into a pantomime. Bethany's plainly disconcerted by the stony faces on the other side of the wall. Ironically, I've discovered, she finds blank, expressionless faces in other people very threatening, and this pair look particularly humourless. Behind them is a bare, colourless garden with a circular gravelled area and not a weed – or a flower – in sight. One lone conifer stands stiffly in the centre, in a white plastic pot.

"Come on, Bethany." I take her arm and gently pull her away, before she pokes her tongue out and rolls her eyes at them. "Let's have a race to the school!"

Babies and liquidisers will have to be shelved for the moment. Bethany is on the brink of another breakthrough – going *into* school!

Bethany's the first to reach the wide, double doors of the school entrance. Standing there, smiling, is Mrs Bryce. She leads us straight into her office. On her desk is a box, brightly wrapped in gift paper. There's a big card which reads: 'To Bethany, our little Mascot. With love from all the Prince's Trust Team.' Everyone has signed it, with a cheery message.

Bethany looks briefly at the card, then tears open the wrapping paper round the box. Her face flushed, she lifts out a set of gardening tools – trowel, fork, secateurs. There's also a large magnifying class for studying insects and a Gardening Week By Week diary. Bethany delves into the bottom of the box. There's a framed photograph of the whole group, arranged on and around the rockery, with Bethany kneeling in front, like a football team mascot. Underneath the photo, the message reads: 'Keep Gardening Bethany!'

Bethany stands very still, holding the photo tight to her chest. She looks at the tools spread out on the desk. Her face is alight.

"And now you can say thank you," says Mrs Bryce. "Nick's on another job now, but he's asked Kirsty to wait for your phone call. She specially wants to say hello to you."

Mrs Bryce winks at me as she dials a number and passes the phone to Bethany. She goes into an inner office.

Bethany's soon engaged in a very long – and one-sided – conversation. I can hear Kirsty's voice crackling at the other end of the line. Bethany's answering "Yes. No. Not yet." Now and then she giggles at something Kirsty's said. I hear Kirsty say, 'Goodbye, Bethany. Be good, won't you!'

"Bye," whispers Bethany. She stands still, looking down at the phone as if still waiting for Kirsty's disembodied voice.

"I'd like to show you something really special, Bethany." Gently, I take the phone from her and replace the receiver.

"What?" She looks towards the entrance, as if planning her escape route.

"It's a nature display. You'll love it."

We're back in the entrance hall. I point down the corridor.

"It's in the library area. On a table. Look, you can just see the end of the table from here."

Bethany stares at me, wary-eyed and suspicious. She looks like a deer sniffing the air for marauding lions.

"You don't have to come if you don't want to. I just thought you'd be interested. There's a huge jar of stick insects!"

"Stick insects!"

Bethany's eyes become as round as saucers. We've been reading about these unusual pets and she's been pestering her poor long-suffering mum to take her to the pet shop and buy her some.

"Come on then!" I urge her.

I start walking slowly towards the library, not looking back. There's a heart-stopping pause when I wonder if Bethany's made a dash for the school gates. But then I hear her soft footsteps padding along behind me.

As Bethany leans over the display table, her eyes light up. She peers into the large glass jar containing the stick insects. She pokes them and tries to prise them off their sticks. Then she walks round the table, examining all the other exhibits closely, picking them up reverently, stroking and tapping and turning them around in her hands.

Holding my breath, I watch her, savouring the moment. Bethany's in school, at last. And enjoying herself! And most important of all, it's been at *her* pace.

Suddenly, a bell breaks into the silence. We both jump. A few seconds later, doors burst open and a rowdy stampede of children floods past us. I cross my fingers, half-expecting Bethany to dive, cowering, under the table. Instinctively, I move closer to her. Bethany shrinks towards me. She stares at the children rushing past her.

Most of them ignore her. A few recognise her and say hello. A tiny, freckle-faced girl appears by Bethany's side.

"Do you like them?" She indicates the stick insects. "They're mine. I brought them."

Bethany nods, speechless.

"I collect them. My dad gets them for me. I can't remember where. He knows a place where you can find them. Do you want one?"

Bethany's mouth falls open. She nods again.

The little girl reaches into the jar and is just about to grab one. Bethany holds her hands out, ready.

"Hang on!" I say. "You must ask Mum first, Bethany. You could ask her if she's got a very big jar – perhaps a sweet jar. And then we can come back tomorrow and meet – what's your name..?"

"Chloe."

"...We can meet Chloe here, and she can give us one or two stick insects, and tell us all about how to look after them. Is that a good idea?"

"Yes," they both chant in unison.

"What class are you in, Chloe?" I ask.

"Mrs Osborne's class. There!"

She points to one of the classroom doors. A double stroke of luck! This class is the one Bethany's supposed to be returning to, *and* it opens out into this library area, where I'm hoping we shall be working one day soon. This proximity will help enormously. Bethany will be able to observe all the comings and goings of the children, getting to know her classmates and Mrs Osborne from a safe distance. At the end of the morning, it won't be too big a step to peep round the door to see what the class have been doing.

"Well, Bethany!" I say triumphantly. "We can meet Chloe here, or in the classroom tomorrow."

Chloe nods. "What's her name?" She asks me.

"Why don't you ask her?"

Once more, I'm crossing my fingers behind my back. If Bethany goes all mute and antisocial at his point, these first tentative beginnings of a beautiful friendship could be ruined.

"What's your name?" Chloe looks at Bethany curiously, as if noticing her oddness for the first time.

"Bethany. What do they eat?"

"Privet leaves. And ivy leaves. I can show you tomorrow. I know a secret place in the playground where you can find the best ones. And," she lowers her voice and looks round for snooping ears, "once, I saw a stick insect in the hedge. We might find one tomorrow. We could catch one for you."

The delight on Bethany's face is unmistakeable. It's touching. I wish we had a mirror handy. Just think, all that earlier monkey-face miming and yum-yum-chocolate-eating, and all we really needed were a couple of stick insects to make Bethany 'do ecstatic'.

"Right, Chloe. So we can come and find you in the classroom tomorrow morning?"

"Yes. What time will you come?"

"Same time, maybe?" I look at Bethany. "Does that suit you, Bethany? Just before lunch?"

Bethany nods. Her face is flushed with this sudden swift moving on of events.

"I'll look out for you, Bethany," says Chloe. With a smile and a wave, she dashes off to join her friends in the dinner queue, which straggles forward from the library, along the corridor, and into the main assembly room, on the other side of the entrance hall, where the meal is being served.

I pick up Bethany's box.

"Who's strong enough to carry this?"

"I am," says Bethany, flexing her biceps.

As we walk back home, I'm on the crest of a wave. The morning's events have exceeded my wildest dreams. And as a bonus, Bethany actually wants to repeat the performance tomorrow! In an exultant daze, I think up ways to capitalise on Bethany's success. It's only as we near Bethany's home that I remember Mrs Webster's frenetic cleaning. My heart misses a beat as I imagine her lying on the ground floor having fallen from the window.

"Hurry, Bethany!"

"I can't. This box is too heavy."

I grab the box from her.

"Why are we hurrying?" whines Bethany. "And we didn't take any photos of the rockery." She looks at me reproachfully.

"No, we didn't have time, but we will, tomorrow. I just want to see if your mum…" I stop just in time.

"If she's had the baby!" finishes Bethany excitedly. "She might have. It might be in the cot!"

"Babies don't come that quickly. Not just in one hour. Mum will have to go into hospital first…"

And the baby will have to be liquidised, I think ruefully, remembering that there's a mystery to be solved here. I'm determined to get to the bottom of this crazy thinking.

'Liquidised.' 'Juiced.' I stop. I stand stock still. 'Juiced.' *INDUCED*! Of course! All is suddenly crystal clear. Bethany heard a discussion between her mother and Mary, the neighbour in the downstairs flat, and tried her hardest to make sense of an unfamiliar word. As children do. It's obvious, really. I sigh with relief.

Yet Bethany's still shown worrying ignorance about the actual birth process. It's essential that she has this knowledge before the baby is born. She needs to understand exactly what's happening if she's around when her mother goes into labour. This belief of hers that babies come out of tummy buttons is totally inappropriate for a girl of nine. I marvel how Bethany has managed to avoid knowledge that most children acquire much earlier, almost by osmosis. Of course, she hasn't been at school during the last eighteen months or so, where she would hear the playground talk. Also, she's the only girl in the family. No older sister to gleefully share the delights of newfound knowledge. And her mother, for all her other sterling qualities, is not naturally inclined to sit down with each of her children and have cosy chats about the birds and the bees. Not only that, she's got eight mouths to feed and four loads of washing to do every day.

As we rush upstairs, Mrs Webster's feeding Joseph. He's grabbing the spoon from her and dipping it into a beige, gooey mixture, then merrily flinging spoonfuls of this into the far corners of the kitchen. Some of the stuff catches the now gleaming windows. Mrs Webster looks quite done-in, hardly managing to concentrate as Bethany excitedly tells her about the stick insects, and barely glancing at the box of presents Bethany thrusts under her nose. I offer to make her a cup of tea, and she accepts gratefully. Has she time for a very quick word, I ask her?

Bethany lifts Joseph down from his highchair, and carries him into the living room. Through the open door, I can see them both crawling energetically round the room. Toys rattle, roll and ping.

As we drink our tea, I tell Mrs Webster about Bethany's interpretation of the word 'induced'. And about the 'tummy button' method of birth.

Mrs Webster looks quite mortified, then embarrassed. Finally she laughs.

"I thought she'd just know," she says.

"I've got some excellent books I can bring tomorrow," I tell her. "But it might be best if you prepared her as soon as possible. Before the baby starts…"

"I'll talk to her tonight," promises her mother, a bit apprehensively.

"Make it into a bedtime story! She'll love it."

As I leave, Mrs Webster's putting her feet up on the settee, while Bethany amuses her little brother.

Tomorrow, having read Bethany my *How a Baby is Born* books, I'll be able to note, with tongue-in-cheek, on my record sheet that we've covered Human Reproduction at Key Stage 2 level.

I just hope tomorrow isn't too late.

Tuesday, 8th June. "What would you like to do for the last ten minutes of our lesson today?" I ask Bethany.

Without a word, she runs into her room and comes back with a large plastic sweet jar. Inside, looking quite at home, are three stick insects, camouflaging amongst some privet and ivy leaves. Bethany places the jar on the floor and kneels down, peering into the top.

When I arrived this morning, Bethany was waiting by the front door. She begged me to take her into school straight away, to collect the stick insects from Chloe. A quick call to the school ensured that Mrs Osborne knew we were coming. We'd arrived at break-time, with most of the children outside. Just three or four remained inside, too few to make Bethany feel swamped and nervous. So, timidly, she'd ventured into the classroom. The stick insects were carefully extracted from Chloe's jar. So intent on this task was Bethany, that she hardly noticed the children who were crowding round, watching with great interest.

After break, we'd sat in the library, researching stick insects in the nature section, and finding out how to care for them. Then we admired this morning's new Show and Tell exhibits. Without any prompting from me, Bethany suddenly asked if she could come into school tomorrow.

"I want to bring something in," she stated, firmly. "To show."

I'm thrilled at this new development. But it still feels quite fragile, as if we're walking a tightrope.

I gather up my bags and say goodbye to Mrs Webster. She tells me that yesterday evening, she read Bethany a story about how babies are born, demonstrating the birth process on her favourite doll. Bethany had been fascinated and wanted her mother to read the story again and again.

Bethany follows me out to my car. There's something about her manner that's worrying me. She's subdued. Tense. I'm disappointed. Surely, she should be more buoyed up by our play-acting, and by getting the stick insects she so much wanted? And Mrs Bryce had kept her promise. She'd presented Bethany with a gold star sticker and a new pencil sharpener, as a prize 'for working well in the library'.

We've packed a lot in this morning. I hope we haven't overloaded her with new experiences, or with too much information. Perhaps she's even more confused about the birth process than she was before. Yet, according to her mother, she seemed to accept and understand it all in a very matter-of-fact way.

I'm in the car, ready to drive off. Bethany comes round and taps on my window. Alarmed, I wind the window down.

"Careful! You're in the road! What is it, Bethany?"

"Nothing."

"Right. Hop back on the pavement, then. I'll see you tomorrow. 'Bye!"

"'Bye."

Bethany skips round the back of the car and comes round to the passenger side. She knocks on the window again. Impatient now, I wind it down.

"What is it?"

"Nothing." Bethany gives me one of her blankest stares.

"Well, goodbye then. Enjoy your afternoon. Oh, and remember to find something for the Show and Tell table tomorrow. Have a hunt round your garden!"

"Bye," says Bethany again. As I drive away, I can see her through the mirror. She's standing quite still, sucking her thumb, staring after me.

Bethany's never come outside to see me off before now. Something is definitely still worrying her...

Wednesday, 9th June. "I don't think this baby wants to be born," says Mrs Webster.

We're in the kitchen having a tea break before I take Bethany into school. Baking tins and mixing bowls are lined up neatly on the work-surface. A large square of shortcrust pastry has been rolled out, ready to be pressed into tins and pie dishes. The oven's on and there's a mouth-watering aroma of baking cakes.

Anita Webster and I are now on first-name terms. We've just had another twenty-minute co-teaching session in the living room. Bethany wanted to enact the birth scene again, from the book her mother had read to her, but this time, following a hunch, I suggested to Anita that we add a few sound effects. With help from all of us, including Bethany, the mummy doll did quite a bit of very realistic panting, grunting and groaning. We likened these labour pains to the effort noises made by a weightlifter struggling to lift a very heavy bar, or to the straining sounds of the World's Strongest Man (one of Bethany's favourite TV programmes) as he pulls a truck uphill. We kept it all as light-hearted and fun as we could, though Anita's labour pains were at times so realistic that once or twice I instinctively reached inside my bag for my mobile phone. Bethany, as midwife, had a central role in the drama, which reached its climax when the baby arrived. It peeped out, shyly, from under its mother's frilly pink dress, as it entered the world and gave its first cry. We all exclaimed with delight over its tiny, perfect toes and fingernails.

At least it all made Bethany laugh. She seems to have brightened up a lot since yesterday. Just now, she's playing with Joseph in the living room, giving me a chance to have a private talk with her mother as we sit at the kitchen table.

"I've never been this late with any of the others," sighs Anita, wriggling her back against the chair cushion.

This sounds like a good opening for me to broach the subject of Bethany.

"I was a bit worried about Bethany yesterday," I say tentatively. "She seemed rather tense. Not herself at all. I wondered if she was worried about you going into hospital."

Anita shakes off her slippers. Her feet and ankles are swollen.

"I'm only in there for a couple of days," she says, "or even just overnight, if it all goes well. Paul won't be able to cope if I'm away any longer. Bethany'll hardly notice I've gone!"

"When you went in last time, to have Joseph, how did Bethany react?"

Anita frowns, thinking back fifteen months. Her contractions, she tells me, had started one evening. Bethany was fast asleep in her room. As the pains became stronger, Anita cried out in agony, yelling and groaning. Bethany woke up and came into her mother's room, where she was trying to stuff some last minute things into a suitcase.

"I can't remember what I said to her," says Anita. "Probably just that the baby was coming and that I was all right. Then Paul came in. He picked up the suitcase and told Bethany to come downstairs with him to Mary's flat. The other children were asleep in bed so we left them for Mary to keep an eye on."

She hoists herself up and opens the oven door. Two trays of golden, beautifully-risen cup-cakes are done to a perfect turn. Anita lifts the trays out and places them carefully on wooden boards on the work-surface. A large cheese, broccoli and onion flan is next to go into the oven. She sits down again, mopping her brow.

"Then we had to call the ambulance," she continues, "I was too far gone for Paul to drive me in. I remember the ambulance drawing up at the front gate with all the lights flashing and making the siren noise. They had to carry me downstairs on a stretcher. I thought I was going to have Joseph there and then, by the front door." Anita's eyes are wide, as she relives every moment.

I catch my breath. This description is so vivid for me – what must it feel like for Anita? And more significantly, how had it been for Bethany, if she'd heard all the goings-on?

I feel I've said more than enough already, and make a move to get up. But Anita is still reminiscing, a faraway look in her eyes.

"Bethany seemed fine, afterwards," Anita says, as if answering my unspoken question. "Joseph was born at half-past nine, half an hour after we got to hospital. Paul brought all the children in to the hospital the next morning. Bethany seemed thrilled. Made a great fuss of Joe. I was home by the following afternoon."

I gaze at Anita in admiration. "I would have thought you'd want to stay in at least a week!"

"They won't let you, these days. Besides, I couldn't leave Paul with the four of them to cope with. You've just got to get on with it, haven't you?"

Bethany's forgotten to find something for the Show and Tell table. Never mind, we can find something along the way to school. As we walk through the park, Bethany skips along happily by my side. I'm feeling up-beat and optimistic. There's a load off my mind. I'd followed a hunch – that Bethany might have heard her mother in labour with Joseph, and possibly with Carlos before – and been confused and terrified by the experience. This next birth too could turn out to be frightening and upsetting, but at least Bethany will be better prepared. And if my theory turns out to be a complete red herring – well, no harm's done, and Bethany has gained some useful knowledge.

I'm still puzzling about my mental block that somehow prevented me, much earlier on, from using this imminent birth of a baby as a superb teaching opportunity with Bethany.

Could the reason be that sometimes I wake in the night with a hollow, sick dread, wondering if baby Darren has found a new, permanent home?

It's odd that, on the rare occasions tutors come together for staff meetings, we never talk about mental blocks. I suppose we're far too busy catching up on other vital information – the number of pupils we have, or the lack of them, or exchanging success/horror/funny stories or phone numbers. Why, I wonder for the umpteenth time, don't we have weekly – or even fortnightly – supervision, i.e. access to a trained educational counsellor. If I were a psychotherapist or social worker or psychologist, regular supervision would be the norm. We tutors, in the course of one day, can find ourselves taking on all of these roles with our pupils. What happens in other parts of the country? Do all LEAs have this penny-pinching, cavalier attitude towards the professional development and emotional wellbeing of their tutors? Sometimes, it would be such a relief not to have to puzzle out *everything* on my own.

Bethany wants to go on the swings, but I hurry her along. We have to be at school before twelve if we're to miss the dinner hour rush. Today, we'll just stay for twenty minutes. We'll look at the nature display and add Bethany's contribution – if she can find one. Then we'll look at a few library books. Perhaps we'll play a word game. Finally, we'll come back to Bethany's house for a short cooking session: I'm still amazed that Bethany's adapted so well to this new routine of going into the school library for up to an hour a day.

However, getting her into the classroom is another matter altogether. Faced with a room full of lively children, Bethany's solitary nature comes to the fore. In inverse ratio to the amount of hubbub being generated, she becomes more and more withdrawn, more…autistic. Sometimes, I wonder whether the idea of Bethany going back into full-time schooling is little more than a fantasy.

Bethany's footsteps are gradually becoming slower and slower. I glance at her face. Is she as tired as I am? Our session this morning has been full-on, intense. She stops by the monkey-swing parallel bars. She probably feels cheated that I haven't let her play on the equipment today. Maybe I should let her, just for two minutes.

Bethany puts one hand on the supporting pole at one end of the frame. She leans against it, looking down and away from me. Anxiously, I lean down and peer into her face. Her lower lip is trembling. She glances briefly at me. One large tear rolls down her cheek.

"Bethany! What's wrong?"

I kneel down next to her. In a low, wobbly little voice, she says, "I heard it come. The ambulance."

I catch my breath. "You heard the ambulance come to take Mum to hospital…?"

"I heard Joseph being born." Bethany twists her body away and grips the pole so tightly that her knuckles show white. "When Mum was going out of the front door. She was screaming. She screamed some more when she was in the garden." Bethany finishes on a half-sob. A shudder shakes her whole body. "I thought she was dying!"

I hold both her hands. Poor Bethany. How terrified she must have been. I can picture her, listening on the other side of the door of Mary's downstairs flat, hearing everything, but not understanding. I wait.

But Bethany's silent now. Another tear rolls down. She's very still. Only the rapid rise and fall of her chest shows her inner turmoil. She takes a deep breath.

"I was scared," she says suddenly, in a tiny, choking whisper. "When Mum went away. I was scared."

"I know. It was scary for you. So scary."

Bethany's trembling. I put my arm round her shoulders. "Joseph wasn't being born then, Bethany. He was born when Mum got into the hospital. You heard Mum having labour pains. But you didn't understand what was happening, did you?"

Bethany shakes her head. She takes a long shuddering breath and bites her lip.

"But you're a bit older now. You know that it can hurt the mother when it's time for a baby to be born? You understand that Mum was having some natural birth pains – hard work pains. Like all mothers have, but that she was all right. She wasn't dying."

Bethany nods, quieter now.

"Here, have a tissue. Your nose is running all the way to school!"

Her body is still stiff, as if held in some vice. I guess there's more feeling locked up there, an ocean of tears still dammed up inside. Perhaps even more terrors that she hasn't yet been able to express. It will take time. She may need some professional help that I can't give her.

Gradually, Bethany's shoulders slacken. Some of her tension releases. A few nose-blows and she's almost back to normal.

"Can you show me your best monkey swing?" I challenge her.

Bethany springs up and catches hold of the underside of the frame. With the ease and speed of Tarzan in the jungle, she swings hand under hand along the length of the frame, and clambers down the ladder at the other end.

"Look over there!" she says suddenly, pointing in the direction of the tennis courts on the other side of the playground. She dashes away across the grass.

I chase after her, but I'm too late. Along one side of the courts is a long flowerbed. As swift as a swarm of locusts, Bethany's deftly snapping off the almost-flowering heads of salvia, wallflowers and African marigolds, leaving behind a conspicuous patch of bare, colourless stalks.

"Bethany!" I shout, horrified, "Stop! You mustn't pick flowers in the park. It's public property!"

Bethany stands up, clutching her bunch of flowers to her chest.

"I know," she says indignantly. "It's public. Not private. Not like opening someone's gate and going into their garden. I don't do that now, do I? Public means it's *everybody's* garden. The flowers are for everybody. So it doesn't matter, does it?"

She gives me a withering look, and skips off towards the park gates.

"They're for the Nature Table," she calls back, over her shoulder.

"Bethany…" I hurry after her. "Bethany, you really mustn't…"

Then I stop. Let it go…

Win some, lose some.

Thursday, 10th June – 7.30 a.m. Though I've been expecting this phone call for weeks, the shrill ringing tones juddering into my dreams still send me into a hyperdrive of panic. I reach for the alarm clock and send it flying. The pagoda of books on my bedside table crashes to the floor.

"Hello?"

A short silence, then, "Yes, um. This is Bethany's father."

"OH!" I sit up in bed. "Hello!" My voice cracks with excitement.

"Yes, er, hello. Um. Anita's had the baby. Born yesterday afternoon at 5.35.p.m."

"That's fantastic news! Congratulations!"

"Yes, er…thank you. So. Anita thinks it's not a good idea for you to come in for Bethany today, or tomorrow. She'll – er – ring you to arrange your next visit."

"Of course. Thank you for ringing. And are they both, I mean…"

"Oh, er, yes. I have to tell you…" a long silence, during which I hear a rustle of paper. Mr Webster seems to be reading from a prepared script. "Yes. mother and baby are both doing well."

"And…?"

For heavens' sake, I wonder, is it a boy or a girl? How is Bethany reacting? But there's a finality in Mr Webster's voice as he says, "Well, goodbye, then."

"Goodbye, and congratulations again. Please give my very best wishes to your wife…" The phone goes dead… "And to Bethany," I whisper, into the silence.

For a moment I sit transfixed, staring out of the window at the gulls wheeling around my window in their early morning search for breakfast titbits. Then I replace the receiver and bounce up and down on the bed, laughing and clapping like a small child.

Thankfully, Anita and the baby are both doing well. But has Bethany now got the baby sister she longed for? And how is she coping with it all? I'm hoping that it won't be too long before I find out.

Monday, 14th June. I'm sitting on the settee in the Websters' living room. For the second time this year, I'm holding the tiniest of babies. She weighs six and a half pounds. Her name is Maria.

Bethany's sucking her thumb and kneeling in front of us, stroking her baby sister's silky dark hair. Maria has the most perfect little fingernails and hands in the world. Just now she's grasping my little finger as if her life depended on it.

Anita sits opposite me in an armchair, her feet propped up on a footstool, looking surprisingly perky, considering she's only been out of hospital for three days. She's filling me in with all the absolutely essential information – length of labour, type of birth, what the hospital food was like – that her minimalist husband had left out when he rang me on Thursday morning.

Anita had gone into labour soon after I'd brought Bethany back from the school on Wednesday. The contractions had started at about 1.30 p.m. They'd been slow at first, and not painful. She'd been very tempted to 'wait and see', but thought better of it, in view of her previous experience. She was able to tell Bethany what was happening and to reassure her. She even remembered – at this fairly early stage – to tell her daughter that these were 'good' pains and that they were there to help the baby be born. When her waters broke, at about three o'clock, she realised that things were moving fast. She gave Bethany the very important task of ringing her dad's mobile number while he was at work.

"Dad got here ever so fast," Bethany says, wide-eyed with remembering. "I was watching out of the window. He whizzed round the corner like a racing car. Then he stopped really sudden and the brakes made a noise like this..." She makes realistic grinding-to-a-halt squealing sounds.

"And then," continues her mother, "Paul drove me to hospital in plenty of time!"

She smiles contentedly. Joseph is asleep in his cot in her bedroom, and if he wakes her husband will see to him. The other children are at school or at nursery. In a couple of hours, her own mother will be arriving by train from London, to hold the fort for a week or two. Mr Webster, at this moment washing up in the kitchen, looks like a cat that's just landed in a pond. It's very plain he can't wait to get back to the more congenial and predictable world of fuse boxes and flexes.

I'd been surprised, and honoured, when Anita rang last night and asked if I'd like to come and see the baby. I'd expected Bethany to be unavailable for at least another week, bearing in mind the disruption a new baby could cause, even in this most regulated of households. But Bethany was longing to show off her new sister. And, her mother said, if I could also fit in a short tuition session, that would be fine, adding that she realised that too much of a gap in our routine would be bad for Bethany.

However, I doubt whether much work will get done today. As always, a new baby takes centre stage. All Bethany wants to do just now is to gaze at Maria, to pick her up and put her down again, to smooth the blankets in her crib and to examine her nappy for poos. Everything, in fact, that any devoted big sister would do for a newborn baby.

Tuesday, 29th June. "It's so tiny, that little baby! Look at my hand – it's the same size as the baby in the picture. My hand comes to eleven cent… centi… what are they called again?"

Bethany thrusts her left hand, palm up, towards me along the table. With her other hand, she's placed a transparent ruler over it, and she's laboriously counting centimetres.

"Centimetres," I remind her, "That's right. And the baby weighs about 100 grams. Remember when Maria was in your mother's tummy? Well, after she's been growing there for seventeen weeks, that's how big she would be and what she would weigh."

"Look, she's got little hands!" says Bethany, excitedly, pointing at the photograph. "And ears and eyes and a funny nose – look, you can see them!"

We're both gazing in wonder at a series of the most amazing photographs. They start with the baby at seven weeks' gestation, just a quarter of an inch long (much more impressive in imperial measurements), and follow the baby through various stages of development up to week 38.

By a lucky chance, I'd stopped at the newsagent at the end of Bethany's road, in urgent need of a chocolate fix. Idly scanning today's headlines, the caption on the front page of one of the newspapers caught my eye. It proclaimed:

'They are the most extraordinary pictures ever, of a baby in the womb, published in a new book, *Watch Me Grow*, by leading obstetrician Professor Stuart Campbell. Here he describes what is happening, week by week….in the baby's own words.'

We sit at one of the low hexagonal tables in the school library, poring over the photographs. We're surrounded by rulers, kitchen scales and balance scales.

"Can you find something in the room that weighs one hundred grams, Bethany?"

Bethany jumps up and begins prowling round the room. She loves this sort of game – anything to stretch her legs and give her the chance to move about. It's remarkable how many maths learning opportunities the photos have provided: weight, length, comparative size, as well as explaining the concept of weeks and months in a way that is meaningful to Bethany. They've added to her newly acquired knowledge about human reproduction, and they've enlivened her maths worksheets on metric measurements of length and weight. Luckily, they happen to be of bugs and insects – creatures dear to her heart – otherwise the moment might have been lost.

Watching her, I try hard to think about the progress she *is* making, instead of feeling discouraged by its slowness. What's worrying me is that these are worksheets that most of her year group would find too easy. Mrs Osborne, Bethany's class teacher, has been showing me what her children are doing in maths. Compared with what we're doing, it all looks incredibly advanced: negative numbers, rounding up of decimals, long multiplication... All of this is way beyond Bethany's comprehension. However will she cope if she does go back into class?

I shouldn't be thinking so negatively. A month ago, Bethany wasn't even doing maths worksheets. She wasn't here, in the library, actually in the school. I must never lose sight of the huge strides she has made, but I must also be realistic. Without extra help in class, Bethany will always be struggling to keep up. What she needs is a Learning Support Assistant.

During break-time, while Chloe drags Bethany off to show her a nest of red ants, I go to find Mrs Bryce. I want to know if Bethany has been 'statemented' yet. This very lengthy procedure of establishing a Statement of Educational Needs is done by an educational psychologist. It's a must if Bethany is to have her own LSA, but the whole process can take forever. Not only are educational psychologists fairly thin on the ground, but there's a long waiting list of children waiting to be assessed. And the whole statementing process is expensive, not to mention the actual cost of employing a LSA to work with a child in the classroom. Even so, considering the pressure being put on Bethany to return to school, I'm amazed that it's all taking so long.

I manage to catch Mrs Bryce in her office during a quiet moment.

"No," she says, "Bethany won't be statemented until she's back at school. That's how it works. Once she is back and we can see that she's struggling, we can start putting things in motion."

"But surely she can be assessed out of school? Then, when she does go back, everything's in place."

Mrs Bryce sighs. "The statementing process moves in its own mysterious ways. We'll just have to be patient and hope Bethany comes back quite soon."

"But she'll struggle!" I exclaim. "Won't we just be setting her up to fail – again?"

Mrs Bryce is looking at the clock. I take a deep breath and ask her if she's had any time to think about an idea I put to her just before half-term.

Mrs Bryce taps her forehead.

"Ah," she says. "It's too soon to give you any definite news. But – fingers crossed – I'll know by next Monday. These things take time. Now, if you'll excuse me, there's a parent waiting to see me. Just be patient," she says again, smiling, as she opens the office door.

Tuesday, 6th July. "Come on, Bethany! You can do it!"

I'm crossing my fingers and holding my breath, watching Bethany's every move.

It's the Sports Day heats for the high jump. Unbelievably, Bethany is lined up, waiting her turn to try and clear the bar. Out of the sixteen girls who started, only eight remain, (the boys having their own separate event).

As I watch the five children in front of her have their turn at jumping, I'm still telling myself that this must be a dream. If it's not a dream, it's little short of a miracle – helped by some lucky timing. Sports Day is just a couple of weeks away, and today the heats are for the high jump, the 100 metres, the sack race and the egg and spoon race.

To my surprise and delight, Bethany wanted to join her class for this occasion. It helped that it's taking place safely outside, on the field which adjoins the new pond and vegetable area.

It happened like this. We'd just started work in the library, when, unexpectedly, the children in Mrs Osborne's class burst out of the door dressed in shorts and sports tops.

"Where are they going?" asked Bethany, her jaw dropping with surprise and alarm at this sudden event

"Don't know," I said. "Let's ask, shall we?"

"Sports practice on the field," said the teacher, matter-of-factly. "Want to come and watch, Bethany?"

A clever move. If Mrs Osborne had asked Bethany to join in, that would have been a leap too far, but just watching was different. And if it came to a choice between doing maths worksheets inside, or going outside on a glorious July day into the familiar territory of the school field – well, in Bethany's mind, there was no contest.

So, hesitantly, Bethany took her place at the end of the row of children, who were sitting on chairs along the run up to the high jump, waiting for this event to start. She looked uneasy and nervous, glancing sideways along the row of watching children as if, at any moment, one of them might do something threatening or unexpected. There was a lot happening all around her and it was all going on at once. Spectators in different parts of the field watching other heats jumped up and down and cheered the participants on. Children and teachers dashed here and there. If it hadn't been for Chloe, who sat staunchly by her side and kept up a reassuring running commentary about what was going on generally in other parts of the field, and specifically about each of her classmates' past form in this jumping event, I'm sure Bethany would have taken fright after two minutes.

To begin with, the bar was set very low.

"Why don't you have a go, Bethany?" I suggested, casually. "Just one little jump, while the bar is so low. Look how easy it is – I bet Joseph could jump it!"

"Yes, go on, Bethany," squealed Chloe, pink with excitement. "I bet you can jump much higher than that! Come on – I'll be first, then you."

There was a lump in my throat as I watched the two of them run up and join the end of the queue of girls waiting to jump. I wanted to capture and freeze-frame forever this historic moment – Bethany joining in with her classmates for the very first time. Even if I'd had a camera, no photo would have done justice to the vivid memory-picture I have now, as I write this: Bethany at the end of the queue, her face a mixture of fear, uncertainty, excitement. The expressions of surprised delight on the faces of the watching children, their sudden nudges that rippled along the row of chairs as all eyes turned towards Bethany:

"Look! Bethany's going to jump!"

"Bethany's joining in!"

After one easy jump, Bethany was hooked. The bar was raised incrementally. Six of the girls were 'out', including Chloe, but Bethany was still there.

Now eight girls remain in the heat. Only four of these, in first, second, third and fourth place, will go through to the final, as there are two other classes in year 4, and they too will select four finalists. A thick blue plastic-covered foam mat is placed on the far side of the bar – suggesting risk and extra challenge. A frisson of new excitement grips the spectators.

I reckon that Bethany might have met her Waterloo. Surely, she's too short to clear the bar now. The other girls are much taller than her. But Bethany takes a long, long run up and lands on her bottom with a whoop of delight. Her classmates laugh and clap.

All eight children have cleared the jump. The bar is raised again and again. Now only five girls are still in. The bar is level with Bethany's shoulders. *Surely* this is far too high for her! Oops – now the first girl to jump has knocked the bar down. There are still four contestants to have their turn, including Bethany. Two more girls clear the bar – just. The third girl, very tall, in front of Bethany, clears it easily.

Bethany's the last to jump. If she fluffs this, there'll be a tie between her and the first girl, both vying for fourth place. Both will be given a second go. This is too hair-raising to contemplate. Bethany needs to get this jump safely under her belt. She takes an extra long run-up, making her classmates laugh as she nearly disappears out of sight. As she nears the bar it seems to tower over her. There's no way she can make it...is there?

With a sudden deft twist of her body Bethany soars off the ground, tummy-side-up, executing a perfect Fosbury Flop! She clears the bar easily, by at least two inches, and lands on her back on the mat. With the grace of a Russian gymnast she bounces herself upright, stretching her arms up high, landing neatly on the same spot. She's grinning from ear to ear.

Shouts of delight from the watching children. I rush up and hug her.

"Where on earth did you learn to do that?"

"I watched it on the telly," says Bethany, as if it were the most normal thing in the world to come out and do a successful Fosbury Flop for the first time ever – with no previous practice at all.

"Well done, Bethany," beams Mrs Osborne. "Would you like me to put your name down for the final?"

Bethany, suddenly finding herself the star of the show, goes pink with embarrassment, but manages a brief nod.

After this, the 100 metres heat is a doddle. Bethany qualifies easily. The egg and spoon race is trickier. Bethany's too eager to get going and drops her egg soon after the start. But a triumphant second-place finish in the sack race means Bethany is in yet another final. She's flushed with excitement – and so am I.

There's one more thrill to come. A surprise I've been hugging to myself since yesterday. With any luck it should arrive just before lunch.

I was hoping that Bethany would file back into class with the other children. Surely, after such an amazing triumph, she must by now be feeling part of the class? But no, this is the real world, not some cloud-cuckoo-land, happy-ending fairy tale. Bethany has quickly reverted to type. She's standing by her chair, a solitary little figure sucking her thumb, watching her classmates whoop and whirl their way back into the school building. Disappointed, I take her back into the library for a short reading session.

At five minutes to twelve, Bethany looks up suddenly. There's a familiar figure standing under the wide arch that marks the entrance to the library area. A young person with a cheeky grin and mischievous eyes.

"LOOK! It's Kirsty!" Bethany stares, mouth agape.

"Hiya, kid. How you doing?"

Bethany, suddenly overcome with confusion and shyness, stares speechlessly at her adored Kirsty.

"So, what are you doing here?" I ask her, as if I didn't know.

"I've come to see this one, of course. Who else?" She whisks her cap off, and plonks it, wrong-way-round, on Bethany's head. "Who's going to show me the vegetable patch, then? I want to see what's growing."

"Let's all go and see it now," I say. "Can you lead the way, Bethany?"

Bethany leads the way out into the midday sunshine.

Kirsty takes Bethany's hand. We walk round the building quietly, so as not to disturb the children who are still in their classrooms.

"What have you planted, then?" asks Kirsty.

"Lettuces," says Bethany. "And radishes. And peas…"

The playing field, so quiet now after the hurly-burly of the sports events, seems to have a magical quality.

'When the hurly-burly's done,
When the battle's lost and won…'

I have a crazy urge to run along inside the white lines of the racetrack. It's like gazing down into the still depths of a swimming pool when everyone's got out, and wanting to hurl yourself into the calm water.

The fluty call of a blackbird pierces the muted throb and hum of midsummer. A wood-pigeon sings its mournful song: 'o-ooo-ooo-*o*-*o*'. The last two notes are emphasised, stern. Fancifully, I hear a message for me. It seems to be saying: 'You'll soon be *leaving*. You'll soon be *leaving*.' There's a sudden 'click' in my brain. All my senses sharpen into a hyper-awareness of colour and sound, scent and form. A rare moment. I catch myself alive.

Kirsty admires the neat rows of runner beans, now halfway up their supporting frame, and the pea sticks which Bethany proudly points out.

"I put those in," she says, sucking her thumb.

Bethany's like a very young child again. It's as if the spectacular young athlete and gymnast of half an hour ago was nothing but a figment of my imagination. She looks uncertain, as if she's not sure how to *be* with Kirsty.

Kirsty seems unaware of this, and keeps exclaiming over the new luxuriant growth, breaking off a couple of young pea-pods and stuffing one into her mouth. She hands the other to Bethany.

"Try it! Good, innit?"

Suddenly, Bethany says, "We had to hunt for the pea sticks in the hedge. They were all the sticks you cut down. We had to cut some of them up. And some of the leaves are what my stick insects eat. I've got seven of them now and they keep having babies."

Her shyness has gone. The links between herself and Kirsty are firmly back in place.

A loud bell signals the end of morning school. The air reverberates with shouts and yells as children spill out into the playground.

Bethany looks at Kirsty. "Are you going home now?"

"Nope. I'm staying for lunch. And for the afternoon. Will you be staying?"

Bethany shakes her head. "Will you come another time?"

Kirsty smiles her broadest smile.

"Like tomorrow? And the day after that? You'll be seeing a lot of me now, kid. Because I'm a volunteer helper. I'll be in school every day from now on."

Friday, 9th July – 12.15 p.m. Getting Kirsty on board has been my masterstroke of the year .

The very idea that Kirsty could come into the classroom as a volunteer assistant seemed, even to me, highly unlikely. For a start, it was fraught with risk. Kirsty at this time was still on probation, though this was soon to finish. Secondly, though her attendance and time-keeping during her stint with the Prince's Trust was pretty good on the whole, there was no way of knowing how committed and punctual she would be as a school volunteer. In making such a bold suggestion to the headteacher, all I had to go on was my intuition. And this was telling me that Kirsty's boisterous energy would go down well, not just with Bethany, but also with a class of lively children.

Something like this hadn't been tried before – not with an unknown quantity like Kirsty. Of course, there were already parent volunteers, and a devoted band of retired folk who turned up regularly come hell or high water. But to put forward someone who had herself dropped out of school very early on and had no qualifications, *and* was on probation – well, the idea was ludicrous, even to me in my saner moments. I'd expected Mrs Bryce to laugh at me and tell me to get real.

However, Mrs Bryce hasn't got to where she is today – head of one of the most successful schools in the area and a candidate for the title of Headteacher of the Year – by being conventional, or by not taking risks. In her book, the pupils come first, in equal place with hard-pressed classroom teachers. For their sakes, if there were *any* means of helping children who were lagging behind in their basic skills, nothing daunted her.

And she too had observed Kirsty in action. Noticed how, out of all the Prince's Trust trainees, Kirsty was the one to ask if anyone wanted to know how deep to dig the trench for the runner beans. It was Kirsty to whom a child came running, crying her heart out because her best friend wouldn't play with her today. Most important, she was one of the few people who understood Bethany.

But first, Mrs Bryce had to convince the staff and the governors. Meetings had to be held – lots of them. The police checks – normal for everyone who wanted to work with children – had added value in Kirsty's case. For Kirsty had a police record. True, this record was 'only' for drunk and disorderly behaviour, and swearing at a police officer while obstructing him in the course of his duty – not to mention a bit of shop lifting. Still, this was enough to send shudders of shock and horror round the governors and powers-that-be. Interestingly, all the teachers themselves were for the idea, no doubt desperate for help from any source. Or perhaps they, too had observed Kirsty, and realised that she was well on the way to becoming a reformed character. All she needed was a bit of direction and purpose in her life. Try convincing the most starchy member of the school governors, however. Not easy.

During all the time I waited for a decision, I'd been on tenterhooks. I felt responsible for starting something that might not work out. But thankfully, Mrs Bryce had considered my suggestion very seriously. And by some miracle of persuasion, she had assuaged the doubts of all concerned.

And now, another miracle is taking place before my eyes – Kirsty and Bethany are queuing up together for school dinner! I'm sitting at one of the tables nearest the arch at the entrance to the library, as the queue files past me. I'm pretending to be looking through some books, but I'm stealing covert glances at the pair of them whenever I can. Bethany looks extremely nervous, glancing round anxiously at me as if seeking reassurance that she is in fact meant to be here, in this long line of very noisy children. I'm afraid that at any moment she's going to break away, and bolt for the doors at the main entrance. She and Kirsty are just filing past these doors now. I hold my breath. Bethany glances towards me. I nod and smile encouragingly, with all my fingers and toes crossed.

Now, at last, they've reached the serving hatch in the assembly hall where the meal is served. The dinner lady is asking Bethany what she'd like to eat. Then, as quick as you can say 'turkey twizzlers', she and Kirsty have both found a seat next to each other on a long table of chattering, ravenous children.

Things have been happening very fast for Bethany. At the end of morning school, as I prepared to take her back and do some more work with her at home, Kirsty swooped down on us and persuaded Bethany to stay for lunch. A quick phone call home to Anita confirmed that this would be a very good idea. Bethany would then stay for the whole dinner hour and her mother would come and collect her before afternoon school started. As the *pièce de résistance*, Anita would bring Maria. Bethany was thrilled by this – at Bethany's age, to introduce a new brother or sister to one's friends is most children's dearest wish.

This opportunity, following so hard on the heels of Bethany's stunning high-jump performance, means that Bethany will be fast gaining class credibility and kudos at an impressive rate. I just hope she doesn't blow it. At this stage, so many things could happen to upset Bethany and we could be back again to square one.

Friday, 16th July – 10.10 a.m. We've changed our routine. As Bethany has now decided to stay for school lunch, I arrive at ten o'clock instead of eleven, so I can take Bethany into school in order to give her two full hours of tuition.

Anita opens the door, holding Maria, who's screaming as if in pain. I can hear Joseph crying in his cot in the Websters' bedroom. Up until now, Anita seems to have coped amazingly well with the two babies, holding them both in the palm of one hand, as it were. But today, she's looking unusually fraught, with dark rings under her eyes, and she's not yet dressed.

"Bethany isn't ready," she says, clutching a baggy candlewick dressing gown around her middle. "Something's up with her, but she won't tell me what's the matter. And I haven't got time to get to the bottom of it. I've got the housing officer coming at eleven o'clock. There's a bigger place come up on this estate, if they think we're suitable."

I'm pleased for Anita. These days, council places hardly ever come up in this area, ever since the government's Right to Buy scheme.

"That's if we get it," Anita shifts Maria on to her shoulder. "So far, other families always get in before us, somehow. Anyway, I've got to get on – Joe's just woken up and he wants his breakfast. After that I'll be able to clear up in the kitchen. I can't have this woman seeing us in a mess. Do you want to wait in the living room? I've told Bethany to hurry up."

"Shall I hold Maria for you while you see to Joseph?"

"Do you mind? That would be great. She's had her feed, but she's got wind. It's not usually this bad. Typical, isn't it, that just when you need everything to go smoothly, the whole bloomin' family decides to play up."

Anita places a muslin square over my shoulder and hands me the baby, still yelling lustily. I sit down with her while Anita hurries off to see to Joseph.

I'm puzzled by the non-appearance of Bethany. She's usually up well before now, and ready and waiting when I arrive. I hope she's not coming down with some bug.

I settle myself into the cushions, patting and rubbing Maria's back, until her yells subside. There's a sudden, satisfying burp – I'm amazed how such a loud explosion can issue forth from such a tiny body. It's a projectile burp and some of it misses the muslin cloth and forms a creamy dollop on the back of the settee. I wipe it off as best I can, and hope Anita doesn't notice. I move Maria on to my lap. Her eyes begin to close, and so do mine. I'm sinking into that state of utter relaxation induced by a tiny baby who's fast asleep in the crook of your arm. A precious moment in which to reflect on Bethany's remarkable progress over the past week.

After last Friday's successful venture into the dinner hall, Bethany decided that this week, she'd like to stay for lunch every day – as long as Kirsty was there with her. The plan was that she'd then stay for another half an hour until her mother, with Maria in the pram, came to collect her. This meant that for a whole hour I would be redundant. So I'm now seeing Bethany earlier.

Bethany and I have been working in the library as usual. The rather long morning has been broken up by more heats in preparation for sports day, which is on Friday next week. I've also managed to persuade Bethany to take part in a couple of indoor P.E. sessions. Because she's in her element on the equipment – vaulting from the springboard, climbing the wall-bars, doing somersaults on the mat – and because she found herself in a controlled situation, with the other children having to behave themselves or else – Bethany didn't find this experience too challenging.

Yet another triumph came on Wednesday, when Bethany actually went into the classroom and stayed for a whole lesson! On that day, the class project on mammals reached its grand climax. Any child who wanted to bring a small, *caged* mammal into the classroom was invited to do so, but they also had to give a short talk on their pet, describing its diet, lifespan, and how to look after it. I suggested to Bethany that we sit in a corner somewhere and watch the children show off their pets. She'd been tempted. I could see her wavering, but no, she decided, in the end, she'd rather not.

I'd compromised and taken her into the classroom during break while the children were out in the playground. Cages occupied by hamsters, gerbils, mice, fluffy rabbits and even rats were placed around the room on every available surface. Two of the more 'responsible' boys had been allowed to stay in the classroom to guard the animals. Bethany and I came in just as one boy was carefully rolling his male hamster and his friend's female hamster up together into a protesting ball, and squeezing them into a small transparent lunch box, so that they could mate. The boys' running commentary was interesting.

Bethany, goggle-eyed, was riveted by this performance, pushing through the two boys and peering right into the container. I was torn between letting the two little scientists go ahead with their dastardly experiment on the basis that Bethany was at last socialising – sort of – with two of her classmates, and on the other hand desperately wanting to rescue the two hamsters, who clearly didn't even like each other. In the end, the hamsters won, and were duly returned to their separate cages, much to the children's disappointment.

However, to show they had no ill-feeling towards me, the boys generously took me on a tour of the pets, with Bethany eagerly in tow. They somehow persuaded her to stay and hear all the children's talks. She listened with rapt attention, mouth half-open, eyes alight with curiosity.

All things considered, Bethany's doing very well. But the most spectacular triumph of all happened on Wednesday afternoon, with Kirsty. I'd gone to see Ivan by then, so I can't claim any credit for this. Kirsty told me the next day that Bethany had actually asked if she could stay for the afternoon. Apparently, there was an end-of-term performance in the assembly hall by a children's theatre company doing their own version of *The Lion King*.

There's no doubt that Kirsty has played a tremendous part in Bethany's newly found enthusiasm to be at school. She's been there for Bethany every afternoon, watching out for her, gauging her mood, knowing when to push her forward just a bit, and when to hold back. And Bethany has blossomed under Kirsty's tutelage.

Just as amazing is Kirsty's popularity amongst the teachers. They're all fighting over her, all wanting her to come and help in their classrooms. She's shown that she has a knack with the troublemakers. Her particular brand of rough and ready humour, her way of somehow sizing a child up in an instant, her blunt, often irreverent way of talking, have somehow won over the most difficult children.

'She's got them eating out of her hand,' said one teacher, in charge of the most difficult class. "I've been trying for six months to get Craig to sit still and read just one page of a book. Kirsty sat him down this morning and they read a whole chapter together!"

So in the morning, while I work with Bethany, either in or out of the library, Kirsty works her magic in different classrooms, while learning her trade. For one thing's certain, she's well on the way to carving out a successful career for herself.

Bethany seems to be taking an extraordinarily long time getting ready. I think I'll go and find out what the problem is. I look round the room for the crib so I can put Maria down in it, but it's been whisked away somewhere. And so have all the neat piles of baby clothes that are usually on the table. I can't even see any of Joseph's toys. In fact, the whole room looks unnaturally tidy – like the dreadful featureless rooms, without heart or soul, in the 'How to Sell Your House' TV programmes. If Anita carries on like this with her clearing-up, the housing officer will assume that she's exaggerated the number of children in the household. Or that she's such a superb manager that she doesn't need a bigger house. Instead, it will go a family in a perpetual muddle with half the number of children.

At last, here comes Bethany, washed and dressed, but something's wrong. She doesn't greet me with her usual catch-it-quick-or-you'll-miss-it smile that utterly transforms her face for the briefest moment. She doesn't greet me at all. When I wish her good morning she blocks up her ears. Her face is set – stony and blank. She doesn't look at me. She even ignores Maria, still asleep in my arms. Plonking herself down heavily on the arm of the settee, she sits with her back to me and her arms folded.

I reckon Bethany's just very tired.

Holding my breath in case Maria wakes, I get up and carry her carefully into the kitchen.

"We're off now," I tell Anita, regretfully. "I'd love to cuddle her some more, but duty calls. Are you picking Bethany up at the end of afternoon school today? Does she still want to stay for the afternoon?"

"I think so," says Anita, wiping her hands on a towel, and taking Maria from me. "That's what she said she wanted to do last night. But I'll just go and ask her. She's certainly dragging her feet this morning."

"While you do that, I'll just pop out to the car, and move some boxes and books from the back seat."

I put my shoes on and hurry downstairs. Since I've been leaving Bethany to stay for lunch, I've been driving her into school, so that I don't have to walk back to her house at the end of the morning to pick up the car. I do miss our walk across the park, but things have moved on since those days. This car ride spells new progress.

I manage to clear a space for Bethany, then go back into the house. Joseph peeps out of the kitchen door, looking at me warily. Bethany is nowhere to be seen. Ominous sounds come from her bedroom.

Anita comes out of the room looking hot and flustered.

"She says she's not going to school. She won't say why. I can't get any sense out of her at all."

"What's she doing? Is she rocking? Or head-banging?" I have a sudden sick sense of déjà vu.

"She's just sitting on the bunk – sort of rocking backwards and forwards. I really can't be doing with all this – today of all days!" Anita looks at the end of her tether.

"Let me deal with it. You carry on with what you were doing. I'll sort it."

With a despairing look at Bethany's shut door, Anita scoops Joseph up and disappears into her room to change him.

Brave words on my part. I'm totally nonplussed. I feel as if the Tardis has transported me back in time and the intervening months were but a dream.

"Bethany," I call, in as firm a voice as I can muster. "Will you please come out here and tell me what the problem is?"

No reply. I can hear the bunk squeaking as Bethany rocks gently back and forth.

I open the door a fraction.

"Please come out now. How can I help you if you don't say what you want? If you tell me, I can help you."

I hold my breath, willing Bethany to do as I ask. Suddenly, it's become the most important thing in the world that Bethany comes out to *me*. If I have to go in to her now, all our painstaking work over the last months will count for nothing. To get over this present hurdle – whatever it is – Bethany must reach out, at least half way, towards me.

"I'll help you, but you must help me too. And yourself. We can support each other."

I wait. Forever, it seems. There's a long silence. Then I hear the bed creak louder as Bethany gets up. She comes and stands in the doorway, leaning against the frame. Her arms are folded across her chest and she looks down at the floor.

"What's the matter, Bethany? Can you tell me?"

Silence. She doesn't move.

"I'm feeling so frustrated that you won't speak to me. It makes me feel like...like, grrrrrrr." Gritting my teeth, I let out a low growl. I'm not pretending, either. This is exactly how I feel and I want Bethany to know it.

Bethany glances at me. Suddenly recognition flickers across her face – a remembering of something half-forgotten.

Without warning, her features twist into an alarming grimace. Her teeth are bared in the monkey-fashion that only Bethany can do so well. She glares at me, thrusting her monkey-face toward me.

"Ah, you're a monkey!" I guess, hoping this will lighten Bethany's mood. "Is that it?"

Bethany shakes her head vigorously. The grimace becomes more exaggerated. Now it's more like the horrible rictus of a grinning skeleton.

"You're a scary skeleton?"

This is becoming more and more like that charade party game where someone mimes a book, a film or a play and you have to guess what it is. But for Bethany, this is no game. She's playing it for real. Her eyes are full of effort and concentration. She brings her hands round in front of her and spreads them out, making clawing movements. Then she flops down on the floor, and prowls about.

"Ah, I see! You're a lion!"

Bethany nods, still grimacing and clawing.

"Is the lion hungry?"

She shakes her head.

"Is it frightened, then?"

Wrong again. Red with exertion, Bethany makes even wilder movements. She's doing her best. It's my fault I've completely lost the plot.

"Can the lion speak? Or make a sound?"

The lion certainly can. Suddenly, it lets out an enormous roar. I jump.

"Goodness, that's a FIERCE lion! What is it trying to say?"

Bethany takes a deep breath. She looks straight at me.

"I – DON'T – WANT – YOU!" Each word is separated by a roar.

I take a step back. I hadn't expected this. I'm not prepared. I stare at her, not understanding.

"I – DON'T – WANT – YOU!" roars Bethany again, hammering the point home with thumps on the carpet with her fist.

"Right."

My knees are trembling. Suddenly, I do understand. I know exactly what's coming next. Somehow I manage to keep my voice level and matter-of-fact.

"That's clear enough, Bethany. Well done, you managed to tell me. Now I can help. Can you tell me what, or who, you *do* want?"

Bethany stands up, and leans against the door frame, sucking her thumb. The lion has vanished. In its place is a small, vulnerable creature who looks startled by her own courage.

"I want Kirsty," she says in a timid little voice.

"Ah, I understand. Of course you want Kirsty. You've been spending a lot of time with her this week. And you'll be spending all this afternoon with her, too. She's looking forward to seeing you."

Still sucking her thumb, Bethany shakes her head. Tears glisten in her eyes.

"I want her now. I want *her* to walk me to school. Through the park. I don't want you anymore."

"But Bethany..." I open my mouth to tell her all the logical reasons why this isn't possible. Like, 'Kirsty doesn't help you in the mornings. She's busy helping another teacher. She can't be spared suddenly, just like that, just because you want her, *now*...'

Bethany's looking at me, straight at me, in that inscrutable way she has. Yet there's something new in her expression, something just beginning to bloom, that I've never seen before. There's a very faint hint of expectation, of trust. And it is this that tells me what I must do. I must continue how I started. From the beginning, I've encouraged Bethany to set the pace, to lead us where she wanted to go. Why should things change now, at this, the most crucial stage in the game? Because all along, this has been about Bethany discovering her own way, her own power.

"Bethany," I say gently. "I'm going to try and arrange it. I'm going to ring the school and ask if they'll let Kirsty come and collect you here. There's a chance that she's too busy in one of the classrooms. But you do believe me, don't you, when I say I'm going to do my very, *very* best?"

11 a.m. I'm driving to the school. Kirsty and Bethany are probably in the park by now, following our much-loved route past the swings, the monkey-frame, the long flower bed by the tennis courts...

Somehow, it had been sorted. Kirsty was tracked down and released, no doubt by an unwilling teacher. How it was achieved, I've no idea. My heart's still thumping from the swiftness and unpredictability of things. I'm in urgent need of chocolate and a cup of tea.

I park the car and walk towards the entrance, mentally preparing some kind of speech. One which explains to Mrs Bryce how one small girl has thrown goodness-knows-how-many people's morning into disarray.

But there, waiting for me outside on the steps of the school entrance, is Mrs Bryce herself. She's beaming. I can't believe it. It's a Red Carpet welcome!

"Well, well, well! This is a turn up for the books, isn't it?"

"Yes." I begin my speech. "I'm sorry about…"

"Don't worry. This is just what we've been aiming for."

We walk up the steps into the entrance hall, both marvelling at this sudden change in Bethany. Outside her office, Mrs Bryce stops and gives me a long look.

"It's you I'm worried about!"

"Me?"

I'm taken aback. Mrs Bryce holds my gaze.

"It's happened quite quickly in the last week or two, hasn't it? All that time and energy you've invested in Bethany. It's suddenly come to fruition. And where does that leave you? A bit high and dry, I expect?"

I nod. I can't speak.

"Let's work something out for you, for next week. I know one or two teachers who are desperate for a bit of extra help. Not in Bethany's class, of course. We'd best keep you two apart for the moment."

"I'm not sure my line manager will allow me to continue. Once a pupil goes back into school, that's it. As far as the office is concerned, my work is now finished, but I'll be glad to help on a voluntary basis."

"I'll ring your office," says Mrs Bryce, "and see what I can do. Meanwhile, go and have a cup of tea in the staffroom. You look as if you need one."

"Thank you."

"You've done well."

A little later, I drive slowly along the seafront towards the Pier Café. I need an extra big piece of chocolate cake before I can face joining the busy holiday traffic on my way home. I'm feeling a rosy glow at Mrs Bryce's kindness and understanding. In our line of work, accolades are rare.

Yet I don't hold out much hope for getting paid next week. Ruefully, I wonder if I'm in the only job in the whole wide world in which the workers are rewarded in inverse ratio to the amount of success achieved.

As has happened so many times before, I've been far too successful for my own good. I've worked myself out of a job.

But as I sit in my favourite café, watching diamonds of sunshine dance on an emerald sea, I too feel like dancing for joy.

Against all the odds, Bethany is back in school!

Friday, 23rd July. Having Sports Day on the very last day of term is a new experiment for Bethany's school. The idea is to kill two birds with one stone. It's a carrot and stick to make sure the children behave themselves – otherwise they won't be allowed to take part. It's also a way to keep the children's interest and momentum going until the very last moment. Often after Sports Day, which for many children is the highlight of the summer term, there's a sense of anticlimax. By moving it right to the end, the school fills that void of the last few days, in which nothing really exciting happens, creating conditions rife with the potential for mischief and hyperactivity.

Once again I'm sitting in a row of small chairs placed along a track. Only this time, the event is the long jump, and I'm sitting next to Kirsty. On my right, at the end of the row, is Anita with Joseph on her lap. He's wriggling like mad, wanting to run or jump like everyone he sees around him seems to be doing. Maria sleeps peacefully in her pram next to her mother.

We're watching Bethany take her turn. She's at the back of the queue, and she gives us a shy, quick wave. Today, even I am included in this wave, and I feel honoured. Bethany has managed, at last, to work out in her head that just because Kirsty is her favourite person and the one who now helps her at school, this doesn't automatically make me into The Wicked Witch of the West. Her natural difficulty in knowing how to relate to the two of us at the same time has been countered by the fact that our paths in the last week have hardly crossed. Whenever we have met, in passing, I've made it clear that I'm happy that she's now in Kirsty's charge, and that I've no intention of whisking her away to a previous life. I can see that Bethany is trying hard to reinvent herself, as a child who now goes to school.

While we watch the girls jumping, Kirsty tells me how Bethany's getting on. I'd expected, this week, that Kirsty would somehow achieve the goal that eluded me right to the end – that of getting her into the classroom full time. But according to Kirsty, this hasn't quite happened yet – Bethany still does no more than dip in and out according to what's going on in there – and I'm not saintly enough to feel disappointed about this. In fact, I only just manage to stifle a guilty feeling of gratification. Well, I'm only human. It would be galling to think that I'd missed some magical trick that could precipitate Bethany into class – or that Kirsty, in one week, had found all the answers to problems that I've been scratching my head over for thirty five years.

Bethany's running up to the jump. She takes off well, and her stride covers a good distance, but she's not doing so well in this event as in the high jump. She hasn't yet perfected her landing technique, and instead of throwing her weight forward, she sits back in the sand, knocking a few inches off her total length. She comes last this time. But who cares, she's already won the 100 metres sprint, the sack race and throwing the welly-boot. And, with another spectacular Fosbury Flop, which had the watching parents shouting with amazement, she's come joint-first in the high jump. She has the makings of a fine athlete. Kirsty and I have been discussing how to get her into a junior athletics club and how to persuade Anita that the extra time ferrying Bethany back and forth would be time well invested.

Kirsty herself has blossomed into a mature young woman who knows where she's going. She's enrolled for GCSE maths and English classes, which she'll start in September. When she's got these under her belt she'll start the training to be a full-time learning support assistant, hopefully picking up more GCSEs on the way. While all this is happening she'll continue to volunteer in the school and support Bethany.

Sports Day is nearly over. Just the toddler race. I've already got through half a box of tissues this afternoon watching Bethany – now I use more when I see her standing behind Joseph holding his hands up in the air as he toddles towards the finishing line. But these are tears of laughter as Joseph breaks away from Bethany when he suddenly spots his mother. He makes a dash towards us, a big beam on his face.

Bethany goes up shyly to receive her four first prizes. I mop up more tears – of pride and joy.

I watch the last hustle and bustle as children, parents, friends and relatives crowd round the tables laden with snacks and drinks. Everyone is relaxing in the sunshine, laughing, chatting, catching up on school news.

Now it really is all over. Not just Sports Day, but my time with Bethany. And it's the end of the school year. No more pupils for me until September. Ahead stretch aeons of time – the long summer holidays.

For a few minutes, I sit very still, overwhelmed by the poignancy and the sweet-sadness of endings.

Bibliography

Quotations from:

Duffy, Carol Ann. Poems *Anne Hathaway* and *We Remember Your Childhood Well,* (taken from NEAB/ AQA GCSE English Language and Literature Anthology 2004).

Levine, Mel M.D. *A Mind at a Time,* Simon & Schuster, New York, 2002.

References to, plus good ideas and inspiration gleaned from:

Brooks, Ruth. *Imagine!,* educational game, Claire Publications, Colchester.

Campbell, Professor Stuart, Photographs of a human embryo developing in the womb. These were printed in full colour in *The Daily Mail,* on 29th June, 2004, and reproduced from Professor Campbell's book entitled *Watch Me Grow*, Carroll & Brown Publishers, London, 2004.

Dahl, Roald. *Danny, the Champion of the World,* Puffin Books (a Penguin imprint), London & New York, 1994.

Deary, Terry, *The Horrible Histories* series, Scholastic, London, publication year according to title.

Finney, Patricia. *Betrayal - The Lady Grace Mysteries,* Delacorte Press Books for Young Readers (a Random House imprint), New York 2004.

Holt, John. *How Children Learn*, Penguin Books, London & New York, (this edition) 1991.

McCullagh, Sheila. *The Puddle Lane Series*, Ladybird Books (a Penguin imprint), London, publication year according to title.

Miller, Arthur. *All My Sons,* Penguin, London & New York, (this edition) 2000.

Sachar, Louis. *Holes,* Yearling (a Random House imprint), New York, 2000

Steinbeck, John. *Of Mice and Men,* Penguin Classics, London & New York, (this edition) 2000.

Tough Guy and *The Forbidden Path* are fictitious novels.